ON THE SET — Ben Hunter prepares to go "on the air" for his daily two and one-half hour television show on KTTV, Los Angeles.

ON THE BEACH — Two hundred miles South of the glamour and heart attack pace of Hollywood, Ben Hunter begins to experience "The Baja Feeling" . . .

THE BAJA FEELING

The
Baja
Feeling

by Ben Hunter

Brasch and Brasch, Publishers, Inc.
Ontario, California 91762

Walter M. Brasch, editor

Illustrated by John Wheeldon

Library of Congress Cataloguing in Publication

Hunter, Ben.
   The Baja Feeling.

    1. Baja California—Social conditions.
2. Public opinion—Mexico—Baja California.

I. Title
HN 120.B3H66   309.1'72'2   78-13211
ISBN 0-89554-005-3

Printed in the United States of America

Dedication

To Margie, whose scribbled logs formed the basis for this narrative, and without whom none of these adventures would have occured.

To Dottie Weichman, who unhinged my dangling participles, exorcised my redundancies, and peppered the manuscript with punctuation.

To my good friends whose chapter-by-chapter flattery kept me at the typewriter.

And, finally, to my mistress—Baja.

Prologue

Roberto has just finished my haircut and departed.

He shows up at ten o'clock a.m. every other Sunday. He has a sly smile as if enjoying a private joke unshared by his clients. He is an artist at his profession, even though he carries his tonsorial tools in a brown zipper bag. I feel like an oil-rich Middle Eastern nabob having my hair cut in the privacy of my own home. No prosaic barber shop for me! But in truth, Roberto only charges $2.00 and the price includes his barberly chit-chat seasoned with a bit of neighborly gossip—in Spanish of course.

Soon Juan will be rapping at the door. He'll be carrying a steaming white pail filled with succulent, meaty tamales made by his wife this morning, and I may buy a few. But right now I'm alone.

I gaze out my two-story window toward the sea. A gentle morning breeze has started to stir the palm fronds and ruffle the glassy surface of the water; porpoises play just beyond the waves, and an island perches on the horizon like a purple beret on the side of the world. The only sounds I hear are the music of the waves as they tumble on the beach and the occasional cry of a gull. The sand is white and clean. I have never known such peace and contentment.

Yet, it seems only yesterday I was caught up in the tenseness and turmoil of the Hollywood scene. There was my successful television show to keep on the air ("What are the ratings this week?"); sponsors to woo; production problems to work out; guests to book; jobs to be hustled, and smog to be breathed. Ulcerville. Coronary Canyon. Most of my friends in "The Industry," as we call it, have had one or the other. The remainder are alcoholics. Alcoholism is an occupational hazard, and A.A. is the fraternal order of Hollywood.

What miracle transported me from that miasma to this paradise?

Are we really predestined? Does an omnipotent Mind-power-force-God really write our destiny in a great book?

TOM: Will die at thirty-six in traffic.

DICK: Will live to eighty-three on his uncle's farm in Idaho.

HARRY: Will leave his wife, paint in Tahiti, and spawn an illegitimate son. Die at sixty-four.

Or does one's fate just happen, like a winning number at Las Vegas? Or like falling in love?

Now I hear my wife, Margie, humming softly to herself as she putters with her plants someplace. The humming stops and I hear her footsteps entering the room. She comes up behind me and rumples my newly-cut hair.

"Having the Baja Feeling?" she said.

"Yeah. I guess so."

That's where it all started. With The Baja Feeling. When it first occurred those many years ago we had no idea it would lead to this. Then, bit by bit, it grew inside us both and finally matured here—in our little corner of paradise.

This is how it happened.

1/ The Baja Feeling

It was a hot August day in 1965. Two California Highway Patrol officers had been chasing a drunk driver. Finally, at the corner of 114th and Compton, in Los Angeles, they got him over to the curb and tried to make the arrest. Suddenly, they were surrounded by angry people. And the throng grew. In minutes there were two hundred people around them. Someone threw something at the officers. They radioed for reinforcements, and the riot started. Black smoke from the ramshackle stores smudged the sky over Watts a dirty gray, and the rioters were shooting at the firemen fighting the blaze. As the nightmarish evening wore on to the next day, television documented it all. Horror by horror. Commentators wondered if this were the start of another Civil War. It was vicious, frightening, insane.

The television show I do on KTTV, Los Angeles, is normally an assortment of movies, games, and interviews. But on this eleventh day in August my show, too, had been constantly interrupted with updates on the riot and pictures of the bruised, the angry, the dead, and the arrested.

When I arrived home, Margie was still watching the holocaust. The flames were still out of control and so were the people.

I switched off the TV set. "Let's get the hell out of this town," I said.

Margie agreed. "Let's just get in the car and keep driving."

There was no long preparation for a trip. We borrowed a double sleeping bag, grabbed whatever food was in the house, some booze, a bucket of ice, a few other things, and set out. As we left Los Angeles behind, we stopped at a supermarket and purchased a box of barbecued chicken. It turned out to be delicious, and lasted us several days. I never thought to inform the studio of this impromptu departure. I just pointed our little four-cylinder Pontiac Tempest south, and we headed for Mexico. Anyplace in Mexico.

Mexico wasn't completely unknown to either of us. We had both been there many times before—Margie as a tourist, and I as a travel agent. But that was Mexico City, Cuernavaca, and Acupulco in eight days. The tourist bit. Smiling, English-speaking tour guides who described the wonders of the pyramids, the history, architecture, and the ancient folk dances also insulated us against the unexpected. They acted as our interpreters, drivers, nurses, shopping consultants, and—for the ladies— dancing or (if desired) bed partners. So our picture of Mexico was a kaleidoscope of First Class Hotels (tour price includes double occupancy), luxury restaurants, and hand-woven baskets bulging with souvenirs that can be purchased for less money in Los Angeles at the Akron.

This was different. We were on our own. The only Spanish we knew was *Buenos días, Buenas noches, and Gracias!* And if we got an answer to any of those, we didn't understand it. Further, we were going down into Baja where the roads were notoriously bad, there were no First Class hotels, and little, if any, English spoken. Instead of Aeronavis de Mexico airliners and stretchout limos, we had my wife's four-cylinder Pontiac. We had chosen her car for the trip rather than my Cadillac, figuring it would handle the bad roads better.

The beautiful freeway that now connects Tijuana with Ensenada was nonexistent in those days. The only road to Ensenada was a curving, rutted, asphalt path, two cars wide, that snaked along the edge of the cliffs from Rosarito (ten miles south of Tijuana) to a little community called La Misíon. At La Misíon, it ducked inland and wound the remainder of the way to Ensenada through struggling ranchos. It took much longer for the trip then, so it was after dark when we reached Ensenada. We had been married in Ensenada (illegal but satisfying) some years before, so it had sentimental attachments for us, but our obsession to get away from civilization was still so strong that we stopped only long enough to refuel the Tempest and buy some tequila. Then we pressed on into the pitch blackness of "The Baja Road."

We have since learned in hundreds of junkets to Mexico that you should never— but never—attempt any Mexican highway at night. They are all unlighted, and your headlights seem to stab out into infinity without revealing the slightest hint as to where you're going. There is usually no "rough shoulder" to the road. Where the asphalt ends, it pitches down a steep embankment which could overturn a car. Even

14

worse, livestock strolls nonchalantly across the road in front of your vehicle in the darkness. This was our first experience with it, and a few miles of holding tensely to the wheel, and staring out into black nothingness, was enough for me. We began to look for some place to turn off.

At length we thought we saw some sort of a dirt path leading off the road in the darkness. Since it went to the right, which was toward the beach, we took it. A few minutes drive, and it petered out against the foot of some sand dunes. We could hear breakers in the distance, but still could see nothing. It was as though the Creator had shut off the moon in disgust with the goings on in Los Angeles. We were very tired now. Wearily we unloaded the sleeping bags, food, ice, tequila, and coffee, and spread out our gear between two sand dunes. One small sip of tequila and we'd go to sleep.

Suddenly, Margie's hand tightened on my arm. "Did you hear that?" she whispered.

"No. What?"

"There's someone here in the dunes with us!"

"You're just nervous, Honey, it's been a long drive."

"The heck I am! There's someone there in the dark. Near us!" She was beginning to sound panicky.

I felt a tightening in my chest. We have never carried a weapon with us in Mexico. "I swear I don't hear a thing," I whispered.

"Shhhh . . . Listen."

Then I heard it! It was the unmistakable sound of the sand crunching under someone's foot. In a split second all the stories I'd heard about bandidos and assorted other Mexican criminals ("They'll kill you for a nickel") flashed through my mind.

"Yeah, I heard it," I whispered. "Let's climb in our sleeping bag and lie very still. Maybe they won't see us."

Silently we slipped into our double sleeping bag and kept very still, straining our ears for another sound, our hearts pounding.

For awhile we heard nothing but the waves in the distance. Then suddenly there it was again! Scrunch. Scrunch. Scrunch. Someone walking slowly, stealthily, toward us!

My mind was racing. I'd go for him first. Before he could get either one of us. I felt my side of the sleeping bag. It was unzipped. Good. I'd work my leg out of it so I could deliver a kick in the balls real fast. That way, if he had rape on his mind—

"Are you Americans?"

15

A male silhouette against the black sky. The accent was Mexican.

I wanted to sound like John Wayne facing the Apaches, or James Cagney against the New York underworld ("Look out, Buster, there's dynamite in these fists!") Sound tough! Sound seven feet tall!

"Yes we are," I quavered.

"Thank God!" he said. "So are we."

"Who's 'we'?" I asked.

"My wife and me. We're from Los Angeles. You know about the riot?"

"Yeah, we sure do." It was almost as if the riot were good news.

"Well, we live in that area, and we were afraid we were going to be killed, so we took off this afternoon."

"So did we," I said.

Now he was much closer. He'd been edging toward us as he spoke. I quickly got to my feet and observed he was slightly shorter than I, and not very fearsome either. He was nicely dressed. His hands were soft looking and his fingernails were polished like the nails of a man who does office work. An accountant, perhaps.

"May I ask a favor?" he said.

"What is it?"

"Well . . . it sounds silly, us being of Mexican descent and all . . . but we're frightened down here. May we sleep near you for company?"

"You've heard those stories about Mexican *bandidos,* huh?"

"That, and worse!"

"Sure. Just bring your stuff over here."

His wife had apparently been waiting in the car. Soon the two of them were puffing and tugging a large double bed mattress out on the dunes. They explained that in fleeing Los Angeles, they'd just stripped their bed and stuffed it in the back of their station wagon. They flopped their big mattress on the dune about ten feet from us, bid us a polite goodnight, and soon were snoring loudly.

We awakened with the sun in the morning and attempted to brew some coffee on a Sterno stove we had purchased at a Thrifty Drug Store. We got it lit, finally, but it looked like it was going to take forever to bring the water to a boil, and we were anxious to get going. We packed and departed coffeeless. Our Mexican-American friends were still snoring on their double bed mattress as we drove off.

The asphalt highway was in pretty fair shape except for an occasional chuckhole, and as the Mexican countryside reeled past our car windows, the charm of Mexico began to set in.

16

Mexico is unique and special in the mornings. Everything seems to get started at an earlier hour. A worker in blue denim trudges to work, a bottle of drinking water in one hip pocket and a burrito in the other. Fresh-scrubbed children stand at the roadside awaiting the bus to take them to school. Their classes begin at 7:30 a.m. Fruit stands are opening up, red chilis are drying in the morning sun, and the farmers are beginning to plow. Above all, there is a certain smell in the air. It's acrid, and yet strangely pleasant. We puzzled over its source for some time and finally concluded that it was the type of wood used for hundreds of wood fires in Mexico. Many of the rancheros can afford neither cooking stoves nor heaters for their homes, so the fire serves a dual purpose. The wood is probably mesquite or manzanita, both of which are plentiful.

The occasional bus you pass is an unforgettable sight. The buses seemed to be U.S. rejects from about 1935, propped up, patched together, and operating on pure determination. They groan slowly up and down Mexican hillsides emitting black balloons of smoke. Inside the buses there is an air of festivity. They are jammed with people, chickens, and— once in a while—a goat or pig, and there is much shouting and laughter as they go rocking by.

To travel in Mexico you must have a Tourist Card. They are free, and are obtained at the Mexican Government Tourist office at the border and in major cities. It is simply a piece of paper that identifies you from your birth certificate (or other proof of citizenship), and states your destination and length of stay in Mexico. They are not required in the border towns, but a few miles south of each border city there's a checkpoint where immigration police inspect, stamp, and sign the document.

As we approached the checkpoint south of Ensenada we realized that in our hasty departure we had neglected to get the Tourist Cards. What to do? An immigration official in uniform was flagging us down. We could speed up and make a run for it; perhaps they wouldn't bother to give chase. On the other hand, if they did and they caught us, our halcyon Mexican holiday might be spent in jail. We slowed down, and decided to face the music.

"*Buenos dias!*" I said, smiling hopefully.

"Good morning," he replied in English. "May I see Tourist Card please?"

"Tourist Card? What's that?" I had decided to play dumb.

"You don't know about Tourist Card?"

"No sir, I don't."

"Well you can not pass beyond here without one."

"Where can we buy one?" Margie asked. She was picking up on the act.

"You do not buy them, *Señora*. They are free. But you must get them at the border."

"Oh Golly," I put on my best crestfallen look, "that's so far back. What'll we do?"

"We can't go all the way back," Margie said plaintively. She was really perfecting our act. "We just can't!"

"Well," he was smiling mischievously now, "there is one way."

"What that?"

"I collect *peectures.*"

"What kind of pictures?"

"*Peectures* of U.S. presidents."

I was a little slow. I didn't get the point, but Margie was already fishing in her purse. She came out with three one-dollar bills, and handed them to him.

"George Washington! One of my favorite presidents," he said, and grinning broadly, waved us on.

This was our first experience with the Mexican *mordida*. It is misunderstood by Americans who refer to it as a bribe. It is a bribe by our standards, but not by theirs. Mexican government officials of all kinds, as well as policemen, accept the *mordida* as a legitimate (or quasi-legitimate) part of their pay. The police, for example, exist on a notoriously low pay scale and have to augment their salaries in this way in order to survive. It is similar to our practice of slipping the *maitre d'* a five dollar bill for a special seat, quick seating, or some other favor in a restaurant. We are bribing him of course, but we call it a tip. Various Mexican presidents have sworn that they would stamp out the *mordida* custom, but they never succeed. It's too much a part of Mexican life.

Gleeful about our success at the checkpoint, we picked up speed and soon had left what little civilization there was behind us. The plowed fields gave way to greening hillsides as the road took us inland, away from the sea. Now and then a jackrabbit skittered across the road in front of the car, or we'd see a skinny horse, belly swollen and rib cage bulging, staring at us mournfully as we passed.

Soon we descended down into a very fertile valley about a mile and a half wide and started up the other side. At the top was an ancient two-story adobe with a gasoline pump to one side. Our map identified the spot as Santo Thomás. We decided to fill the car with gas, and try to get a cup of coffee.

Typical of all countryroad gas stations in Mexico, there was no choice of Regular, Premium, or Unleaded. Just one pump with some pinkish Brand X fluid in it. The pump was of the 1930 variety that requires vigorous pumping by hand to get the liquid (that you hope is gasoline!) up in the glass chamber at the top, and ready to be gravity-fed to your gas tank. The Mexican youngster who manned the pump spoke no English, but we got the idea across with gestures and he started to fill the tank while we went inside for a look around.

The coffee you get in Mexican luxury hotels is about the same as our own. In the Mexican countryside, however, it's quite different. They start with whole, fresh coffee beans, roast them, and then grind them up in a kitchen grinder attached to the wall. The grounds are then dropped into a pan of boiling well water and allowed to bubble for awhile. When the heat is finally turned off, and the grounds sink to the bottom of the pan, the coffee is ready for drinking. The taste of chicory is very strong, and Mexicans usually add lots of milk and sugar. We take our coffee black, and that first cup left us clawing the air and gasping for breath! But we had the feeling that a great adventure awaited us just ahead, so we drank it hastily and departed.

Today, a highway runs all the way from Tijuana in the north, down the spine of Baja, and right to the very tip. But in those days the pavement ended at a town called Cabo Colonet, a short drive from Santo Tomás. When we got there, I was a bit disappointed. I had heard blood curdling tales about the fearsome, dangerous "Baja Road," and it looked like nothing I had envisioned. It was simply a graded, dirt road, and quite passable. A piece of cake.

Five miles later, the grading ended, and it lived up to its reputation. Thirty-five years of tire tracks on top of tire tracks had hammered the pink Baja dust into just the semblance of a road. There were huge rocks and bumps in the center of it that could knock out an oil pan or transmission with one blow; there were chuckholes that could swallow an entire wheel; dust, piled like snow on either side of the tracks would drift in around your tires making them spin helplessly. This hideous monster of a wild road meandered off to the south, a skinny ribbon stretching as far as the eye could see. Scores of other drivers, despairing of the original road, had started driving beside it on virgin soil creating yet another set of impossible tracks adjacent to the original, and just barely passable. There was not a sign of life for miles in any direction.

Dropping the Tempest into low gear, we began the trek.

"How about a drink for the road?" asked Margie.

"Make it two!" I said.

So with Margie trying to tend bar in the lurching, halting, skidding, bumping car, we continued to crawl southward at a snail's pace. The pink dust swirled in the air behind us, and dust devils danced across the landscape. The sun was now high in the sky. After about two hours of this I had an idea:

"Y' know what?"

"What?"

"We haven't seen the ocean for ages. What do you say we just turn off the road and drive across this wilderness until we find it?"

"Why not? We know it's somewhere out there." She pointed to the right.

I swung the car to the right, bounced over the last set of road bumps, and felt the car smooth out as we started over land untouched by man or vehicle.

"Just think," I said, "our tire tracks are the first ones here. In a few years maybe others will be following our tracks." I didn't realize at the time how right I was!

Ever since we had crossed the border—and with increasing intensity—Mexico had worked a special kind of magic on us. The Watts riot, the concerns of the nation and the world, our own personal problems (we had many then), job—money—house—bills,—and all other concerns seemed to belong to another world, another place in time. They were no longer part of us. Neither was the future. We felt as if we existed soley in the present. We were as carefree as feathers, wafted on the warm breezes of Baja, savoring every moment. And there was a great welling of love. Love for Mother Earth, everything in it, and greater love for each other.

We laughed, sang, and played games as we drove. Then after a time, we saw the great, blue Pacific Ocean, slightly rippling, and stretching out to touch the sky somewhere in infinity. I stopped the car and we opened the doors to hear the crashing of the waves on the rocks below.

I kissed her. And then, like kids, we made love on the front seat of the car.

Then we slept a little, and when we awakened that same wonderful feeling was still with us.

"Did you ever run around outside naked?" I asked.

"Not since I was a little girl."

"Me either. But I think it would be fun . . . there's no one around for miles."

"Let's do it!" Margie was already moving out of the car.

Hand-in-hand we walked, farther and farther from the car, feeling the sun and the warm air on our bodies.

"It's like taking an air-bath," Margie said.

As I looked at her golden body with the sunlight glinting on it, I was again overwhelmed with a feeling of love. I took her in my arms and we embraced. We would probably have made love again, right there, but suddenly I saw an incredible sight over her shoulder!

"Don't move!" I said, "Let's just stand like this."

"I like it too."

"I didn't mean that. There's someone coming toward us."

I could feel her stiffen. "Whaaaat?"

"Are you ready for this? It's a school bus full of kids!"

"Oh my God! What'll we do?"

"Well, we'd look ridiculous racing back to the car. Your back is toward them, so all they can see of you is your cute fanny."

"Well I don't like that."

I started to giggle. "Maybe they'll think we're a new kind of statue or something!"

We were both standing there in that position giggling as the school bus went by. Twelve pairs of big, brown eyes stared at us curiously, twelve little noses mashed against the windows, and then the back of the bus disappeared along the cliff.

Back in the car and clothed again, we concluded that there must be nesters—fishermen or small farmers—with homes scattered along that cliff, and of course their children, too, had to go to school.

As we resumed our drive southward on "The Road," we talked about that wonderful feeling we had—a high that no chemicals could ever produce—and we decided to call it "The Baja Feeling." Many years have passed since that first trip, but we still get "The Baja Feeling" every time we cross the border. I don't know why it happens, but it does. Other people we know say it has happened to them too.

Maneuvering the car at five miles per hour around cavernous chuck-holes or rocks, over huge bumps, and through soft, pink dust made the time go quickly. So did our conversation. We laughed a lot, and we sang. We exclaimed over the wonders of the vast, bleak wilderness. Now and again we'd pass through a little settlement; the Mexicans call them *poblados*. There'd be perhaps a dozen tiny houses, usually with potted geraniums in front. Often we'd see the *Señora* busily sweeping the dirt floors and yards with a homemade broom. Everybody waves at you in

Mexico. There were always adults and kids waving at us when we passed. Sometimes the settlement would boast a gas pump of the type we'd seen in Santo Tomás. If so, we'd stop and fill up with that *Brand X* ping-producing gasoline. Once we saw a Mexican worker in his blue denims and *sombrero* trudging from somewhere to somewhere else on "The Road" and we offered him a ride. He got in gladly, but spoke no English, refused a drink of tequila, and was obviously a little nervous riding with *locos gringos* who drank tequila while driving. At the next *poblado* he got out of the car.

Late that afternoon we saw what appeared to be a very lush and fertile ranch. It was the first of these we'd seen since leaving Santo Tomás. It covered quite a few acres, and was completely surrounded by tall, shade giving tamarisk trees. There was obviously plenty of good water there, so we decided to look in and see if they had any ice cubes. Ours were dwindling fast in the Baja heat. Turning off "The Road," we followed a well-tended track through the tamarisks to a cluster of buildings. It was easy to spot the main building. It was larger and had two enormous whale bones crossed to form an arch over the walk leading to the front door. The garden was typically Mexican. Someone long ago had planted flowers with some sort of basic landscaping scheme. Then with benign neglect, the flowers had flourished, crossed, spread in all directions, and created an immense bouquet of reds, golds, pinks, corals, and greenery that threatened to engulf the entire house. The roofs of all the buildings were paved with large, sun-bleached clam shells. We passed under the whalebone arch and knocked on the door. To our astonishment an American woman greeted us with "Welcome to Santa María Sky Ranch!"

There were ice cubes aplenty. There was also booze, lodging for the night, and some of the best Mexican food we've ever eaten.

Over a cooling drink, we learned that Santa María Sky Ranch was a haven for American business and professional men who liked to fly their own airplanes down into Baja, land on Santa María's dirt landing strip, and spend a few days hunting the waterfowl that abound in this region. Pictures of these stalwarts, standing beside their planes, or holding up their bags of game birds, were hung on all four walls. When we arrived, we were the only customers in the place.

The charming propietors were Mr. and Mrs. Scott. Although Americans, they ran Sky Ranch with a gentle Mexican touch and a delightful sense of humor. On one wall, for instance, was hung a wall telephone. The sign attached to it said in large block letters: "FREE PHONE CALLS TO ANYWHERE." Then in smaller letters down below,

22

it said: "You make both sides of the conversation." There was absolutely no telephone service in this part of Baja at that time, and I'm sure the phone gag resulted in a lot of hilarious phone calls to the President of the U.S., or a wife left at home. Against another wall stood an ancient upright piano which had probably served as accompaniment for a thousand tipsy community sings.

As we chatted with the Scotts, a group of Mexicans came in speaking excitedly in Spanish. They sat at one of the tables, opened a brown paper bag, and removed some prickly-looking oval-shaped fruit. Then they began slitting the fruit open with their pen knives.

"What the heck are they doing?" Margie asked.

"They're about to enjoy one of the great delicacies of Mexico," Scott said.

"What's that?" we asked.

"It's the fruit of the *Nopales* cactus," Mrs. Scott said. "They call them *Pitahayas*. They taste much like pears."

"They're even better when they're chilled, I think," Scott added.

"How do you find them?" I asked.

"Well . . . you know what *Nopales* cactus looks like? It's just the most typical cactus there is. The kind with the big, spiny leaves."

"Yeah?"

"Well," he continued, "if you look at it closely, you'll see the fruit. You just pick it."

Mrs. Scott chimed in: "When you pick it, be sure to use leather gloves or something to protect your hands, or you'll never get those stickers out of them."

Margie and I shared the *pitahaya* that afternoon at Sky Ranch and it was delicious. In fact, from that moment on we kept looking for *Nopales* cactus wherever we went in Mexico.

As the sun lowered in the sky, the planes from the States began to arrive. One by one they circled Sky Ranch, and then bounced in on the dirt landing strip. Soon the main building was filled with happy guys, drinking and talking, and planning their bird hunting for the following day. Margie and Mrs. Scott were the only women in the place. Having already had several drinks, and caught up in the happy mood of the place, we told the Scotts we'd like to stay overnight.

The drinking at Sky Ranch was handled in a novel way. They had a small, traditional bar, but no bartender. When you wanted a drink, you went to the bar and mixed your own. Drinks were twenty-five cents each, but no money changed hands. You had a small cardboard box at the bar

23

with your name on it, and there was a large bowl of dried beans on top of the bar. Each time you mixed a drink, you'd place one of the beans in your box. Then, when it came time for departure, the Scotts would count the beans in your box, multiply by twenty-five cents, and add it to your bill. It was strictly the honor system, and I'm sure no one cheated.

By the time the sun went down and the local generator had the two lightbulbs glowing, Margie and I had become well-acquainted with nearly everyone in the room. If you had to get sick in Mexico, this sure would be the place. At least half of the flier-hunters there were doctors. One of them, a surgeon from Long Beach, California, was a regular customer of Sky Ranch and our self-appointed "Guide to Baja." He told us that the place was jointly owned by an American and a Mexican. The American was Ken Hansen, owner of the famous Scandia restaurant in Hollywood. The Mexican owner, he said, was an old gentleman named Hussong, a German whose family was one of the earliest settlers of Ensenada back in the 1800s. In fact, it was his family who owned the well-known Hussong's Cantina in Ensenada. Then the doctor started raving about the food at Sky Ranch and insisted that we come back in the kitchen and meet the cook.

Her name was Lily. An incongruous lily she was! She weighed in at close to two hundred pounds, and had a moon-shaped, chocolate brown face continually split in a wide smile that revealed a fortune in gold-capped teeth. Our doctor friend explained that Lily could never have afforded all that dental work, but one of the flying dentists, visiting Sky Ranch from Los Angeles, had done her dental work at no charge to relieve her discomfort. She spoke no English, but she communicated in a way anyone could understand—with the language of superb cuisine!

As we entered her kitchen (and it was hers), there were large, four- or five- pound lobsters creeping about on the floor. Gabriel, one of the young workers on the ranch, would pick up a squirming lobster, deftly remove the meat and hand it to Lily before the lobster knew what had happened! So fast was he, you could scarcely see the knife move. Lily then chopped the fresh lobster meat into smaller pieces and placed them in a buttered skillet with onions and other seasonings. Wheat tortillas, as light as French crepes, were heating. For just a few moments she stirred the lobster meat, cooking it lightly, then scooped it up and placed it in a tortilla, creating the most succulent, mouth-watering bit of taco goodness I have ever enjoyed. We devoured so many of them we nearly foundered ourselves and finally, about 9 p.m., staggered off to our room.

If our room had had the pat, assemblyline luxury of a Holiday Inn,

24

we'd have been disappointed. Even so, we weren't quite prepared for our accomodations! We had a cell-like room with cement walls and a naked light bulb hanging from the ceiling. They shut off the generator at 9:30 p.m., so if you wished to stay up later you had to use a flashlight. Our double bed against one wall looked like a large, collapsed balloon with one loose spring sticking straight up out of the middle of the bed as if it were growing there. Would that spring be our Mexican bundling board that night? A foreign intruder that would preserve our sanctity? Or would someone awaken in the morning with its circular imprint on his thigh? (Margie carried the imprint for half a day!)

The Mexicans seem never to have quite understood bathrooms. Even in a number of luxury, American-oriented hotels I have encountered some plumbing surprises. One hotel in Acapulco had the toilet placed conveniently in the shower. You could bathe and relieve yourself at the same time. The beautiful María Isabel Hotel in Mexico City offers a luxurious bathroom replete with a gold telephone. But the toilet paper roll is mounted in the wall across the room from the toilet so you have to waddle across the room with your trousers at half-mast to tear off a few squares! The Hilton in Guadalajara features a cavernous bathroom with the floor sloping sharply to a large drain in the center of the floor. Its purpose must be to swallow any overflow of water from the shower.

Our bathroom at Sky Ranch featured a toilet and a cardboard box. The box was for used toilet paper because if you flushed the paper down the drain it could stop up the plumbing. There was a shower in the corner, but it was obviously an afterthought. It had been prefabricated of galvanized metal and simply stood in place in the corner like a tall sentinel guarding the toilet bowl. Nevertheless, after a couple of days on the road in the Baja dust, a shower was most welcome. By the time we were finished, the lights had gone out, so we groped our way to bed.

With the total honesty prevalent among the Mexicans of Baja and the guests of Sky Ranch, there was no need for locks on the doors, so there were none. Female guests with the gentlemen were a rarity there also. The men usually slept alone or shared a room with a friend, and got up early to go hunting. By 7 a.m., the rooms would all be empty. We were awakened abruptly at seven the next morning by a young Mexican girl coming in to clean. Seeing a man and woman unclothed and in bed together embarrassed the poor girl worse than it did us. She blushed, almost upset her water bucket, and backed hastily out of our room.

We arose, enjoyed one of Lily's hearty breakfasts, brushed our teeth, paid our bill, and bid our charming hosts goodbye. In the years that followed, we visited Sky Ranch many times and, in fact, became "regulars."

As this is written, Sky Ranch stands in ruins, and a 160 room luxury hotel complete with swimming pool, riding horses ("Our beautiful golf course will open soon"), and other tourist appurtenances is just a short distance away.

"The Baja Feeling" still with us, we jounced again down the rutty road heading southward, ever southward, at a breakneck five miles per hour. We couldn't see the ocean, but we could smell the fresh salt air, so we knew it couldn't be far away.

"I'm getting tired of just driving," Margie said, "What do you say we turn off, drive toward the ocean, and look for a place to camp?"

"Done!" I said, and turned toward the sea.

The profiles of the two coasts of Baja are completely different. On the Gulf side you have brush-covered land leading to sand beaches that are usually fairly flat. On the Pacific side of Baja you find either high cliffs with waves smashing on the rocks below, or if it's a sand beach you find great billows of sand dunes. Fortunately we hit upon a sand dune beach. I ran the little Tempest as far as I could without getting stuck, then parked it, and lugged our gear out on the beach. We made camp between two sand dunes.

Outside of that first night when we'd slept in the dunes south of Ensenada, this was our first camping experience. We were woefully ill-equipped. Our camp really consisted of my large golf umbrella, a couple of beach towels, and our double sleeping bag. We were never able to make the Sterno stove work at all. Fortunately, however, we had brought with us our portable barbecue and an ample supply of charcoal briquettes. It worked well for all our cooking, and served as a table when not in use.

Despite the makeshift nature of our equipment, our little nest in the sand dunes shortly began to feel like home. Our days were spent lolling on the sand getting suntanned, or bathing in the ocean. At night we cuddled in our sleeping bag and stared at a black sky studded with trillions of stars, like sequins on black velvet. Having enjoyed our brief experience with nudism, we played Adam and Eve on the beach and never saw a soul.

Well, almost never.

I have often wondered why our Creator, in forming anything as beautiful and graceful as the human body, couldn't have thought of a more dignified way of disposing of the sewage. But he didn't, so we had purchased a Jonny Pot before leaving Los Angeles. This "camper's friend" consists of a traditional toilet seat mounted on collapsible legs, and fitted with a plastic bag. After use, you simply (sometimes not so simply!) detach the bag, twist its top, and fasten it with one of those wire "twisties." Then you bury it.

On one particular morning I had, as usual, taken the Jonny Pot, some toilet paper, an old copy of *Life* magazine, and a shovel a couple of dunes away from camp for the morning meditation period. I was returning to camp, the Jonny Pot slung over my arm, my stomach bulging over my bathing trunks, and a very good stand of whiskers on my face, when two Americans—total strangers—dressed in suits and neckties came strolling over the dunes toward me.

"Hey!" one of them said, "I know you! You're Ben Hunter."

I pretended to be deaf. Or Mexican. Or George Spelvin from Milpitas, and kept on walking, eyes straight forward.

"Hey, Ben Hunter!" (*"Keep walking! Don't look back!"*)

By the time I got back to our friendly camp and dared to look, they were gone. We never saw them again.

Our only other visitors were two little Mexican boys. They were brothers. One was about ten years old, the other about eight. "Ten" spoke some English, and was the salesman. "Eight" spoke no English, and was the laborer. He was dragging a large gunnysack filled with corn.

"Corn for sale," said "Ten," as "Eight" struggled with the big sack.

"Some barbecued corn would be great, Honey," I said to Margie.

"How much?" she asked "Ten."

"Fiffy cent."

"Fifty cents?"

"Sí."

"For how much?"

He just pointed at the bag and shrugged.

"Just give him fifty cents and see what you get, Darling," I said.

Margie fished into her purse and found the money. She handed it to him.

"Thank you," he said, and they departed, leaving us with the entire sack full of corn!

We sat there agape at the size of our purchase, and as the two little figures got smaller and smaller walking across the fields to their adobe home somewhere, I told Margie I could just imagine Big Brother saying in Spanish: "You see, Little Brother, how easy it is to earn lots of money when you speak English?"

That night we soaked some ears of the corn in seawater and barbecued them in the husks. They had stayed too long on the stalk. The kernels were as big as marbles and just as hard. We couldn't eat them without breaking our fillings. So perhaps "Ten" drove a hard bargain after all!

The days slipped by like sand through our fingers. Lazy days on the beach hearing only the cry of the sea birds, and making love at night with only the stars to see. Little things became great adventures.

One morning we awakened to discover tiny, tiny footprints all around our sleeping bag. The prints were no larger than a fingernail, and were of only two feet. They were not bird prints, so we concluded it was some tiny animal like a kangaroo rat hopping on its hind legs. We pictured this little creature with pink, twinkling nose, hopping around and round the two snoring giants on the sand, his heart palpitating with fright, but his curiosity even greater than his fear. Then, probably, sometime during the night one of us had turned suddenly, or thrown an arm out of the sleeping bag, and our wee visitor had fled in terror to the brush from where he had come. Each evening after that we smoothed the sand around our sleeping area in hopes of finding his prints there again in the morning. But, a lesson learned, he never returned.

At length, our food supplies began to dwindle and, like a specter lurking in the darkness, the necessity of returning to the world began to seep into my consciousness. I would have to explain my long, unexcused absence from my television show (if I still had one!), and Margie would have to shop for groceries. There'd be housework and social obligations, and our personal problems would reassert themselves. We decided it was time to pack our gear and start the homeward trek.

Every time we've ever gone to Mexico—even if just for a weekend—we've found that the trip there seemed to take an instant, and the return trip seemed forever. So it was this time.

"My God, I didn't realize we'd driven so far!" I said a hundred times as our car ground slowly northward toward the States and reality.

We had one frightening moment.

While bouncing over one particularly treacherous stretch of road we heard a stone fly up and clang against the underside of the car. I kept going.

"You better get out and check the car," Margie said.

"Why? It was just a stone hitting it. We're probably okay."

"Check it! I just have a feeling."

I know Margie's "feelings." She has a lot of ESP and when she says she has a "feeling," there's usually something wrong. I stopped, got out, and peeked under the car as soon as the dust settled.

Oil was dripping steadily out of the crankcase. The stone had apparently punctured it, and at the rate it was dripping, there was no way our oil would last until we could find civilization.

"What is it?" she called out of the window.

"Punctured crankcase. We're losing oil fast."

She got out of the car and joined me. "What'll we do?"

"I'll think of something," I said. I said it to reassure her. I didn't know what in the hell to do. Cars went by on this road very rarely, and even if one came along, what could he do to help? We were stuck! We stood there quietly, listening to a distant cricket, each of us occupied with his own thoughts.

"Remember the school bus, Darling?" Margie said.

"How could I forget!"

"Well, if you remember, we said at that time that there were probably little houses hidden out all around here, even though you can't see them. Maybe some of those people could help us."

"I doubt it . . . But how are we going to find them, anyway?"

"Just look."

"Okay," I said, "you stay here with the car, and I'll start walking."

"No way! I'm coming with you!"

We started walking across the desert in the general direction of the ocean, straining our eyes against the sun's glare, searching for some sign of life. We had only gone several hundred yards when we saw a tiny shack. It so blended with the desert scenery that we could have missed it altogether. It was over a small rise, so there was no way we could have seen it from the road. As we approached, a Mexican emerged from the doorway and stood watching us curiously. Soon it was apparent to him that we weren't just taking a stroll in the desert heat but were coming to him, so he moved lazily toward us.

"*Buenos días*," I said.

"*Buenos días*."

"We have car trouble." I pointed to the car. "Broken. Won't run. Understand?"

The Mexican just gazed at us.

I picked up a stone. "Stone came up from road." I demonstrated. "*Bang!* Hit crankcase." I whacked the stone against my palm. "Oil dripping out. *Blub. Blub. Blub.*" I made motions of oil dripping out of my palm.

The light of comprehension dawned in his eyes. "*Momentito,*" he said, and disappeared into the house.

"I think you just won an Oscar," Margie said.

"I'm going to Spanish school before we ever come down here again," I replied.

The Mexican emerged from his house, carrying a bar of old fashioned, yellow laundry soap.

"What the hell is he going to do . . . wash the car?"

"I don't know," Margie said, "but he's our only chance."

"Soap?" I said to him increduously.

'Está bien," he said, and started walking toward the car. We followed him, and as we walked, a rotund, pleasant-looking Mexican woman came to the doorway of the shack and gazed at us. It was probably her soap.

When we arrived at the car, he bent over, looked underneath, and nodded his head sagely as he saw the oil dripping down.

"Está bien," he said again.

He immediately flopped on his back in the hot, red dust, and pushed with his feet until he had worked his body under the car.

I bent over to watch.

Grasping the bar of soap, he started rubbing it back and forth over the leaking oil. The heat from the crankcase melted the soap gradually, and allowed it to seep into the crankcase. In just a few minutes it had ceased to drip. It not only stopped losing oil then, it never lost another drop for three months after we were back in the states. When we took the car to Pontiac to have a new crankcase installed, they couldn't believe it!

The Mexican scrambled to his feet, grinning, and trying to brush the dust off his clothes.

"Oh gracias, gracias, gracias!" I bubbled. I could have kissed him! Instead, I reached into my pocket and drew out a five dollar bill. "It's yours," I said, and put it in his hand.

"No, no. Gracias." He handed it back.

Perhaps the money had offended him.

"Can I give you a drink of tequila?" I waved the bottle.

He smiled. "No me gusta. Hay cigarillos?"

"Cigarettes? Sure!" I reached in my pocket and gave him the remainder of the pack. He pulled one out and I lit it for him.

"Gracias," he said, and turned to go.

Margie produced an unopened pack and thrust it at him. "For mañana," she said.

He accepted it, said gracias again, and went on his way.

"Golly, he got filthy!" Margie said. "His wife is going to have a fit

30

when she sees those clothes."

"They've got the laundry soap," I said.

In hundreds of trips to Mexico since that day, we have discovered that once you get away from the big cities, Mexican people will not usually accept money, except as pay for whatever type of work they do normally. Life in the countryside is hard—especially in Baja—and the people are accustomed to helping each other, because their existence depends on it. They love American cigarettes, and they always need lead sinkers for fishing. So they gladly accept these small gifts. We always keep them with us in Mexico, along with an ample supply of hard candies for their children.

The rest of our trip was long and uneventful. Soon we were home, plunged back into reality, with Baja just a memory. But the charm of Mexico had worked its way into our hearts. That first cup of Mexican coffee with the smell of chili cooking; the friendly, waving people in the little *poblados*; the worker who was frightened of the *locos gringos* drinking tequila while driving; little "Ten" and "Eight," the corn salesmen; Santa María Sky Ranch; and Lily's lobster tacos; star-filled nights on the warm sand, and the dusty, brown angel who'd fixed our car. But, most of all, that wonderful, light, loving, carefree "Baja Feeling." We couldn't recapture it at home, but we could remember those ten days. We would feel it again some day. We would return to this lovely wilderness as soon as possible.

2/ The Biggie

On my first day back on my television show, things went well—at first. My crew told me that the studio had called on my good friend Don Lamond to stand in for me during my unexplained absence, and that he had done an excellent job. Between commercials and other business of the show, I relaxed in my comfortable set and regaled the crew with tales of our Mexican odyssey. However, all of this serenity came to an abrupt halt midway through the program when a page handed me a note saying Jim Gates, the program director, wanted to see me in his office as soon as I signed off.

In television, all performers are referred to as "talent," no matter how impoverished they might be in that area. All talent survives at the whim of the program director who, if he desires, can sever your career by invoking the cancellation clause that exists in all talent contracts. These thoughts flickered through my mind as I made my way toward Jim's office, and tried to think of a good lie to explain my appropriated vacation.

Jim was not known for screaming, waving his arms, and chewing the rug as were some of his colleagues. When angered, he was more apt to be cold, distant, and icy. When I entered his office you could have chipped icicles off his ears.

"I want to ask you a favor, Ben," he said before I could speak.

"Sure, Jim. What?"

"The next time you're planning to take a few days off, give us a little notice, will you?"

That's all he said.

In the year that followed that first trip to the interior of the country, Margie and I became Baja freaks. We read everything we could find on the subject and we visited the area time and time again. There was a limit as to how far into Baja we could drive because we didn't have a four-wheel drive vehicle. However, it's surprising how much territory we covered with the Tempest. Its feather weight, as cars go, seemed to make up to some extent for its lack of power.

I hadn't carried out my promise made on that lonely Baja road to go to school and learn Spanish. However, through association we both began to learn some of the language. The first things you learn are the road signs. One hard jolt and you remember that a *Vada* is a dip in the road. When your car is winding snakelike around the eyebrow of a cliff with rocks a hundred feet below, it isn't difficult to figure out that *Curva Peligrosa* means "Dangerous Curve." And so it goes.

We also purchased a Spanish-English dictionary, and were constantly looking up words in it and trying to speak Spanish. The book also has a brief explanation of Spanish grammar on the first few pages. The explanations are heavily pedantic, but once you have waded through it, you begin to understand. We still have that dictionary today, and it still rides in our car with us to Mexico. It's dog-eared, torn, and patched with masking tape, but we wouldn't part with it for the world.

We made some funny mistakes. One time, we were passing through a town when we saw a sign saying *Taller Mecánico*. The word *mecánico* was obviously "mechanic," and we reasoned that *taller* was the mechanic's name. Since it wasn't a Latin name, we decided he must be an American living in Mexico. George Taller, perhaps. But then in other towns we saw other *Taller Mecánico* signs, and sometimes *Taller Electrico*. George was both a mechanic and an electrician?

"He must be rich," I said. "He's got a place of business in every town."

Finally we had the good sense to look up *taller* in the Spanish part of the dictionary. It is pronounced "tah-yair," and it means a "workshop." We've never forgotten that word either!

Another time we noticed signs every so often pointing to some place named *Micro Ondas*. If it was a town, why were there so many of them? And in different locales? We puzzled over the towns named *Micro Ondas* for some time. Again, the dictionary saved us. It means "micro-wave" and the signs were pointing to transmitters.

As time went by, I learned to speak Spanish fairly well. I got so I could say just about anything that needed saying. The only problem was, when I got a reply I couldn't understand it! It was frustrating. Margie was just the opposite. She had difficulty speaking the language, but could understand nearly everything that was said. Together we were a conversational team. I would address our Mexican friends in my proper Spanish. Then when they'd reply, I'd turn to Margie and say quickly, under my breath: "What'd he say?" She'd tell me briefly, and the conversation would continue. Conversationally speaking, we were like a sack race, each with one foot in the bag.

Thus, linguistically lame, we laid plans for "The Biggie." We had decided we were going to rent a camper and travel the entire West Coast of Mexico. This was to be no madcap dash into the wilderness like our initial trip. There were plans and counter-plans, marked maps, and lists of supplies. No French Leave from the studio this time. I arranged a legitimate vacation—a long one, for this trip.

We wanted to get "The Baja Feeling" as soon as possible, so instead of driving over to Arizona and crossing the border at Nogales, which would have been quicker, we planned to cross at Tijuana. From there we'd follow Mexican Highway 2 eastward to the point where it joined Highway 15, Mexico's highway to the south.

Margie found a place in Canoga Park which rented campers with trucks, and we inspected our future home. At that time of our lives we had no idea of what the inside of a camper should look like, and this one looked to us like the Hilton Hotel! There was a sink, a four burner stove (no oven), and an icebox. It even had a toilet. The toilet consisted of a toilet seat, recessed in a tiny closet area, and suspended over a bucket. You filled the bucket with a couple of quarts of water and deposited some pills in it. No flushing. You just dumped the bucket. Rent for the whole rig, including the truck, was $150 per week. Not bad.

When the day of departure finally arrived, we were as excited as kids going to the circus. Margie picked me up at the studio on a Friday afternoon as soon as I'd signed off my show, and with farewells from my crew, we were off on our great adventure. One of my sponsors at that time was "Chicken Delight," and they kindly provided us with a gratis bucket of delicious fried chicken for the trip. Our adventures always seemed to begin with chicken!

Outside of learning how to drive the truck without the benefit of being able to see out the back window, the first leg of our trip was without problems. Since we began the journey in mid-afternoon, it was nearly dark when we reached Tijuana. I am not a night person, and neither is Margie. When it gets dark our eyelids begin to get heavy, so we pushed ourselves just far enough to get out of Tijuana and start the eastward trek. Then we pulled over to the side of the road, ate some fried chicken, and went to bed.

Early the next morning, the roosters were singing their morning serenade, dew was heavy on the fields, and those lovely, familiar dawning sights of Mexico were starting. A wreck of a school bus loaded with laughing children lumbered by, and that wonderful euphoric, carefree, loving "Baja Feeling" engulfed us again. We sipped delicious camper coffee and soaked in the atmosphere through our pores.

The town of Tecate is known to most people for that tasty Tecate beer. To us, it's better known for a mishap that occured there. We had purchased a pair of leather gloves for the purpose of picking the *pitahayas* from their spiny cactus hosts, and were *pitahaya* picking veterans by now. As we approached Tecate, we espied an enormous stand of cacti. They stood ten to twelve feet high and covered about a third of an acre. Never—anywhere—have we seen cacti as old, large, and as numerous as in that one spot. Someone had hacked his way into the cactus forest with a machete, creating a dark tunnel that went back out of sight into the huge thicket.

"Obviously, that tunnel was made by *pitahaya* pickers," I said.

We stopped the camper, put on the leather gloves, and with paper bags in hand entered the tunnel. As we groped our way along in the half light, we envisioned our paper bags filled with the juicy delicacies, and how good they would taste after chilling in our camper icebox.

After walking a short distance, we discovered that the only cactus fruit there was above us way out of reach. Moreover, there was a terrible smell in that tunnel . . . as if someone had used it as an outdoor toilet. We decided to give up on the *pitahaya* hunt, and return to the camper. On arrival at the camper I discovered that I had stepped in feces left in the tunnel and it was plastered all over my shoes. The smell was intolerable. I removed the shoes, and Margie and I both worked over them for a long time. We scraped them as clean as a dog's bone; we washed them; we even scuffed them around in the desert sand, but the stench remained. When I climbed back into the cab and we closed the doors, the smell was enough to drive us outside again.

We thought perhaps they'd have something at a gas station we could use to remove the smell. Maybe even gasoline would do it. So we turned into the first Pemex station in Tecate.

I did not know a polite word for feces in Spanish. The only word I knew was the street-word, *cagada*.

To the questioning glance of the attendant, I said: *"Tengo cagada en mi zapatos."* [I have shit on my shoes.]

I didn't need Margie to interpret his answer. He shrugged and walked away.

We then had another bright idea. Tecate is filled with cute little shoeshine boys. They practice their art on the sidewalks of the town, and the only English they speak is "Shine?" Perhaps some nice, strong-smelling shoe polish would eradicate the odor.

It wasn't hard to find one of these young businessmen. To his query, I said *"Si,"* and placed my offending shoe on his box.

He started to remove the polish and brush from inside, and then jumped up as if he'd sat on a cactus.

"Cagada!" he said, and made a wry face. This was followed by some rapid Spanish I couldn't understand, but the intent was clear. He wasn't going to shine *those* shoes. No, sir. Not for *any* amount of money! *"Adiós Señor."*

We finally left the shoes, which were brand new, beside the road somewhere in Mexico.

To some people the drive across the state of Sonora, Mexico, might be boring. It's mostly desert. In fact, we surmise that it is a continuation of the great Arizona desert. Highway 15 is a black, shimmering strip that bisects this wasteland clear to the skyline—a skyline you never seem to reach. The desert on either side of it is studded with different types of desert growth, but that's all. The sky is cloudless, and the sun beats down unrelentingly. There seems to be no life, except for the occasional buzzard circling high in the sky. If you stop your car, there isn't a sound. Not even the chirp of a cricket.

We made many stops as we crossed the desert. Sometimes we stopped to have a bite to eat, sometimes to use the bucket facilities astern, and—at least once—to make love, basking in the sheer delight of our aloneness and the rugged beauty of the desert. During one of these stops we peered, from inside the camper, at the limb of a desert tree touching our window and saw a large, green iguana staring back at us. On another occasion, I spotted what appeared to be a bright red spot of blood on a cactus. And then it started to move!

"It's a cochineal bug," Margie said.

"What's that?"

"It's a bug they make a red dye from. The red dye is used in a lot of different ways."

"I'll be darned. How did you know that?" I asked.

"I don't know," she said, "I just knew it."

A very familiar sight on all Mexican roads is the truck driver fixing his own truck. Keeping ancient, complaining vehicles running is a necessary Mexican pastime, and nearly all the owners are excellent mechanics. Necessity has taught them to compel broken-down engines to run again by using wire, string, pieces of paper, pen-knives and even soap for tools.

At first, when we'd come to a stalled truck we'd stop and ask the driver if he needed help. But we soon learned that he had the situation under control, and in an hour or so he'd be rolling again. Meanwhile, it was pleasant working under the truck in the shade.

After about six hours, the desert crossing terminated at the seaport of Guaymas. We had many traveler's guides with us, and one of these publications informed us that *Bocochibampo* meant "sea serpent" in the Mexican Indian tongue, so we decided to camp at Bocochibampo Bay near Guaymas. Today, Bocochibampo is crowded with hotels, but in 1966, it was unsettled. We jounced off the road and parked the camper in a little cove next to the water, never dreaming that in the morning we'd see the sea serpent!

We were hot and dusty from the long desert drive, so we peeled off our clothes and plunged into the cooling water of the Gulf for a bath. We toweled off, and then sat in our camp chairs sipping a drink and watching the sunset. At times like that I feel that the Earth is a beautiful toy, and we are its masters. When the last orange light in the sky faded, we barbecued hamburgers, ate them, and went to bed.

When camping in Mexico, we try to conserve water by washing the dishes (as well as ourselves) in the ocean water. So the next morning after breakfast we were squatting at the edge of the bay doing the dishes when we saw it! Margie was concentrating on the scullery more than I, so I saw it first.

"My God! There's the sea serpent!" I said.

Margie looked up. "It *is* a sea serpent!"

The morning breeze had not yet ruffled the surface of the bay. It looked like a mirror. And there, cutting through the water and creating a small wake, was a long line of dorsal fins undulating in and out of the water in a line. It was the classic artist's conception of a sea serpent, and just off shore!

For a few moments we stared at it in awe. "Go get the camera," Margie whispered, "otherwise no one will believe us."

I sprung into action. I was back beside her in a moment, ripping the camera out of its case. Too late. The waters of the bay were flat and undisturbed again. The sea serpent was gone.

Discussing it later, we decided it was probably just porpoises, swimming one behind the other and creating the illusion of a long, serpentine creature having a morning swim. It had fooled the ancient Indians, and it had fooled us.

But what were porpoises doing out of the open ocean swimming in a small, calm bay? Why were they swimming in a straight line? Porpoises usually cavort and splash next to each other, not single file, and they like the open sea. Scientists believe that such creatures as giant sea serpents actually exist. Could it be that there really was a sea serpent there?

We left Bocochibampo and decided to check out the San Carlos hotel before continuing on. At the hotel we had a flat tire that marked a milestone in our Mexico travels.

The *Posada San Carlos* (*Posada* means "Inn") basks on the sunny strand of San Carlos Bay, a small inlet about five miles north of the city of Guaymas. It is owned by an American attorney from Tucson, and its clientele is mostly American. Nevertheless, it manages to capture the spirit and feeling of Mexico. No high rise here. There is one main building housing the dining room, bar, and hotel registration, and a series of rooms spread out along the beach north and south of it. The architecture and decor are pure Mexicana, with flaming red bougain-villeas climbing over the white adobe walls. Seaward from the rooms is snow white sand, caressed by the warm waves of the Gulf. The setting was so beautiful, and the people so hospitable and charming, we decided to stay overnight. Our decision to stay was also influenced by the prospect of a warm, fresh water shower for a change!

When we checked out in the morning and bade our hosts farewell, we discovered that during the night one of our tires had breathed its last breath. Immediately, we were surrounded with smiling Mexican tire changers volunteering to help. With much chatter and laughter, they changed our tire in minutes, and gladly accepted the tip we proffered. We bade them goodbye and went in search of tire repair. It wasn't hard to find. On the outskirts of Guaymas was a Goodyear dealer.

"You know how Mexicans are," Margie said as we drove into his service area, "they never want to do business with a woman—"

"Yeah, the land of *machismo.*"

"Well you take the tire in to be fixed and I'll tidy up the camper while I'm waiting for you."

"Okay," I said, and dragged the flat into the repair shop. The owner was an affable gent who offered me coffee and conversation while I waited. He particularly wanted to discuss civil unrest in the U.S., and American politics. Who did I think was the best president since FDR? What about American involvement in Vietnam? I struggled to be very objective with my answers, but I fear my personal political bias poked through just like the nail in the tire in the next room. We had a grand conversation for about twenty minutes while the men worked on my tire. Then it was done; the repaired tire was placed on my truck, and we were on our way again.

As we pulled onto the highway, Margie said "How did you get along?"

"Fine. Why?"

"Did he speak English?"

"No—" only at that moment did I realize I'd been talking Spanish for twenty minutes and *understanding!* I hadn't needed Margie as an interpreter. I had been thinking in Spanish while I talked, and thus hadn't realized anything was different. The brain, that marvelous computer, had chosen the occasion of the flat-fixing to usher in The Dawn Of Understanding. The caveman, receiving his first answering grunt from his cavewife, could not have been more elated than I. The barriers were down! The sack race was over and won! Communication was the order of the day! That is, until we got to the city park five minutes later.

Every Mexican town big enough to call itself a town has a park, and every park seems to have an heroic statue. The park and statue in Guaymas are especially charming. The park is divided into two parts— one-half for kids, and one-half for adults. The kid-half is loaded with outdoor toys, always in use, and the usual *vendedores de banqueta* [sidewalk vendors] selling sweet drinks, candy, tacos, and heart of watermelon on a stick. The adult-half is serene and cool with tree-shaded park benches, many flowers, and a striking statue. It depicts a mother with her children. She smiles fondly down at them, and a gentle hand rests on one tousled head. The plaque underneath the statue says something to the effect that it was commissioned by the wife of the president of Mexico, and is dedicated to "The Mothers Of Mexico."

We had planned to continue our jouney southward, but couldn't resist stopping at the park for a moment. There was one lone man in the adult-half of the park, and I resolved to talk with him.

Casually, Margie and I strolled among the flowers, working closer to the gentleman, seated on a park bench. Finally we were within earshot of him.

"*El día está bonito,* no?" I said. [It's a beautiful day, isn't it?]

40

No reply.

This time I looked him directly in the face, smiling: "*Me gusta la estatua de la madre y ninos, especialmente.*" [I especially like the statue of the mother and children.]

Still no reply. Was this going to be the first rude Mexican we'd ever met?

Then he smiled sadly, and pointed to his ear.

He was deaf! Using the deaf sign language, I asked him if he knew how to sign.

His face split into a huge grin, and he nodded vehemently.

I then signed that my oldest son is deaf, and that Margie and I often talk to him in signs even though he reads lips and speaks.

He signed to us that he went to a special school for the deaf in the border city of Juarez, but now was living in Guaymas. He was a carpenter, he said, but had difficulty finding work because he could not communicate.

Margie and I signed with him for a little while, feeling that perhaps he felt at this moment just as I had five or ten minutes before. He would tell his friends that he had talked with two *norteamericanos* who knew the sign language.

Our signing ability is rather rudimentary since our son is able to read lips, and soon we found ourselves running out of things to talk about. We shook hands with our new friend (who almost shook our arms off), and took our leave. On the way out of the park we purchased a delicious watermelon heart on a stick from a *vendedor de banqueta*, and it dripped in our laps as we continued our push south to the port city Mazatlán.

At Guaymas you enter the states of Chihuahua and Sinaloa. These states are blessed with water in ample supply, and endless fields of fertile farmland reel by your car window. Wherever a river nears the highway you see the women kneeling on its banks doing their wash. Hard, yellow laundry soap and a rock are the only cleansing agents they use. Then the wash is spread on top of bushes to bleach in the sun. Their white things are "whiter than white" without detergents or Clorox. They laugh and sing as they work, and there's no tattletale gray here.

Many years before this, in Mexico City with a tour, I had wanted to make a snapshot of a very interesting looking old lady. Her face was creased into thousands of lines that bespoke years of squinting at the sun. But she was very poor and her clothes were in tatters. I had found that in many countries they disapproved of pictures taken of their poor, so I asked my tour guide if it was okay.

41

"Of course, *Señor*, make the picture," he said.

"Should I ask her permission?"

"No it is not necessary. Just go ahead."

"But she's so very poor."

He looked at me evenly. "*Señor* Hunter, she does not know she is poor."

I remembered this incident as I watched the women with their wash, and I told the story to Margie. "These women are like that," I said. "They don't know they're poor."

Robert Frost once wrote: "Something there is that doesn't love a wall." No walls at all, and very few fences circumscribe the Mexican countryside. The result is that cattle are constantly strolling contentedly across the highway, day and night. When it happens at night it's often instant hamburger. In the daytime, however, cars and trucks screech to a stop and wait impatiently for the animal to complete the crossing. Bossy, meanwhile, chews on a straw like a country bumpkin and stares at the traffic with bovinely stupid eyes. It's almost as if she were saying, "What's the matter, honey? Y'all got someplace to go?"

Our lovely, silly "Baja Feeling" was in full flower, of course, so we found it hilarious when trucks bound for the market, businessmen on important errands, and tourists bent on pleasure had to wait interminably for one peaceful cow to amble across the road. Sometimes, a frustrated driver would leap out of his car and give her a hard slap on the rump to get her going. She'd do a quick little foxtrot and halt again. Still in the highway. Still chewing. We'd howl with laughter.

Soon, we had reached Mazatlán and were driving along the *malecón*. Literally, *malecón* means "dike" or "seawall," but in Mazatlán they apply the word to the beautiful boulevard that extends north and south, next to the seawall, on the ocean front.

Never has the ocean been clearer or bluer. Never has the sky been so breathtakingly beautiful. We were now in the tropics in the early summer, the time for tropic rainstorms, so here and there were great, bulbous clouds, tinged with gray, edged in silver, and framed by a turquoise sky. Sea birds wheeled and dipped over the bay while children squealed and played in the warm surf. We turned left at the beginning of the drive and continued south past small boys diving off rocky crags into the clear water, and *vendedores* selling colorful seashells spread out on the seawall. Quaint, horse drawn carriages, like those seen in Central Park, clip-clopped merrily down the *malecón*, their passengers enjoying the scene as much as we. At the part of the beach where the fishermen sell their catch, still flopping from the sea, we saw one of the most beautiful little girls we've ever seen. She was about eight-years-old with shiny, raven hair, sparkling white teeth, and large, mellow, amber eyes. She was selling a fish. We were admiring her beauty when she took a step and we saw she was badly crippled.

Besides just enjoying the beauty of this picture postcard city, we were looking for some place to purchase ice. The ice block in our camper had shrunk to the size of a snowball and needed replacing at once. After making a few inquiries, we found to our astonishment that with all those beautiful hotels and magnificent restaurants there were no ice cubes to be had anywhere, and only one ice house. We got the address of the ice house from a friendly policeman, but finding it proved to be an adventure in itself.

In Mexico, street signs are rarely on posts or curbs as they are in the United States. The name of the street is usually printed on a metal plate about eight or ten inches long and tacked somewhere on the side of a building. Sometimes the street name is never put up at all. Besides, the name of the street may change in mid-course. *Calle Primero* at one end of town may be called *Calle Mendoza* at the other (*calle* means "street"). So just knowing an address isn't too helpful.

After much driving around, and even having to stop and get out of the camper to read the street name on the side of a building several times, we finally reached a point where we could *see* the ice house, but we couldn't maneuver ourselves in front of it. This was because the ice house was at the top of a steep hill on a one-way street going the wrong direction for us. This required more maneuvering on other one-way streets in heavy traffic to get to our destination. The frustrating experience taught us two new words: one-way streets are always marked with a sign that says *Circulación*, and an arrow indicating the direction of the traffic flow. The two-way streets are labeled *Preferencia* and have the right-of-way. This language lesson consumed the better part of an afternoon.

The ice in the ice house was brown—about the color of weak tea—but the gentlemen there assured us it was *puro*, so we made our purchase and hastily departed the city with its maze of one-way streets to find a place to camp before dark.

We didn't have to go far. The beach where we parked is called Sabalo Beach, and today it is ringed with lovely hotels for American tourists. We stayed on that beach for a week and never saw a living soul except for one man—flourishing a knife!

We did have some other visitors though. And they liked coffee. They were the largest land crabs I've ever seen, and they seemed to be nocturnal. When we'd arise before the sun each day, we'd see them scuttling about by the hundreds all around our camp. Since each one was about the size of my fist, it was rather eerie to see so many. Then, as soon as the morning sun struck the beach, they would completely disappear. We never throw refuse on any beach, but Margie says coffee grounds are biodegradable and good for the soil, so habitually she throws them out, even at home. Here at Sabalo Beach, the grounds would no sooner strike the sand than these huge crabs would start fighting for them. Eventually one crab would prevail, and the coffee grounds were his. He would sit there, picking them up with his claws, and placing them in his vertical slit of a mouth, like an old Chinaman eating rice with chopsticks. It was fascinating to watch.

From the start, we wondered how the crabs disappeared so fast when the sun came out, so we set up a watch. We'd take turns sitting on the steps of the camper, binoculars in hand, staring at our "friends" and waiting for the sun to strike them. When we finally discovered their secret, we were amazed. Each crab had his own hole. He dug it himself, and it was deep! It curled its way down into the sand at least six feet. Maybe more. One day we tried to dig one of the crabs out by following his tunnel, but it just went down, and down, and down. He finally outdug us.

All of those days on Sabalo beach were lovely and lazy. After our crab-watch at dawn, Margie would make us a huge breakfast. Then we'd go for walks along the beach, picking up shells, and watching the sea birds fishing beyond the breakers. About mid-afternoon when the sun was quite hot we'd go nude, enjoying the feeling of the warm sun and air on our bodies. No one to see us. One day Margie gave me a haircut as I sat in my swimming trunks on a barber's chair we'd built of sand. The warm breeze blew the tufts of hair down the beach, so she called it "an air cut." Another time we spent hours making photos of one of the crabs digging his hole. We discovered he was right-clawed. He never used his left claw to dig. And so the days passed.

About 4 p.m., the gentle breeze would become a wind; the clouds would close out the sky; lightning would flash, thunder roll, and the rain come pelting down. Sometimes the thunder claps were so loud they actually rocked our camper, and the lightening would illumine the beach like daylight. We'd lie in our bunk at night with the rain beating a tattoo on the outside of the camper, and finally go to sleep. Then when we awakened in the morning, the storm would be gone, the sun would shine,

44

On a cool morning, Ben and Margie Hunter, in the never-ending quest for "Beasties," explore one of many tidepools near their camp.

and another gorgeous day would be upon us. It happened day after day. It's often that way in the tropics.

"The Baja Feeling" was at full peak as our lovely beach days slipped away, but on the day before our departure a frightening thing happened.

It was well before dawn. I was in that deep sleep that occurs just before you awaken when Margie began shaking me.

"Wake up! Wake up!" she hissed in my ear.

"Mnnnnf. Wha—"

"Shhhhh! Wake up, but be quiet!"

I was coming out of it fast. Something was amiss. "What is it?" I whispered.

"Listen!"

I strained my ears, but could hear nothing but the breakers. "I don't hear anyth—"

"Shhhh!" She was pulling the curtain back from the window of the camper. She placed her lips right in my ear and breathed, "Look out there!"

I peered into the darkness. Nothing. Then suddenly the moon moved out from behind a dark rain cloud and I saw him.

"My God!" I gasped.

He was a large man. Mexican. Naked to the waist. The sudden bright moonlight revealed an ugly scar across his face and a two- or three-day growth of beard. But what my eyes riveted on was a large knife hanging loosely from his right hand, its blade glistening in the moonlight! *And he was standing stock still, staring at our camper!*

"What'll we do?" Her lips at my ear.

"Nothing right now." My lips were at her ear. "Let's just lie very still. Maybe he'll go away."

As we laid there, our hearts pounding, thoughts went rushing through my head: Had he, perhaps, been concealed in the underbrush during the day, ogling Margie's beautiful body as we played naked in the sand? Had he been laying plans? Was he going to kill me and rape her? Maybe he was just a Mexican-American like the one we'd encountered on the dunes outside Ensenada. Nothing to fear.

No way! He was no Mexican-American. Not looking like that! All the tales we'd heard of rape and robbery in Mexico—tales we'd come to disregard—streamed through my mind. This was the showdown. The final confrontation. Well, he'd probably win, but he'd have a damn good fight first!

He may have only stood there a minute, but with the adrenalin flowing,

46

it seemed like hours. Finally he began to move slowly north along the beach and away from us, looking back over his shoulder once or twice. In unison we sighed in relief.

"Let's get out of here before he comes back," Margie said.

"A-men!"

We climbed out of the bunk and started to dress. "Don't turn on the lights," I said. "Dress in the dark."

The sky was getting quite gray now. Soon it would be crab-watch time, and then the sun would be emerging and drying the rain puddles from last night's rain. Margie was brewing coffee and it sure smelled good.

"We can't leave without coffee," she said, "You'd crack up the car."

Over coffee and cigarettes we began rationalizing. Perhaps he was just a fisherman. The knife was for cleaning fish. Maybe he was just admiring our camper. Our fears were probably for nothing. Why should we leave our lovely camp a day early? We'd probably never see him again.

That's where we were wrong.

By the time we'd had quite a few coffees and performed our morning ablutions, the sun was full up, it was another spectacular Sabalo beach day, and we'd talked away our fears. We decided to stay. At least until nightfall.

I insisted that we keep our bathing suits on that day, but otherwise we pursued our usual activities; soon the man-with-the-knife was forgotten—or at least pushed back into our subconscious.

About four o'clock that afternoon, the rain clouds, as on schedule, began to gather, and the wildest lightning storm we've ever seen took place. There was no rain. Just huge, rolling claps of thunder and sheets of lightning that emblazoned the whole sky. It was frightening, but fascinating. The weather was still warm, so I poured stiff drinks of tequila for us, and we sat on beach chairs outside, watching the light show and drinking. Why try to drive with a storm like this brewing? We'd stay another night, we decided.

On the third or fourth drink we saw him coming toward us down the beach. He was carrying a five gallon tin can on his shoulder, and the large, ugly knife had been stuck in his belt.

"What'll we do?" I said. "Ignore him?"

"I don't know. Let's wait and see if he comes toward us."

In another moment we saw that he was indeed coming toward our camp. Shortly, he'd be within twenty-five feet of us.

47

"Maybe he's just a fisherman," I said. "He's probably got fish in that can.

"Oh yeah? Where's his fishing pole?" Margie said, and gulped her drink. She was getting jittery.

He stopped and stared at us.

"Hola!" [Hello!] I shouted above the wind.

"Hola!" he shouted back. But he didn't smile.

Suddenly the booze took its toll. I was filled with liquid courage. *"Quiere un tragito de tequila?"* [Do you want a little snort of tequila?] I shouted.

"You shouldn't have said that!" Margie hissed.

He took a couple of steps forward. *"No me gusta. Hay cervesa?"* [I don't like it. Do you have beer?]

"Si," I said, and went inside to open a can.

Margie was inside the camper with me in a flash.

"Don't leave me alone with him out there!" she whispered.

While I was at it, I poured each of us another tequila. Then we rejoined our "guest" outside. I handed him the beer and he took it with a nod. He didn't sit down. He just stood there drinking it thirstily.

"Tiene pescados?" [You have fish?] I ventured, nodding at the can.

"No pescados. Son nopales." [No fish. They are nopales], he said.

I peeked into the can. Sure enough! It was filled with *nopales* cactus—the kind with the fruit we enjoy so much. But his can contained no fruit, just the broad cactus leaves.

"Como usa esos?" [How do you use those?] Margie said.

That seemed to relax him a little. He sat down on the sand and began to talk with us.

He was a *nopales* picker by trade, he said. Each morning he set out early and spent the entire day cutting off those broad, succulent cactus leaves. "With that knife!" I said to Margie in English. She nodded

He then had to remove all the spines from the leaves, and pack them down tightly in the five gallon tin. He would sell this tin of *nopales* for ten pesos [eighty cents for a hard day's work!].

Mexicans chop these cactus leaves up in small pieces called *nopalitos* and eat them as a vegetable. They can be boiled in salted water and served with butter, or even put in salads. They are quite tasty, and may even be purchased, canned, in markets.

I asked him how he removed the spines from the cactus, expecting to see some special device, or at least a pair of pliers.

"Con este," [with this] he said, and produced that long strip of metal you

roll off the top of a coffee can when you open it. He showed us how he cut the strip into smaller pieces which he then bent in the middle, and used like pinchers. He used the same pinchers to remove the spines which invariably penetrated his hands and fingers.

There was a brief lull in the conversation while I went inside to mix more drinks and open another can of beer.

As I emerged from the camper he said "Only this morning I was admiring your beautiful camper."

I nodded, and handed him the beer. How well we knew!

"Tiene familia?" [Do you have a family?] Margie asked.

"Si," he said. His name was Antonio Alonzo, and he had a wife and six children back in Mazatlan. It was hard to support his family on only ten pesos a day, but things were better in the winter. During those months, he said, many touristas came from the States and he then made much money as a fishing guide. But a man must always work.

I wondered how he functioned as a fishing guide when he could speak no English, but I didn't inquire.

As it grew dark and the lightening increased, he taught us two new words. The word for bolt lightning is rayo, and the word for sheet lightning is relampago. Since this was relampago, there was nothing to fear, he said.

Finally it began to rain. He thanked us for the beers, said how pleasant it was to meet norteamericanos who could speak Spanish, and added that he must be going. His wife would worry. We thanked him for the visit and wished him well. He picked up his can of nopales and started trudging homeward in the rain. He had only gone about fifty feet when he stopped and called back to us over the storm: "Cuidado de los rateros!" [Beware of evil men].

"Si!" I shouted back. "Gracias." Margie and I looked at each other ruefully.

In the morning we broke camp. We were reluctant to leave our little paradise at Sabalo, but our desire to see more of Mexico was stronger. We returned to Mazatlán and went—unerringly this time—to the ice house for more brown ice. Then to a supermercado [supermarket] for supplies, and finally to the highway south for more adventure.

From Mazatlán, the highway moves away from the sea, and as the landscape unwinds before you it becomes more and more tropical. The adobe houses begin to have thatched roofs, and palm trees dot the roadside fields. Soon, you see more palms, some of them standing in groves. Everyone is barefooted, and the air is warm and moist. By 3 p.m., we were pretty warm and moist ourselves and beginning to dream of a cool dip in the ocean. The previous night's storm had apparently been the biggie and the sky was washed clean and blue. There'd be no rain to cool us off this night.

"Where shall we sleep tonight, Babe?" I asked.

"Beside the road, I guess." She was studying the map. "I don't see any other place."

"God, I'm hot! Look at my shirt!" It was sopping wet.

"I know, Darling, I'm the same way," she said.

"How far would you say we are from the beach?"

She studied the map a moment. "I don't know. Maybe twenty miles?"

"I've got an idea."

"I know what it is," she said. "We'll take the next road we see that leads toward the beach."

"Right!"

It wasn't a road, really. It was just a couple of tire tracks, but they led beachward so we turned off, little suspecting what we were in for. It was awful! Treacherous! It reminded us a lot of the old Baja road we had driven for the first time a year before, but this wasn't any little four cylinder Tempest. This was a Dodge truck with a heavy camper on it. As I attempted to maneuver us around deep chuckholes and over huge bumps, we could hear the dishes falling and crashing back in the camper. It was low gear, five miles per hour, all the way. The hot afternoon dragged on. We were drenched in our own sweat and covered with dust which seemed to cling to everything. Now and then I'd stop the truck long enough for Margie to tend bar. The drinks helped keep us cool, and probably gave us courage for what was to come!

The road suddenly ended at a deep gorge with a torrent gushing through it. The banks of the gorge were so steep there was no way to work yourself down to the river, and even if you did you'd be swept away in the raging water. Crossing the gorge at the point where the road ended was a bridge that beggared belief! It consisted simply of two large beams, a car's width apart, laid across the gorge from bank to bank. The idea, apparently, was to position your vehicle with two wheels on each beam, and then creep across the "bridge" with the water roaring twenty feet below. Each beam was just a few inches wider than the truck's tires.

Maybe it was the booze. Maybe it was our desire to get to the beach. But we never thought of *not* crossing it.

"If the Mexicans can drive their cars across that thing, we can too," I said.

Margie got out of the truck and directed me until the wheels were as straight on the two beams as I could get them. Then, she walked ahead on one of the beams, keeping her eyes riveted on our wheels, and directing me as I inched the camper forward. Keeping those wheels straight was obviously the name of the game! When we were directly over the water, neither of us looked down. The bridge was about two and a half carlengths long, but crossing it seemed to take an eon. Then, suddenly, we were on the other side. Margie got back in the car and we continued along the track toward—we thought—the beach.

Soon, it became dark. We continued creeping along, our headlights stabbing out into the darkness to reveal more darkness. We stopped and strained our ears occasionally to hear the welcome sound of surf. Nothing. We had just about decided to call it quits and go to sleep right there on the "road," when we drove into a tiny town. The effect was eerie because the town had no electricity. We could see the shapes of buildings around us, but no people. It was like a ghost town. Suddenly, as we rounded a corner, our headlights revealed three men standing beside a building. They shielded their eyes from the unaccustomed glare, so I switched the headlights off. As our eyes began to adjust to the darkness we saw that there were quite a few people. We had stopped next to a tiny park, and some of the town's inhabitants were gathered in the park for a bit of after-dinner conversation. Adobe homes and stores with thatched roofs surrounded the park.

Finally, one of the men broke away from his friends and came toward us. I stuck my head out of the window of the cab:

"*Donde esta la playa?*" [Where is the beach?] I said.

He looked at us curiously and just pointed in a direction away from the plaza.

"*Queremos hacer un campo allá,*" [We want to make camp there] I said.

He smiled. "Come. Follow me. I'll direct you," he said in Spanish, and started moving down one of the streets.

I switched the headlights back on and followed.

The little streets were two or three burros wide, a perfect distance for door-to-door conversation, and women were standing in their doorways chatting as we passed. Since the sides of our camper almost touched the sides of the adobes, they'd step back inside, stare at us curiously, and then when we'd gone by, resume talking. As we passed the last house on the block we were again plunged into total darkness. We could see nothing except our new friend beckoning us ahead in the headlight beams. An archangel on stage.

Soon, he held up both hands for us to stop. *"No más! La arena es flojo aquí."* [No more! The sand is soft here.] he called. I shut off the engine and we could hear the surf. We got out of the truck, and felt a cooling breeze blowing off the ocean.

I thanked our friend and attempted to give him a tip, but he refused it and went back to rejoin his friends.

"Suddenly I'm sleepy," Margie said.

"Me too."

"You still want to go in the ocean?"

I yawned. "Hell no! Let's go to bed dirty. We can bathe in the morning."

We opened the back of the camper, climbed in, and went to bed without dinner. We were probably sleeping within thirty seconds.

The next morning while we were drinking our juice and coffee, we began to hear sounds of gaiety outside our camper. I put on an ancient, worn bathrobe, and with hair mussed from sleep, and clutching my coffee cup, I stepped outside the camper into the middle of a Fiesta!

There was a merry-go-round; a booth where you throw baseballs at wooden milk bottles; another booth for throwing darts at balloons; dozens of stalls selling food and soft drinks; and many other carnival games. This included that ride where seats are suspended by chains from the top of a pole and whirled round and round in widening arcs. This latter device was whirling its customers right over the front end of our camper at the moment. The booths were scattered all around us.

"Hey, Margie!" I called, "Look outside!" Her tousled head emerged from the camper door. "We're parked in the middle of a carnival!"

"I think we might be the star attraction," she said. "Come inside and get some clothes on."

We quickly splashed some cold water on our faces, combed hair, and put on some clean clothes. Just in the knick of time, too. The first polite knock on the door came within five minutes of the time I had first stepped out of the camper.

Our visitors were all male, very polite, and very shy. We had suspected that they were looking at our camper in order to give a complete report to their wives, who were even shyer. We learned from them that the name of this little village was Teacapán. They all earned their living as fishermen, and this carnival was the *Fiesta Marinera*—the Sailor's Celebration. We were quite a novelty for two reasons: Americans never visited Teacapán, so—except for one *gringo* gentleman who had lived there until he died—we were the first Americans most of them had ever seen. It followed, therefore, that this was also the first camper any of them had ever seen. Our camper was rudimentary by today's standards, but to the people of Teacapán it was a miracle on wheels. One by one, they filed in and stood looking embarrassed as Margie displayed the stove and the icebox, and I attempted conversation. They shuffled their bare feet about, thanked us for the hospitality, and beat a fast exit. I'm sure that each *señora* later received a detailed description of our camper interior!

Our final visitor of the day was wearing shoes and was obviously a gentleman of some importance. He introduced himself as Seymore, and we invited him to stay for a drink or two. He accepted our invitation with relish. Seymore, it developed, was the owner of the carnival. He had a complete list of all the Fiesta days in every small town of Mexico (a prodigious list!) and simply moved his caravan of carnival attractions from one town to the next for each celebration. He proudly pointed out the trucks he used to transport his carnival to every village in Mexico. We asked if he brought those trucks over that bridge to Teacapán. "Of a certainty! How else could one get to Teacapán?" He crossed it every year, he said.

Seymore had *macho* too. *Macho* is a difficult word to translate into English because it combines all the Latin concepts of masculinity in one word: Male, virile, brave, daring, and a winner with the ladies. Those having *macho* will usually tell you about it, and Seymore told us.

"*Cuántos años tiene?*" [How old are you?] he asked me.

I reluctantly admitted to forty.

"*Mire!*" [Look!] he said, and pointed first to my thinning hairline, highlighted with silver, and then to his own luxuriant growth of glossy black hair.

"My hair is younger than yours, and I am sixty-nine years old," he said in Spanish. "Why do you suppose that is?"

He didn't wait for my answer. "It is because of the lives we lead. Yours is the life of the city and mine is the life of the country. It is the country life that makes one young."

As his essay on the pursuit of life continued, he told us that he was married to his fourth wife (he had outlived the other three) and she was just twenty-one years old. He pointed her out through the camper window. She was a beautiful girl, and she was holding a young baby.

"The baby is yours?" Margie asked him.

"*Naturalmente!*" You can bet your bippy it was. I was beginning to find the old geezer a little tiresome with his constant bragging about his youthfulness. But we had to hear all about the other children, the other wives, and on and on. Finally, he said his young wife would have his supper ready so he had to be going.

"Let's go for a walk on the beach," Margie suggested, and soon, hand in hand we walked barefooted along the beach with the waves slapping at our toes, and the water sparkling in the moonlight. Back at camp, the *Fiesta Marinera* was closed down.

After breakfast in the morning, we decided to push on to our ultimate destination, Guadalajara. We packed our load tightly for the bumpy road ahead, broke camp, and set out, waving goodbye to our new friends as we departed. In about half an hour we reached that awful bridge and it looked just as frightening in the cold light of dawn as it had two nights before. In fact, we concluded that we must have been bombed when we crossed it the first time. It was either make the crossing or stay in Teacapán indefinitely, so we started across using the same strategy as before—Margie walking ahead and leading the way, I following in the truck and *keeping* those wheels straight! Again, it seemed to take forever to cross, but I never once looked down. I couldn't. It was too scary. When we finally made it, I shut the engine off, kicked the door open to let in the breeze, and slumped in the seat.

Margie has severe acrophobia and I could see she was shaken too as she slipped in her side of the cab. "Never again!" she said.

A couple of drinks later we were happily spinning along the Mazatlán-to-Guadalajara highway in search of new adventure. After two or three hours of driving, a roadside sign seemed to beckon the adventure we sought. It pointed toward the beach, and it said San Blas.

The road to San Blas is a dark ribbon through a dense, tropical forest. As you travel about twelve miles toward the sea, a jungle of purple flowered lignum-vitae, mahogany, ebony, brazilwood, rosewood, palms, and bananas crowds you from either side. Orchids hang from branches, and overhead large colorful parrots zoom and screech as you invade their domain. It's as if you were entering another land.

Back in the sixteenth century when the Spanish had first conquered the Indians of Mexico, they made San Blas into one of their major seaports. To give them dominion over the sea as well as the land, they built a major fortification on the hill above what is now the town of San Blas. As was so often the custom with the Spanish, it was a combination church and fortress, built of heavy stone blocks carried and dragged to the top of the hill by the slave labor of the Indians. Bronze cannons were mounted on the fort's ramparts. We had read about it, and heard that ruins of the old fort/church could still be seen, so we looked for a possible turn off as we drove.

We rounded a turn and saw a rutted, eroded set of tire tracks leading off the road into the jungle.

I executed a left turn, and once again we were driving off-the-road. It was little more than a jungle trail, just wide enough for our camper with the brush scraping our sides at times. In much of the area the trees had grown clear over the top of the road, closing out the sky and leaving us in darkness. We turned on the headlights and continued. Soon we rounded a curve and the road began to rise ahead of us. We could see blue sky at the top. Another five minutes in low gear and we were there. We stopped, turned off the engine, and stared at an incredible sight, the vestigal remains of the ancient fort/church.

In the four hundred years since the conquistadors built this fort, the jungle has been slowly, inexorably, reclaiming the land. Here and there you see a giant banyan tree, its mighty roots locked around the remnants of a wall. It's difficult to see where wall ends and tree begins. Enormous green iguana lizards sun themselves on the ruins and seem undisturbed by the presence of humans. Only one cannon remains, and its barrel has pitched off its cradle. Even the jungle noises are silenced here. You feel as if you should speak in hushed tones, or not at all, and that perhaps you will hear the ghostly voices of the ancient conquistadors on the wind.

"Darling, look!" Margie pointed at a crumbling wall.

"What about it?"

"Well, you can tell from the shape of the window that it was a wall of the church."

"Yeah?"

"Well, now, look at that vine!"

And then I saw what she meant. A jungle vine had started from the ground and crawled up the side of this one remaining church wall, reaching the gaping window, and then spreading out in all directions until it embraced the entire wall . . . in a giant crucifix!

"My God! That's eerie," I said.

We strolled out past the motionless iguanas to the rampart on the ocean side of the fort. Looking down, we saw the tiny town of San Blas slumbering in the noonday sun. Beyond the town were palm groves reaching clear to the sandy beaches in both directions. We'd sleep under palms tonight.

We got back in the camper and drove back down the hill onto the highway and followed it into town. The crumbling old fort with its lizards, its fallen cannon, the encroaching forest, and the ghosts of the conquistadors was left behind, but the picture of it remains with me vividly today.

It was siesta time when we pulled up and stopped at the *plaza principal,* so the park was full. We strolled about like everyone else, people-watching, and enjoying the shade of the trees. Here, a man was selling warm tortillas from a tin can hung from a pole over his shoulders; there, a young girl squeezed fresh orange juice while you waited beside her pushcart under a tree; little shoeshine boys were doing a brisk business among their elders, seated on park benches. It was a scene of complete urban tranquility, and the two *gringos* who wandered into the park didn't even cause a head to turn.

We enjoyed their siesta with them for an hour, then set forth again to find a place to camp for the night. We drove toward the beach, then turned south, driving through groves of palms trying to decide where to make camp. Actually we could have stopped anywhere. It was quite isolated. We were weaving our way through the trees when I spotted a horseback rider in my rear view mirror. He was about a half a mile away, but was galloping toward us as fast as he could make the horse go.

"Oye! Oye!" [Hey! Hey!] he was yelling.

I stopped the camper and waited for him.

As he approached, I saw he was a teenager, about sixteen, and riding bareback. He pulled the horse to a stop beside our truck.

"Que pasa?" [What's wrong?] I said.

"Su paquete de cigarillos!" he said breathlessly, and showed me an old cigarette pack I had crumpled and thrown away a mile back.

"Si?"

"Hay un otro cigarillo!" [There is another cigarette!] He carefully unfolded the remains of my crumpled pack, revealing one badly wrinkled cigarette inside. Proudly he presented me with his prize, then turned his horse to go.

"Le gusta cigarillos?" [Do you like cigarettes?] I asked him.

"Si."

I took three uncrushed cigarettes out of the working pack and presented them to him. He thanked us profusely and galloped off. When people ask me about bandidos, and about the honesty of Mexicans, I like to tell them of the little boy who galloped a mile or more to return a cigarette he thought I'd lost.

We made camp beneath some tall palms about fifty yards from the sea and, overcome by the lazy ways of life in Mexico, resumed siesta time with a nap. We awakened about four that afternoon and discovered one of the reasons San Blas is a *winter* resort!

The reasons are numerous, and they are all named *jijenes*. They are similar to what midwesterners call "no-see-ums"(tiny little insects small enough to fly through wire screens) that appear in clouds on late summer afternoons and swarm around your face, stinging you until you're a mass of welts. Our camper was filled with them when we awakened. Out came the Flit gun and thousands perished to be replaced by other thousands. We rubbed insect repellent on ourselves, and it helped just a little. We decided that the only thing to do was shut up the camper and fumigate. We'd walk into town for dinner, and by the time we returned they'd be dead. We could then sleep if we kept all the windows closed. So we closed everything down tightly, sprayed well with insect killer, and slipped out the door.

On the way to dinner, we noticed that the locals, out for an evening walk, were very casual about the annoying *jijenes*. They all carried large bandannas which they skillfully swished around their faces as they walked. It seemed to work better than the insect repellent, so we stopped at a store, purchased two bandannas, and swished like everyone else.

The restaurant was clean and reeked of insect spray. It featured *mariscos* [shellfish] and the service was good, but I was startled when the young waitress taking my order suddenly slapped me smartly on the shoulder! She had spotted a stray *jijene* there and was dispatching him swiftly. She saw one on Margie too, but instead of a swift slap, the *jijene* died from a long, gentle press. It seemed that the manner in which a *jijene* died depended upon who he landed on!

The dinner was delicious and the choice of wines excellent.Afterwards, we strolled along the ocean front, swishing our bandanas, to our now bug-free camper, and retired.

In the morning we broke camp to leave for Guadalajara, but before departure we decided to take the river trip. It is a regular tourist attraction of San Blas, and everyone we'd met had advised us not to miss it.

Our boatman's name was Francisco, but he liked to be called Paco. We parked our camper beside the dock, scrambled into his little boat and shoved off. Paco gave a quick tug on the starter rope, and the outboard motor sprang to life and began pushing us up the river, deeper and deeper into the jungle. A giant white flamingo, startled by our sudden presence, took to the air and soared downstream from us.

At first, the river was fairly wide and took us by some banana plantations. Then it became much narrower with the jungle closing in on us and putting us in semi-darkness. It was rather like the jungle ride at Disneyland, but it was real. The bedlam of screeches from Myna birds and parrots was real, and so was the occasional cry of the big cats, or the splash of a bull alligator in the river. Paco said there were boa constrictors there too, but we didn't see any. Once we saw a huge ball of mud about eight feet in diameter. Paco said it was a termite nest. One time he cut the motor and just allowed us to drift quietly, listening to the jungle sounds. While we were drifting, he stood up in the boat and broke one of the branches off a tree. It was garlanded with orchids, and he presented it to Margie. There were oriole nests hanging down over the river and one bird followed us, flying just over our heads all the way to the end of the river.

The river had its origin deep in the forest in a beautiful little pond fed by a spring. The water was clear and cool, and you could see large fish swimming about. A family lived back there on the edge of the pond and someone's grandma, with silver hair that hung to her waist, was sitting in the sun brushing her long locks. Paco exchanged brief greetings with grandma, circled our boat around, and headed back downstream. In what seemed like a few minutes we were back at the dock. We thought we'd been gone about thirty minutes, but it had been over three hours! We paid Paco, thanked him for the trip, and with Margie still carrying her native orchids we got in the camper and resumed our trip.

Guadalajara has been called "The Queen City of Mexico," and the "Paris of the Western Hemisphere." It is all that and more. We had both been there before, but we had always arrived by plane and been whisked about the city in limousines or tour buses. This was our first approach on land, and we were enraptured. The main north-to-south highway (Mex. 15) becomes *Avenida Vallarta* as you reach the city limits, but you really know you're in Guadalajara when you come to *La Gloria*. It is a huge traffic circle with boulevards like spokes going off to all parts of the city. In the center of the traffic circle is a gigantic statue of the goddess Minerva, framed by a huge curtain of water creating shimmering rainbows that dance in the sunlight. It's a spectacular welcome to a spectacular city, and it sets the mood for what is to follow. As you continue south on *Avenida Vallarta* around *La Gloria,* you pass through a stately, ornate arch that brackets the four-lane boulevard, and you discover that this main thoroughfare is lined with trees and flowers, beautiful mansions, and parks. At every intersection monuments and fountains salute you, and vendors are selling flowers on street corners.

Jaws agape in wonderment, we rounded the *Gloria*, passed under the arch, and had proceeded about a block when a police car pulled us over to the curb. In situations like this I often pretend I speak no Spanish. The theory is that they may be more lenient if communication is a problem.

"What did I do wrong, officer?" I said.

He spoke some English. "Nothing yet, *Señor* But if you buy this leetle card," he held up a card, "you weel not get in trouble."

Ah hah! It was our old friend, the *Mordida!* "How much does it cost?" I asked.

"Two-feefty."

"Dollars?"

"*Si.*"

The family treasurer was already getting the money out of her purse. She handed it to me and I gave it to him.

He tipped his hat and smiled. "Keep the leetle card on your winsheel," he said, and handed it to me. Then he climbed in his prowl car and was gone.

We kept that card in the windshield as long as we were in Guadalajara, and it served us well on several occasions. The *policia* upheld their end of the bargain.

Today, Guadalajara is replete with all types of superb hotels, ranging from the familiar Holiday Inn to the super-luxurious *El Tapatio*, but in those days there was just one luxury hotel. It was the Guadalajara Hilton. Our plan was to check in there, shelve the camper for a week, and rent a car to see the sights as we'd never seen them before.

Besides being the nicest hotel for tourists, the Hilton was also the "in" spot for the Mexican social elite to go dining. The curved driveway in front of the Hilton was lined with black limousines depositing their tuxedoed, gowned, and jeweled well-to-do occupants for an evening of dining and dancing. Liveried attendants greeted each car, opening the doors and assisting the patrons inside. In the midst of this elegant scene we arrived. Our camper was muddy, bug-besplattered, and weary looking. We, too, were grimy and probably looking and smelling as if we hadn't bathed for four days (we hadn't!). Despite our appearance, the attendants were impassive. Each of them opened a door of the cab, and we slid wearily out.

"Welcome to the Hilton." (Perfect English!)

"Thank you," I said.

"Do you have bags?"

"Not really. But we do have some clothes. In the back."

I opened the back door of the camper and removed our clothes on hangers from the closet. He took them from me and, holding them high, started for the lobby.

"Follow me, sir."

We followed him in, too embarrassed to see whether any of the elegant patrons were staring at us!

In Mexico, the numeral 13 is lucky. Therefore, contrary to the states, all of the hotels and buildings have a thirteenth floor. Our room was on the thirteenth with a magnificent view of the city. As soon as we were ensconced in our attractive room I called room service and learned a valuable lesson.

"*Servicio?*" said the voice on the phone.

"*Me gustaría unos cubitos de hielo en mi cuarto. Es número—*"

"Are you saying you'd like some ice cubes in your room, sir?"

"Yes, that's what I was saying." I was a little deflated.

"What is your room number, sir?"

I told her.

"It'll be right up." A click and a dial tone.

We had been gleefully speaking Spanish with all comers for the last two weeks, but now at the Hilton we discovered it was the English tongue that had the clout. Never again in that hotel did we speak anything but English, and the service was excellent.

There was, however, one exception to the above. That exception was Emilio. He was a bellboy, quite young, who had never mastered English. He seemed delighted at being able to talk with us in Spanish and became our willing slave during our stay there. He fetched food, ice, and sundries for our room: he directed us on shopping excursions; he kept my shoes polished like mirrors, and seemed to be smiling and greeting us every time we turned a corner in the hotel.

The morning after our arrival, we ate breakfast and then discovered a Hertz U-drive just two blocks from the hotel. We rented a VW, complete with city maps and brochures, and began our Guadalajara holiday.

Many days were spent becoming acquainted with this beautiful, fascinating city. We visited the cathedral and churches, some of them dating back to the sixteenth century; we fed pigeons in the plaza; we marveled at the beautiful new buildings, and the stately old ones; we dined at the *Copa de Leche* restaurant, sitting in a bank of flowers and watching the traffic on the street below. We shopped at Woolworth's— bigger and more modern than any we've seen in the United States—and we visited the *Mercado Publico,* a public market where you can purchase anything from a love potion to a live jaguar. We found under-the-street shopping in white tiled catacombs where you can become lost in a maze of little shops, and we sipped tequila in sidewalk cafes while listening to the music of *mariachis.* We drove to Lake Chapala, watched the fishermen's boats on the water, and dined on Chapala's famous whitefish in a patio restaurant.

On Sunday, we decided to visit the small suburb of Tlaquepaque. When we arrived at the Plaza in the center of town, there was a celebration. All the streets leading to the plaza had been blocked off, and were filled with carnival rides, gambling booths, games, and vendors. It was thronged with people enjoying the fun, and *mariachis* were strolling about serenading anyone who would listen. We thought we had stumbled on some sort of special Fiesta as we had in the little town of Teacapán. I saw a police officer and asked him.

"*Es un día de Fiesta?*" [Is this a festival day?]

"*No, Señor. Solamente es Domingo.*" [No, sir. It's only Sunday.]

We sat on the plaza with everyone else, sipped tequila, were serenaded by *mariachis,* and a man twisted a silver wire into the name "Margie." She wore it like a pin.

On the way out of Tlaquepaque we spotted a furniture store that was open. It was called *El Tular.* Margie loves to shop, so we went inside for a look. The furniture was all hand-made and beautiful. We particularly admired one dining room set. There were six chairs, a large table, and a sideboard. The frames were of rosewood, and palm fronds had been hand woven into a kind of parquet pattern for the seats of the chairs, the top of the table, and the front of the sideboard cupboards. It was stunning. The price of the entire set was only $150, but we hated to part with that much cash before the end of our trip. We talked with the store owner, a lady named María Elena, and she offered to ship us the entire set for a $20 deposit! We gave her the money and our address in the States and hoped she'd do as she promised.

Three months after our return to Los Angeles, the dining set arrived. We immediately mailed her the balance, and have the furniture to this day. We have been offered four times as much for it.

What we didn't realize at that time was that ten years later we would again be negotiating with María Elena. This time for the purchase of her home at Lake Chapala.

When the end of our stay finally came, and we were checking out of the

Hilton, we had a sudden sobering thought. We had neglected to purchase a block of ice for the camper. Moreover, we hadn't the foggiest notion where some ice could be purchased. What to do? Outside, a tropical rainstorm was pelting the streets and sidewalks, and the gutters were high with water. It certainly wasn't a day to go cruising through Guadalajara searching for an ice house, even if there was one. We turned to Emilio for help.

"No problema," he said. We were to go to the camper and wait for him. He would join us soon with ice.

We made a mad dash through the pouring rain, opened the back of the camper, and got in. We were drenched from just those few steps. We sat there listening to the rain hammering on the metal roof, and looking out the window for Emilio. After awhile he appeared, a small figure struggling with a large crate behind the hotel. He hurried toward us through the rain, and soon we could see that the crate was loaded to overflowing with ice cubes from the hotel kitchen. We poured them into the camper icebox, but Emilio wasn't satisfied. He was stealing the cubes, he said, and he might as well steal some more so we'd have plenty for our trip. Back he went. Soon the crate, refilled, was back in the camper again, and we had enough ice cubes to throw a coctail party for the entire clientele of the Hilton Hotel!

We thanked Emilio, and tipped him, but we felt he'd gone way beyond the call of duty in proving his friendship. As we pulled off down the street, he was still standing there in the parking lot, the rain drenching him to the skin, waving goodbye.

As we reached the outskirts of the city half an hour later, the rain ceased as quickly as it had begun, and we saw for the first time the bottling plant of the Sauza Tequila Company. Since we ranked ourselves among their most enthusiastic consumers, we decided to stop for a look around.

Anyone who has ever visited Mexico, no matter how briefly, soon realizes that Mexicans are the all-time masters of mosaic work. Whether it's the mosaics on the walls of the University Library in Mexico City, the walls of a private garden, or a public lavatory in a park, they are everywhere. And they are exquisite. The entire outside wall of the Sauza bottling plant was one huge, colorful mosaic depicting the evolution of this historic drink from the harsh fermentation of the ancient Indians of Mexico to the present day delicately flavored potion with which we're familiar. We ogled the mosaics for a few minutes, then went inside and inquired if it might be possible for us to visit the distillery and see the tequila made.

"Well there are certain visiting days, Señor, and this is not one of them—"

I explained that we were on our way back to the States and had no time to return another day.

"Ah, what a pity. But perhaps Señor will return to Mexico another time, and then—"

I decided to use an old ploy that has always worked well at home. "I have a television program in Los Angeles," I said, "and I should like to make pictures of your distillery for my show."

It worked. Eyes flew open with a new respect, and there was a flurry of activity including a mysterious phone call. At length, all smiles, they told me a private tour for us had been arranged. They gave us directions for finding the place, and told us to ask for Margarita (the girl, not the drink) when we arrived. We thanked them and departed.

As we drove off, Margie said, "Now you're stuck. You promised to take pictures, so you'll have to do it."

"I know it," I said grimly. "When we get there I'll get out the movie camera."

Tequila is not made from cactus. It is made from the maguey plant, also known as the agave or century plant. It is about three or four feet in diameter, and is actually a member of the lily family. The ancient Indians of Mexico did not know tequila. They used the juice of the maguey to make a stronger drink called mescal. When mescal is sold today, there is usually an embalmed maguey worm (a little white creature found in the heart of the maguey plant) floating about inside the liquor. The beverage known as tequila is named after the town of Tuiquila where most of the maguey plants are grown. Later its name was changed to Tequila. Driving north from Guadalajara, we soon saw thousands of acres of maguey under cultivation and we knew we had arrived.

Tequila is a small town with a pronounced Mexican colonial flavor. There are cobblestone streets, white adobe walls, and tile roofs. It's very clean. I suspect that the majority of the population either works in the distilleries, or services those who do. The Sauza distillery was easy to spot. We pulled the camper up in front of it and parked.

"I guard your car meester?" It was a cute little urchin with a bright face and snapping black eyes. He was barefooted and wearing a huge sombrero and oversized clothes.

"Yes you may," I said. "You stay right here with the car until we return. Understand?"

He didn't. Apparently "I guard your car meester" was the only English he knew. I translated my orders into Spanish.

"Sí Señor! Con mucho gusto!" And he drew himself to attention like a soldier, placing himself in front of the camper.While I'd been talking to the child, Margie had been unloading the movie camera, tripod, lights, and other gear. We went inside the distillery, lugging it with us, and asked for Margarita.

After an impressive fifteen minute wait, she appeared and introduced herself in perfect English. Margarita Sauza.

Margarita Sauza! Great Scott! She is *Número Uno!* That is like going to the Jack Daniels distillery and being greeted by Jack himself! We were flattered indeed.

After a brief chat we started our tour, filming all the way. Margarita was beautiful, knowledgeable, and charming.

We learned that it took the maguey plants eight to ten years to mature and be ready for making Sauza. The leaves were stripped from them leaving just the heart, which looked like an enormous pineapple. These giant hearts were then halved and placed in a cooker where they were steamed until soft and pulpy. Then they were placed on a conveyor belt which carried them through machines that ground, mashed, chopped, and extracted all the juice and pulp. The resulting liquid was placed in vats with yeast to ferment.

The fermented juice in those vats, strictly speaking, would be *mescal.* But it is then distilled. The clear liquid which emerges from the still is the liquor known as tequila. Some of it is bottled as is, and some is tabbed for aging in oak casks like whiskey. The top of the line at Sauza is a product they call *Commemorativo* which has been aged for fifteen years. Margarita took us into the cellars where the *Commemorativo* was aging, and allowed us a sip from a fifteen year old cask. Nectar of the gods! Then on our departure she presented us with a gift bottle of it.

It had been a long tour, made even longer by the necessity of filming. We had been inside the distillery for several hours and had forgotten all about our "guard," but when we returned to the street there he was. He had fallen sound asleep, but was lying protectively across the entrance to our camper.

We awakened him, paid him a few pesos for his excellent guard job, and started on our way. We'd only gone three or four blocks through the town, however, when I glanced in the rear vision mirror and saw one small brown hand and a tip of a nose at the back of the camper. He had apparently jumped onto the rear steps as we were pulling away, and was hanging on for dear life. We stopped.

Margie was first out of the truck. *"Qué estás haciendo?"* [What are you doing?] she said to him.

"Quiero ir á Estados Unidos con ustedes," [I want to go to the United States with you] he said.

Margie is wonderful with children. She reasoned with the little guy, explained what a long journey it was, and finally convinced him to release us and go home to his brothers and sisters. As we left the town of Tequila we saw him idling his way back up the street, kicking a rock ahead of him with his bare feet.

The rest of our trip was uneventful and—like the other trips—seemed interminable. We finally made it, unpacked the camper, returned it to its owner, and sent the film out to be developed. I kept my word and showed film of the Sauza distillery to my audience.

Some weeks later we were reminiscing about the trip when we asked ourselves what it was about Mexico that so enthralled us. Foremost had to be that wonderful "Baja Feeling" that made each day seem like a honeymoon. It worked its magic even on the Mexican mainland. Second, we decided, was the Mexican people with their delightful friendliess. People like Antonio Alonzo the cactus picker, the simple people of Teacapán, the cute waitress who killed bugs on us in the restaurant in San Blas, María Elena with her furniture store, Emilio the bellboy, and our little "guard" at Tequila. We swore we would never forget them.

Yet, the most unforgettable character we have ever met in Mexico was an American. His name was Emmy.

3/ Emmy

The remainder of the summer of 1966 was spent zipping down to Baja in Margie's little Tempest whenever I could get away from my television show for a few days. We had become fairly expert campers by now, and had accumulated some of the equipment one needs to make camp life a little easier. But what frustrated us on these trips was our desire to go where our vehicle was unable to travel. Time after time, as we lugged our camping gear from the car onto the sand, we would say how nice it would be to have a four-wheel-drive auto that could just drive us out there. With such a car, we could just drive the beaches—go from beach to beach on the sand—and find even more isolated places to camp. Sometimes a particularly beautiful or interesting piece of landscape would beckon, but had to be bypassed because the Tempest couldn't handle the terrain. Finally we decided to buy a four-wheel-drive car, but something happened that made us postpone our plans.

At this point in our lives, I had not yet had the good sense to sell my travel agency. The influx of charter tours and travel clubs had eaten into our business severely, but the business was still absorbing a lot of my time. As the Mexicans say, *"Mucho trabajo y no dinero"* [Lots of work and no money]. Once again it made a demand on our time. We had just sold a fairly large tour to Acapulco on Princess Cruises, and as the resident experts on Mexico, Margie and I were "elected" to conduct the tour.

We were not breathless with excitement at the prospect. We had conducted tours to Acapulco many times before, and knew the spiel of the tour guides by heart. Also, we were not crazy about ship cruises. When we're traveling some place, we like to get there fast and then relax. All those days at sea, with the social director organizing fun and games, leaves us cold. Finally, if you're a concientious tour conductor, you sublimate your own pleasures to the desires of your tourists. After all, they paid a lot of money for the trip, and it's up to you to see that they have a good time. This includes filling in at cards or shuffleboard when needed, picking up some drink checks, introducing people to each other, and spending time with the lonely ones. In short, you are their host. We resigned ourselves to our fate, however, and dutifully boarded the ship at sailing time, never dreaming that just around the corner another exciting adventure awaited us.

The first night out we gave a cocktail party for our tour so they could become acquainted, and so we could look them over. They were a typical tour group. There were no single men, but a large number of single ladies middle-aged and older, and a few couples. Included among the ladies was my mother and three of her pals. They would be no problem on the tour. They'd be playing bridge from port to port. Margie and I circulated about, introducing ourselves, chatting, and telling our passengers not to hesitate to call on us for anything they needed. By the time the party was over, we concluded that we had an exceptionally congenial group of people.

At the time of this trip, the Princess Cruises were owned by a Canadian firm. Consequently, many of the personnel were either Canadian or English.

Also at our party was the ship's social director, a charming English girl named Helen who seemed to find everything "teddibly smashing." That very first morning she organized some of the passengers to take a brisk morning hike around the deck. Helen, in sensible English walking shoes, was setting a fast pace. Red-faced and puffing along behind her was her flock. "Briskly now!" we heard her say, "Isn't this salt air smashing! Makes one enjoys one's breakfast." We slipped deeper into the covers and went back to sleep.

Our first full day at sea brought us our first problem. Two elderly ladies on our tour became ill. One of their worried friends contacted me.

"They're so sick," she said, "and we can't find the ship's doctor."

I reassured her, saying that I would find him and that the ladies undoubtably had just a touch of *mal de mer* and would be okay in a few hours.

Neither statement was true. The ship's doctor could not be found for the entire trip, and the two ladies just became sicker and sicker. Among her many talents, Margie is also a nurse. So it became her unpleasant task to care for the two ill passengers. The ocean was like a lake and the ship moved slowly through the water with scarcely a roll, so Margie doubted that their problem was seasickness. The food aboard was not gourmet. It was simple, hearty, English food, so stomach problems from rich food were unlikely. Both ladies were running temperatures, so Margie concluded that they had picked up a touch of intestinal flu before sailing. Whatever it was, most of my poor wife's time was spent fetching containers for them to throw up in, and administering to their comfort as much as possible.

Thus far, things were going about as we had anticipated. I socialized and Margie carried bedpans. When the ladies slept, Margie would slip quietly away and I'd buy her a quick drink. We'd tumble into bed at night exhausted.

All passenger ships have fire drills. You are instructed that when you hear the ship's whistle blowing repeatedly, you are to don a life jacket and run—not walk—to your assigned lifeboat station. One afternoon, when the ladies were sleeping, Margie and I met secretly in our cabin for a drink, made love, then fell asleep. That was the moment they chose for the fire drill! We awakened on the last three toots of the whistle, threw on some clothes as fast as we could, and ran to our lifeboat station fastening our life jackets on the way up to the deck. By the time we arrived, the drill had been over for some time and the people seated about in deck chairs stared at us curiously. It was embarrassing.

Our first stop was the port of La Paz at the tip of Baja California. As the ship eased into the dock, the *mariachis* struck up a musical greeting. Then, when the gangplank was lowered and the tourists started to descend to the dock, the trumpeters played the bugle call used at the start of a horse race. It was certainly appropriate because the passengers literally charged down the wharf to the waiting taxis, impatient to spend their money on souvenirs. To the tradesmen of La Paz, that ship arrival must have been a welcome sight, indeed. Margie was able to leave her unfortunate patients for a few hours, so we joined the thundering herd. We shopped and acted as translators for one group of our tourists, and joined a different group for luncheon at the beautiful *Los Cocos* hotel on the beach.

Our ship put in to the harbor of Puerto Vallarta at six in the morning. Margie and I were awakened by the rattle of the anchor chain as it paid out into the clear waters of the bay.

"Welcome to Puerto Vallarta, Darling," I said.

"Listen! Do you hear what I hear?"

I listened for a moment. "My God! It's *mariachis!*"

We both got up on our knees and peered out the portholes. There was a boat drifting just about a hundred yards from our ship, and it was loaded with *mariachis* playing their lungs out.

"Those poor devils," I said. "They were probably up until 2 a.m. playing in some bar, and now they've been hustled out of bed at this hour to serenade us!"

Margie giggled. "It sounds like one of them hasn't got his lip working yet this morning."

It was true. They were blowing some clinkers all right, but we certainly appreciated the gesture.

At breakfast, Helen was hustling about, full of English vim and enthusiasm, marshalling her troops for a sightseeing excursion.

"—the shopping is absolutely smashing!" she was saying, "And we'll take the boat to Mesmaloya. That's where the cinema *Night Of The Iguana* was made."

"Is that where Elizabeth Taylor and Richard Burton—?" One of the ladies left the sentence pointedly unfinished.

"Of course!" she chortled, "The scene of historic hanky-panky!"

Seated three tables away, Margie and I chuckled at Helen's phrase. I have stolen it for reuse many times since then.

Then the loveliest thing happened! Into the ship's dining salon came Margie's two sick ladies. They were a bit weak and wobbly, but rouged and dressed for a shopping spree, and determined to eat some breakfast.

"If they can eat, they're okay," Margie said, "and that little chore of mine is over." We watched with satisfaction as the ladies ordered and enjoyed a light breakfast.

Margie and I decided to pass up the tour. With our entire flock off on an excursion, it would be lovely to have a day to ourselves—our first since leaving port in Los Angeles.

Small things often lead to large consequences. The decision not to go on the tour that day affected the entire course of our trip and led to our adventure.

We went back into the salon, had a leisurely cup of coffee, and then returned to our stateroom to sit around for awhile, basking in the contentment of having nothing to do. Finally we decided to catch a shoreboat into town, have lunch, and look around a bit.

At that time in Puerto Vallarta the taxis were not metered. There was just a flat fee of five pesos (forty cents) for the ride, no matter where you wanted to go. We caught a cab at the pier and went straight to the Iguana restaurant for lunch. It's always been one of our favorites, and boasts a complete Kosher menu along with other selections. It's the only Kosher menu we've ever seen in Mexico.

After lunch, we cabbed back to town for some shopping and wandering. Puerto Vallarta is most picturesque. The little town is dominated by a beautiful church topped with a two-story crown, lacy and golden, which seems to catch the sun's rays and reflect them in the happy faces of the people. The streets are cobblestoned, and lined with colorful vendors selling fruit and flowers. Happy faces are everywhere. A wide, shallow river bisects Puerto Vallarta and serves as the laundry tub for the poor. Like the laundromats at home, it is a place for meeting, chatting, and exchanging gossip. Here you see a beautiful woman and her little girl shampooing their hair in the river; there, you see Papá has built Mamá an elaborate "laundry room" in the stream, complete with sun shade from an old sheet and a table on which to place her freshly-scrubbed garments. He sits on a stone reading the newspaper while she does the laundry and chats with friends. There is laughter and singing and when a horse crosses the stream and urinates in the water, nobody notices or cares. We strolled along the stream, joining in the fun and admiring the whiteness of the wash as it dried, spread out on bushes next to the water.

The food on the ship had really been quite uninteresting, so we decided to change our clothes and go out that evening to the Cuatro Vientos [Four Winds] restaurant, internationally famous for its gourmet cuisine.

We arrived back aboard the ship to change clothes at about six o'clock. Except for a skeleton crew, it was nearly deserted. We were walking down the deck toward our stateroom when we heard loud, angry voices. There, at the entrance to the dining salon, was the English purser of the ship, barring the door of the salon to an attractive, well-dressed Mexican couple. There was much shouting back and forth, and absolutely no communication. We decided to see if we could help out

We talked first to the Mexican couple, Daniel and Michelle Castallanos, who were celebrating their wedding anniversary. All year long Daniel had promised his wife that when the ship came to Puerto Vallarta, he would take her aboard for their anniversary dinner. He had hired a

71

launch, come out to the ship, and now was being refused entrance. He said he could pay for his meal, and was indignant at being insulted by this officer. I patiently explained all of this to the purser.

"I'm sorry, Mr. Hunter," he said stiffly, "we can not allow these people from Puerto Vallarta aboard."

"It couldn't hurt anything," Margie said.

"It's just regulations, Mrs. Hunter. Those are the rules."

Margie and I glanced at each other. We were both getting the same idea at the same moment. "What if they came aboard as our guests?" I asked.

"Well, that would be different of course," the purser said. "As a passenger, you may invite anyone you wish."

"Okay," Margie said, "Mr. and Mrs. Castellanos are our guests for dinner this evening."

"Very well," said the purser, and opened the door for us.

We were the only diners in the salon, so we selected the best table in the place. It was one which afforded our guests the most beautiful view of the city by night. I shuddered as they both ordered Cantonese food. With the pallid food we'd been served thus far on the trip, what would the Cantonese be like? It appeared to have been dumped on their plates out of a can, but they ate it with gusto.

Since then we have learned something about Mexican taste. Contrary to what most Americans think, Mexicans do not subsist on enchiladas, tamales, and chili relleno, such as is served in Mexican restaurants in the States. The campesinos [peons] eat beans and tortillas because they are low cost and high in protein. But the upper and middle-class Mexicans prefer Continental dining and Cantonese fare. Cantonese food is, by far, the favorite, and any city with enough people to call itself a city will have at least one place offering the Chinese food. Furthermore, we have found that Chinese food in Mexico, generally speaking, is superior to that in the United States.

Daniel Castellanos was chunky and clean-shaven, making him appear somewhat younger than his twenty-five or so years. He had a firm handshake and a warm smile that made you feel like a friend at once. His wife, Michele, was tiny and peppery, with an impish smile, raven hair, and eyes that sparkled when she talked. We immediately dubbed them "Danny" and "Mich." The four of us sat at the table talking long after the runny sherbet and weak coffee had been served.

We told them about our love of Mexico, my television show, and the tour we were conducting. They told us about themselves. Danny was a very successful young businessman. He owned a gift shop at the airport [a lucrative location], plus a flourishing hamburger stand on Puerto Vallarta's shimmering white beach. He and Mich were obviously deeply in love. Both of them had come from upper-class families with profitable family businesses in Mexico City. They achieved black-sheep status with their families when they decided to spurn the family businesses and strike out on their own in Puerto Vallarta. Despite family disapproval, they worked side by side in the gift shop and at the hamburger stand, were proud of what they had accomplished, and dreamed of even bigger things.

Margie and I were immediately attracted by their youthful enthusiasm, and they seemed equally fond of us. In that short time we became fast friends.

Finally, the hour was late, the waiter was stifling yawns, and the passengers were beginning to come back aboard. The Castellanos said, reluctantly, that they had better leave.

"We are indebted to you for this night," Danny said, "so I have a plan. Tomorrow in Puerto Vallarta you will be our guests, and we will show you a Puerto Vallarta you have never seen."

I was heartsick. It was such an exciting prospect, and the ship was sailing the next day. "We can't, Danny," I said, "we sail for Acapulco tomorrow."

"Oh, I'm so disappointed," Margie said, "There's nothing I'd love more."

"Yo también" [me too] I said.

"How long will you be in Acapulco?" he asked.

"A week."

"Well then," Danny said, "when your tour ends in Acapulco, you and Margie can fly back to Puerto Vallarta and join us. Verdád?"

I shook my head. "No, Danny, I have to return to my television show after that."

"Phone and tell them you can't come back yet," Mich suggested.

"Why not, Darling?" Margie added, "You have two more weeks vacation coming."

Now I became enthusiastic. "Okay, I'll do it! I'll phone the studio from Acapulco."

"And you will join us after that?"

"We will."

It was settled then. Danny said he and Mich would meet us at the airport in Puerto Vallarta when we returned. We bade each other goodbye, and they descended the ladder to the waiting launch and their

73

return to shore.

We spent the remainder of the cruise "doing our thing" as tour conductors. We had the sun and the sea, dinners and dances, shuffleboard, horse racing (a betting game), bridge, and especially nice passengers. Nevertheless we were impatient to be off and gone, so time seemed to drag.

As our ship entered the harbor of Acapulco, all the passengers rushed out on deck to view it, and we were struck once more by the beauty of this most beautiful of ports. There was the enormous bay of crystal-clear, blue water, the brilliant white sand beaches, the palm trees, and the giant half-circle of luxury hotels backed by a cloudless sky.

I remembered a time several years before when I had learned to scuba dive in Acapulco. My instructor, a Mexican diver, had worked with the crew of divers that attempted to salvage the Andrea Doria. I can't recall his name, but he modestly called himself "The Prince." After many practice dives in the hotel pool, he took me out for my first dive in the bay. To my astonishment I saw a huge statue of the Virgin Mary on the ocean floor in about fifty feet of water. She had been there a long time and was entwined with seaweed, encrusted with shells, and encircled with brightly colored tropical fish who stared at us blandly, and without fear, as we descended into their realm. "Prince" told me she was the "Diver's Virgin." As the little tugs towed our giant passenger ship into the bay, I wondered if we were passing near her—perhaps over her head.

After docking, our whole tour group scrambled into taxis, waiting for them on the wharf, and headed for the hotel. My mother and her friends rode in our cab, and it was the first chance we'd had to talk with her on the entire trip. She was having a ball.

As we approached the hotel, we saw parachutes sailing over the water. The parachute ride was new in Acapulco at this time. The rider is strapped into the harness of a brightly colored parachute and towed by a speedboat. The chute fills with air as the boat moves, and he floats like a human kite high above the waters of the bay. I had no desire to try it.

The days that followed were filled with the usual sightseeing excursions for our group. We went to La Quebrada to see the high divers. La Quebrada is actually a night club near a cliff overlooking the ocean. 135 feet down the sheer face of the cliff is a tiny inlet that only fills with water from the surge of the sea. One moment it's deep enough for a dive, and the next moment it is nearly empty with jagged rocks jutting upward. The divers must leap off the cliff into this inlet with split second timing, or be crushed on the rocks below. A number of divers have died in this spectacular manner.

The tourists sit at tables, sipping their drinks and watching as a diver slowly climbs to the top of the cliff. At the top is a small shrine to the Virgin Mary. He kneels before it in a brief moment of prayer. Then he arises, and a hush falls over the audience as he approaches the extreme edge of the cliff. He stands, watching the surge and planning his timing. He leaps! Spectators hold their breath as he falls in a graceful swan dive. He strikes the water at sixty miles per hour—and surfaces in triumph! Afterward he greets the tourists at the door with an ocean-wet handshake, and hopes for a tip. The tips are usually generous, for the spectator feels he has just grasped the hand of a man who has flirted with death.

We took our group to the Club Esqui [Ski Club], where the stage curtain is a giant spray of water, and the floor show features some of the most spectacular water skiing ever seen.

We took in the classic Ballet Folklorico, where the visitor sees costumes and dances that have their roots in ancient Aztec rituals, performed by dancers who carry the blood of the Aztecs in their veins.

With all of this there was the usual city tour, the shopping tours and the boat rides. Then, to conclude the week, Margie and I gave a dinner party for our passengers at the Focolare restaurant. Some of the people were continuing to other parts of Mexico, and some were returning to Los Angeles either by plane or ship. So this was the end of our tour. Tomorrow, Puerta Vallarta!

The fates willed otherwise.

I discovered in the morning that no direct flight to Puerto Vallarta was available. We had to fly to Mexico City, lay over a night, and then catch another plane to Puerto Vallarta. It was a disappointment, but we made our reservations.

Then began the phone calls. The first was to KTTV studios in Hollywood to have my vacation extended. They were so cooperative about it I felt a little uneasy about my job security! The next phone call was to Danny Castellanos to tell him the hour of our arrival and our flight number. A phone call to Puerto Vallarta in those days was an experience in itself! There were only one or two phones in the whole city, so you had to call a call service. The "service" consisted of just one phone. Not a switchboard. When you finally got past the constant busy signal, you would tell them whom you wished to talk with, and they'd dispatch a small boy (retained there for such purposes) to fetch that person. Then you'd hold the line—message units ticking away—while the little boy supposedly ran to get your party on the line. I pictured him ambling down the street, peeking in shops, and forgetting his errand, so I was very relieved when I heard Danny's familiar voice on the phone. I told him about our necessary delay en route, and gave him the flight information. He said he and Mich would be waiting for us.

When you go on a sea voyage you very nearly have to empty your closets at home. You require a tuxedo for the Captain's dinner, scores of sport jackets and slacks, plus a varied assortment of beachwear in rainbow hues. With your wife it's even worse. She seems to require several formals, cocktail dresses galore, plus casuals (whatever they are), beachwear, accessories of all kinds, and purses. During the tour our luggage had been conveniently handled for us, but now that we were on our own, I looked at the small skyscraper of assorted suitcases crowned with a few bulky items we'd purchased along the way, and wondered how we would ever manage. The bellboy got us to the street and into the cab (we had to sit with the driver since our luggage filled all other space), and the cabby got us into the airport. I watched the luggage move inexorably out of sight on the conveyor belt and hoped, secretly, that some of it would get lost before we landed.

We were tired. Not so much from all the running around on the tours, but from the pressures of being responsible for all those people, changing plans, making phone calls, getting plane reservations, packing, and sweating over all that damn luggage.

At Mexico City International Airport it was worse. The airport is huge, crowded, and impersonal. Everyone is busy hurrying somewhere. So there we were with stacks and stacks of suitcases and other impediments, and no one to help. Finally, with the aid of *muchos pesos*, we got ourselves and our bags stuffed into a cab and on the way to the hotel. This was mid-November, and Mexico City was dressed up for the Christmas holidays. It is one of the most exquisite sights in the world. Festive lighting creates giant nativity scenes, Christmas trees, or wisemen with the star, from the top to the bottom of the tall buildings. One thirty-story building was wrapped like a Christmas present with neon lighting for ribbons and the bow on top. We had never been to Mexico City at this time of year, and we rode all the way to the hotel with our noses mashed against the taxi windows, ogling the sights.

At six the next morning we were up and gone. When we deplaned at the tiny Puerto Vallarta airport we were surprised to see quite a large crowd waiting. Anxiously we scanned the faces of the crowd to find Danny and Mich. They came up behind us.

"Bienvenidos!" [Welcome!] they said in chorus.

76

After we had greeted each other Margie asked, "Who are all these people?"

"Well it's this way," Danny explained, "This was the first time a jet plane ever landed at Puerto Vallarta, and they weren't sure it could make it. It's a small landing strip."

Margie looked at me silently, but I could read her mind. "Oh yeah?" she was thinking, "How're we going to get out of here?"

"Come!" Danny said, beckoning, "My car is parked over here."

His car was proof of his affluence in Puerto Vallarta. In a town where the majority of the population walked, rode burros, or traveled in horse-drawn carts, Danny was the proud possesor of a brand new Datsun truck. With the efficiency of one used to giving orders, he had our tons of luggage loaded in the back of the truck, tipped the recruits he'd found to carry the load, seated us all, and started for town. We rode four in the front seat, I with Margie on my lap.

Our first stop was a tiny travel agency called Pacífico.

"This is the office of a friend of mine," Danny said, "He'll store this luggage for you. You won't be needing it in Puerto Vallarta."

Margie selected one bag, and the overnight case containing our toilet articles. The rest of the mountain of suitcases disappeared into the back of the tiny office. I could almost feel the pressure letting up as I watched it vanish. Then we all got back in the truck again.

"Danny, I never thought to make a hotel reservation," I said, "Do you suppose—"

"No problema," he said. "But we'll get to that later. Right now it's time for lunch and a drink."

More pressure eased up. I was even starting to notice the flowers along the way now. They were in full bloom and beautiful.

Luncheon was at the Tropicana. We sat on comfortable wicker chairs scattered about a patio at the edge of the beach. A gentle, perfumed breeze cooled us as we sipped our drinks, watched people playing on the sand, and listened to the soft music of a combo playing for diners. As my icy tequila went down and I stared, hypnotized, at the waves curling on the beach, I took root. I didn't care if I ever moved from that chair for the rest of my life.

Margie looked at me suspiciously. "Are you getting bombed?"

"No, Babe. It's just that the kinks are coming out."

At this time Puerto Vallarta hadn't become the popular tourist resort that it is today, and fancy American-type hotels with all the amenities did not exist. We stayed at the Oceana, the best of the hotels available. It was typically Mexican, built around a central tiled patio. There were no elevators, just outside stairs leading up out of the patio to the various floors above.

Danny let us off at our hotel after a long, lingering lunch. He said he'd pick us up in the morning for some fun. With the last bit of strength we had, we lugged our bag and overnight case up the stairs to the second floor (Thank God we weren't on the third!), opened the door to our room, and flopped onto the bed. Neither of us opened an eye until six the next morning.

When Margie and I are staying in hotels, we always carry our own coffee and juice with us so we don't have the intrusion of a bellboy at the early hours we awaken. It is always my pleasant morning task to mix the instant coffee and stir up the Tang in the melted ice from the previous evening. It was especially good that we adopted this practice at the Oceana hotel, because there was no bellboy, and no way to summon one!

When I arose at six and started my little chores, it seemed rather dark for that hour of the day in the Tropics. It was then that I realized that the rooms at the Oceana were all equipped with heavy, thick outside shutters to preserve the darkness and quiet for the hotel guests. As Margie stared dreamily from the bed, I made my way to the large window, put down my coffee, and started to struggle with the shutters. Suddenly they swung wide, the sunlight streamed in, and a cacophony of sounds from the street filled the room. There were church bells clanging; roosters crowing; burros braying; babies crying, and children laughing and chattering. All the morning sounds of Mexico combined in one loud, discordant concert. It brought Margie bounding out of bed for a look. Together we stood at the window, sipping our coffee, and watching and listening as Puerto Vallarta awakened. For the first time since we'd left Los Angeles, I began to feel faint stirrings of "The Baja Feeling."

Danny and Mich picked us up after a leisurely breakfast and there began a day of meeting their friends and exploring some of the little known (to the tourist) byways of Puerto Vallarta.

On one occasion, he said he wanted us to meet a couple of Americans he knew. He said we would find them interesting, but didn't explain why. The Datsun truck wound its way along the cobblestone streets to the "low-rent district" and a line of white, tiled roofed apartments that all looked alike. All had large, wide windows, unglassed and unscreened, and open-air patios hanging like flower boxes above the street. He knocked at the door of one of them.

"Entre!" called a muffled female voice.

We entered, climbed the stairs, and met Dolores and Fred.

Dolores was an American artist living in Puerto Vallarta, an attractive girl, inclined toward funky clothes and cheap, bangly jewelry. Her husband, Fred, a Black, was a former sailor in the U.S. Navy. But the astonishing thing was her art work.

She painted eerie, psychedelic designs on human bones!

I held in my hands a human skull, grinning at me toothlessly, emblazoned in bright colors suggesting a look through the bone into the brain. With some persuasion, she brought forth other bones similarly decorated. They were—should I say *beautiful?* No, they were fascinating. Eerie. Thought provoking. Unforgettable. No adjective is really adequate to describe them.

I noticed something else strange. Her voice, normally light and vivacious, dropped to a deep monotone, and seemed to take on a gentle ghoulish quality as she discussed her work. Or did I imagine it?

"Dolores, where in the world did you get these human bones?" I asked.

There was a pause. A mischievous light in her eye. "A medical student gave them to me.

A medical student in Puerto Vallarta? Odd. There is no medical school there. A picture flashed through my mind: Midnight in the cemetery. Out of the shadows slip Dolores and Fred; he carrying a spade. He starts to dig. All we hear is the sound of the soft earth being turned and Fred's panting. Then suddenly a clunk. He drops his spade and reaches down into the darkness. He brings up a human skull, its eyes dark holes, its pate shining in the moonlight. "That's it!" she whispers in that creepy voice. "It's perfect. Now quickly! Let's get out of here!" And carrying their grisly burden, they vanish again into the darkness.

After we left their apartment, I told Danny my suspicions and imaginings, and I asked him what he thought about it.

He just shrugged. *"Quien sabe?* But I thought you would be interested."

I certainly was, and I shall never forget Dolores and her art work!

Our first full day with Danny and Mich had been delightful and fascinating, but it was also tiring. By nine o'clock that night, Margie and I were both gulping back yawns. We finally asked our charming hosts to excuse us, returned to the hotel, and went to bed. The light had just been off a few minutes and I was starting to doze when I felt Margie's hand on mine.

"Darling, are you asleep?" she whispered.

"Yeah. Sort of. Why?"

She sighed. "It seems like we're always with people—never alone together. I haven't felt 'The Baja Feeling' yet on this trip."

I agreed. We talked it over and decided that the next day I'd ask Danny if there was someplace near Puerto Vallarta where we could be alone for a few days.

That decision made, we both went instantly to sleep, never suspecting that we had just taken the final step toward the adventure we'd been seeking.

I popped the question to Danny the next day.

"I know of a place that is *perfecto!*" he said.

"Near here?"

"Just a short boat ride. It is a little island called Yelapa. *Qué bonita!*"

"Well how do we get to this island?

"Every morning at nine, a small boat leaves for Yelapa with mail and supplies. The driver of the boat will take you there for fifteen pesos."

"And how do we return?"

"One day when the mail boat arrives at the island, you go aboard, and for another fifteen pesos he will bring you back to Puerto Vallarta."

"Well if there's mail, there must be people living there."

"It is a very small *poblado*. Perhaps a hundred persons."

"Do we sleep on the beach?"

"No there is a small hotel. It accommodates five parties. But you will be quite alone . . . oh—one other thing."

"What's that?"

"Sometimes you will see those people. Those—how do you call them?"

"I don't know what you mean."

"The ones who wear their hair like women."

"Hippies."

"*Sí*. Hippies. Sometimes they go there."

"Why?"

"Because there is no law there."

"You mean to smoke marijuana?"

"*Sí*. And to buy. In Mexico our laws about marijuana are much harder than yours in the United States. If you are caught with it, you may go to prison for a very long time. But in Yelapa there is no *policia*."

"Do they just sell it on the streets?"

He laughed. "There are no streets in Yelapa, Benito." He lowered his voice. "They say there is a man there who calls himself 'God.' They say that this man sells them the weed." He paused and looked at me sharply. "You do not use marijuana, Benito."

"I never have, Danny, but I might. I just might."

80

"Be careful, *amigos*."

At this time back in the States, Timothy Leary was espousing his "drop out and turn on" philosophy, and thousands of adolescents were running away from home, existing on welfare abetted by macrame and ceramic sales, and smoking pot. The nation was scandalized and predicted they would all become hard-core dope fiends—a total loss to society. Today, those dropouts are nearing thirty-five, and most of them have become worthwhile citizens. But the great furor in the media over the pros and cons of marijuana had aroused our curiosity. Margie and I had discussed it often, and said that sometime before we died we'd like to try smoking a joint and see what the big attraction was. We discussed it again in our hotel room that night, and decided that Yelapa might be the ideal place to try it—if we could find the nut who called himself "God."

The next morning we checked out of the hotel and walked to the pier to catch the mail boat. Probably for the first time in history the boat had departed on time, and we were five minutes late. We weren't about to allow anything to delay our plans, so we looked about and eventually found a man who sold speedboat rides to tourists. We engaged his boat to take us to the island. Our driver was a very young boy named Jesús. He was a cute lad with snapping black eyes, and a mischievous look about him, but he took his job very seriously, and scarcely talked as he sped the boat out of the harbor and south along the tropical shore. As all signs of civilization faded astern and the tropical sun warmed us, we felt a wonderful feeling of elation.

"Jesús is taking us to find God," Margie giggled, "It sounds like Yelapa must really be heaven!"

She was sitting in the stern in her bikini with the white wake of the speedboat foaming off behind her, looking like a luscious water sprite.

The long dormant "Baja Feeling" had again begun to emerge in full flower.

Our boat was speeding about half a mile offshore, paralleling the coastline so we could watch the scenery unfold as we journeyed south. The homes of Puerto Vallarta had vanished quickly, but every now and again you could see a simple dwelling of some sort nestled in the tropical jungle and looking out at the sea. A vista like that in California would cost $150,000 or more, and that Mexican settler probably got it for nothing. In Mexico, much of the land along the seashore is called *ejido* land; homestead land. A citizen may occupy it, build a dwelling, and it's his. The jungles are full of coconuts, papaya, mangoes, and other fruit. You grow a few vegetables, and catch fish for your protein. Not a bad life.

Cove after beautiful cove sped by. At one of the larger ones, Jesús took the boat on a slow, wide sweep, coming quite close to shore. On the cliff, back in the jungle, was a large thatched roof.

"Mismaloya," our taciturn driver said.

Soon we could make out what appeared to be a number of small islands on the horizon.

"Es Yelapa?" I asked Jesús, pointing in their general direction.

"No. Los Arcos," he answered.

"The Arches. That's an odd name for islands," I said to Margie.

But soon we saw why. These islands were actually giant rocks sticking up out of the ocean, and each one was a perfect arch! The sea, through millions of years, had in its inscrutable way hollowed the center out of each of them. You could actually pass "under" the island in a tunnel.

Jesús dropped the boat's speed so we half-drifted through each arch. Inside them it was dark, and the sea birds making their homes there went screeching out into the sunlight at our approach, their voices and ours echoing off the walls. On one occasion we were able to view the tropical shore through one of the arches. It made a rugged frame for the picture of white sand beach and green jungle. It was breathtaking. For the umpteenth time during our visits to Mexico, I longed to be able to paint.

In the past we had bathed on the Riviera, drunk wine on the beaches of Majorca, and lounged on the sands of Hawaii and other South Pacific paradises. We have camped on many of Mexico's beautiful beaches. But never had we seen anything as beautiful as Yelapa. Clouds, like huge gobs of whipped cream, hung motionless on the tops of purple mountains in the background. In the foreground was a glistening white beach, fringed with a tropical jungle of palms, bananas, frangipani, orchids, and lavishly adorned with garlands of red bougainvillea. A warm, gentle breeze wafted the fragrance of the flowers over the water to us. From back in the mountains, a sparkling river tumbled over boulders, making its way to the sea, while egrets and herons with their long pink legs, stepped like ballerinas in the clear water.

Jesús expertly swung the boat into the entrance of a small cove, cut the engine, and dropped anchor. He waved to three men on the shore, and they started pushing a large dugout down the sand. Apparently they were going to breach the giant waves pounding the beach to come out and pick

Margie Hunter on the boat to Yelapa.

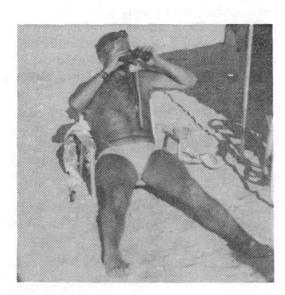

Ben Hunter scans the horizon for seagulls.

us up.

They waited for one huge comber to smash itself on the sand, and then quickly launched their dugout in the foam, their trousers soaked to the hips. Then, with handmade paddles, they started paddling furiously to get beyond the breakers before the next wave. It was already humping to gargantuan size and starting to curl over them. One great, last effort, and the dugout shot over the crest of the wave and came crashing down as if dropped from a balloon. It made a loud smack, and the spray shot out like a fan, creating instant rainbows. And then the dugout was alongside. We tipped Jesus, who remained silent to the end and only nodded in appreciation. Then, with the men steadying her, Margie (and the tote bag) got aboard, followed by me with the cameras, and we headed back toward the shore. We hadn't gone fifty feet when Jesús had the anchor up, and was speeding full throttle back to Puerto Vallarta.

Expertly, the men backpaddled while one wave expended itself on the shore. Then with the next one rising beneath our stern, they dug in their paddles again; we caught the wave, and were propelled toward the beach, nose down, as if a mighty sea monster were pushing us from the rear. We breathed a sigh of relief as the bow grated on the sand. We had both been so absorbed in the landing procedure that we hadn't noticed a man standing on the beach awaiting us.

"Welcome to Yelapa!" he said, "I'm Emmy."

I couldn't believe what I saw. A little man—an American—in his late fifties or early sixties was smiling gaily at us. His wispy hair was covered with a sailor's cap that bore the autographs of countless friends. He was wearing trousers which originally had been ankle length, but were crudely severed at the hips so that the pockets hung below the frazzled ends of his homemade bermuda shorts. Tanned, knobby birdlegs extended from the shorts beachward into long, black stockings and shiny black shoes! To top off his natty ensemble, he carried a walking stick. We introduced ourselves, then I asked, "Does the hotel have liquor? We'd like you to join us for a drink."

"Oh my yes. They certainly do," he twittered, "but I never drink. Never, never."

"Well perhaps you'll join us for a bottle of pop or something."

"Well . . . very well. But only one." He put his arm around Margie and started guiding her across the beach to the hotel. I struggled along behind.

The lobby-bar-restaurant-coffee shop-kitchen was just one structure. It was about thirty feet by forty feet in size, and consisted of

84

poles hewn from local trees as uprights, covered with a roof thatched of palm fronds. No walls; no floor. One corner had been squared off to be a kitchen area; a bar had been erected in another corner; and tables and chairs were scattered about. Clumps of bananas, picked in the jungle, hung from the crossbars between the poles. It looked like a scene from *Rain*.

Palm-thatched shelters such as this are used extensively in the tropical part of Mexico. Why have walls and windows when the air is always sweet and balmy? Why have screens when there are no insects? Why have locks where everyone is honest? These shelters offer shade from the sun, and dryness from the tropical rains. They are sturdy, and only need to be reroofed every ten years. Who needs more? The Mexicans in the tropics call such a shelter a *palapa*, a word unknown to many Mexicans in the northern or inland areas.

Emmy introduced us to the manager and his wife, Roberto and Choyo, who both spoke a little English. Roberto constantly carried his one-year-old son, Robertito (little Robert), proudly on his arm.

"These are your new tenants," Emmy said.

"*Bien*. You would like to go to your room?" asked Roberto.

"Well, we'd like to see it," I said, "but first we're going to have a drink with Emmy."

We picked out a table and sat down. As it turned out, the three of us sat drinking for nearly an hour.

"How did you come to live on this island?" Margie asked.

"Oh it's not an island, my dear," he said.

"It isn't!"

"Oh my, no. It's part of the mainland."

"Well, we were told—"

"I know, I know," he interrupted. "The locals in Puerto Vallarta call it an island because it's only accessible by boats. We're completely cut off from everything here, but we are part of the mainland."

Later, he freely admitted that he was gay. He also told us that he was a former purser in the merchant marine. On one of his trips, he said he'd discovered Yelapa and always said that's where he was going to retire. He had been as good as his word. With his mustering-out pay, he built a beautiful home on a cliff which afforded him an unparalleled view of the beach and the bay. He didn't always come down from his cliff to greet strangers, he said, but he'd spotted us in the boat with his binoculars and decided he'd like to meet us. We were the kind of people he would like. We accepted the flattery, and didn't ask how he could come to that conclusion just looking through binoculars.

"You must come up to my little cliffhouse and see the flowers, Margie," he fluttered, and touched her lightly on the arm. "They're so beautiful!"

Though I felt like extra baggage in this new friendship, we both agreed we'd visit Emmy the next morning.

"Excellent! You can't miss it. It's that beautiful house at the south end of the beach. I'll have the ladder down for you."

Then he thanked us for the drinks, and with his sailor cap set at a jaunty angle, he minced his way back down the beach toward his home, merrily swinging his walking stick.

We both wondered what ladder he would have "down" and why, but concluded we'd have to wait until our visit to find out.

To find our room, Roberto told us to just follow a dirt path leading away from the palapa and into the jungle.

"We will need a key?"

He smiled. "No key."

Still aglow from the drinks, "The Baja Feeling," and enchantment with our new-found paradise, we started up the path which ascended gently upward into the jungle. It was lush and beautiful beyond words. There were stands of ferns on either side of the path, and showers of bougainvillea over our heads. Fragrant frangipani perfumed the air, and Margie stopped to sniff every blossom and inspect every bloom. Then we rounded a curve in the path leading out to the sunlight. There below us, the waves were crashing on the rocks; above us, on our right, was our "room."

It was a palapa like the main building, but smaller. It boasted a small patio with a hammock of coconut fibers slung between two uprights. One could lie and swing in that hammock by the hour, staring with fascination at the flowers, and the ever changing sea below.

Two double beds almost filled the room. There was a chest of drawers, and a kerosene lamp. One could lie in bed at night and peer out from under the palm fronds at the stars, so low in the sky you felt you could almost touch them. The bathroom was the only walled area, walled off from the rest of the room by thick cement set with hundreds of abalone shells. Abalone shells were used for soap dishes in the shower and over the wash basin. The bathroom window was unforgettable. A line of Vodka bottles had been cemented into the wall, giving light to the room, but defying anyone to see through. The whole palapa was unique, picturesque, and charmingly Mexican. An electric light dangled from the ceiling of the bedroom, but it didn't work.

We slept that afternoon, but were awakened by the electric light turning on. So *that* was it. They started the electric generator when the sun went down. We dressed in our best bermudas and tops, and descended the jungle path to the main *palapa* to have dinner and meet the other hotel guests. They were chatting quietly over drinks when we entered. We sat down, ordered a drink, and introduced ourselves.

There were only three other parties in the hotel. As the days went by, we discovered that all of these people enjoyed the same things we did— aloneness, the beach . . . and the sun. We would have lively chats with them at the cocktail hour each day, and the rest of the time we rarely saw them.

They all filled us in on the hotel operation. There was no menu for any meal. At breakfast and lunch you just asked for what you wanted, and if it was not available, you had to substitute. For dinner, you had whatever they'd been able to catch that day. Sometimes it was a wild pig from the jungle, sometimes a sea turtle, other times fresh-water shrimp from the river. It was always a surprise, and always delicious. The herbs and vegetables were grown in a little plot behind the main *palapa*. If there was anything you needed, like film for your camera, Roberto would catch the mail boat into Puerto Vallarta to get it for you. Our waitresses were three teen-age girls from the village who were painfully shy; plates were placed on the table with much blushing and giggling.

As our new friends described the hotel routine to us and displayed their knowledge of Yelapa, I was tempted to ask them if they'd heard of the man who called himself "God." I abandoned the idea, however, thinking I might shock them by revealing our secret plans.

Because of our long nap that afternoon, Margie and I weren't sleepy. So after a magnificent dinner of freshwater shrimp cooked in garlic and butter, we went for a walk on the beach. The tropic moon was big and silver, and the phosphorescence made dancing lights in the waves. We walked on the wet sand and the warm water of the Gulf washed our feet as we strolled. Then it was back up the jungle path to our *palapa*, into bed, and staring at the stars until we fell asleep.

After so much sleep, we awakened before dawn and were lying in bed listening to the waves and waiting for the sunrise when we heard a twig snap outside.

Margie gripped me tightly. "Someone's out there!" she whispered.

"Naw, Honey," I said quite loudly, "It's just a little animal or something." I hoped my loud voice would scare away whatever it was.

Then there was no mistaking it. Someone *was* outside our *palapa*!

"There's someone there!" Margie said insistently. "If you don't believe me, get up and look!"

I didn't want to appear as cowardly as I really was, so with a display of bravado, I got out of bed and stepped out into the moonlight.

"Who's there?" I said loudly.

"*Buenos días.*" A little white-haired Mexican gentleman, his arms loaded with coconut shells, approached me in the half light.

"*Qué estás haciendo?*" [What are you doing?] I asked.

"*Soy Manuel. Vengo hacer el fuego.*" [I'm Manuel. I come to make the fire].

"*El fuego? Porqué?*" [The fire? Why?]

"*Para agua caliente.*" [For hot water]

"*Oh! Gracias.*" I was beginning to get the picture. Up on the side of the hill above our *palapa* was a hot water heater with a gravity feed to our bathroom. Manuel was going to build a fire under it so we'd have hot water.

The old gentleman struggled up the hill to where the little hot water heater stood, placed the coconut shells under it, poured oil or something over them, and lit them. They began to burn merrily. We'd have hot water for our shower in twenty or thirty minutes. This was a part of the hotel operation our friends hadn't told us about.

Since they didn't turn on the generator in the mornings, there was no way Margie and I could make our customary cups of coffee in the room. So, then and there, we made arrangements with Manuel to bring us juice and coffee each morning when he came to start the fire. The familiar sight of this handsome, white-haired gentleman coming up the path with our coffee each dawn is something we'll never forget. We became very fond of him.

This was "Visiting Emmy Day," so after breakfast we started down the beach toward his house. It was then, in the daylight, that we discovered the reason for his reference to a ladder the day before. Situated on a cliff above the beach as it was, his home was only accessible from the beach by a fifteen foot wooden ladder. We weren't half-way there when we saw the ladder being lowered from above. Emmy had spotted us.

Margie went up the ladder first, and was greeted effusively with an embrace and a kiss on the cheek. "Good morning, my dear, how lovely you look!"

I joined them. "Good morning, Ben, it's nice to see you, too. Did you sleep well?" He didn't sound as if he cared.

"Beautifully, Emmy," I said.

"Come now, Margie, let me show you my flowers!" He grabbed her by the hand, and off they went to his beautifully-terraced garden.

Margie has a green thumb, talks to flowers, and can identify every single one by the shape of its leaf. I have a brown thumb, tend to step on flowers, and am unable to identify the most common species. I decided to let her do the flower inspection without me. "I'll wait in the house!" I called after them.

They didn't hear me. They were exclaiming over the plants, and both talking at once like women at a tea party. I went up the stairs into the house.

It was beautiful, indeed! No *palapa* this. His house had been built of stone, and was as sturdy as the rock cliff on which it perched. All across his living room were large windows, without glass or screen, giving Emmy a vista of the distant horizon beyond the sea, and the rolling breakers on the sand below. His flowers *were* beautiful, blooming everywhere, and threatening to take over the house. The binoculars stood on the window sill. I suspect that was their permanent place. For awhile I just stood there staring at the ocean and listening to their happy voices in the distance. Finally it sounded as if they were approachinng the house again, so I flopped into a deep leather chair near the window.

They burst into the room. "Oh Ben, his garden is exquisite! I promised to send him some seeds as soon as we get back to the States. Don't let me forget!" Margie said.

Emmy told us many interesting things about Yelapa. It is one of the few settled areas in the entire world where the wheel is not in use. There are not only any cars or motorcycles in Yelapa, but there are not even bicycles! Everyone walks, or rides a burro. There is a settlement of people up in the purple mountains behind Yelapa who took up residence there to avoid paying any Mexican taxes. They live there, fiercely independent. Once or twice a year they descend from the hills and demand tribute from the people of Yelapa in return for their lives. The tribute consists of chickens, pigs, and other foodstuffs. The people of Yelapa are rather proud that they have their own exclusive *bandidos*.

"And have you seen our Yelapa waterfall?" Emmy asked.

"No, where is it?"

"Well it's quite a walk from here. Perhaps an hour or so. But it's really worth it. It's soooo beautiful!"

"We must see it sometime," I said.

He snapped his fingers. "I've got an idea! Can you two come by my house again tomorrow morning?"

"Of course we can, Emmy," Margie said.

"Well then, come here about this same time tomorrow, and I'll have Matilde guide you to the waterfall."

"Who is Matilde?" I asked.

"He's my houseboy. He's in the village now doing some shopping. But he'll be here tomorrow and take you to the falls. He speaks English, too. I taught him."

Thanking Emmy for his kind offer and his hospitality, we agreed to be at his house in the morning, and departed.

Walking back up the beach toward the hotel, I wondered ruefully if we were going to find the man who called himself "God."

The remainder of the day was spent lolling in the sand, chatting with our newly-found friends, and soaking up the sun. Back behind the main palapa, the three little teen-age waitresses were picking vegetables and herbs for dinner. They sang in harmony as they worked, and their pretty voices formed a background for the shush of the waves, and the gentle breeze in the palms. The afternoon evaporated.

In the morning we met another guest of the hotel. An unwelcome one!

Manuel had delivered our early morning coffee and juice as arranged, and we had sipped it while waiting for the hot water to heat. Finally, I got up and went into the bathroom to shave and shower. I had just begun showering when I heard a blood-chilling shriek from the bedroom!

"Ben! Ben!"

There was no mistaking the sound of terror in her voice. I leaped out of the shower naked and soaking wet, and dashed into the bedroom. "What is it?!"

"Look!" she pointed.

There on the floor, moving determinedly toward my terrified wife, was one of the largest scorpions I've ever seen. He carried his stinging tail arched over his back like a man advancing with dagger raised. Margie was backed into a corner. My God! It looked as if that scorpion was really going to attack her! Wildly I looked around for something to kill him with. We wore no shoes, and had none with us. Then I spotted a pair of rubber sandals just a few inches away from the advancing scorpion. Slowly, very slowly, I moved my hand toward one of them.

"Be careful, Ben!"

Then, one of the sandals was in my hand. The scorpion hadn't wavered from his path toward Margie. Gripping my improvised weapon firmly, I brought it down squarely on top of the creature as hard as I could. It didn't kill him. He started lashing out with his tail. Again I

90

brought it down. Again and again.

Finally, he lay still.

Margie was covering her face with her hands.

She shuddered. "Get him out of here!"

I found a piece of paper, gingerly slipped it under him, and tossed him out into the jungle. Thereafter, as long as we were in Yelapa, we turned back the covers of the bed before retiring, and shook out our clothes before dressing. We didn't want any more surprises!

Later that morning, at Emmy's house, we met Matilde. He was a tall, powerful-looking Mexican, with a great gentleness about him. He spoke English, as Emmy had said, but doled it out sparingly, as if each word came from the abysmal depths of his memory. He was wearing the usual white shirt, denim trousers, and leather sandals (guaraches).

"Come!" he said laconically, and started up the path leading from Emmy's backdoor. We followed.

We were actually traversing the road that led to the village. But "road" it was not. It was more like a trail around the side of the mountain, so narrow that we had to walk single file. Occasionally, someone would pass us carrying a load of coconuts, or riding a burro, and we'd have to step off the trail and stand on the side of the hill until he passed. At length we came to a spot where a small, gurgling brook crossed the path and tumbled down the side of the hill to the ocean. Matilde turned, and started climbing the rocks up the hill beside the water.

"Does this stream come from the falls?" I called out to Matilde.

He looked back and nodded, smiling.

"Hell, it's not anywhere as big as the river back by the hotel. I can't see how there could be much of a waterfall," I said, noting there were water lilies and other plants of all descriptions growing in the water next to the rocks and boulders.

The climb became steeper and steeper, so Margie and I lapsed into silence, each of us occupied with our own thoughts. Margie was, I'm sure, thinking of flowers, birds, plants and other things of beauty. The only plant I was thinking of was "grass." I was wondering whether I dared pop the question to Matilde about the man called "God." The man from whom we hoped to make a purchase. Matilde was so quiet it was hard to figure him out.

Up, ahead of us, he stopped and beckoned. "Come!" he said again.

As we approached him he reached down and picked up a small, baseball sized rock.

"Chicle," he said. Then he bashed the trunk of a tree with the rock, and white, gummy sap began to drip out.

"*Chicle* is rubber, isn't it?" I said.

"Yes," said Margie, "Let me feel it, Matilde." She put her hand next to the tree trunk and allowed some of the sticky stuff to drop in her palm. It was amazing. You could stretch it out like a rubber band, or roll it in a ball and bounce it.

"We go now," said Matilde, and started to climb again.

We continued our climb up the river for about half an hour, with Margie exclaiming at the plant life. For a time, Matilde was climbing faster than we and out of our sight, but we assumed he was just ahead. Rounding one particularly large rock, we were startled to find Matilde waiting there for us.

"Here!" he said, and pointed upstream.

We could see nothing. "Where?" I said.

"You go first," he said.

Margie and I started around the next turn of the stream with Matilde bringing up the rear, and suddenly there it was! At our feet, a crystal-clear pool about fifty feet across, and the falls spilling like a long bridal veil into the pool from a height of about one hundred feet. The smallness of the stream made its falls the more lacy and beautiful as they trailed down the moss-covered rocks in the drop to the pool. Emmy was right. It was breathtaking.

I sat down to catch my breath from the climb, and to drink in the beauty. Margie started scrambling around the side of the pool to look at more flowers, leaving Matilde standing beside me. This would be the perfect time to ask Matilde if he knew the man we were seeking. But did I dare? Why the hell not? It was now or never. I looked up at Matilde standing above me.

"Matilde?"

He looked down at me.

"Do you know a man in Yelapa who calls himself 'God'?"

He just stared. He didn't nod or shake his head. There was no evidence of comprehension. Perhaps my English had been too complicated. I decided to try Spanish.

"*Conoce usted un hombre quien el se llama 'Dios'?*"

A long pause, then impassively, "*No sé.*" [I don't know].

I was deflated. He knew all right. He just wasn't about to admit it. "Okay, Buster," I thought to myself, "I'll just ask someone else."

I set up my camera and took pictures of the pool and the falls; we waded in the cool water to soothe our feet, hot from hiking, and then started the long walk back down. I didn't bring up the subject again.

Matilde delivered us back to Emmy's house, and this time we accepted his offer of a soft drink. We chatted for awhile, and I began to find myself really liking this bubbly, eccentric little man. He seemed less cool toward me, too. Perhaps he sensed more acceptance on my part. We thanked him again and went on our way, nothing mentioned about pot, or the man called "God."

That night, cuddled together on the coconut hammock on our patio, Margie and I whispered about it under the stars. The next day, we decided, we would go by ourselves into the village. It would be interesting to see what it looked like, and we'd ask the people for the whereabouts of our man.

It's not like any other village in Mexico we have ever seen. The typical Mexican village is a cluster of adobes around a central square, usually with some sort of park. The trail starting back of Emmy's house which we had trod the day before was the only street of Yelapa. As we continued into the village area, its appearance didn't change a bit. It continued to be a winding path about one burro wide. The village simply consisted of perhaps fifty *palapas* scattered above or below the trail, and nearly hidden by the lush foliage. There were no stores as such. There was a sandal maker, a tortilla maker, and some other small businesses, but in each case the proprietor operated the business from his own *palapa,* with his children running about.

The tortilla maker was a woman. She was making them the old-fashioned way, slapping the dough back and forth between her palms until it was sufficiently flat, then placing it on a griddle heated by charcoal to cook. We could smell the tortillas cooking way down the trail, and decided to buy some. Our noses led us to her *palapa.* After the purchase, I inquired, as if asking for an old friend:

"*Conoce usted un hombre quien el se llama 'Dios'?*"

She had been affable and chatty while we were buying the tortillas, but now suddenly her cooking seemed to absorb all of her attention. There was no answer.

"Let's try someone else," Margie said.

Munching our tortillas as we walked, we continued through the village asking the same question. But each time we asked, we either got no answer at all, or the individual asserted he knew no such person. In a village so small, it would be impossible for everyone not to know everyone else.

"I don't know what this conspiracy of silence is all about," I said, "but it

93

looks like we're not going to find our man this way."

"I agree," Margie said, "Let's go back to the hotel."

We turned and starting walking back along the winding path around the mountain, when he stepped out from behind a clump of bushes. He was large. Well over six feet, and weighing perhaps 280 pounds or more. He had a full, flowing black beard, and was wearing a tunic made of burlap, tied in the middle with a leather thong. His feet were bare. Before he spoke, I suspected he was our man.

He spoke in Spanish: "They say that two Americans who speak Spanish are asking for the man called God."

"Yes, we are the ones," I replied. "Are you the man?"

"I am."

"A friend has told us that we may purchase marijuana from you."

"It is not so."

"But he said—"

"There is no marijuana for you. There is no marijuana in Yelapa."

"You do not sell it?"

His deep voice almost thundered, "I do not sell!"

He glared at us a moment, and then stalked off.

"Now what do you make of that?" I asked Margie.

"I got the message. He doesn't sell!" she laughed. "I guess we bombed out."

"But I wonder why. You'd think he'd sell it to us if he sells it to other people."

"All I know is we'd do a heck of a lot better buying it from one of your musician friends."

"How true," I said ruefully.

I still puzzled over it as we made our way back to the hotel. Perhaps the *federales* were cracking down on Yelapa at this time and he—and everyone else—were afraid they'd get busted. Or perhaps he was just a religious nut of some sort, and the stories about him selling pot were untrue. Or, dealing with Hippies as Danny said, he was used to hearing English, and mistrusted Americans who speak Spanish. Whatever the reasons for his refusal and the strange behavior of the people of Yelapa, we never found out.

(As a postscript to this piece, I'll add that Margie and I finally satisfied our curiosity about grass three or four years later in the privacy of our home. Its effect was so tame that we returned happily to tequila.)

After meeting with "God," the lazy days at Yelapa just drifted by. We spent quite a lot of time with Emmy and grew to like the odd little guy more and more. We also spent much time exploring the area.

One day we decided to take a walk up the river near the hotel to see if it had a waterfall as pretty as the other one. On the way up we watched varicolored tropical birds flying overhead, and pecking for food among the water hyacinths in the river. We chased a family of piglets on the river bank, and watched, fascinated, as the women of Yelapa obtained drinking water for their homes. A woman would dig a deep hole in the soft sand beside the river. Then she would wait patiently until the water seeped through the sand into the hole. The sand, of course, was a natural filter for the water. When the hole was filled, she would ladle her clear, freshly-filtered water into a bucket, place the bucket on her head, and walk gracefully up the hill to the village. I was reminded of pictures I've seen of American models learning how to walk gracefully by balancing books on their heads. They could learn a lot from the ladies of Yelapa who balance a pail of water weighing twenty-five or thirty pounds on theirs!

We went upstream as far as we could, but found no waterfall, so we turned back. On the way down, we surprised the three little teen-age girls taking a bath in the river. They were very modest and were wearing their slips—completely covered—but they shrieked and hid from us as we passed.

On one occasion, Margie found an odd stone. It was odd because of its very light weight. She found a shallow little eddy in the river and dropped it in. To our astonishment it floated! We decided to take our "floating stone" home as a memento of Yelapa.

Our week in Yelapa slipped by like a day, and suddenly the day of departure was upon us. Before leaving, we climbed up the cliff to bid Emmy goodbye.

He bestowed a kiss on her cheek. "Don't forget to send me those seeds, Margie."

"I won't, Emmy."

I had a sudden thought. "Emmy, I know you gave Margie your post office box number in Puerto Vallarta. But shouldn't we have your full name to address the package?"

"Not necessary," he smiled. "Everyone knows me as Emmy. That will work fine."

"Well what does 'Emmy' stand for?" I asked, "I'd really like to know."

"My secret," he said coyly.

95

"Please, Emmy," Margie said, "I'd like to know too. Is it an awful name? We'd never tell anybody."

"No it's not awful. But you'd never believe it."

"Try us!" I said.

"Well . . . all right." He stood up and suddenly looked very serious. "It stands for Ralph Waldo Emerson III."

"You mean you're related to—"

"I am. A direct descendant. You see? I said you'd never believe me."

"I do," Margie said.

"I do too," I said. We checked it out later, however. We made a few discreet inquiries, and it apparently was true!

After telling Emmy goodbye, we went back to the hotel for farewells to Roberto, Choyo, and the other hotel guests. Margie kissed little Robertito, then we climbed into the dugout with our few belongings, and the men shoved off. Even the surf was down, and it was an easy ride out to the mail boat. As the boat pulled out of the cove and pointed its bow toward Puerto Vallarta, we could make out a small figure, binoculars in hand, waving goodbye from the house atop the cliff.

In a little over an hour we were back in Puerto Vallarta, and thanks to the miracle of jet travel, we were sitting in our own living room that evening, our bags stacked all around us.

There's always a letdown after a wonderful trip. We just sat and stared for awhile.

"I just hope I can remember everything," I said.

Margie's face brightened. "I have something to help you!"

She went over to the Mexican tote bag sitting atop the luggage, fished around in it for a moment, and then flourished an object in the air.

It was an ash tray from our room in Yelapa. She had stolen it. I remembered remarking one time about how unusual they were. Each ashtray was made of pottery in the shape of the dugout that first brought us to shore. Now every time we saw that ashtray we'd remember the dugout, and all the adventure it brought us. Margie removed the "floating stone" from her purse, placed it in the ashtray, and set it on the shelf.

Today, the Trans-Mexico highway has been pushed through, and Yelapa is accessible by car. A luxury hotel has been erected on the beach, complete with chic shops for the tourists. It wouldn't surprise me if those shops were manned by the *bandidos* from the mountains who used to demand tribute from the villagers. They're now getting their tribute from

96

the tourists. Regularly scheduled tour groups of ten to twenty persons at a time now go to see the waterfall we visited with Matilde.

Emmy is dead. It's my guess the coming of the fancy hotel and the hordes of tourists did him in. We have discovered that our "floating stone" is in reality a burro turd, hard-baked by the sun. But it still reposes in the little dugout ashtray on the shelf where Margie put it years ago. Each time it catches my eye the memories come swarming back of beautiful Yelapa, our *palapa* in the jungle, and—most of all—Ralph Waldo Emerson III.

4/ Taco and the Toy

We were restless, anxious, and eager to do something, but we didn't know where to begin. We wanted a four-wheel-drive car, but we had to sell the Tempest first; we wanted a dog, but were living in an apartment, so we needed a house.

After much discussion, Margie deemed the house our top requirement, and I gave in. We owned a house up on the high desert. It was a genuine white elephant. We couldn't rent it, and we couldn't seem to sell it at any price. Meanwhile, we paid taxes on it and the flash floods chewed up its backyard. Margie took out a classified ad offering this house as a down payment on a house in the city. To my astonishment, our telephone nearly rang off the hook! One of our callers was a most pleasant gentleman named Barney. He was a building contractor in temporary financial difficulty, and—if we liked his house—he'd accept our high desert loser as down payment. Moreover, it appeared he was going to accept it sight unseen! We inspected his house and it was a beauty.

While all this was transpiring, I had put the Tempest up for sale by tacking an advertising card on the office bulletin board at the studio. One of the secretaries seemed to like the car.

My choice in dogs has always been mongrels. In my opinion they tend to be more intelligent, and certainly hardier than their pedigreed brothers. A friend of ours had a dog named Betsy who was about to have pups. Betsy was a cross of nearly every pedigree in the American Kennel Club (you couldn't even identify her predominant strain), and he offered us one of her pups.

Fate seemed to be taking a hand in solving our problems.

Next, the secretary purchased the Tempest, and I had cash in hand for a down payment on a four-wheel-drive car. We spent each afternoon after that trudging through auto show rooms, checking out the 4 x 4 cars, and listening to the sales spiels.

In the evenings we visited Barney, rechecked his house, and dickered a little. He had over-priced his home, but we were unloading that white elephant in the high desert, so the question of who was taking advantage of whom was moot! We finally closed the deal. I liked Barney, and I really hoped that our white elephant would turn into the goose that laid the golden egg for him.

It all clattered into place at once. Within the space of three weeks, the puppy was born, the four-wheel-drive was delivered and we moved into our new house.

We had a name for the dog before it was born. In Hawaii they call mongrels "poi dogs." We had always thought the Mexicans should do something similar, like calling their mongrels "taco dogs." Since they didn't, we resolved that our pup at least would be named Taco.

When Taco was weaned from her mother and delivered to us, we found that Mother Nature had prepared a canine surprise. Through the magic of genes, Taco was a throwback to some distant relative who must have been a prize-winning poodle! To this day we have difficulty persuading veterinarians and dog groomers that she's just a mongrel. The groomers always want to give her a poodle cut, but we refuse. We wanted a mutt, and by God she's going to look like one! She has the looks, charm, and winning ways of a poodle, combined with the hardiness and intelligence of the combined strains she represents. She has learned many commands in both Spanish and English (which delights our Mexican friends), and she has taught herself to say "I want" quite distinctly in English. Most of all, from her actions, plus the intelligent look in her eyes, we know that she understands nearly everything we say. She has travelled with us to all parts of Mexico again and again, and developed into a fine camping dog.

I fell in love with the Toyota Land Cruiser at first sight, so it was only natural that Margie would refer to it as "Ben's toy." With Taco and the Toy we enjoyed some of the most exciting and rewarding Baja explorations of our lives.

Although 4 x 4 cars and dune buggies existed in those days, off-the-road driving wasn't the popular sport it is today. We were in the vanguard of off-the-road driving, so about the only instruction or advice we could get was the word-of-mouth variety from others who'd been at it a little longer. Today, there are publications galore to help the novice get started. The first thing I was told by the salesman was "Put your car through its paces someplace where help is immediately available. Then, once you've learned its capabilities thoroughly, you can head for the boondocks." That's what we proceeded to do. We took a number of short runs to various locations of soft sand and steep hills where I could determine the vehicle's climbing and traction characteristics within walking distance of a telephone and the Auto Club. I was amazed at how well it climbed. It could go straight up an almost vertical slope, like a cat climbing a tree!

My most invaluable advice came from my brother-in-law, Bob Trimble. He was a dune buggy fan at the time, and he told me to *always let the air out of the tires* when driving in the soft stuff. I had purchased extra large balloon tires with the car, and by dropping the air down to about ten pounds, I discovered I could handle the softest sand. I purchased a gadget that utilizes the engine compression to blow the tires back up for the highway. One time I saw two young fellows with a brand new, bright-red Jeep pull up to the edge of the beach at San Felipe. As if they'd rehearsed it many times, they got out of the car, and each one locked in the hub on his side of the vehicle (the hub actuates the four-wheel-drive), returned to the car, started the engine, and pulled off onto the beach. They hadn't gone ten feet when the car sunk in the sand up to its crankcase. They had standard tires on the car, and hadn't let out the air. They were rescued from their predicament by an old Mexican in an ancient, one-wheel drive Chevy truck with big tires that were nearly flat. He drove out on the sand and pulled the Jeep out.

As further insurance against getting stuck someplace, I had purchased a heavy duty Warn winch, mounted on the front bumper of the Toy. It had 250 feet of cable, and was capable of pulling 8,000 pounds. We got to use it for the first time in a most unexpected way.

One Sunday, we took Taco, a picnic lunch, and some other refreshments, and went tooling around on the Mojave Desert. I figured it would be very similar to the terrain we'd be covering in Baja. We had stopped on top of a rise for a drink and a snack when we spotted a large camper way below us making its way across the desert.

"They're going to get stuck, I bet," I said.

The words were scarcely out of my mouth when we saw the camper bog down. Two small figures emerged from the cab, inspecting their predicament hopelessly.

"Shall we try out our new winch and rescue them?" I said.

"Let's do!" Margie replied. Then, as I started the engine and began speeding down the hillside on the rescue mission, she sounded the bugle call for "Charge!"

We pulled up behind the camper and switched off our engine. "Do you need help?" I called.

They came out of the camper. "I'll say we do!" said one.

I fastened the cable to their rear axle and winched them out. We then towed them about a mile and a half to some hardpan, warned them against any more driving on sand, and departed.

A half hour later, we found more trouble. We were crossing a dry riverbed when we saw an old car containing two people bogged down in deep sand. We recognized the signs of what had happened. They had pulled their car under a large shrub on the bank of the riverbed to make love. When the lovemaking was over they'd discovered they were stuck. We winched them back to safety also.

Incredibly, we had a third rescue mission that same day! Crossing back over that same dry riverbed several miles south of where we'd been, we found a pickup truck in trouble. In it were two worried teen-age boys. They appeared to be about fifteen or sixteen years old. They confessed to us that they'd swiped their dad's truck and gone out on the desert to try drinking some beer (there was a partially-consumed case in the bed of the pickup). Then, a little silly and careless from the effects of the brew, they had tried to cross the wash and had become stuck. By the time we arrived they were in danger of having their misdeeds discovered, a little scared, and quite sober. We didn't moralize to the lads. They'd learned their lesson. We just winched them out.

So the first time we'd ever used the winch, we'd used it three times in one day!

When I was recounting my winch caper at work, one of my friends said innocently, "That winch is real neat, Ben. But how do you winch yourself out when you're on a beach?"

"Oh you can usually find a rock or something to winch to," I said nonchalantly, but my heart sunk. What, indeed, would I winch to out on the sand? The chances of finding a suitable rock were practically nil. Had I laid out $400 for a gadget I'd never be able to use? I thought about it the rest of the day, and on my way home from work the answer came to me. I stopped off at a marine supply store and purchased a large, heavy U.S. Navy anchor. The shank detached from the flukes for easy storage, but when sunk in the sand it would hold firmly. The harder you pull on those anchors, the deeper down they go. That anchor saved our rig twice in the years that followed.

Margie and I were very much aware that what we were dreaming of doing was quite risky. We were going to use the Toy to venture deep into an unforgiving wilderness where there was little or no water, no civilization, and no help for many, many miles. Stories were rife in those days about bleached bones, and rusted hulks of cars being found in the Baja badlands. Even today, with more roads and civilization, it happens occasionally. So we did everything we could to prepare ourselves for any eventuality. We obtained the most reliable camping gear we could find, and we practiced using it. We read books on survival techniques, and learned how to get water from certain types of cacti, or how to dig a hole and line it with plastic to capture moisture. We even learned how to improvise a snare to trap small desert animals for food.

To me, the chuggings and puffings that occur beneath the hood of an automobile have always been an abysmal mystery. This worried me a lot. Even though the Toy was new, and supposedly dependable, wouldn't it be ironic to be stuck out in the Baja boondocks trying to survive because of a simple mechanical malfunction that most teen-age boys could diagnose and fix quickly? Here again my brother-in-law came to the rescue. I obtained a shop manual for the Toy, and Bob gave me a crash course in mechanics. I still don't deserve the cognomen "mechanic," but at least I am able to diagnose and repair the simpler ailments that afflict autos in Baja. Indeed, this ability may have saved us a great deal of discomfort on our very first trip.

After some months of learning and practicing on weekend junkets near the city, we decided we were as ready as we'd ever be for our big adventure. I arranged a long vacation from the studio and packed the Toy to the roof with supplies. Our jumping-off place was to be the sleepy little fishing village of San Felipe on the Gulf of California. There were paved roads that far. At San Felipe we were going to hit the beach and simply drive the beaches south until we'd left all civilization behind and found an idyllic place to camp.

A year or two before, we had camped right on the main beach at San Felipe. We used to just park the Tempest at the end of the paved road and lug our sleeping bags out on the sand. It was such a small place, and none of the residents had noticed us or cared. We were therefore shocked to see what had happened to the town in our short absence. A motel had been built, and there was a string of trailer parks all along the beach front. We were there in an off season, but even so, the trailer parks were about one third filled. They were all Americans, and there were a couple of dune buggies and one trail bike in evidence. Never mind. Where we were going, we'd soon leave them all behind.

People sunning themselves on the beach stared at us with idle curiosity as we stopped at the end of the road, let the air out of the tires, dropped it into four-wheel-drive, and set out across the sand. Despite all of our practicing on the Mojave Desert and elsewhere, a wild, wonderful feeling of exhilaration came over me as the little car zipped down the beach without a problem. We were heavy, loaded to the rooftop with supplies and camping gear, but we had passed through soft, deep white sand without a falter.

Now we were on the wet sand, hard as a freeway, and I shifted back into standard drive and increased our speed.

"God, what a great car!" I shouted above the sound of the wind and the car's engine.

Soon we had left the dune buggy tracks behind, and San Felipe was just a small spot in the rear-view mirror. We came to an estuary extending from the water's edge back into the sand dunes that line the beach. It appeared to be several feet deep.

"We better stop and see if it's okay for the car to cross that water," Margie said.

"Aw, to hell with it!" I said. "Let's just plunge through it and see what happens!"

I put the Toy back in four-wheel-drive, and we hit the water with a huge splash. Water showered over the entire car, engulfing it for a moment, but the wheels kept turning on the muddy bottom, and we soon emerged on the other side and continued streaking along the beach, laughing like idiots as we drove.

Now the sand dunes on our right gave way to towering sand cliffs, sculptured by wind and water, that made us and our vehicle seem tiny indeed as we dashed along the beach, waves lapping at our tires. Suddenly the beach ended, and we faced a cliff that extended upward at a very steep incline, but I knew from our practice runs that the Toy could handle it. I picked out a spot that seemed more passable than the others, put the car in four-wheel-drive again, and gave her the gun. Up the incline we went, the Toy almost standing on her tail, her front wheels churning on the sandy slope. Then we were at the top. We stopped the car, got out, and stared at the beautiful vista back toward San Felipe. The little town was just a dot against a rock butte, backed by a teal-blue sky that extended into infinity.

Then it was back into the car and on again. The coastline we were driving consists of a series of coves guarded at each end by cliffs, and sparkling white sand in between. We would cross the sand, climb the cliff, and then descend to the beach on the other side. Climbing to the top of one of these cliffs, we looked down on the prettiest beach we'd seen yet. The white sand was unscarred by print of man, beast, or vehicle. Clear, blue water lapped gently on the beach, and sea birds wheeling and diving for fish in the little bay were the only signs of life. It was a paradise.

"That's our beach," Margie said.

We descended from the cliff to make camp.

A person used to camping with tent and sleeping bag might feel inclined to laugh when he looked at our set up. It was funny looking, indeed. But we had planned it carefully, and were able to enjoy a great many luxuries and conveniences tents do not allow.

We had installed a long metal slot, running from the front to the back of the car along the line of the roof. Into this slot we slipped one edge of a fairly large canvas. We then stretched it straight out from the car, holding up the other end with tent poles. This was the roof of our "tent." Using suspender grips, we hung three more pieces of canvas to the three sides (the fourth side of the tent was the car), and staked them to the ground. We now had a waterproof, windproof canvas "box" actually attached to our car. During the heat of the day we could remove the three sides and just have the roof for shade. Or, if there was wind blowing, we could leave the windward side on, and remove the other two. Many different configurations were possible, and we could enter the car from inside the tent. To keep it firm, we had purchased special tent stakes called "sand hogs" that keep their grip in soft sand.

Our camping gear and supplies were carried inside the car stacked above and below a pair of specially-cut plywood panels. I had cut them myself to fit inside the auto. With the load removed, these two panels were extended from the back of the car to the dashboard (with the front seats folded down). On top of this plywood "bed frame," we placed air mattresses which we inflated with a foot pump. Then we made up the bed with sheets, blankets, and pillows. From our "living room" we could enter the "bedroom" without stepping outside.

Keeping things cold for a couple of weeks, and having ice for our tequila, was a problem on a hot Mexican beach. We worked it out this way: Salad things like lettuce were not chilled until needed. They were carried to the campsite and stored, rolled in newspapers for insulation, in brown paper bags. The ice chest contained a twenty-five pound chunk of ice which we placed atop a cake rack so the ice wouldn't wallow in its own melt. On top of it we placed a large slab of dry ice wrapped in newspaper. If we hadn't wrapped the dry ice it would have frozen the chest shut. We then packed the ice chest with frozen foods. On the beach, the ice chest was placed atop two thick wooden blocks (off the hot sand) and stored in the shade under the car. Even with temperatures hovering around 100 degrees it was several days before the ice began to melt. When it did, we immediately drew it off into a plastic bottle to use for ice water.

Water conservation is a problem in parched Baja. We carried it in five gallon saddle tanks on the sides of the car, plus several one gallon bottles squeezed inside. Water was used for drinking purposes only. Dishes, pots and pans, clothes, and us, were washed in the sea. The various liquid detergents seemed to work fine with the cooking utensils and dinnerware. For shaving, I kept a plastic bottle of sea water sitting on the sand in front of our camp. By ten o'clock each morning the sun had heated it boiling hot. It gave a good shave.

I built a portable cooking table that would hold the Coleman stove and still provide working space on either side of it. We didn't use the various prepared or freeze-dried foods because of the shortage of water. Besides, Margie enjoyed the challenge of whomping up fantastic cuisine on a camp stove.

The only holdover we had from the old Tempest days was the Jonny Pot with its supply of plastic bags. When not in use it served as a "table" for our portable tape recorder which provided soft dinner music to blend with the sound of the waves as we sat at our portable dining table enjoying the gracious life.

Setting up the living room, bedroom, dining room and kitchen was a well-rehearsed routine. We each had assigned jobs, and had timed ourselves for efficiency. We could get the entire camp together in twenty minutes.

We found our spot on the beach, put up camp, and then sat in beach chairs sipping a drink, and watching the sky change colors as the sun went down. Then we marveled again when the sky became black, sequined with trillions of stars. To light a fire and spoil that view would have been sinful, so we just sat in the dark, talking softly, and staring at the stars until we couldn't hold our eyes open any longer.

I awakened in the morning to the happy spatter and heavenly aroma of ham sizzling in the frying pan. Peeking out of the window of the car, I saw Margie in her pink bikini, cooking breakfast and humming happily to herself. There is something wonderfully satisfying to me to awaken to happy kitchen sounds, so I just stayed in bed, savoring it for awhile.

"Wait til you see the ocean!" Margie bubbled excitedly.

"The ocean?" I reached for my bathing trunks. "What about the ocean?" I had no sooner uttered the words than I saw what she meant. It wasn't there!

This was our first experience with the extreme tides on the Gulf of California. When we'd camped at San Felipe two years before, it had apparently been a period of little or no tidal change. Suddenly this! The night before, we had made our camp about twenty feet above the high tide mark. Now it was low tide, and the water had receded over a quarter of a mile! The floor of the ocean was laid bare for hundreds of yards.

"Mother Nature dropped her pants and exposed her bottom," I said.

She laughed. "How poetic! But just imagine all the weird sea beasties we might find out there!" We decided we'd have a Beastie Hunt as soon as we'd finished breakfast.

Margie's breakfast was a gourmet triumph! Using nothing but the Coleman stove and some ingenuity, she had produced delicious Eggs Benedict topped with a truffle, just as you see in the finest restaurants. We finished it up, and Taco licked the plates clean (which makes dish washing easier), then the three of us started on our search for strange creatures from the bottom of the sea.

We hadn't gone a hundred yards when we saw one of the most unusual sights I've ever seen! First we just noticed strange tracings on the wet sand, as if someone had drawn a line with his fingertip the way children write their names on the beach. The next thing we noticed was that the wiggly lines all pointed toward the distant water. And then the surprise! At the end of each line was a clam. And each clam was standing on edge and *actually moving* toward the water! It wasn't a fast movement. You had to stare intently for a few minutes in order to see it move. But move it did! Any clams I've ever caught in a lifetime of living near beaches had been buried and had to be brought up with a shovel. Here were hundreds of them on edge, on the surface, pushing their way toward the sea like a child pushing a scooter. We reasoned that the fast tide change must have left them suddenly high and dry, and—in a panic—they started migrating toward the ocean.

It only took a few minutes to teach Taco to watch for the movement, grab the clam, and place it in our bucket. She seemed to enjoy the fun, and it was the easiest clamming we've ever done. The dog did it all.

Leaving Taco happily catching clams, we continued strolling on the newly-revealed sea bottom looking for other goodies. Soon we saw something else strange. On the surface of the sand was etched a perfect five pointed star. No artist could have made that pattern in the sand more perfectly.

"See if there's a beastie underneath it," I said bravely.

Unlike me, Margie has no qualms about digging up unknown critters with her bare hands. She slipped her hand under the star, took a large scoop of sand, and turned it upside down. There atop the heap of wet sand squirmed a strange little creature. The center of its body was almost perfectly round, and about the size of a marble. Then, in a star formation, its five wiggly legs stuck out in each direction.

"Maybe it's a baby octopus," I said.

"No, it would have to have eight legs. But I wonder how it makes that star pattern on the ground."

"We'll put him down on the sand, and watch him."

"Okay." She carefully laid him, right side up, on a flat piece of beach. Immediately the little creature started doing a kind of hula, inching himself into the wet sand until he was out of sight. When he was completely buried, his five legs had left the perfect star-mark on the spot where Margie had placed him. Now that we had found him, we began to notice other similar patterns around us. We had fun digging them up, too, and watching them do their hulas.

Months later, we discovered that these are not rare creatures at all. They are called Brittle Stars, and we have found them on many beaches. We have even found Brittle Stars that have been washed up on the beach, died, and then been dried by the sun into a star shaped shell. We've collected quite a few.

Taco, tired of clamming, left her bucket half filled with clams, and came splashing through the puddles to join us. This was her first experience on a beach, and she was loving it. We found a little crab in a pool left by the tide and showed it to her. There then ensued a very funny battle. The crab was plucky. He wasn't about to scuttle off; he was going to stay and fight. He held his pincers aloft like a fighter, inches from Taco's tender nose, and dared her to come closer. Some basic instinct kept Taco wary and she stayed just far enough away to avoid being pinched, but barked and barked at the spunky crab. She would sniff, he would feint; she would bark, he would sidle to a better position. Then the whole performance would begin again. We watched for awhile, then wandered on.

The next thing we came to was what appeared to be a sea anemone. These are animals which look like the bloom of a flower. You can see hundreds of them clinging to rocks in the coves of California beaches. But growing out of the sand? That was something new.

"Let's see if he closes up on your finger like the sea anemones at home," I said, and stuck my finger into the center of the "bloom."

Instead of closing up, he sucked out of sight into the sand, leaving not a trace behind him.

"Quick, Ben! Get the shovel and see if you can catch him!" Margie said excitedly.

We always carry a collapsible camp shovel with us when beastie hunting. Quickly I began to dig as fast as I could in a wide circle around the spot where he'd disappeared. When the hole was about a foot and a half deep and two feet across we found him. The "bloom" part that we'd seen on the sand was attached to a long, reddish stem about an inch or so wide. It looked like a giant phallus, and when I grasped it to remove it from the hole, the end of it squirted water at me!

"Good grief!" I said, dropping it on the sand, "What do you suppose that is?"

"I don't know. Maybe a weird kind of sea cucumber. Put him back in his hole."

I threw him back in the hole and filled it in.

The rest of our beastie hunt revealed nothing unusual other than a frightened baby octopus cringing under a rock, and myriad unidentifiable shelled creatures. Margie collected a few of the latter for her ever-growing, useless shell collection, and with the bucket of clams in hand we returned to camp. The strangest creature of all would be discovered a couple of days hence.

We stripped down, took a bath in the warm ocean water, and then romped naked on the beach. We had decided to name our little paradise, "La Playa Cazadores" [Hunter's beach].

We were almost too lazy in Baja! Hours were spent just sitting in our beach chairs staring at the sea. While all the events and worries of the rest of the world faded into obscurity, little things in our beach world took on great importance.

A stick driven into the ground helped us keep track of the various heights of the tides as we noted their rise and fall.

Each day a school of porpoise swam past our cove as the tide changed. We noted that they swam north with the incoming tide, and south with the outgoing.

Once, I spent hours gaining the confidence of a lizard sunning himself on a rock so I could get close enough to him for a snapshot.

Watching the sea birds was a never-ending fascination. We noted that the pelicans (The Mexicans call them "The Mexican Air Force") flapped their wings fourteen times and then glided. They all did this without exception, and we wondered if it was because of the strength of the wind at that time, or the flying characteristic of the bird.

One flock of sea birds—a type of gull—had a trainee in their midst. We named the trainee Charlie Brown. When this flock visited our beach, we always recognized them because of him. They would come swooping in with graceful flight, and land gently on the water without a splash. Charlie Brown flew awkwardly about four bird-lengths behind the group, and landed in a flurry of flying feathers and feet, making a huge splash. Using the binoculars, we studied him carefully to see if he was injured. He apparently was not, so we concluded he was just ungainly, but would "straighten up and fly right" some day.

Whenever we catch clams, we let them sit overnight in a bucket of sea water before cooking them. That way, they spit out the sand during the night and you can enjoy them the next day without "true grit." Our second night on the beach, Margie steamed the clams. She placed a large rock in the bottom of a cook pot filled with boiling salted water. Then she placed the clams on the rock so they'd steam without falling in the water. When they were steamed open, she bathed them with butter, lemon, and garlic. They were delicious, and what a feast we had! Taco had gathered too many, however, and we couldn't finish them, so we left the remainder on top of the dining table when we went to bed. In the morning they were gone.

We scanned the ground around the table for telltale footprints, but the sand was so churned by our own footprints that we couldn't make out anything. All day we speculated about what type of creature could have stolen our food. A bird, perhaps, landing on the table? A tiny mouse running up the leg of the table for a gourmet mouse-feast? Just at dusk that day we had our answer.

You don't really see a sunset on the Gulf side of Baja because the west is behind you. However, the setting sun creates a beautiful light show of oranges and golds in the east that is lovely in its own way. Margie and I call it a "reverse sunset." I had made us some potent but delicious daiquiris, and we were sipping them and watching the reverse sunset when Taco started to bark.

110

"What's the matter with her?" I said.

"I don't know," Margie looked worried. "That's her 'I-want-to-go-out-and-play' bark."

"I know. It's the same sound she makes when there's a doggie friend outside at home."

Then all three of us saw them at the same time. A mother coyote and two pups came onto our beach about 150 yards away. Taco was off joyfully to join them for play!

"Here, Taco! Taco, come here!" we both screamed, but the dummy was off to join her "friends."

"Catch her, Ben! Those animals will tear her apart!"

I was off at a dead run down the beach. Fortunately Taco was just doing her puppy trot, with plume waving. If she'd been really running I could never have caught her. I made a diving leap and landed on the sand with the squirming black puppy in my arms.

Margie had already retrieved Taco's leash from the car. We tied her, and started watching the coyotes through the binoculars.

That's when we saw another amazing sight. Those coyotes were drinking the sea water! Thinking that perhaps they were really hunting for clams or something and only appeared to be drinking, we studied their actions very carefully. There was no mistaking it. Their tongues were out and they were actually lapping the ocean water. We reasoned that since water is so very scarce in the Baja bush, these animals had learned to ingest, and benefit from, that salty water.

"They're the robbers who stole our clams," I said.

"I guess if they can drink that water, they can enjoy garlic too!"

Suddenly, I had an idea. "Tonight let's put out some bait for the coyotes and see if we can get a snapshot of them!"

Margie was enthusiastic. "We can use that partly empty can of Taco's dog food."

Excitedly, we laid our plans. We'd place the dog food can in a spot about eight feet from the window of the car. Then we'd put the flash and the telephoto lens on the camera, focus it on that spot, and wait. We decided to sleep in shifts, taking turns manning the stakeout. Sooner or later that mother coyote and her pups would be attracted to the food. Then, whichever one of us was standing watch would snap the shutter. *Pow!* The photo would be ours!

When we went to bed that night we tied Taco inside the car so she wouldn't leap out the window for fun and games with our prey, and we gave her a long lecture about *not* barking if we had visitors. It was 9 p.m.

when we retired. I stood the first watch, and Margie was soon fast asleep.

My first hour went fairly fast because I was excited, and expecting coyotes any minute. Nothing happened. At the end of the hour I shook Margie awake.

"Your turn," I whispered.

"Okay," she whispered back, and was immediately alert.

Taco's buzzy little snore from the foot of the bed told us we hadn't disturbed her. I handed Margie the camera, plumped up my pillow, and was asleep in a moment.

It seemed like five minutes later she was shaking me awake.

"Are they here?" I whispered excitedly.

"Not a sign of 'em. It's your turn to stand watch."

"It's been an hour already?"

"Yup." She yawned, handed me the camera, and fell asleep at once.

I looked at my watch. Eleven o'clock. It had been another hour all right. Well, those coyotes ought to be along any minute now, I thought, and took up my vigil at the car window.

This time the hour dragged on and on. Once, thinking the hour had passed, I checked my watch. It had been twenty minutes. There was the dog food can, shining in the moonlight. Damn those animals! I waited some more. After what seemed an eon, the watch's hands pointed to midnight. Thank God!

"Your turn, Margie," I whispered in her ear.

"Hmmm. What?" She was coming out of it slowly.

"Your turn to stand watch."

"Mmmm. Oh. Okay." She sat up and reached sleepily for the camera.

"Are you okay? Awake?" I whispered.

"Sorta."

"G'night." My head dropped into the pillow like a shot.

Again it seemed I'd scarcely gone to sleep when I felt her hand on my shoulder.

"Wake up, Darling, it's your turn."

"Okay," I groaned, and assumed my position at the car window.

The moonlight was relentless, bathing the whole beach in a mellow glow. Beyond our camp, the shush of the waves made music on the beach, and inside the car Taco's gentle buzz made a peaceful, sleepy sound. I tried to peer into the shadows of the brush along side the beach to see if the critters were lurking there. Nothing. My eyelids felt as if they were weighted with lead. I arched my eyebrows in an effort to hold them

112

open. Once I awoke with a start and realized I'd actually dozed off for awhile. Anxiously I checked the dog food can, but it was still standing in the moonlight. I started telling myself stories to keep awake. Then I couldn't remember them anymore. Then I didn't care.

Soon it was dawn. I had been sound asleep at the car window for hours. Margie and Taco were still snoring. The dog food can! It was upset, tossed on its side, and licked clean! The coyotes had out-waited us.

At breakfast we decided that we would not attempt a stakeout again. It was too much of a strain, and this was supposed to be a vacation. Who wants a coyote picture anyway?

"You can clip one out of *National Geographic,*" Margie said.

"Coyote!" I shouted back at the brush, "You is the winner!"

We thought we heard a "Yip-yip-yipee!" from back in the badlands.

We soon met another camp visitor. We had bathed, romped, made love, and were lying together on a beach towel, enjoying the caress of the warm breeze on our bodies when I saw him.

"We have another visitor," I whispered.

"What?"

"Not a 'people' visitor, a beastie."

"Where?"

"Under the car. By the box of canned goods."

She rolled over on her tummy for a better look. "It's a chameleon!"

"How can you tell?"

"Look! He's turned the color of the box!"

The chameleon, capable of changing his color to match his background, had been hiding next to a cardboard box that had formerly contained cans of Campbell's Tomato Soup. On his back was a reproduction of part of the tomato insignia, and part of the word "soup." We decided to photograph him and send his picture to the Campbell Soup Company. We got his picture, alright, but we frightened him away. Also, since he was in deep shade under the car, the picture didn't come out too well. Only we can realize its significance.

About the only exercise we ever got on this junket was strolling along the beach at low tide looking for what Margie calls "goodies." These consisted of an occasional sun-bleached shark jaw-bone, different-shaped shells which she always seemed to recognize, and an assortment of stones of different shapes and colors. She seemed to consider each item a real find, and exulted and chortled over every one. It pleased me to see her receiving so much pleasure from these bits tossed up by the sea, and I kept trying to find one to please her, but to no avail.

"Oh that's just a *limpet*," she would say. "I have several of *those*."

Or, "Yes it's pretty, but see? There's a little chip out of it. I'd like a perfect one."

I finally gave up trying to find something to please her and resorted to making weak jokes.

Once I found an old shoe washed up on the shore. Was this all that was left of an unfortunate fisherman washed overboard? Or did someone just lose a shoe? Holding the shoe dramatically, I assumed the classic pose from *Hamlet*, and intoned: "Alas poor Yorick! I knew him, Horatio: a fellow of infinite jest, of most excellent fancy . . . "

It received an absent-minded chuckle, which was all it deserved.

Another time I found a large rock shaped like an ostrich egg.

"I have a story to tell you, so listen!" I said, concealing the egg-shaped rock behind my back.

She stopped and looked up.

"Millions of years ago," I began, "there lived on this barren peninsula, in this very spot where we are standing, one of the largest birds ever known to man. It was the dreaded Roc bird, with a wingspread so gigantic it could swoop down and carry off a live hyena to its aerie. It was the scourge of the area, and all the animals were paralyzed by fear when they saw the shadow of its wings and heard its ear-piercing screech."

I paused, but she seemed to be enjoying the story, so I continued:

"So fearsome had the Roc become that all the other beasts of Baja joined together for the only time in history in a concerted effort to rid themselves of this terror. Rabbits, hyenas, and field mice met in temporary friendship for their common cause, and they evolved a plan. They would have a great Spring fiesta. There would be all manner of revelling and debauchery. Then, when the great Roc heard all the singing and laughing, he would be attracted to the party in hopes of achieving his greatest slaughter."

I paused again. "You want to hear the rest?"

"Of course!" Her eyes were sparkling. She has many child-like qualities, and loving being told a story is one of them.

"Well, sir, they had that party, and it was a dinger! The hyenas were laughing, the rabbits were doing what they do best, and what do you suppose the field mice were doing?

"They brought the grass!" she laughed.

114

"Yes they did. They not only supplied grass, they recited dirty poems by Eugene Field. Naturally, with all this going on, the Roc was attracted, just as they knew he'd be. He circled around a few times building up his appetite, but they pretended not to notice. At length he swooped in, taxied for a landing, and came to a halt right at the edge of the fiesta. On a given signal from a horned owl, all the animals of Baja descended on the ugly old Roc. The field mice tickled him, the rabbits thumped hell out of his ribs, and the hyenas attacked in a pack—"

"I guess the horned owl didn't give a hoot."

"Right! At any rate, with one last, heart-rending screech, the dreaded Roc died. Never again would he terrorize the other residents of Baja." I stopped.

"Is that the end of the story?"

"Almost. There was one secret the animals didn't know. The Roc had laid one of its giant eggs right here on this very beach. If that egg hatched, there'd be another Roc bird in Baja."

"Did it hatch?"

"No. Fortunately for all of us, Mother Nature took a hand. She turned the Roc's egg to solid stone, and left it here all these years."

I bowed and presented her with the egg-shaped stone. "Mrs. Hunter, you are now the proud possessor of the only Roc-rock known to man!"

I had scored! She laughed delightedly, and put it in the bucket with her other goodies. That was many years ago, but she still has the Roc-rock today.

We were walking that same stretch of beach another day when I spied something silvery on the sand, right at the water's edge.

"Look, Honey," I said, "There's a little sardine or anchovy there. A bird must have dropped it."

Its tail flopped.

"It's alive!" Margie exclaimed. "Poor little thing. I'm going to throw it back in the water."

She reached down to grasp it by the tail, and it was at that moment we discovered another strange creature of the sea.

We hadn't realized it at the time, but its head was buried. When she pulled it out of the wet sand by the tail, its astonishing head was revealed. The head was enormous for that tiny body. It had pop eyes, and a large lower jaw which extended way beyond its upper jaw giving it a bulldog appearance. This vicious-looking lower jaw was lined with oversized, sawlike teeth. A grotesque head like this on the body of what appeared to be a sardine was an oddity indeed!

"My gosh! I wonder what he is," Margie said as we stared at him.

"Who knows!"

"I'm going to put him in my bucket with some water so we can watch him."

That was when the next amazing thing happened. She placed the little fish on some wet sand in the bottom of her bucket, and it immediately started using its shovel-like lower jaw and huge teeth to bite its way into the sand again! When we pulled its head out of the sand a second time, eggs were pouring out of its ugly mouth!

Margie's maternal instinct surfaced. "Why she's a mother, trying to lay her eggs in the sand!" she said. "I'm going to let her go free." With that, she dumped the creature eggs and all into the water, and it darted off.

"I didn't even get a picture of it!" I wailed.

"C'est la vie," she said laconically.

The lovely, lethargic, lazy days continued to drift by.

Taco perfected her crab-hunting techinique and actually caught a few, but ate only the claws. Soon "The Baja Feeling" would take over again, and she'd return to camp to snooze in the shade.

I tried some fishing from the shore and found the fish cooperative. They didn't bite, which left me time to stare at the sea.

Margie continued to pick up goodies along the shoreline at low tide.

The rest of the time we just lazed in camp, making big events out of non-events, and wondering at how fast the time slipped by.

We forgot to wind the watch, so it stopped, but we didn't care what time it was. We arose early each morning and sipped coffee as we watched the glorious sunrise, and we retired when the sun went down. That's why I'm not sure when it happened, but it felt like the middle of the night. Taco started barking. It was not her happy bark; it was the angry dangerous-sounding one she reserves for strangers at the door. Instantly we were both awake.

"What's the matter with her?" I said.

"Shhhh!" Margie clamped Taco's jaws shut, reducing her bark to a snort and a growl. "Be quiet, Taco!"

"What is it?"

"Listen! There's something out there!"

I listened. There was an eerie sound in our camp! It sounded like several apes grunting at each other, but there couldn't be apes in Baja.

"What can that be?" Margie whispered.

"Damned if I know. Let's see if we can see anything."

Taco was quiet now. She was standing at the back end of the car looking out the rear window, her tail between her legs. We scrambled back beside her and saw them!

"Javelinas!" I breathed.

"They look like pigs."

"They are a type of wild boar. They say they're one of the most vicious animals in the world. One of the few that will attack a human being without provocation." I had never seen a javelina before, but I had heard that there were some in Baja. According to reputation, they will attack almost anything that moves. Hunters tell stories about these animals climbing over the dead bodies of their comrades to continue an attack. One hunter told me: "The way to kill a javelina is to shoot him right between the eyes . . . and then run!" "But what are they doing here?" I asked.

"I don't know—oh yes, I do!"

"What?"

"Yesterday I discovered that one of our heads of lettuce had spoiled, and I buried it right there."

"That's it, then. They're rooting for the lettuce. Just be quiet, and for God's sake hang onto Taco."

"Don't worry about her. She's scared."

"She ought to be!"

We watched as they rooted up the lettuce, fought for it between themselves, devoured it, rooted around some more, and finally disappeared into the shadows. Sleep was difficult for me the rest of that night. I kept imagining I'd heard them return.

The next day was our last one at *La Playa Cazadores* and we tried to make the most of it, savoring every minute. In the evening, Margie (who often expresses her feelings cooking) produced the greatest dinner ever. It was ham, baked with a crust of brown sugar and rum, candied yams, Boston brown bread, and green beans. If you want to know how she achieved that on a Coleman stove, you'll have to ask her. It beats me! We stayed up later than usual after dinner, knowing that bedtime was the start of goodbye time to our beach. We watched—for the last time—the "reverse sunset" and Baja's star-splashed sky. We both avoided saying how much we hated to leave, but we felt it in our hearts. Finally we went to bed.

In the morning, it was quick breakfast, followed by breaking camp. We spent a little extra time cleaning up our campsite, because so often we have seen piles of cans and bottles, bearing American brand names, marring an otherwise lovely beach. We didn't want to be identified as Americans in that manner! Edible garbage was left out for the animals. The rest, including cans and bottles, would ride in a plastic bag beneath Margie's feet until we reached the city dump at San Felipe. We sped off down the beach in silence, with only Taco looking back. She'd miss those lovely crab hunts.

At the end of the beach I put the Toy in compound low gear for the climb up the cliff, when it happened! Suddenly there was no throttle. The car slowed to an idle and stalled.

"What's the matter?" Margie said.

"No goddamn throttle. Look!" I banged it up and down with my foot. "Nothing! Son of a bitch!"

"Calm down, Darling. You can fix it if you try."

I had lost my cool completely. "Oh yeah? With *what*?" I shouted, "Is the little old master mechanic going to wave a magic wand or something?"

Now she became angry. "Well if you just sit here like an idiot, swearing at it, it won't fix itself. Do you want to just wait to be rescued?"

I didn't answer. With a snarl, I got out of the car and threw up the hood. It was an especially hot day. There seemed to be no cooling breeze at all, and the perspiration was pouring into my eyes. I couldn't see a thing.

Margie called from the car, "I'm fixing us Bloody Marys!" "Bloody Marys at a time like this?" I thought, "Christ!" Then suddenly the humor of the situation got to me. Here we were stranded on a Baja beach a million miles from nowhere, with a broken automobile and the possibility of no rescue for days or weeks, and my beloved was mixing drinks! A picture flashed through my mind: Two explorers discover the rusted hulk of our car, and our bleached bones on the beach. "Look, Sam," one of them says, "Each of those skeletons has a glass in its hand!" I laughed aloud.

"What're you laughing about, Ben?"

"Because you've got class, Baby. Real class!"

I wiped my streaming face with my sleeve, and started studying the engine. At this point, my crash course in mechanics began to help. I located the throttle lever inside the engine and used a piece of wire to connect it back to the foot throttle. In a few minutes the car was operable again, and I was sipping that drink. We got the rest of the way home without incident.

Some weeks later I described the little sardine-like fish with the grotesque head to my brother, John, who has a doctorate in marine biology; he is a scientist highly respected by his colleagues. If anyone could identify that fish, he could.

Johnny listened intently to the whole story, then said, "Ben, there are over five hundred unclassified species of marine animals in that Gulf, and it sounds like you and Margie found one of them. I wish you hadn't thrown it back in the water."

I looked at Margie accusingly, but she just smiled.

5/ The Padre's Beach

Many times, as Margie and I have sat on those beautiful Baja beaches with the warm waters of the gulf lapping gently on the sand, I have felt shore-bound. "Lord, if we only had a boat," I would say. Then we'd talk it over again, and again we would decide it was impractical. If we attempted to tow a trailer behind the Toy it could bog down—or bog us down. The roof of the Toy was too small to carry a boat. It would be like putting a saddle on a cat. We discussed it many times but never came up with a solution. The solution finally came from my good friend and television director, Bill Chesnutt.

"Why don't you get an inflatable boat?" he said.

"A life raft? No thanks. I want something I can put an outboard motor on."

"Ben," he said patiently, "if you'd ever go to one of those sports shows, you'd know that an inflatable boat is *not* a life raft. It's a real boat with a motor—any size motor you want!"

The light dawned. "Like Jacques Cousteau uses!"

"Right!"

That was the answer, of course. The only remaining problem was where to carry it. When we headed out on our trips in the Toy, the interior was always completely loaded. A luggage rack on the roof was no good either. We'd bought one at the time we first purchased the Toy, and it lasted about one-quarter of a mile on the Baja roads before falling in a dozen pieces to the ground. One of my cameramen solved that problem. In a few days he presented me with a monstrosity. It was a deep cage, constructed of one-inch extruded steel rods welded together. This basket-like contraption exactly fitted the roof of the Toy and was strong enough to support a dancing elephant. Four heavy steel legs extended down the sides of the car and bolted into the frame in eight places. Before that monster got jounced off the Toy, the car itself would have to fall apart! Margie took one look at it and dubbed it "The Bird Cage" (for a one-ton canary).

Our inflatable boat was, when inflated, ten feet long with a four-foot beam. It came complete with a foot pump, collapsible oars, and a transom for an outboard motor. The whole business folded into a duffle bag that weighed about fifty pounds. For power we purchased a three horsepower Seagull outboard that weighed about thirty-four pounds. Both of these items, plus a lot of other gear we had added, would ride on the roof of the Toy in "The Bird Cage."

Our boat adventure was to begin with San Felipe again. We would hit the beach there just as before, but this time we would drive farther south than ever before and discover a new paradise. The trip from our home to San Felipe takes a boring eight hours, so we set the alarm for 1 a.m. and were on the road a half hour later. With little traffic at that hour we made good time and were on the beach letting the air out of the tires by 9:15 that morning. Some of the Americans camped at San Felipe stared at us curiously. With our heavily overloaded vehicle, we must have looked like a scene from The Grapes of Wrath. Nevertheless, the Toy handled the soft sand without a slip or groan. In a few moments we were on the hard, wet beach picking up speed and leaving San Felipe behind. Once again that wonderful feeling of exhilaration came over me.

We came to the estuary we had splashed through on that first trip and we splashed through again. Then the familiar sand cliffs appeared, towering over us. This time I recognized the way up the cliffs at the end of the beach, and took the Toy up them without hesitation. At the top we didn't even pause to look back at San Felipe as we had the first time. We were anxious to pioneer new territory so we just kept going. Down the other side of the cliff we plunged, across the beach, and up the next side. After awhile we came to our old campsite—the beach we'd named "La Playa Cazadores." It was nearly as beautiful as we remembered, but this time it was traced with the tracks of dune buggies. The incursion of the duners was spreading ever southward. On we went.

From this point on it was all new country to us, but similar to what we'd seen before. It seemed to be a series of coves embraced at either end by a cliff. If there was no way up the cliff, we'd find a way around it. Otherwise we'd climb it, and descend to the beach on the other side. Some of the beaches were a mile or so long, others as small as a hundred yards. Some of them were glistening white sand, while others were studded with large rocks we had to pick our way around. Many of them could have made perfect campgrounds, but we were determined to go farther south.

The tide was receding rapidly as we drove, and I kept inching the car farther out on the sand flats thinking I'd be driving on harder sand. We were zipping down the exposed flats of one of the longer beaches, doing about thirty-five miles per hour, when suddenly it became as soft as quicksand! Our heavy Toy immediately sank in way above the hub caps and began to slosh to a stop.

"My God! We're sinking in!" Margie yelled.

"Don't you think I know that?" I said irritably.

"Fight it, Darling!"

"I'm fighting! I'm fighting!"

I slammed the car into four-wheel-drive, but we were now almost at a standstill. If I turned the wheels sharply to get back on hard stuff it would snowplow and bog down completely. I had to try to keep the car moving and make a slow, easy arc until I could find firmer ground. It felt as if the Toy were sinking in deeper with each turn of the wheels. A picture of something we'd seen near San Felipe flashed through my mind: somebody's beautiful four-wheel-drive car mired in the mud with the tide waters up to its roof. God, was that going to happen to us? The car struggled for another minute or two threatening to sink in and stop at any second, and then, just as suddenly as it had become soft, the sand became hard again! Once more the wheels were turning with ease. I stopped the car and we got out.

"Look at our tracks!" Margie exclaimed.

Like a pair of twin canals they stretched back across the flats, two feet deep in places and filling with water. There were already huge muddy pools wherever our wheels had spun.

After such a close call, I decided we could take no more chances. Margie and Taco would have to walk ahead of the car, testing the sand for firmness until we had completed our crossing of the treacherous flats; in this manner our strange little caravan resumed its trek. Now and then Margie would sink in up to her knees, and we'd have to stop and look for another route. Taco just splashed along, enjoying the exercise. Finally we made it to the other side.

After a few more coves without incident, the character of the beach changed drastically again. It was our first experience with what they call "ball-bearing sand." The entire surface of the beach consists of billions of ground-up shells. From a distance it looks like ordinary beach sand, but when you drive on it your wheels get no traction at all. It's as if you were driving on a mass of ball-bearings. We hit it suddenly and the Toy began to yaw, skid, and slip. I put the car into compound low and four-wheel-drive, and we were then able to move precariously along. It was not a relaxing drive, because I was fighting the churning wheels every inch of the way. That was when Margie said: "Ben! Stop the car!" She sounded excited.

"Stop the car? I might never get it going again!"

"Oh." There was disappointment in her voice.

"Why do you want to stop?"

"There's a whole family of sea turtles up there above the beach."

That did it. "Sea turtles!" I stopped the car.

She started to whisper. "Be quiet so we don't disturb them. There's a mama and two babies."

I looked. Sure enough. They were sitting there motionless, staring out to sea. "I'll get the camera!" I whispered.

With the camera set and ready for action we crept stealthily over the rocks toward the little turtle family. It was odd. They didn't seem to move at our approach at all. Had we been that quiet? Soon we were very close to them and we saw why.

I'll be damned!" I said. "They're dead!"

"It looks like they're petrified!"

We scrambled over the rocks for a closer look. There was no evidence of foul play at all. None of the shells was punctured by spear or bullet. All three turtles sat comfortably on the sand, their necks arched upward, sightless eyes staring out at the ocean, scanning the horizon for some sign of rescue. They weren't actually petrified, but the sun had dried them out as stiff as boards. There wasn't even any smell. We speculated as to what could have happened, but couldn't even come up with an intelligent guess. It was as if mama and her two turtlets had come happily ashore for a little sun bathing and been suddenly struck dead. We took snapshots of them and rejoined Taco in the Toy, leaving these sad statues to their silent vigil.

The first town south of San Felipe is the little village of Puertocitos. There is a main road of doubtful quality linking the two towns. It's a forty-mile drive which takes anywhere from two to four hours, depending on the road condition at the time (and the shock absorbers on your car!). We had not used that main road, of course. We made the entire trip via the beaches and arrived some six hours later, about 3:30 p.m. Puertocitos is apparently a retirement haven for a number of Americans. We saw their small, American-style houses, and noted that the streets had names like "Old Tequila Bottle" and other bits of Gringo whimsy. We filled the Toy with gasoline at the one pump in the town and continued south.

The travelguide warned us about the road south of Puertocitos. We learned that the road was considered to be the most dangerous of any section of the Gulf Route. The road was apparently cut through volcanic slag, and the unevenness of it has been a barrier to all but the sturdiest vehicles. But that was not all. The guide also informed us that there were short steep grades, with sharp rocks.

So, we decided to challenge it, believing we had the experience and equipment to overcome this natural barrier to migration.

We had only been on the road for about an hour when two American motorcyclists, road-weary and covered with dust, approached us from the other direction.

"Turn back! Turn back while you can!" they shouted as they bumped past us.

We were moving about five miles per hour in four-wheel-drive. The "sharp-edged rocks jutting from the surface" mentioned by the Auto Club were granite shafts eight or ten inches high, spearing our tires mercilessly as we drove. We wondered how long our tires could endure this kind of punishment. On top of that we were dead tired, and didn't know how long we'd have to drive to find a place to camp.

"Let's take their advice and turn back," Margie said.

"We wanted to see what it's like farther south."

"I know, but we can try it tomorrow morning after we've had some sleep. I'm exhausted."

I was too, as we'd been driving since one o'clock that morning. We decided to head back to Puertocitos and camp for the night. I crept the car back and forth until I'd turned it around on the narrow road, and we headed back for Puertocitos.

The beach there wasn't particularly appealing to us. It appeared to be very rocky at low tide and there was too much civilization around, but at that point we didn't care. We pulled out on the beach, threw a couple of beach towels on the sand, lay down and promptly went to sleep. I don't know what time we awakened, but it was dark. Groggy from sleep (or lack of it), we dragged enough stuff out of the car so we could make up the bed, munched some cheese and crackers, and went back to sleep.

Margie and I are morning people. We awaken early, ebullient and eager to start a new day. At sunrise I always feel as if the Creator had fashioned a new world for me to enjoy. Yesterday's problems belong to the past and the new-born day is worry-free. As we rejoiced in the dawn, even the awful road south of Puertocitos seemed tame. After a couple of hours on it we found a beach to drive and began searching for a campsite. It didn't look too hopeful at first because these beaches seemed very rocky—not what we had in mind at all.

"Let's go back and camp in one of those coves we passed yesterday," Margie said. "They were really pretty."

Just ahead of us loomed a sheer rock cliff with a reef extending seaward from its toe. The reef would be underwater at high tide and the tide was coming in fast.

"Okay," I said. "We'll go around that point up ahead and if we don't like the beach on the other side we'll turn back." "We'll have to hurry. It's going to be underwater pretty quick."

I maneuvered the car around some large boulders, skirted the reef on wet sand with waves lapping at the tires, and we discovered our paradise.

It was a small beach—perhaps two hundred yards long. Steep cliffs at either end smashed by waves at high tide sealed off our cove from the rest of the coastline. The sand was white, the water clean and clear. At low tide there would be lush tide pools for crabbing and goodie hunting. But the most remarkable sight of all was a giant saguaro cactus standing alone on a bluff overlooking our beach. It had the exact silhouette of one of the old Franciscan Fathers who had pioneered Baja over four centuries before. His robe was loose, he was wearing his cowl, and his head was bent in meditation. He seemed to be asking a blessing for our private paradise. Then and there, we named the beach *La Playa Del Padre*, and we made our camp at his feet.

Most people have a dream world where they can retreat from realities—at least in their thoughts. But imagine being able to enter your dream world and actually live in it! Our beach world is our dream world. From the moment our camp was completed, it was as if we had never left the beach a year before. That wonderful, languorous "Baja Feeling" enveloped us and we picked up our dream right where we'd left it. The tide closed us off from the world, and we played, naked, on the beach the rest of the day. We laughed, we splashed, we loved, and we remembered good things.

Late that afternoon I was sprawled in the shade putting an eye splice in a piece of tent line when I heard Margie start to laugh.

"What is it?" I called.

"I won't tell you. Just come here and look!"

Lazily I got up and strolled to the other side of the car where Margie had been unpacking the suitcase.

"Look!" she said, and pointed to the open suitcase on the sand.

There on top of all the neatly-folded garments was a big, ugly bone! The scraps of meat on it were starting to rot, and dirt still clung to it from being buried.

"Taco did her own packing!"

"Didn't you see her put that bone in there when you were packing our clothes?"

"I swear I didn't. She must have just slipped it in there."

We called her and she came out from her shady spot under the car. We handed her the bone and she took it back under the car without looking back.

The "reverse sunset" was even more beautiful than we had remembered, and provided backlighting for our cactus padre. Silhouetted against a blue sky washed with orange and gold, he seemed to be the central figure in the stained glass window of a church—a holy assurance of peace and security. We slept contentedly that night, never dreaming that in four days we'd feel we needed his protection.

We were awakened in the morning by loud screeching!

I sat bolt upright in bed. "My God! What's that?"

Margie rubbed her eyes. "It sounds like seagulls, but there must be thousands of them!"

Taco was up and wagging her tail excitedly as she peered out at the beach—a sure sign something interesting was happening.

It was a very low tide that morning. The water had receded at least half a mile from the high of the night before. The morning sun created a reddish path across the water and shimmered in the puddles on the exposed sea bottom, but left the rest of the beach in semi-darkness. Whatever that screeching was, it was way out on the sand flats somewhere. With camera in hand we set out to see what it was.

It was an amazing—and somewhat frightening—sight. Somewhere along the coast a fisherman's net had broken and literally hundreds of dead fish had been washed up by the tide. They were good-sized—three or four pounds at least—and had attracted many hundreds of seagulls. The shrieking birds were having a feeding orgy. Crazed by the presence of all that free food, they squawked as they leaped from fish to fish, fighting each other over what was plenty for all. The ravening birds were so wildly bold and so numerous, we felt as if they might attack us at any minute. We could approach within one or two steps of any of the gulls and he wouldn't budge. He'd just glare at us with baleful eyes and screech angrily as if to say: "One step closer and I'll peck your eyes out!" It wasn't an idle threat, because that is what they did with the fish. The eyes were pecked out before a single morsel of the flesh was eaten. We wondered if this was an instinctive protective measure, or were fish eyes some sort of gull delicacy? I took a few snapshots, but we felt increasingly uneasy with these hundreds of wild, aggressive birds, so we retreated to our camp. In camp we watched the orgy with binoculars. It continued until the blessed tide came in and swept the flats clean. We felt strangely relieved when the screeching ceased and the birds departed.

Driftwood is very scarce on Mexican beaches. There are no trees growing near the shore to drop branches in the water, and the bits of flotsam and jetsam that might burn are quickly picked up by Mexican fishermen encamped here and there along the coast. Therefore, much of our wandering-around time on the beach is spent in picking up bits of sticks, twigs, or whatever other combustible items we can find for our nightly campfire. The best time to find them is in the morning after the previous night's high tide.

On the morning of our second day, it was my turn to hunt for firewood. The previous night's tide had been generous and there were quite a few sticks to pick up. Soon I had an armload, and was quite a long distance from camp when I heard Margie scream.

My heart thumped. What could have happened? "I'm coming!" I shouted. "I'm coming!" I dropped the firewood on the beach and started sprinting for camp. As I got closer I could hear her sobbing.

I dashed up to the camp, ripped the tent flap open, and saw one of the saddest—funniest—sights I ever have seen! Apparently she had been sitting there innocently reading Sunset magazine when the pot had collapsed without warning, dropping her squarely into the center of its contents. Too dirty, disgusted, and angry to move, she was just sitting there in the mess crying. I bit the inside of my cheeks to keep from laughing.

"How did it happen?" I said.

"There's a snake in here!" she said between sobs.

Sure enough! Coiled under the car, and probably more frightened than Margie, was a baby rattlesnake! "Well, get up out of that mess," I said,

128

"and then I'll get the snake." I extended my hand to help her.

"Don't touch me!" Gingerly she arose as if getting up out of a bed of cactus. She started to weep again.

"Now just stand there until I get the snake."

I have heard that baby rattlers can be just as deadly as their larger relatives and will strike quicker. We never carry weapons in Mexico, and I didn't want to get as close to him as a camp shovel handle. Also, I didn't relish the idea of blood and gore inside our tent if I did kill him, so I decided to spare his life. I took a long tent pole, stuck the end of it under his belly, and flipped him back into the brush whence he came. Then I turned to my pathetic spouse standing there nude with the pot contents plastered all over her fanny. "Now exactly what happened, Honey?" I asked.

With the snake disposed of, she became angry. "I was sitting on the pot when the goddam snake came into the tent. It made me jump, and when I jumped, the goddam pot collapsed and dumped me into the shit. And look how goddam far I have to walk to the goddam water to get clean!"

I started to chuckle. "It *is* kind of funny, you know."

She drew herself up haughtily. "I see nothing funny about it." Then, with soap, scrubbrush, and dirty potty seat in hand, she started to walk the half mile to the water, waddling like a child with dirty diapers. I decided the discreet thing to do was remain in camp and let her do her bathing in privacy. As I watched her wend her wretched way to the ocean, I noticed that even after suffering the ultimate indignity, she held her back straight and proud, and I loved her dearly.

Later that day the lovely tide came in, washing the beaches clean and obliterating memories of unpleasantness. We sat in the shade of our camp, laughing over the snake-and-pot incident, watching the sea birds circling lazily in the sky, and loving our languid life.

"When are you going to take the boat down out of the 'Bird Cage' and go boating?" Margie asked.

I sighed. "When I feel ambitious. Right now I don't feel like doing anything."

And so the day passed.

The next morning at breakfast, Margie launched us on our most ambitious project.

"I wonder if we could build an island," she said wistfully.

"An island?"

129

"Right here. In front of our camp."

"You want to build an island in front of our camp." I thought a moment. "I'm afraid I'm losing the thought somewhere."

"With the tide. Couldn't we dig a canal so that when the tide comes in, it will run up our canal and make an island? We could use it for picnics and stuff."

Aha! I got the picture.

It became a serious project. We decided on an island about twelve feet across. The canal surrounding it would have to be fairly deep, and we'd use the excavated sand to make the island higher. It would remain dry when the tide was full in. We took turns digging with the camp shovel and smoothing, tamping, and finishing. So intent were we with our work that we didn't even remember to stop for lunch. We were hastening to complete the job before the tide came in. We finished construction just in time. As Margie threw the last shovelful of sand atop the island the water reached the entrance of our canal, so we retired to our camp to rest and see what happened.

Margie pulled up a camp chair and sat down. It was then the problem became obvious.

"What's the matter?"

"I think I have a little sunburn."

"Let's see."

She stood up. We had been so excited about starting our project that we hadn't bothered to put on any clothes. We had been digging, with our bottoms up, in the hot sun for nearly five hours, and Margie's cute fanny was sunburned cherry red! Mine was sunburned too, but not quite as bad as hers.

To our delight, our planning was perfect and the canal was a success. The tide came in, circled around the canal, and our private island emerged. We put sunburn lotion on our bottoms, donned bermuda shorts, and waded out to our island with a couple of drinks. There we sat, despite our sunburns, until the sun went down.

In the morning, the gentle breeze that blows off the sea and keeps us cool was quite a bit stronger, and the ocean was dotted with whitecaps like bits of fluff. It gave me that old urge to go to sea. I climbed up to the "Bird Cage" on the roof of the Toy and unloaded the inflatable boat and motor. We laid the boat out flat on the sand, attached the foot pump, and took turns pumping up each compartment. It took about half an hour of lazy work to get the boat inflated, the oars assembled, and the motor mounted on the transom astern. In this short time the wind had increased markedly. The water, which normally laps gently on the shore, was beginning to look angry, and three- or four-foot waves were smashing the beach. The whitecaps were very numerous now, and grains of sand were beginning to blow down the beach.

"Do you think we can launch the boat in these waves?" Margie asked.

"Nothing to it," I said. "I've been handling small boats all my life. Just do as I say."

We loaded Taco and the fishing tackle into the boat and began to wade it out through the waves.

It was true that I was very experienced at handling small boats, but they had all been wooden-hull boats which tend to cut through the water. The inflatable was quite another story. It danced and bounced on the top of the water, leaping the waves like a jackrabbit.

"Hop in and man the oars!" I shouted.

Margie attempted the order just as a large wave came crashing over all of us, filling the boat with water, soaking the engine, frightening Taco, and washing us all ashore in a sodden mass.

Both members of my crew obviously wanted to try the boat launching on a calmer day, but I was now determined to show Margie what a capable boatsman I am and insisted that we try again. We dumped the water out of the boat, dried off everything as best we could, and coaxed a reluctant Taco back into the bow of the craft.

Now the waves were even higher and the wind stronger. I decided on a new tack. I put Margie in the boat too, holding the oars at ready and keeping Taco calmed down. I then walked the boat myself through the waves as far as I could, gave it a shove, and dove into the stern sheets head first.

"Row!" I shouted.

Margie immediately bent to the oars. A large wave was coming.

"Harder! Faster!" I shouted.

Too late. It broke over us. This time, however, it didn't wash us ashore. Margie's last big effort with the oars had pulled us beyond the breakers, where we drifted like a bloated, floating bathtub.

I had tied cooking pots to the thwarts of the boat before launching so we'd have something to use for bailing, if needed. I set Margie to bailing the water out while I pulled on the oars to get us farther away from the breakers. As soon as I felt we were safe, I shipped oars and attempted to start the drenched outboard motor. Two or three pulls of the starter cord availed nothing. It didn't even cough.

"Did you open the gas line?" Margie asked.

131

"Of course I did!" I said, feeling it with my fingers at the same time. It was closed. I twisted it open, gave the starter cord another pull, and rejoiced at the happy song of the little outboard. As we went bouncing happily over the waves, Margie didn't even say "I told you so." I was grateful for that.

The three-horsepower motor propelled the light inflatable along at a pretty fast clip, but the wind was becoming so strong it threatened to blow us off course, and the usually calm Gulf waters were heaving up into angry, white-topped mountains. The only intelligent thing to do was get the hell off that ocean and head for the safety of our cove. I swung the boat around, steered for our beach, and expertly caught a wave which washed us up on shore high and dry. We dragged the boat above the high tide line, drove a stake in the ground, and tied it up. Then I tied the duffel bag securely over the motor to protect it from blowing sand.

The wind was really howling now, and grains of sand were whipping our bodies, stinging us like thousands of bees. Our camp chairs had blown way down the beach, tent stakes had pulled out, and the canvas—still fastened in the slot on the Toy—was flapping wildly in the gale. Our fire pit from the night before had vanished—filled with sand. Margie made a dash for her "kitchen," retrieving lost or sand-filled articles, and I ran down the beach to recover our camp chairs. They were bounding like tumbleweeds in the wind, but I managed to capture them. Walking back to camp against the wind was a struggle, but I ducked my head down, so the swirling sand wouldn't cut my face, and dug my feet in doggedly.

We tried to put our tent back up. I held the lashing canvas—or tried to hold it—while Margie hammered the tent stakes into the ground. It was no go.

I can't stand this anymore!" Margie shouted over the wind, "Let's get in the car."

We fought the car door open against the wind, lifted miserable little Taco in first, then climbed into the bed after her.

This was the start of a dreaded *chubasco*. It is a particular type of storm that frequents the Gulf of California. Its main characteristic is high winds that may peak at 110 miles per hour or more. With very little warning it hurls its fury against small seacoast towns—ripping off roofs, beaching and shattering fishing boats, and leaving destruction in its wake.

It was hot in the car, but we didn't dare open the windows, for the car would have filled with sand in just a few minutes. The three of us just lay there on the bed watching the storm ravage our beach. The wind, its mighty force turned on anything in its path, would set up little eddies like tiny whirlwinds at the base of an object. Like speeding drills, these miniature whirlwinds would spin the sand away from the base until a large cavity was created. The object would then topple into the cavity, be covered with sand, and eventually disappear. It was as if the furious gale was bent on obliterating everything in sight on our beach. One by one we watched rocks and some of our belongings disappear, and still it continued to blow. Awed by the howling *chubasco*, we tended to talk very softly even though it was difficult to be heard over the storm.

"Can you see the boat?" I asked, "I hope it's alright."

Margie peered intently out her window. "I can't make it out. There's too much sand blowing. I hope that stake holds."

"No way. The wind probably dug up that stake first thing. But maybe the weight of the motor will keep it from blowing away."

"Thank God you put that duffel bag over the motor. Did you tie it well?"

"As well as I know how. If that duffel bag blows off, the motor is ruined."

Suddenly there was a sickening lurch, and the car was listing at nearly a 45-degree angle. "What happened?"

"Climb to the high side! Hurry! We might topple over!"

We scrambled around so that we were both sitting crosswise in the car, throwing our weight to the high side.

Margie picked up Taco and held her. "What happened?" she said again.

The only thing I can figure out is that the wind dug a big hole under our tires and the car slipped into it. Just like it does with rocks and everything else."

"Lord, how much longer?"

We were cramped now, and uncomfortable with the car leaning way to one side, but we didn't dare change our position for fear of causing it to fall completely on its side. We would then be marooned on this beach. We lapsed into silence and just stared at the blowing clouds of sand and the angry sea. Sometimes I caught Margie, who was raised as a Catholic, staring intently—perhaps reverently—at the cactus padre on the bluff above us. He was standing firm in the storm and still praying. Buffeted by the wind, the car began to tremble, and I made up a silent prayer of my own.

One hour passed. Two hours, and the gale roared on. After three hours it seemed to be lessening a little, or was it our imagination? We waited a little longer. No, there was no doubt. The howling had diminished considerably and the clouds of blowing sand were beginning to settle. Still we waited. At last we felt it was safe to get out and survey the damage. Cautiously we struggled out of the high side of the tilting car.

"My God, look at this beach!" I said.

Gone were the canal and our private island; gone were the rocks we had used as tide markers; our boat was almost completely buried with just the top of the duffel bag on the motor showing; and the beach was swept white, even, and clean. It was as if a new beach had been born amidst the fury of the winds.

"Our padre is still standing," Margie said. "He got through the chubasco okay."

"Yup. Still meditating too. Maybe it was the padre who saved us."

I was joking, but Margie took it seriously. "Maybe he did."

As for our car, it was as I had surmised. The gale had tunneled under the windward side of the tires, dug deep holes, and that side of the car had slipped into them. Sand-blasted by the storm and pitched over on one side like that, our little car looked forlorn, like a plaything cast aside by the wind. I decided to level it out by digging under the wheels on the high side. While I was doing this, Margie sifted through the sand with her hands to recover various lost objects.

Soon the Toy was level again and the wind had abated enough to put our tent back up. That job was no sooner accomplished than it started to rain. The wind ceased completely with the coming of the blessed rain, and we sat in our camp chairs sipping a badly-needed drink and listening to the happy patter on the roof. As the rain fell and the sea calmed down, our spirits rose. Margie made a marvelous dinner, and we enjoyed a couple of after-dinner drinks, then retired.

We awakened to a glorious morning. The rain had swept the skies clean, the sea was calm, the birds returned, and sunlight danced on the water. Our boat, though buried in sand, had survived the storm, so we decided to dig it up and attempt another launching. Using the technique of the previous day, I loaded Margie, Taco, and the fishing tackle into the boat and walked it out through the gentle waves. All went smoothly. I gave it a shove, hopped aboard, and soon we were well beyond the breakers. This time I remembered to open the gas line, and the outboard started with the first pull of the starter cord. I opened the throttle about three-quarters, and the little boat skipped daintily over the swells and out to sea.

I steered the craft in a long, lazy northward arc. We watched the retreating shoreline and speculated as to what might be the best fishing spot. We finally decided on a place about half a mile off the end of a reef, cut the motor, and rigged the lines for fishing. We hadn't bothered to get any bait so I just put shiners on the lines. We would jig for fish. We drifted, casting and reeling in the lures, for about half an hour without a nibble. Just about the time we'd decided to reel in and try another spot, Taco began to bark furiously. She was looking down at the water, so we followed her glance and witnessed an astonishing underwater ballet! Just below the surface and plainly visible in the clear water was a giant school of manta rays. They were swimming by us in matched pairs hooked together by the flukes, apparently engaged in their own curious mating dance. Hundreds of these hitched pairs glided by us "hand in hand" as we sat and stared.

"They look like big frying pans in love!" Margie said.

"They sure do. If only I'd brought the movie camera!"

"We could make dirty fish pictures."

"They'd be called 'fin-flicks'," I punned.

She laughed. "And the title of the film could be 'A Piece Of Fish Tail'!"

We watched them for awhile, then reeled in, started the motor and continued on our way. About the second cove we passed seemed to have some sort of life ashore. Margie studied it with the binoculars.

"It's a fish camp!" she said. "I'll bet that's the fisherman who lost his net the other day."

"Let's go ashore and talk with him," I said, swinging the boat around.

Another fifteen minutes or so and we were ashore, walking toward the camp with Taco trotting happily ahead of us. In an arroyo near the beach was a palapa-type structure similar to what we'd seen at Yelapa—four cacti uprights, narrower crossbeams, and desert greenery tossed on top to provide shelter. It was about lunchtime, and the smell of tortillas cooking was heavenly. A Mexican in his early thirties emerged. He was bare foot, shirtless, and had a two- or three-day growth of beard. He bent over and started petting Taco (she's always our best ambassador).

"Buenos días," I said.

"Buenos días." He didn't smile. His attitude was one of suspicion or wariness—I couldn't tell which.

We asked in Spanish if he was the fisherman who had lost a net two days before.

He replied that he was. He hadn't lost the net, he said, it was just very old and had broken in several places. It had now been patched and was

135

working again. As we stood there chatting, he seemed to become less wary of us and more affable. He told us how the *chubasco* had torn his camp to pieces and how they had repaired it. Finally, he explained that he usually felt uncomfortable with *norteamericanos* because he spoke no English, but since we spoke Spanish he felt quite at ease.

We introduced ourselves, as a small group gathered nearby.

"*Su familia?*" Margie asked, nodding at the others.

"*Sí.* Permit me the pleasure to introduce you," he said formally, but in Spanish. "This is my wife, Henrieta." He gestured, and a very pretty Mexican girl came shyly forward to shake hands.

"*Mucho gusto,*" I said, "*Somos Benito y Margie.*"

"*Pueden hablar español!*" [They are able to speak Spanish] Pedro said. She blushed and murmured, "*El gusto es mío.*"

"And these are my children," he continued, "Little Pedro—"

A six-year-old boy with enormous brown eyes stepped up politely and shook hands like a grown man. He was obviously Pedro's favorite.

"And these are my daughters, Dora and Patti." Two slightly older girls clapped their hands over their mouths, suppressing nervous giggles.

Pedro frowned, and we smiled at them. "*Mucho gusto.*"

"The baby is Rita and she sits in the lap of her grandmother."

An older woman feeding the baby a bottle looked up and smiled.

"And this is the children's grandfather who helps me with the nets."

The older gentleman came over and shook hands vigorously. "*Bienvenidos,*" he said.

As so often happens with very shy people, there followed an awkward pause while we all stood there trying to think of something to say. Pedro's wife broke the silence.

"*Le gusta cerviche?*" she asked.

We told her we didn't know whether we liked *cerviche* because we didn't know what it was.

She then insisted that we stay in their camp for lunch and try some. The smell of tortillas was driving me wild, so I thanked her and accepted for us. She smiled, and returned to her cooking.

"Look at the stove!" Margie said to me in English.

It was ingenious. The bottom of an old oil drum had been removed and welded back in about a foot below the top. They had then cut a hole in the side of the drum just above it. It made a perfect firebox, and when the wood was burning inside, the top of the drum was hot as a griddle. Henrietta was cooking the tortillas there.

Soon, everything was ready and we sat down to what has now become one of our favorite dishes. *Cerviche* is the Mexican way of preparing raw fish. Generally they use *sierra* [Spanish mackerel]. They fillet it and place it to soak in the juice of those slightly sweet, green-yellow limes you find only in Mexico. After the fish has marinated in the lime juice for several hours, it is more or less pickled. Then they chop it up in a bowl with chilis, onions, small chunks of tomatoes, and salt and pepper. I swilled it down with handfuls of piping hot tortillas and never tasted anything better in my life!

After lunch, Margie retired to the other area of the *palapa* with the women and children, and I chatted with the two men. I asked Pedro how he kept his fish fresh for the market.

He pointed to a huge ice chest. It was about five feet by twelve feet. "When the ice box is full, I take the fish to San Felipe and they are still fresh," he said.

"That box is filled with ice?"

"*Sí. Mucho.*"

I told him I thought Margie and I might run out of ice in a few more days and then we'd like to buy a piece from him.

"*No se puede,*" [It is not possible] he said. "You are my friends. For friends, the ice is free."

When it was finally time for us to depart, Margie invited all of them to visit our camp the next night when the tide was low. She told them that since they had entertained us, now it was our turn to entertain them. Delighted, they accepted.

After we were back in the boat and headed for our cove I said, "How in hell are you planning to entertain all those people in our tiny camp?"

"We don't have to feed them. Low tide will be after their supper time."

"I know. But even so—"

"Don't worry. I'll think of something."

We landed at our beach, bathed while the tide was still fairly high, and then lazed around camp the rest of the afternoon. When the tide receded late in the day, we went on a long walk across the sand flats and through the tide pools. Margie found some interesting looking, orange, spongy stuff growing on the rocks, and Taco resumed her tireless crab hunting.

Perhaps because she felt less secure on other beaches, Taco had always left the tide pools whenever we did. This time, in our secluded cove, she refused to return to camp with us. As we sat in camp, enjoying a couple of drinks before dinner, we could just make out a little black spot darting here and there on the reef in search of crabs. Finally Margie could stand it no longer.

"She'll be exhausted and sick!" she said, calling for Taco.

The small black dot paused a moment, perhaps to look back, and then went on to another tide pool.

"Taco! Here, Taco!" Margie looked at me. "Honestly, Ben, she's just like a child."

I had a quick flash of myself as a child on Balboa Island. I was a little butterball, impervious to the cold, and could stay in the water for hours. My poor mother would try to call me out. I begged for an extension of time—"Please, Mom! Let me stay in a little longer. Pleeeeeeease!" I knew just how Taco felt. "Let her play a while longer, Darling," I said.

An hour later, Taco returned to camp. She was wet, bedraggled, and thirsty. She lapped up all the drinking water in her dish, licked the sides of it, crawled under the car and went asleep.

The morning sun ushered in another lazy Baja day. It's amazing how two normally active people like Margie and me can suddenly become devoid of all ambition. It even seemed like too much work to take the boat out. We spent the entire day bathing, loafing in the sun, or just staring at the beautiful sea. Perhaps it is the hypnotic effect of the gently moving water with its ever-changing colors and its soaring sea birds that induces our lethargy. Like sand in an hourglass, the time slipped away from us, and soon the "reverse sunset" was beginning.

"Hey! I just remembered!" I said, "you're giving a party tonight."

"I know." She yawned.

"Well, have you decided what we're going to do?"

"Oh, yes. I thought it out awhile ago."

"You want to let me in on your secret?"

"Well, since they will have had supper, I'll serve that watermelon for dessert for all of us . . . "

"That's a good idea."

"And then you can make drinks."

"I'll fix tequila, lemon, and salt for the men. That's easy. But should I serve that to the women?"

"Why don't you make them a sweet rum drink of some kind?"

"Okay. And the kids?"

"We have that Delaware Punch."

Using leftovers, Margie made us a quick dinner, and we got ready for our guests. At her suggestion, I changed the configuration of the tent so that it was just one big tarp overhead. We didn't need it for protection from the elements, but Margie said it would make our guests feel as if they were really in our home. I got out the booze and we waited.

The tide was way out and the sun nearly extinguished when they appeared walking around the point at the end of our cove. The two dogs came first, bounding and barking. They were followed by the three children—Dora, Patti, and Little Pedro—laughing and chasing each other. Then came Pedro and Henrieta holding hands, with Grandpa and Grandma bringing up the rear. As usual, Grandma was carrying the baby.

It was a cute sight, but the most charming to us was that this simple fisherman's family had really dressed up to visit our camp. The men had shaved and were wearing neatly pressed, worsted trousers and clean white shirts. Feet, calloused and splayed from a life of going barefoot, had been squeezed into boxy mail-order catalog shoes which must have caused agony at every step. Henrieta and Grandma, also usually barefooted, were wearing long stockings and high-heeled shoes (walking through sand!) as well as their finest dresses. They had allowed the three children to remain barefooted, but they had all been scrubbed squeaky clean and were wearing their nicest clothes. Both little girls had bows in their hair. Here we were on a lonely beach, miles from anywhere, and this little family had gone to this much trouble to honor us. We were very touched.

We greeted each other effusively, and I exchanged *abrazos,* a masculine embrace traditional in Mexico, with the men. We seated the ladies in our two camp chairs, while the men inspected our camp with polite admiration:

The car: "Two transmissions, no? How much does such a car cost?"
The Coleman lantern: "With such a *lámpara* I could fish at night."
The Coleman stove: "Henrieta would no longer cook on the oil drum."
The winch: "It has much power, no? How many kilos does it pull?"

Meanwhile, Margie had cut the watermelon and served the children, directing them to spit the seeds into a hole she'd scooped out of the sand. This was something new to them and became somewhat of a game, keeping them occupied.

Then when we were all seated on the sand we began the conversation by getting names straightened out again. My name is easy. I just tell them it's "Benito." They can handle "Hunter" too, if you spell it "Junter." Margie's name was a problem. The "G" sound in "Margie" doesn't exist in Spanish and their tongues simply couldn't handle it. Her name came out "Marshe." She said she liked "Marshe" better anyway, and ever since then has always introduced herself in Mexico by that name. Grandpa and Grandma told us their names again but it didn't stick. They were very simple Mexican names, but we always referred to them in private as "Grandpa and Grandma," so that's all we remembered.

The watermelon was welcome on that warm evening and was soon devoured by all. I cracked out the booze and the Delaware Punch, and Margie produced some peanuts. That gave me an idea for amusing the children. I performed the only magic trick I know.

"Aqui, yo tengo un cacahuate," [Here, I have a peanut], I said, holding it aloft by my thumb and forefinger. *"Ahorita, mire!"* [Now watch!]

I placed it carefully in the palm of my left hand and closed my fingers over it. Then holding my two fists out toward the children, I said, *"Ahora, dónde está?"* [Now, where is it?].

Of course they all chose the left hand and I showed them it was empty. Then they quickly chose the other hand, but it was empty too. I proceded to produce the missing peanut from Patti's ear.

You'd have thought I was the reincarnation of Houdini himself! There were shrieks of amazement and laughter, followed by pleas that I do it again—heady wine for an old ham. Naturally, I performed it again. And again and again. Soon I was beginning to tire of doing my one and only trick, but each time I tried to stop I got another curtain call. *"Otra vez! Otra vez!"* Margie finally rescued me. She produced some old *copies of Life* magazine we had in camp, and the kids were soon poring over every picture. The baby had long since gone to sleep in Grandma's lap, her pacifier still in her mouth. At last it was quiet so the adults could talk.

We talked of the children, our families, the fishing, the beach, and the trips to market at San Felipe. Finally I happened to say: "Pedro, will you always fish, or is there other work you do?"

He became very serious. "Benito, it is in my heart to become a singer. Someday, if I am lucky, I will be a very important singing star and we will all live in Mexico City in a beautiful house."

"Would you sing for us?" Margie asked.

"I have not yet enough money for a guitar, but—?"

"Sing without a guitar, Pedro, we'd like to hear you," I said.

He sat up very straight on the sand and held his arms as if he were cradling a guitar. Then with his right hand he began to strum the air for his imaginary accompaniment and sing. His singing voice was much higher than his speaking voice. It was young, melodic, and beautiful. Bathed in golden moonlight he sang from his heart, with the gentle shush of the waves his accompaniment. His song was *La Golondrina*, the story of the swallow, and when it ended, I was so entranced I almost forgot to applaud.

"Did you like it?" he asked.

"It was beautiful. Please sing some more," Margie said. I could tell she had been affected too.

He sang another song. This one we had not heard before, but it was very sad and very beautiful. So great was the magic of the singing I wished it would never end. It concluded on a high note which Pedro muted until you could barely hear it, and then finally it blended with the sound of the waves. I have never known a more beautiful moment.

This time we collected ourselves in time to give Pedro the applause he deserved. Grandma had dozed off during the song, the baby still cradled in her arms. Pedro touched her on the shoulder to awaken her, took the baby in his arms, and told us it was late and they'd better be going. Margie gave the children the *Life* magazines that had so enthralled them, we all bid each other good night, and the little family started the long walk back to their camp. The last we saw of them they were picking their way around the rocks at the end of our cove in their party finery.

As I have mentioned, our cove was only accessible at low tide, and at this time the lows were occuring very early in the morning and late in the afternoon. That may be the reason we didn't see Pedro and his family for several days. Or perhaps they were merely respecting our privacy. At any rate, we fell back into our Baja routine of loafing, loving, and staring. We took the boat out a few times and had slightly better luck with the fishing. Our catch consisted mainly of corbina and perch. I'm not overly fond of either, so after one fish barbecue, we started throwing them back when we caught them. Mother Nature gave me a birthday present, however. On the morning of my birthday I caught a good sized *totuava* [Mexican sea bass], one of the most delicious fish in the ocean. That night we had a feast of *Totuava Almondine* as only Margie can prepare it.

With such total privacy, we never bothered to put on clothes, except for boating, and our sunburned tails had turned tan. We decided it wasn't as much fun to be tan all over, because without a white patch you couldn't tell how tan you were. One early morning low tide we were seated nude in our camp, sipping coffee, when we heard the sound of a car's engine coming our way! We made a fast dash for our clothes and scrambled into them just as the most incredible truck I have ever seen rounded the point and headed straight for our camp.

141

The truck had been put together with what the Mexicans call *refacciones* [spare auto parts] to such an extent that you couldn't identify its original pedigree. The cab was one brand, the hood another, the truck bed yet another, and all of them strictly vintage. It looked as if one severe bump could trigger an automotive eruption and send its pieces flying in all directions! Strangest of all were the tires. Oversized carcasses of old tires had been placed around the outside of the regular tires, stuffed with straw, and wired together! I surmised this was for the purpose of driving on soft sand. The owner of the vehicle apparently had no way of deflating the truck's tires and pumping them up again for the road, so he had used this peculiar device for traction in the soft stuff.

This contraption that would have caused heart attacks in Detroit pulled up in front of our camp and stopped. At the wheel was Pedro.

"*Buenos días*," he said getting out of the cab.

"*Buenos días. Qué tal?*"

"*Bien. Ustedes?*"

"*Bien. Muy bien. Su familia?*"

"*Igualmente.*" [The same.]

These are the usual greetings. When seeing a friend after a few days, you must always inquire about his health and the health of his family, and perhaps even engage in a brief discussion of the weather. Then, and only then, you can get down to business. Americans are much too inclined to plunge into the purpose of their visit before exchanging the amenities. I was about to inquire how the fishing was going, but this time Pedro was anxious to disclose the purpose of his visit.

"*Tengo su hielo*," he said.

The ice! After all the days that had passed since my chance remark, he had remembered that we were going to need ice! He had timed it just right, too, becasue our block had shrunk to a watery snowball.

"Oh Pedro, *gracias!*" I said with true gratitude. "Please permit me to pay you for it."

"I told you, Benito, with friends the ice is free."

He unloaded it from the bed of the truck and carried it over to our ice chest. Margie opened the chest and he dropped it in.

It was apparent I wasn't going to be able to pay him for the ice, so I tried another tack. "Thank you for the ice, *amigo*, but you had to bring it in the truck. Gasoline is expensive, so permit me to pay for the gas."

After much discussion he finally agreed to accept five pesos (at that time about forty cents) for the gasoline, and the matter was settled.

"When do you return to the United States?" he asked.

142

"In another week."

"We leave the beach in two more days," he said sadly.

"Why?" Margie asked.

"The fishing is bad. We return to my father-in-law's house in San Felipe. I will look for other work."

My mind was racing. We had to think of some way to help this man. A way to help him without seeming to. But how? How? "We will come to your camp to say goodbye before you go," I said, stalling for time.

"*Bueno*. My family and I will be expecting you." He shook hands, got back in the cab, and the strange-looking truck departed.

Off and on the rest of that day Margie and I discussed how to repay Pedro for his kindness. To buy him a guitar was not possible. He could have probably afforded one of those cheapies. He obviously wanted a good guitar and we didn't have that much money with us. To mail money into Mexico is most unwise. Letters are often torn open and the money removed. We would certainly be ineffective at finding him a job. There must be some gift we could give him—something we could do.

"I've got it!" Margie said at length.

"What?"

"Remember the night of our party?"

"Who could forget?"

"Well, you told me that he admired our Coleman lantern that night."

"That's right! He said he could use it for night fishing."

"Well, let's give him the lantern."

"We'll tell him we don't need it, so we want him to have it."

That was more or less true. We retire very early when we're living on the beach, and if we do stay up once in awhile, we always have our campfire for light.

The next day we took the lantern and a supply of fuel for it and boated north to Pedro's camp. When we arrived the tide was still fairly low and the whole family was out on the rocks. They would turn a rock over, reach down, pick up something, and place it in a sack. We strolled over for a look.

They were not gathering clams. These were round, flat creatures with many triangular legs sticking out from the center. Each one looked like a sunburst.

"*Qué es?*" Margie asked one of the children.

"*Estrellas.*"

"A starfish with all those legs?"

"*Sí,*" the child smiled, "*treinta y dos.*"

143

"Now what in the hell do you suppose they do with a thirty-two-legged starfish?" I said to Margie.

Pedro came over to us. "With the fishing bad, we harvest the *estrella*," he said. "A *norteamericano* pays much money for them when they are dried."

"He sells them for souvenirs?"

"*Sí.* In the United States."

Forgetting the lantern back in the boat, we offered to help the Camacho family with their harvest. It would be fun to do and would help swell their coffers. So for several hours, until the tide came in, we gathered the strange-looking starfish. Finally, the water covered the rocks, our backs were aching, and the bags were filled. The family gathered around to thank us and say goodbyes. Then I remembered the lantern. I sprinted over to our boat, got it and the fuel out, and presented them to Pedro with a little speech I had planned beforehand.

He was overcome. "Benito, it is the finest gift I have ever received." He could think of nothing else to say, and everyone stood there silent and a little embarrassed. Grandpa stepped into the breach.

"As you know," he said, "we leave for my *casa* in San Felipe tomorrow. Benito, you and Marshe must come to see us before you return to the United States."

We agreed that on our way back we would stop by to say one more farewell. Using a piece of broken shell, Grandpa scratched a map of San Felipe in the wet sand and made a big "X" where his house was.

"Memorize it, Darling," I said to Margie. "We can't take this map with us!"

Then, once again, there were thanks and goodbyes, and we left.

Margie memorized the improvised map alright, but just to be sure she sketched it on a piece of paper when we got back to camp.

The remainder of the week it was just Taco, Margie, and me; the beach, the sun, the sea, and the birds. We loafed and loved and the cactus padre bestowed his blessings on us and our paradise. Before we knew it our last day had arrived and the necessity of returning to reality loomed like a dark cloud. Our one respite would be a brief stop in San Felipe at Grandpa's house.

The wheels of the Toy were pretty well dug into the sand because of the *chubasco,* so after breaking camp I had to shovel out in front and back. The little car started without a whimper after its long rest, I dropped it into four-wheel drive, and we pulled out of the sand hole and started on our way.

"So long, Padre! Thanks for everything!" I shouted, and our beautiful campsite began to disappear behind us.

The trip back to civilization seemed to take many hours longer than it had taken us to get there. Actually, it took less time because we drove the road rather than the beaches. In San Felipe we knew we'd found Grandpa's house before we saw it because Dora, Patti, and Little Pedro were playing in the dusty street. As soon as they saw us approaching they came running and laughing up to our car.

"Marshe! Marshe!" Disappearing peanut trick notwithstanding, Margie is always the favorite with kids.

The house was a small one-bedroom home made of stucco. How all of them slept there remains a mystery. When we arrived, the adults were sitting on the front porch awaiting us and the baby was inside having a nap. Once again there were effusive greetings and abrazos, and Grandpa served cold beers to cut the dust of the road. We told them nothing much had happened on the beach since they'd left, and Pedro said he was still looking for a job. We agreed that we must keep in touch. Pedro said he would write, and I said I would answer his letters. I gave him our home address in the States, and he gave me his apartado postal [post office box] number in San Felipe. We chatted a little longer, finished the beers, and rose to depart.

"Momentito!" Grandpa said, and disappeared into the house. He emerged a moment later and presented us with a two-kilo (four and one-half pound) bag of big, frozen shrimp!

Like Pedro when he was given the lantern, we were too dumbstruck to say anything at first. At today's prices for shrimp, that was a generous gift indeed! Finally, we thanked him as eloquently as we were able in Spanish. Then we said goodbyes for the umpteenth time, but this time we really left.

We had been home a little over two weeks when a letter with colorful Mexican stamps arrived. Excitedly, I tore it open. It had been painstakingly printed in pencil. Something had been placed under the lineless paper so that each line of printing was absolutely even. Each letter of each word was a tiny work of art.

Estimado amigo, [Esteemed friend]
We miss all of you very much. Did you enjoy the shrimp? I still do not find a job. The fishing is poor too, but perhaps we may set the nets another place. Henrieta, the children, and of course I send love to you,

Marshe, and little Taco. Please write soon.

Your friend,
Pedro

Translating the letter from the Spanish wasn't too difficult. One of us read it aloud, and when we *heard* the words we knew their meaning. Writing a letter back in Spanish was another ball game! Having learned what little Spanish we knew by ear, we hadn't the foggiest notion how to spell the words we wanted to use. Each one had to be looked up in the Spanish-English dictionary, and my typewritten answer to Pedro must have taken as long to write as his carefully handprinted letter.

"*Estimado amigo,*" I began, taking the cue from him, "The shrimp are delicious." Then I told him that we missed him and his family, we hoped the fishing would improve, and that we were looking forward to returning to the beach very soon and seeing all of them again. We sent our love to him, Henrieta, the children, and "the grandfather and grandmother." I signed it "*Su amigo, Benito.*"

Thus, our letters went for quite a long period of time. They certainly were not brimming over with a wealth of news, comment and information! For my part, I didn't discuss my life or my job in the states because I felt he just wouldn't understand. It would be like trying to explain the Dow Jones average to a man from another planet. Pedro must have felt somewhat the same at his end. Nevertheless, our uninformative letters trickled back and forth for nearly two years.

I don't know whether I stopped writing first, or whether he did. No matter; it was inevitable that it end. One day I realized I hadn't heard from my "*estimado amigo*" in a long, long time. But we have never forgotten the Pedro Camacho family. How they welcomed us—two gringo strangers on the beach—into their family to share their food; how they gave us ice and shrimp from their simple larder; how they honored us by donning their party finery to visit our camp; and the magic of Pedro's singing that night on the beach. We said that one day we really would return and see them again.

That was quite a few years ago. Recently, Margie and I returned to the area for the first time since that trip. We couldn't find Grandpa's house and—dammit—still couldn't remember his name. We inquired everywhere about Pedro Camacho and Henrieta, but no one in the stores, gas stations, or private homes seemed to know them. Then we drove the beaches, checked the fish camps along the coast, and asked in the various trailer parks that now proliferate the area. Nothing. No one had ever heard his name.

We wondered if perhaps his big dream had actually come true. Perhaps he was even now singing for enchanted diners in Mexico City. Or perhaps he had simply moved his family and his nets to another part of Baja.

I suppose we shall never know.

6/ Los Barriles

One of Margie's favorite sayings is "Things always work out for the best." I'll admit that it's banal and pollyannaish, but in our case it seems to be true. Any number of seeming misfortunes we have suffered have eventually brought about some sort of improvement in our lives. But is there anything good about a heart attack?

I had one. On June 1, 1971, I awakened about two o'clock in the morning, feeling as if I needed a truck load of bicarbonate. Margie checked the vital signs and called the doctor. Despite my protests that "You're all nuts! It's just indigestion," I was carried out feet first a short time later.

I was in my forties, slightly overweight, and a smoker with a family history of coronary problems. It was a textbook case. The doctors diagnosed what they called a myocardial infarction, and I was to be held in the Intensive Care Unit for about a month. During that time I hallucinated quite a lot, but when I was conscious, I looked up to see Margie's sweet, sad face looking down at me. She seemed never to leave the side of my bed.

Once before, during my prolonged absence from the show, Metromedia attempted to bring in different actors and personalities as stand-ins for me. The results had been disasterous, and ratings had bottomed out. By now they had learned that Don Lamond was the only one who could step into my show as host and carry it off successfully. So, once again, dear old "Donsie" was summoned to fill the breach, and the show rolled smoothly on as if I were there.

There had been a long struggle to keep my heart operational, and the doctors finally determined to install a temporary pacemaker. As I understand it, a pacemaker delivers a small electric shock to a certain part of the heart muscle which causes it to contract. Then, when the current is off, the muscle relaxes. They turn this current off and on rhythmically, thus forcing the heart to keep beating. Pacemakers are usually implanted in the chest of the patient. In my case, however, they merely pinned it to my pillow with its wires entering the artery on the inside of my right arm and proceding from there to the heart. The minute it was installed I felt better. I liked to listen to it pulsing beside me on the pillow and felt as if it was a kind of twin brother—our hearts beating in unison. I named it "Charlie."

Each day the doctors would come in and shut Charlie off for a while to see if I could make it on my own. If I couldn't, the pacemaker would have to be implanted permanently. It looked as if that's the way it was going to be, because when Charlie stopped, so did I!

One day during one of these tests I said, "Hey Doc? I've got a request."

"Yes?" He was feeling my pulse.

"I'm used to having a couple of highballs before dinner, and I'm really missing it. Any reason why I can't have one or two here in the hospital?"

He thought a moment and scratched his head. "I can't think of any reason why not," he said.

"Well, write it down somewhere so the nurses will know. Margie can bring the booze and the nurses can furnish the set-ups."

He didn't reply. He just finished his checking and turned Charlie back on.

"Don't forget the highballs!" I shouted as he went out the door.

That very afternoon when Margie returned to my bedside she had, as per my orders, a flask of tequila in her purse. The doctor had been as good as his word, and the nurse popped in to see what kind of mixers we wanted. "Just ice, water, and glasses," I said. Margie mixed the drinks and we sat there in the Intensive Care Unit chatting and sipping just as if we were ensconced on one of our favorite beaches.

Two or three days of this 4:30 cocktail hour, and I was able to function without Charlie. Another couple of days and I was released from Intensive Care! Maybe my sudden recovery was coincidental, but I submit it might never have happened without that joyous juice that has buoyed up the Mexican nation for centuries!

Then another nice thing happened. During my six weeks recuperation in a regular hospital room I was visited by Al Krivin, president of Metromedia. It was not only flattering to receive this attention from the top executive of our conglomerate, but Al told me that the company had decided to continue me at my regular salary until I could return to work. Since nothing of this sort is provided for in my contract, it was certainly a generous thing to do.

Finally, the six weeks were up and I was going to be able to go home. The doctor came into the hospital room for his final visit.

"I have two questions, Doc," I said.

"And they are?"

"How soon can I have sex, and how soon can I go to work again?"

He sighed. "Those are the first two questions every man asks after a heart attack."

"It's nice to be part of the crowd."

"Well, to answer them, you can have sex immediately. It can't hurt you at all and it's possible it could even be beneficial."

"Neat! And my job?"

"Two or three months."

I was shocked. "You mean two or three *weeks.*"

"No, *months.* I believe it's possible your condition may have been aggravated by overwork. Take two or three months, walk a lot, gradually increase your exercise, and watch your diet. Keep your weight down!"

I scarcely heard his last remarks. I was thinking, "Wow! Two or three months off with full pay for the first time in my life! Oh wow! What a bonanza!"

Margie has very strong mothering instincts, and after the doctor left, she began planning my days: the daily exercise session, the calorie-counted meals, and being tucked into bed early. I listened to it until I could stand it no longer.

"Now look, Margie," I said, "We have a beautiful paid vacation ahead of us and I'm damned if I'm going to spend it like an invalid. We'll go to Mexico. I can take my walks on the beach instead of in the smog, and I'll eat lots of fish. That'll keep my weight down."

"Darling, you can't four-wheel drive after a heart attack. It would be too much for you."

"Okay. Then we'll fly somewhere and find a hotel."

A spirited discussion ensued. Margie put up a very good battle, and we finally ended with a compromise. I would follow her regimen at home for two weeks—no more—then we'd fly someplace in Mexico for a vacation.

Those two weeks were deadly. She insisted on that blasted daily walk, and she purchased a pedometer which dangled from my bathrobe and prevented me from lying about how far I'd walked. I did my walking in the house, starting from the master bedroom and proceding through the bathroom, kitchen, family room, living room, and down the hall to the master bedroom again. Around and around the circuit I went with the pedometer ticking off the distance. Before long I was doing a full mile on my track. To avoid boredom I read a sexy Harold Robbins novel as I walked, glancing up occasionally to keep from bumping into walls.

The calorie-counted diet wasn't as bad as I had anticipated. Margie accepted the idea of producing low calorie gourmet meals as a challenge, and before long the book shelf where she stores her cookbooks began to slop over at the ends and stack up in the middle with literature on calorie counting. Just as she had succeeded on a camp stove, she prevailed over low calorie foods, and her dishes were delicious. I started typing the recipes on cards to use in a future book.

As those two interminable weeks dragged by, we discussed where in Mexico we would go. Airlines fly to places where many tourists go, and after many years in the travel business we've seen most of those spots and don't care for the usual tourist routine. But how could we avoid it? A plan finally evolved—we would catch a plane to La Paz, rent a car, and simply explore our way southward toward the tip of Baja until we found a little town to our liking, and stay there! The only reservations we made ahead of time were on the airline.

A medieval Spanish romance tells of a fabulous island named California "on the right hand of the Indies, very close to the terrestrial paradise," inhabited by a tribe of Amazons. So, back in 1535 when Hernan Cortez, the conqueror of Mexico, sailed across the Gulf from northern Mexico and discovered a bay filled with pearls, it wasn't surprising that his *conquistadores* believed they had discovered the fabled island of California. They named the bay Santa Cruz; they formed a colony; and they wrote letters home about a "lake" filled with pearls, and mountains of pure silver guarded by an Amazon queen who lured men to their destruction. (However, it wasn't the Amazon queen who did them in. It was the hostile Indians who killed them or drove them off, and resisted all efforts at colonization for another 150 years.)

Things have certainly changed!

The bay Cortez named Santa Cruz is now known as La Paz. The pearls are gone, but the government has started a program to redevelop them commercially. Instead of being called the Island of California, it is known as Baja Sur; instead of hostile Indians, we find hundreds of smiling Mexicans welcoming us to their beautiful beaches which boast some of the best fishing and most luxurious hotels in the world.

Our past trips to La Paz had always been the same—arrive by ship, dash for the waiting taxis for a fast trip to town for shopping and lunch, then back to the ship and on to the next port. We hadn't really seen much of La Paz on those trips, so we resolved to remedy that situation right at the start. We rented a VW at the airport and began a leisurely cruise of the area.

Our first stop was the landing where we had previously come in by cruise ship. We wanted to see it for once without crowds.

The area is called Pichilingue—a deep water cove at one end of the bay of La Paz. During World War II, Pichilingue furnished moorings for the United States fleet, but today it serves only the cruise ships that come to port occasionally. No ship was expected for several days so the place was deserted. Remembering the cacophony of vendors selling their wares, taxis honking, luggage-handlers shouting, and *mariachis* warbling for the tourists, made the silent dock seem almost ghostlike. A lone seagull eyed us suspiciously from his perch atop a piling, and a stray dog roamed listlessly along the wharf. Otherwise there wasn't the least sign of life. Our voices echoed from the walls when we spoke.

"I didn't remember this terminal building being so beautiful," I said.

"I didn't either. I guess we were always too busy with our passengers."

"Look how it was made!"

"Amazing. It looks like the building site was carved out of solid rock."

"I'll bet that originally this was just a big granite cliff sticking out above the water. Then they came in with explosives and machinery and simply blasted out a platorm in the cliff for the terminal."

Margie shivered involuntarily. "It's pretty, but I'm getting the creeps. It's kind of spooky with no one around."

"Well, we've seen all there is to see anyway. Let's go."

Just as in Mazatlán, there is an ocean-front drive in La Paz. It, too, is called the *malecón*. Leaving the ship terminal building, we drove the *malecón* past panoramic views of sparkling beaches studded with palm trees and caressed by the warm waters of the Sea of Cortez. We watched the sea birds diving into the crystal clear water and saw—for the first time in Mexico—spear fishermen wading hip-deep in the bay to spear fish. Poised motionless, with spear held high and the blue water and breakers behind him, one of the fishermen reminded me of a watercolor I had seen of a South Pacific island. Then we reached the city. It was summer—off season in La Paz—so there were few tourists. Everything seemed placid, and people moved sleepily in the heat. Like a gentle zephyr, "The Baja Feeling" encompassed both of us; time, sightseeing, and all our plans no longer had any meaning.

At the La Perla Hotel, we slouched in comfortable wicker chairs with a view of the ocean, and sipped an icy drink. Neither of us spoke. We just sat and stared, soaking up the peace and beauty through our pores. Thoughts of my recent illness, and other cares and worries, drifted away from us like jetsam at sea. There was only the lovely, flower-scented present to be savored.

The La Perla Hotel is a very old-fashioned building which has been standing in the center of La Paz for many years. Despite the ocean view, it isn't really on the beach, and we are certainly beach people. So instead of staying where we were, we made our way to the Continental hotel just outside of town. It is right on the beach, has a charming Mexican colonial atmosphere, and a beautiful tree-shaded dining patio just a stone's throw from the water.

After the bellboy had checked us into our room and departed, we discovered an amusing anomaly. La Paz has one of the best, most modern water purification systems in the world. The tap water there is probably purer than Los Angeles tap water. Yet there on the table was the usual bottle of drinking water labeled "pure." Doubtless, it had been placed there to reassure Americans wary of Mexican drinking water, and had probably been filled from the tap.

We didn't bother to unpack. We simply left our bags in the room and headed for that beautiful patio. There we remained, listening to the Mexican trio playing soft music beneath the trees and watching the changing colors of the sea until the sun went down.

We checked out early the next morning, eager to begin our new Mexican adventure, but we hadn't driven ten minutes from the hotel when Margie wanted to stop.

"Why?" I asked.

"See that building? There's something interesting going on in there."

Set back from the road was a small, innocuous building with a corrugated steel roof. The door was partially open and you could make out brightly colored cloth of some kind, and people moving about. It certainly wasn't a store of any kind.

I pulled the car beside the building and stopped. Nobody came out to greet us, so we just pushed open the door and entered. An older man and a boy were hard at work inside. The older man was spinning cotton on a spinning wheel, the boy was making rugs on a loom.

"*Buenos días*," I said to the man.

He looked up and smiled. *"Buenos días."*

Margie immediately plunged into conversation with the man, and he seemed to delight in explaining the whole operation to her. His name was Fortunata Silva, and he had been in this business all his life. The boy was his son, an apprentice, and would some day take over the entire operation. The cotton was fed into the spinning wheel in exactly the same manner as it was done by the early American colonists. The cotton threads turned out by the wheel were then dyed various bright colors in vats at the back of the building, and hung to dry. When they were thoroughly dry, the boy used the loom to make them into beautiful carpets.

We thanked him for his hospitality and started on our way again. I thought the stop was fun because it was our first chance on this trip to speak Spanish (English is used in the hotels). Margie still talks about the unique spinning wheel and the beautiful, inexpensive carpets. When we left Mexico at the end of the summer, we completely forgot to stop by again and purchase one because we were so excited about two remarkable events that had just occurred . . .

With Margie consulting maps and doing the navigation, we drove back to the heart of the city, rounded the plaza in the center of town, and made our way through crowded streets to the highway. It was two-laned asphalt in good condition, so in no time at all we had left La Paz behind and were winding up through the mountains. Every few hundred yards there were signs threatening *derrumbes* [landslides], but all we ever saw was an occasional football-sized rock in the highway. They either exaggerated their landslides, or had a most efficient road crew. But we never knew when a rockslide could occur.

Like a twisting black ribbon, the highway snaked around lush, tree-covered mountainsides and through valleys choked with luxuriant vegetation, bringing us at length to a tiny, crumbling, but picturesque little town of perhaps five hundred persons. The little houses were whitewashed adobe and the dusty streets baked in the sun. A burro nibbled grass beside the road and twitched flies off his rump.

Our travel booklet informed us that El Triumpho was a big mining town back in 1874 and shipped $50,000 in silver every month to La Paz. The mines became flooded and were abandoned in 1926, but you can visit the old smelter and mine workings.

About five miles later we came to a larger town. It definitely had the Spanish colonial look—white walls, tile roofs, a plaza, and a church. The streets were dirt, but there were a number of stores and quite a few people moving about. There was an air of prosperity about the place. Pretty teenage girls talked and giggled under the shade of a large tree on the edge of the plaza.

The city was San Antonio, at one time the capital of Baja California. It was a silver mining town like El Triumpho, which finally ran out of silver. San Antonio was the first non-Indian community in Baja because the Spaniards wouldn't let the Indians work in the mines. The city now exists on transistors. They manufacture them here. Everyone's working in the transistor business. We decided to look around.

We parked the VW and began our stroll, smiling at the girls under the tree as we passed. One of them whispered something to another, and a fresh burst of giggles heralded our visit to San Antonio. Except for the girls, the plaza was deserted. It was wall-to-wall cement, swept clean and white, and bracketed by an ornamental iron fence. There were a number of large trees creating lacy patterns of shade on the pavement, a statue of one of Mexico's past presidents, and a church built by the Spaniards a century before. As usual, the Spanish had made their church into a fortress bristling with cannons. They could say their prayers and kill Indians at the same time. It was in good repair and apparently hadn't changed any since the first stone had been laid. There wasn't much else to see in San Antonio, and there certainly wasn't any place for us to stay, so we returned to the car and continued on our way.

We didn't have to consult the map to realize we were in the tropics. The hillsides bristled with palms and other lush vegetation reminiscent of Hawaii. One particular valley had a wide river tumbling through its heartland, its hillsides fringed with palm trees, and its bottomland covered with hundreds of acres of papayas, mangoes and other exotic fruits. A small sign indicated that this was the community of San Bartolo. We stopped there and chatted with a farmer who told us that his fig trees bear fruit five times yearly in this beautiful valley. He was selling avocados at the time for four pesos per kilo, about 14.5 cents a pound.

From San Bartolo, the highway started turning toward the Gulf, and in just a few minutes we reached the top of a hill where we could look down on the Sea of Cortez and a large, beautiful bay. It was several miles long and arched like a bow. The beaches were white sand with groves of palm trees nodding gently in the soft breeze off the water. The ocean was slightly rippled and glinted by the sun, giving it the look of rumpled blue satin. It was a scene of beauty and tranquility.

Sr. Silva shows Margie Hunter how to spin yarn.

Back on the beach, Margie dries her hair after a refreshing ocean dip.

From the highway, we spotted what appeared to be a tiny settlement at the north end of the cove. We descended the hill toward the ocean and began looking for a place to turn off the highway to get to it.

The paved road Margie and I had been driving south from La Paz was quite new at that time. Prior to the paving of the road, the only access to any part of the Baja coastline was by four-wheel-drive vehicles or airplanes. Four-wheel-drive cars weren't so numerous in those days, but planes certainly were. So fishing resorts have dotted the Baja coastline for quite a few years. They usually consisted of rather basic accommodations with meals included, boats, fishing guides, and an all-important dirt landing strip. Their supplies (often including water) had to be trucked in over those impossible roads, but each weekend the flying American fishermen came winging in to stay, fish, and make the whole enterprise financially possible.

The asphalt road took a swing to the right paralleling the coast; on our left was a dirt landing strip. A cluster of buildings nestled in the tropical trees next to the strip was labeled Bahía de Palmas Hotel. We turned off the highway, bounced across the muddy landing strip, and stopped for the rest of the Summer.

The minute we had sighted the hotel there had been no doubt in our minds that this was the spot for us because it was so reminiscent of our beloved Yelapa of several years past. Like Yelapa, the hotel was set in a tiny jungle of palms, bouganvillea, plumeria, and other exotic trees and flowers. The walls of the buildings were of white adobe, and the roofs were thatched with palm fronds. Each hotel guest had his own individual "house" with a view of the ocean, and winding paths took you from your tropical abode to the tiny dining room or the cantina [bar]. The cantina was a circular palapa on the edge of the jungle looking out to the sea, and smaller palapas were scattered about the white sand to furnish shade for those enjoying the beach. It was truly a paradise.

When we entered the office to check in, we discovered other parallels with Yelapa. The manager of the hotel at Yelapa had been a young, proud father named Roberto who always had his baby son with him. Julio, the manager at Bahía de Palmas, was about the same age as Roberto, also proudly carried his baby son on his arm, and like Roberto, Julio spoke a little English. His eyes widened slightly when we told him we had come for the whole summer, but he immediately made us a special low rate. Since it was a weekday, there were no other guests in the hotel and we had our pick of all twenty rooms. We chose one of the largest, right on the beach. It boasted a fireplace (which we never needed) and a fishnet hammock strung between two uprights on our patio. It rained nearly every afternoon at four that summer, and I would often lie in the hammock listening to the rain pelting down on our thatched roof and feeling like a character in *Sadie Thompson*. At those times it wouldn't have surprised me a bit if Rita Hayworth had sauntered sexily up to my side. She didn't, of course, but Margie did some sexy sauntering that was good enough for me!

The little town we had observed from the hill overlooking the bay was Los Barriles. Our hotel was well within the city limits (if there were any!), but we didn't get around to familiarizing ourselves with the village for quite some time. We were too busy settling into our new way of life.

We discovered puffer fish quite by accident. The hotel furnishes free face masks and snorkels for the pleasure of the guests, so we went snorkeling soon after our arrival to have a look at the ocean bottom in front of the hotel. First we discovered that there was a picturesque underwater reef about fifty feet out from the high tide line. Multicolored little fish were swimming in and out of the crevices in the reef in their never-ending search for food. They seemed to have little fear of us and would allow us to swim very close before darting away. One type of fish was not brightly colored like his friends, but an innocuous brown shade that blended with the color of the rocks. One of these allowed me to approach so close that I reached out my hand and tried to touch him. He immediately sucked water into his body until he swelled to five or six times his normal size, and spines emerged from his body, sticking out in all directions! From a very typical little fish five or six inches long, he had become a football-sized pincushion. This was obviously the little fish's means of protection and was designed to discourage any larger fish from attempting to swallow him. I surfaced and looked around for Margie. She was snorkeling just a few feet away, so I tapped her on the shoulder. She raised her head out of the water.

"Honey, did you see those plain looking little brown fish down there?"

"Yeah?"

"Well, dive down and make a pass at one of them."

"Why?"

"Wait and see. Just wave your hand by him as close as you can get."

"Tell me why," she insisted.

I grinned. "I won't. Just do it!"

I stuck my head back under the water and watched. She waved her arm near one of the little fellows and he went into his prickly balloon act. I saw a burst of bubbles from her face mask and knew she was giggling. She surfaced hurriedly.

"That's amazing!" she laughed. "I'll bet you could pick one of them up when they're all puffed out like that."

"What about the spines?"

"Well, you'd have to be very careful."

"Okay, I'll try it!" I said.

That's when we discovered the chink in the puffer fish's armor. In the first place, when the fish is swelled up, it cannot swim and is completely helpless. In the second place, those deadly looking spines are fakes! They are soft and fleshy so you can grasp the little rascal with ease. We played with those cute, silly fish by the hour. We'd make one puff up, grab him, and play with him like a beach ball, tossing him back and forth. Soon he'd tire of holding all the water inside and squirt it out like a syringe. At this point he would become a little fish again and wriggle away from us. Then we'd dive and get another one.

Our days were punctuated by a loud gong that summoned us to meals three times a day. As it was in Yelapa, there was no menu here. Your meals consisted of whatever the cook felt like preparing that day. Since we were the only ones in the hotel much of the time, the cook occasionally would take requests. Then, when the food was served, he would sit at the table with us eyeing each bite and awaiting his well-deserved praise.

I have a tendency to get amnesia about unpleasant events. They absolutely disappear from my memory and I have difficulty recalling details about them even when reminded. Thus the heart attack that had made this trip possible vanished from my mind. If I thought about it at all it seemed to be something that had happened to somebody else, not me. Margie, who remembered it all too vividly, however, constantly forbade me second helpings at meals, and insisted on long daily walks along the beach. One time we went farther along the beach than usual, rounded a rocky point, and saw a cluster of buildings in the distance.

At first we thought it might be a large private home, but then we saw the ever-present landing strip and knew we had stumbled upon another resort.

Soon we could see that the landing strip was paved—an unusual bit of class for Baja. There were many large buildings, and perhaps a dozen fishing boats riding at anchor near the resort's beach. It was certainly more luxurious than our hotel, but not as atmospheric.

As we got closer, we could see three people seated on the patio in front of the large restaurant/bar. They appeared to be Americans. As we approached within earshot one of them waved.

"Welcome to Rancho Buena Vista!" he called.

"Thank you," we said, joining them.

"Care for a drink—on the house?" It was a generous offer.

A waiter was summoned, drinks were ordered, and introductions were made all around. The man who had welcomed us was the owner of this famous Baja resort and a most pleasant gentleman. Everyone called him "Colonel." His two guests were Ray Cannon, author of *The Sea of Cortez*, perhaps the most famous book ever written on the fishing in this area, and his lady traveling companion/secretary. It didn't take much prodding on my part to get the grizzled old fisherman spinning his fish stories, and it was a great thrill for me—a fan of his book—to sit on the shore of the Sea of Cortez and listen to the man who had immortalized it.

Ray's secretary had apparently just returned from Mexico City where she had a face peel, and he constantly interrupted his fish stories to comment on it.

"Look at her!" he would say, "Doesn't she look wonderful?" She would beam. "Had that face peel just a few weeks ago, and she looks ten years younger!"

True enough, she seemed to be a woman past middle age with a wrinkle-free face, pink and newborn. Moreover, his calling our attention to it didn't seem to bother her a whit. Coming from the Hollywood scene where facelifts and peels are nearly as commonplace as shoe shines but never ever mentioned, I found their frankness refreshing.

After a couple of drinks and a few hours of Ray Cannon's salty yarns there was a marked increase in the humidity signaling the coming of the four o'clock downpour; we quickly left for our hotel.

The tide had come in quite a bit during our conversations at Rancho Buena Vista, so it was necessary for us to wade through hip-deep water to round the rocky point we had traversed on dry land earlier. I was leading the way when Margie called out—

"Ben! Quick! Come here!"

I stopped. "What?"

"Come here and look!"

She seemed quite excited, so I sloshed back to her side.

"Look!" she said again, pointing to the water.

There, in the opalescent water surrounding her, was an enormous school of baby swordfish. Each one was about one and a half inches long and sported a perfect, tiny sword. They were swimming determinedly past her against the tide as if bent on some important mission.

"I didn't know baby swordfish had swords!" she said.

"Where did you think they got them?"

"Well, I thought they grew them as they got older."

"Nope. They're born with them. I ate smoked baby swordfish as *hors d'oeuvres* once in Mexico City. You hold the sword in your fingers like a toothpick and—"

"How could you do that? They're so cute!"

"Easy. They were delicious."

Then they were gone as suddenly as they had appeared, and we began our walk back to the hotel again.

Often, when the afternoon cloudburst arrived, we would make our way to the hotel *cantina*, order a couple of drinks, and chat with Hectorito (Little Hector), the bartender, until the storm passed. Hectorito, with his slight build and boyish manner, seemed about sixteen years old. Alone in the bar for most of the day, he would sit there strumming a cheap guitar he had purchased, trying to sing. He could neither carry a tune nor stay in rhythm. On top of that he played all the wrong chords. At first, it nearly drove us away from the bar, but as time went by we seemed to become inured. Splashing our way through the downpour to the snug haven of the *cantina*, his discordant sounds began to seem almost pleasant, bespeaking a few hours of interesting conversation and drinks as the raindrops fell.

Hectorito knew the English words for various drink orders and could make change in dollars or pesos, but otherwise spoke only Spanish. Since we could speak Spanish with him, we had long talks on those rainy afternoons and became friends. On weekends when the American fishermen arrived, we acted as Hectorito's interpreters.

A fisherman would say "Hey, gimme a whiskey sour."

"Yes sir," Hectorito would say, and proceed to mix it expertly.

"How long do you think this rain's gonna keep up?" the fisherman would ask.

Hectorito would just look at him blankly. Then we would explain that he only understood "booze-English" and interpret the question for him.

The other denizen of the *cantina* was an ancient Mexican dog. His pedigree was unidentifiable; he was overfed, round as a sausage, and spent the entire day snoozing on his belly with his legs spread-eagled.

One time when we were alone with Hectorito, he told us he would show us something very funny. First he cautioned us to be quiet. Then, suddenly, in a loud, excited voice he shouted, "*Cachora! Cachora!*

Cachora!"

The fat old dog leaped unsteadily to his feet, his sleepy eyes rolling in his head, and began to dart madly around the room looking this way and that as if he were being chased by a swarm of bees. It really was a funny sight. Finally his ancient engine ran down, and the old fellow flopped on the floor and went back to sleep.

"Will he do it for us?" I asked Hectorito.

"For a certainty."

I tried it. "*Cachora! Cachora! Cachora!"*

The whole comic performance was repeated.

At the time Margie and I assumed that "*Cachora*" was the dog's name and that was the way he reacted to being called. Later we looked up the word and found that it means "lizard." The dog was chasing an imaginary lizard! We had lots of fun the rest of the summer sending the animal on his frenzied lizard hunt. I told Margie it wasn't cruel because it was the only exercise the poor old thing ever got.

The first clue we had that Hectorito was older than sixteen was when he started telling us about his wife. Her name was Lupe, a school teacher in a nearby town; she was beautiful, and had red hair!

"*Pelo rojo!"* I said teasing him, "Mexicans don't have red hair!"

"Ah but my wife does, Benito, and she is most beautiful!"

"That is something I must see, Hectorito."

"Very well," he said, "you and Marshe will come to my house for dinner and you will meet my beautiful Lupe."

A date was set for the following week.

This was when Margie and I realized that we hadn't even looked over the town in which we were living. We decided to take our daily walks in that direction.

The town of Los Barriles consisted of thatched-roof houses, most of them with dirt floors, scattered about among the palms on the edge of the beach, and in the low hills back of the hotel. There was no business section and no plaza. Those who were in business simply hung a sign proclaiming the nature of their business on the front of their house. The other citizens seemed to be fishermen, farmers, or employees of the hotels.

All Mexican communities, no matter how small, have an *abarrotes* store. These are general stores which sell everything from basic food needs to clothes and tools. The one in Los Barriles was fairly large, well-stocked, and had wood floors. We chatted with the elderly Mexican woman who owned it and she claimed that the hotel had been built illegally on her land. She said she owned the land through an old Spanish land grant and that some day she would hire a lawyer and reclaim it. Then the hotel would be hers, she said. We listened politely, but didn't believe her.

In the center of this haphazard sprinkling of tropical houses was a small cement block building about ten feet square with a large cement pad in front of it. From a distance it appeared to be a public lavatory and we fully expected to see the customary signs on the doors—*Damas* and *Caballeros*. However, as we got closer we saw there was just one sign on the building. It was old, split and faded by the weather, but it proclaimed proudly in large block letters: Palacio Municipal.

"Now what in hell does a little burg like this need with a City Hall?" I said.

"And what does the City Hall do with this cement pad?" Margie added.

We had no sooner spoken when the door opened and a Mexican sauntered out and leaned against the door jamb eyeing us levelly, his arms folded across his chest. He was middle-aged and rather distinguished looking with tight, curly gray hair. His manner was definitely proprietary.

"I'll bet that's His Honor the Mayor," I said. "Let's go talk with him."

We crossed the cement pad to the door where he was standing.

"No spik Ingles," he said for openers, without a smile.

"*Podemos hablar poquito español,*" (We can speak a little Spanish) I answered. He still didn't say anything, so I rushed on. I told him we were staying at the hotel for the summer and how much we loved Mexico and especially Los Barriles, and how pleased we were to meet the mayor of this beautiful city.

"*Gracias,*" he said. He was a man of few words.

"How do you use this cement pad?" Margie tried.

"*Bailes.*" [For dances.]

"They are city dances?"

"*Sí.*"

"How often do you have them?"

"*Todos los meses.*" [Every month.] He then said there would be a dance a week from Saturday. He seemed to be warming to us (and the subject!) He even showed a partial smile, asking us to attend.

"We are invited?" I wanted to be positive he was extending an invitation.

"*Sí. Cinco pesos.*"

"*Gracias, señor,* we will be there," I said. I was beginning to get the

164

picture of how the mayor's salary was paid.

"*Por nada.*" He actually smiled. He tipped a non-existent hat and re-entered the building, his official mayoral duties done.

"Having a monthly dance sure beats the hell out of paying property taxes," I said as we turned back to the hotel.

"I think the dance will be fun." Margie replied. Neither of us realized then what was in store for us at that dance.

Hectorito had invited us to dinner on a Saturday evening because the beautiful red-haired Lupe would not be teaching school that day. (His inseparable pal, Elodio, would tend bar for him during his absence.) It was sunset, the afternoon rain had cleared the sky, and the tips of the palm fronds were tinged with orange and gold as we started the walk toward Hectorito's house. We had only gone a short way when we saw a charming and fascinating sight.

One of the American fishermen at the hotel had caught a large marlin that day and, having no use for it, had given it to the city of Los Barriles. The large swordfish had been laid atop a flatbed truck and the little children of the town had gathered around it, chattering and playing. Soon the man of the hour arrived. He was the one delegated to cut up the fish and distribute it. Seriously he climbed onto the truck and stood there for a moment studying the task before him. Then, as he bent to his work, the children fell silent, watching and waiting.

Like a skilled surgeon, he deftly made his first incision with a razor-sharp boning knife. Then, seemingly satisfied with this first cut, he began to wield that knife with astonishing speed and precision—so fast at times that the shining, curved blade was just a blur! In only moments the head and entrails disappeared and a large swordfish steak emerged. Another quick turn of the knife and he had cut a handle in the meat so a child could carry the steak like a valise.

"*Paco!*" he called out.

A tiny little boy with snapping black eyes ran up to the truck holding up his arms. The chunk of fish, half the size of the boy himself, was handed to him. Then holding his steak by the specially carved handle, the little fellow scampered for home. Another large steak with handle appeared.

"Angelina!"

A little girl wearing a freshly-ironed dress, her shiny black pigtails tied with orange yarn, came up to the truck. She was handed her piece of fish and off she ran.

And so it went. One by one each of the waiting children was given his family's portion of the fish. As in the Biblical story of the loaves and the fishes, the supply seemed inexhaustible. At length it had been distributed equally and the children were gone. The champion with the boning knife stuck it in his belt, clambered down from the truck, and headed down the beach with a large piece he had saved for himself. The generosity of the American fisherman provided many meals in Los Barriles that week.

Hectorito's house looked like all the others. It was nestled among the trees and consisted of one large room of adobe walls with a palm-thatched roof and dirt floor. This room was just for sleeping and eating. The kitchen consisted of an adobe oven and grill set between the trunks of three large trees apart from the house. The oven looked somewhat like a kiln, and was the source of delicious homemade breads. Everything else was cooked on the grill. The source of heat was, of course, a wood fire. The ever-present outhouse was secluded in brush at the back of the property.

Hectorito spied us coming down the path and ran out to greet us.

"Benito! Marshe! *Bienvenidos!*"

"And where is the beautiful red-haired wife?" I asked.

"She prepares the dinner. Come! You shall meet her!" He led us across the yard to the oven between the trees.

"Lupe, *están aqui!* They are here!" he shouted.

She turned away from the stove and greeted us graciously. She wasn't shy, as so many Mexican girls are. She seemed to have a poise and wisdom beyond her years—a contrast to the youthful, ebullient Hectorito. And she was lovely, indeed. Her eyes were wide-set and a deep, velvety brown. Her hair hung loosely below her shoulders, shiny— and black as a raven's wing.

"Hectorito told us your hair is red," I said after introductions.

"He always says that," she smiled.

"But it is!" Hectorito insisted. "Come!" He grabbed Lupe by the hand and pulled her out of the shade. *"Fijase!* Observe, Benito!"

The orange rays of the setting sun shone on her beautiful hair, and here and there I could discern an auburn gossamer glinting midst the black.

"For a truth she has red hair!" I said.

Lupe smiled at Hectorito indulgently. "Now, if we've had enough of this, I will return to the dinner."

"And I will help," Margie said.

Hectorito and I opened two cans of beer and chatted while the women put dinner on the table. He revealed that he was actually twenty-six years old, Lupe was twenty-five, and they were expecting a baby (their first) in eight months.

The dinner was typical fare throughout Mexico's working class—chopped-up beef of some kind mixed in a gravy with chilis and beans, with freshly made tortillas to sop it up. It was utterly delicious. I was amazed to discover that his home was lighted by electricity.

Hectorito explained that it is a law of Mexico that if one has more electricity than he can use, he must share it with his neighbors. In this case it was the Bahia de Palmas hotel doing the sharing. They had two large generators which supplied much more electricity than was required, so wires had been strung south along the beach, and each of the little, round palm-thatched *casas* had an electric light. With the light showing through their glassless windows, they looked like large Halloween pumpkins winking among the trees.

"You will stay for the speech?" Hectorito said after dinner.

"What speech?"

"The speech of *Presidente* Echeverria." He produced a small transistor radio.

I looked at Margie and her eyes said, "Let's go home."

"We are tired, Hectorito," I began, "and I think—"

"It is a most important speech. It is said that the president will mention Baja California," Hectorito said.

I gave in. "Well, for just a very short time."

"*Bien.*" He started getting out some more beer.

At that moment there were cries of greetings from outside the house, and the neighbors began to pour inside. It seemed that Hectorito had the only transistor radio in the neighborhood, and so had invited his friends in to hear the speech. He introduced all of them (I remembered not one name), cans of beer were passed about, and the transistor radio was placed under the electric light on the dining table like a centerpiece. It was tuned to a La Paz radio station, and happy *ranchero* music mingled with the chatter in the room. Then after a while the music broke off, there was a long pause, and an announcer said in stentorian tones:

"*Señoras y Señores, el presidente de los Estados Unidos de la República de México, Señor Luis Echeverría Alvarez!*"

Prolonged applause followed the announcement and our little group gathered quietly around the dining table to listen to the speech.

It can never be said of a Latin politician that "he drones on." He seems to regard his rostrum as a giant stage and his voice a solo instrument to be played with consummate skill. He carries his audience to great heights of emotion and buffets them with repeated crescendos which then descend to a whisper as soft as a heartbeat. His voice is rational, then frenetic,

167

then broken with emotion. He is a storm beating on the senses of his listeners as he threatens, cajoles, soothes, and pleads. He is grandiloquent, histrionic, and—I'm sorry to say—interminable. But you'll never see a Latin audience chewing gum and staring around, or lost in personal thoughts. Caught up in the magic of the speaker they listen—rapt—until the end. So it was that night. President Echeverría went on for over an hour, dramatic and bombastic from the throat of the transistor radio, but Hectorito and his neighbors sat drinking in every word.

I was not so enthralled with Sr. Echeverría's polemics, so after a few minutes I allowed my mind to wander. At first I mused at how they all stared at the radio as if they were watching television. It was almost as if they hoped by staring hard enough, they could transport themselves through the tiny speaker to the feet of the president as he spoke. Then I remembered how as a child I, too, had stared at the radio while listening to *Chandu The Magician* or *I Love A Mystery* (television was not yet invented) and I thought: "Generations upon generations are growing up staring at electronic devices."

Then as it had so many times before in Baja, the wonder of our present situation struck me. Margie and I were foreigners. Our skin color, clothes, and language were different from theirs. Their combined yearly incomes didn't equal what I earn in a week, and our way of life was completely unknown to these simple people. We were *"gringos"* from the hotel. Outsiders. Yet they had invited us to share their food and their friends. They had accepted us as equals, and were now allowing us to share what was—to them—an important part of their life. It was a rare privilege and I resolved to memorize this scene so I would never forget it. A tiny village in a Territory of Mexico—an adobe house with a thatched roof—the one electric light dangling from the ceiling, a big tropical moon peeking through a window—and our friends gathered quietly around the table rapt in the speech of their president. Then Echeverría's speech concluded and I hadn't heard a word of it. There was a rasp of applause from the radio speaker and Hectorito and his friends joined in. All agreed it had been an excellent speech and Echeverría was a fine president. He would do much for Baja. We thanked Hectorito and Lupe for a lovely evening, bid everyone goodbye, and left.

As we strolled back toward the hotel in the moonlight I asked Margie, "Did you listen to the speech?"

"Parts of it, but my mind wandered."

"Mine too. Did he say anything about Baja?"

"Oh yes, I heard that. He said he had roots in Baja and that he was going to do all kinds of wonderful things."

"What kinds of things?"

"He wasn't specific. Or if he was, I didn't hear it."

"Well, I hope he's careful about it."

"What do you mean?"

"The wrong type of improvements could ruin Baja. Can you imagine the Grand Canyon with a housing project? Or the Garden of Eden with a freeway through it?"

I didn't know how close I had come!

During that summer at Bahía de Palmas, there were two events that had a profound effect on our lives. The first of them occured during that week prior to the dance. It was the arrival of Mr. and Mrs. Jack Rudicelli and their son John.

Rudicelli was an avid fisherman who had been spending his yearly vacations at Bahía de Las Palmas hotel for some time. They were down this time for a week. Each morning the father and son would get up early and go forth in search of the wily swordfish. Mrs. Rudicelli joined them some of the time, but seemed to prefer to sleep in and just have a lazy day lounging on the beach. Then, in the evenings, the whole family would join Margie and me for cocktails in the *cantina* and we'd swap stories about Baja. They were most charming and we thoroughly enjoyed their company, but we were intrigued most of all with little John.

John was nine years old and small for his age. He had a crewcut that stood up straight as a currying brush, and wore black horn-rimmed spectacles atop his pug nose making him look like a small, brush-topped owl. He was a "gifted" child and possessed a fund of knowledge and vocabulary way beyond his years. He was the only nine-year-old I have ever known who could sit at a table engaging in conversation with adults, and fit in as well as if he'd been an adult instead of nine years old. It was almost as if the creator, in a touch of divine whimsey, had placed a college professor in the body of this little boy. His particular interest was science and he could expound interestingly on a wealth of scientific subjects. He was a skilled fisherman, like his Dad, and enjoyed all the usual boyish activities.

One afternoon, after we'd known the Rudicellis for several days, as Margie and I were spread out on the beach watching the sea, I noticed she'd been quiet for a long time. She's usually chirping happily about a shell she's found, a sea bird she's watching, or something else.

"Why so quiet and pensive?" I asked.

"Oh I was just thinking about little John."

"He's a curious little guy, isn't he?"

"Yes he is. And so smart!"

"Jack says he reads books all the time. Avariciously."

"He should be on television."

"Doing what?"

"I don't know. That's what I was thinking about when you asked." She was quiet for a few moments. "Why he could even be the anchorman on a newscast! Wouldn't that be cute? Little John with all those adults?"

"I guess. But forget it. They'd never hire a child for that—no matter how smart he is."

There was another long pause while we both stared at the ocean. Suddenly she turned to me excitedly. "Darling, I've got it!"

"What?"

"Let's produce a children's newscast! Children reporting news of interest to other children. Not adult news, kid news! Little John can be our anchorman!" She paused again. "Well? What do you think?"

"Let me cogitate a minute."

This was 1971. At this time, television was going through one of its many paranoic reversals. The cries against "violence on children's television" had become particularly strident, the FCC had laid down a few "guidelines" (which the frightened industry tends to regard as *laws*) for kid-vee, and fearful TV stations were editing "pow!" and "bam!" out of the children's cartoons. Popeye could no longer slug his villains, and Bugs Bunny had to treat his victims gently. Margie's idea was certainly a nonviolent program, and yet should have a definite appeal to youngsters because it was *their* news. News for them and about them.

Thus, a show was born. Entitled "The Elementary News" it started on the air on KTTV in Hollywood just one month later. It was an instant success and has been the recipient of numerous awards including three Emmys, and has just received the ultimate compliment. NBC decided to do a similar show in 1976, in accordance with the revered television programing formula: "If it's good, copy it."

The only sad footnote to this tale is that little John did not become our anchorman. We called him in to audition with other children, but the moment he faced a live television camera his *savoir-faire* departed like a bird taking flight, and he was too frightened to speak.

During the week before the dance we discovered the community's means of communication with the outside world. We had been away from home for many weeks by this time and Margie felt she should send some word to her sister in Los Angeles that we were okay. Letters were unreliable and there were no telephones. The Rudicellis solved that problem for us when we mentioned it one night at the *cantina*.

"Oh, you've got to meet Jack and Marie Larson," Jack Rudicelli said.

"Who are they?" I asked.

"They're a retired American couple who live down here. Jack has a short-wave radio he uses to talk to the States and he's the only means of communication in Los Barriles."

"What does he charge?"

"Nothing. He just does it for fun and to be helpful. Anytime anyone in this whole cove needs to communicate with someone else they go see Jack."

"Where do the Larsons live?" Margie asked.

"Come here," Jack said, getting up, "I'll show you."

I followed him outside the *cantina* into the moonlight, and Jack pointed south along the beach. "See that spot about half a mile south where there's a house sitting out on the bluff?"

"That big place looking out to sea?"

"That's it. That's the Larson place."

The next day we walked down the beach and scrambled up the cliff to the Larsons' house. It appeared to be a house that had started small, then sprawled in all directions as the owners tacked on additional rooms and afterthoughts. Wide windows in the front offered an unbroken vista of the sea, and flowers of all kinds in a passion to outdo each other climbed the walls, scaled the roof, and embraced the whole structure. The lot was large and a lone burro nibbled grass contentedly in the back of the property.

"Hello! Anybody home?" I called as we reached the top of the cliff.

"We sure as hell are!" called a jovial feminine voice, "Come on in!"

We entered and met Marie. She was a large woman dressed in a simple house dress, apron, and rubber sandals. She had an expansive smile and a hearty laugh that rang from the walls. I liked her immediately.

"Jack's out in the back working on our generator," she said, and stuck her head out a back window. "Jack! Company!" she hollered, then turning to us again, said, "He'll be here in a minute. How about a beer?"

"That'd be mighty nice," I said. "It was a hot walk this morning."

She poured three beers, passed one to each of us, then sat down. "It's hot everywhere today. Wind hasn't come up yet. And our air conditioner won't work til Jack fixes that damn generator. You folks from the hotel I guess?"

We said that we were and briefly explained our purpose in visiting.

"No problem, honey," she smiled at Margie, "Jack'll get you through to your sister and you can have a nice long chat." She picked up an ancient edition of *House Beautiful* and started fanning herself. "Well, what do you think of our little paradise?"

"We love it," Margie said. "It's just beautiful."

"How long have you been living here?" I asked.

"About seven years now. Jack was in the manufacturing business back in Southgate and about seven years ago he decided he'd had enough. So we just pulled up stakes, sold everything, and moved here. We've been here ever since."

"Do you own this property?"

"Oh no. You can't own property next to the ocean in Mexico. We lease the land."

"Ninety-nine year lease?"

"No such thing in Mexico. It's a ten year lease, renewable for another ten."

"Well, what happens after the second ten years?" Margie asked.

Her laughter rocked the room. "We'll be dead! That's what!" Then she became serious. "Of course if we're not dead, we'll get another ten years somehow. The Mexicans are pretty casual about that law."

Jack entered the room wiping his hands on an oily rag. He had the face and demeanor of an executive and the hands of a working man, toil-worn and calloused. Obviously a self-made man. His hair was gray, his face unlined.

"These are the Hunters, honey," Marie said. "They're from the hotel and they want to make a call to the States."

"Nice to meet you," he said, shaking hands. He spoke very softly, but his voice had authority. "I heard you discussing the lease law. You folks planning to live down here?"

"Oh no," I said, "We were just curious about it."

"Well, just this year—last April, I believe—they passed an amendment to their constitution so foreigners can own land in Mexico," Jack said.

"I didn't know that!" Marie said, "Why didn't you tell me?"

He smiled at her fondly. "You didn't ask. The way it works is this. You buy the land and take title to it. The land is then yours to use as you wish. But you don't get to keep the title in your possession. The Bank of Mexico holds the title for you in trust for a period of thirty years. They call it 'The Thirty Year Trust'."

"Is it renewable like the ten year lease?" I asked.

"I believe so—if you live that long." He clapped his hands together. "Well, what do you say we call the States?"

"Okay!" we chorused, and followed Jack out to the patio.

His transmitter/receiver covered about a third of a rickety-legged card table under the overhang of the roof next to the house. He sat down at the table, twirled a few dials, and then began to speak into the microphone:

"This is the Wahoo off the coast of Baja California calling the marine operator in San Pedro. This is the Wahoo standing by." He flipped a switch and waited.

"Off the coast of Baja?" I thought to myself. "What's he talking about?"

"Marine operator," said a feminine voice over the speaker. Jack spoke into the microphone again, placing the call. Then we heard the phone ringing at the other end and Margie's sister answering it.

"Is this Mary Lou Trimble?" Jack said.

"Yes?"

"This is an overseas call. When you are through speaking, say 'over' and then do not speak until the party at the other end has finished. The other party cannot hear you when he is speaking. Do you understand?"

"Yes I do." Mary Lou's voice sounded a little tremulous.

Then he turned to Margie. "Okay, there's your call," he said.

It was Margie's first time on a microphone and she was a little flustered. She forgot half of what she wanted to say, but at least got the point across that we were okay, having a wonderful time, and would be home in a few weeks. When she was through and Mary Lou had hung up at her end, Jack took over the microphone again and concluded the call with the marine operator.

"I have a question, Jack," I said when he had turned off the set.

"What is it?"

"What did you mean when you said you were the Wahoo calling from off the coast of Baja?"

He smiled. "The Mexicans are a little sticky about gringos having short wave radios here, so I just pretend I'm a yacht named the Wahoo. Nobody knows the difference, and it saves a lot of trouble."

We invited the Larsons to join us for cocktails that evening, thanked them, and returned to the hotel.

The hotel was nearly deserted the night of the dance as all the help had been excused so they could attend. The dinner consisted of cold cuts—

something the cook could throw together in a hurry—and then he too disappeared. Even our friend Hectorito was missing from his usual place at the bar. He had been replaced with a young boy we'd never seen before, a non-dancer no doubt! We left the other hotel guests chatting softly over after dinner drinks in the *cantina* and headed for the Los Barriles City Hall where—unknown to us at the time—a second event would occur which would profoundly affect the remainder of our lives.

As we approached the City Hall we saw at once that this was obviously a major social event in the little town. An enormous crowd had gathered, dwarfing the small cement pad used for dancing, and they were all well-dressed. Boys and girls, accustomed to swaying through the palms barefooted and free, had donned neckties, jackets, shoes, and their finest dresses. The party was in full swing when we arrived. Countless cases of beer had been stacked against the side of the building and the beer was being handed out as fast as a couple of sturdy volunteers could handle it. A rock band, which had been imported from La Paz, was ensconced atop a flatbed truck, blaring discordant music from two oversized loudspeakers. But the incongruous thing was the dancing itself. Rock band notwithstanding, the simple people of Los Barilles had never learned modern dancing! Each boy clutched his partner closely and stepped one-two-three, one-two-three around the dance floor like they danced back in the Thirties!

"Bienvenidos!" cried the mayor as he relieved us of our admission charge, and waved us into the party.

In a moment we were caught up in the laughing, shouting, dancing crowd. Someone thrust a can of beer into our hands.

We scanned the crowd for a familiar face, but they all looked so different in their party clothes we could recognize no one. For awhile we wandered aimlessly through the crowd and were just about to return to the hotel when Hectorito came charging up to us pulling Lupe by the hand. They had been dancing, and sweat was streaming down his face. Lupe's cheeks were flushed bright red.

"Benito! Marshe!" he shouted, and hugged us both.

At this moment the band (which was truly the worst I have ever heard) chose to take a break and it became somewhat quieter.

"We were about to return to the hotel, Hectorito," I said.

"Porqué? It is still early. There will be music for many hours more. Come! Let us sit down until it begins again."

We made our way over to a large palm tree and sat on the ground. "When do you and Marshe return to the United States?" he asked.

I sighed. "Our vacation is nearly over. Just a couple of more weeks."

"I never want to leave," Margie added.

"Don't leave!" Hectorito said. "Buy a lot and live here with us like the Larsons."

"That's impossible, Hectorito," I said, "I must work."

"Besides, where would we find a lot here?" Margie asked.

"Mine! You remember my house?"

We both nodded.

"It was a large lot, no? Well I will give you the other half. Half of my lot is now yours, Benito!" He grasped my hand and shook it. "It costs you nothing, and I will help you build your house."

I was stunned. Was this little guy actually offering to *give* us a piece of his property? Perhaps I had misunderstood the Spanish. "A piece of your lot is a *regalo*, a gift, to us?" I said.

"*Si. No problema.*"

"Hectorito, that is the nicest gift I have ever been offered, but I cannot accept it. If we are to have a lot in Los Barriles, we must buy it."

Hectorito looked puzzled. It was apparently incredible to him that anyone could turn down the offer of a free piece of land. "Ah, now I understand," he said after a moment, "You wish to be on the ocean like all the *norteamericanos*. Very well, you shall be!" He leaped to his feet and dashed off.

In a moment he had returned; a tall, handsome Mexican with him. "This is my friend Martín Verdugo. He will sell you a beautiful lot on the ocean."

"*Mucho gusto,*" I said, shaking hands.

"Nice to meet you. I speak English," Martín said. "You would like to see my lot?"

All of a sudden we were becoming involved in a real estate transaction. How the hell did that happen anyway! "No, Martín, I don't believe—"

Margie interrupted. "Yes, Martín, we'd like to see it."

"Very well, Mrs. Hunter. I'll meet you at the hotel in the morning." He bowed, smiling, and left.

Fortified with a few beers, the rock band began to assail our ears again and Hectorito was eager to be off dancing.

"*Qué fantastico, no?*" he shouted over the music, "Now you and Marshe will have a beautiful lot and we will build a house on it. You will never have to leave Los Barriles! But tonight we dance!"

He and Lupe began weaving their way back to the dance floor and

Margie and I slipped away from the party in the shadow of the palms.

During the many years that we had been exploring Mexico, much of our time had been spent talking about someday living there permanently. Our conversations had been mock-serious. After all, weren't many American retirees living there now? Living in Mexico was far less costly than living in the United States, and there were so many beautiful places to have a home. Perhaps we could have that home now and use it for vacations, then retire there some time in the future. Then we'd talk about what kind of a home it would be. There'd be an office for me, and a playroom for Margie's arts and crafts. We'd have a fireplace, of course, and a view of the ocean. And so it went. But we never actively looked for a place to live or investigated how it could be done. It was just a dream that was going to occur in an undefined distant time called "someday." A child will say "I'm going to be an astronaut when I grow up," but deep in his heart he knows he probably won't. Thus it was with us.

Now suddenly—just in the past week—we seem to have been propelled into taking a step. First there was the conversation with the Larsons about how land was purchased. Then tonight came the astonishingly generous offer from Hectorito to give us half of his land, and finally Martín Verdugo with a beautiful lot to sell. Perhaps what surprised me the most was Margie's ready acceptance of the invitation to see the property. Was this it? Were we about to take the step? Did all that talk about buying or building in Mexico have substance after all?

"What are you thinking about?" Margie said, "You haven't said a word all the way back to the hotel."

"I was thinking about you wanting to see that guy's lot tomorrow. Are you serious? Would you consider buying it?"

"It can't hurt us to look. And maybe . . . Well, wouldn't it be wonderful to have a vacation home here?"

I tossed and turned all night dreaming of that very thing.

Verdugo was at the hotel looking for us shortly after breakfast the next morning. "Are you ready to see my lot?" he asked.

"We sure are, Martin," I said. "Where is it?"

"On the beach just north of here. Follow me." He started off up the beach at a brisk pace and we followed. I was glad he spoke English, I thought to myself, because I could get totally lost in Spanish with words meaning "escrow" or "title insurance" and the like.

Just like an American realtor, he started selling as we walked. "You will love the property," he said, "it's beautiful. There is sweet water just below the surface. I will dig you a well and you will have your own water

176

supply."

"Would we need a generator for electricity?" I asked.

"Not necessary. You will be entitled to use the hotel's supply, but if you want your own generator I can get one for you." His pace slowed. "There!" he said, pointing. "That is the lot there."

I glanced quickly at the property and then searchingly at Margie's face. Her expression told me that Martín Verdugo had a winner.

"What are the boundaries?" she said, her eyes glistening.

He paced them off for us. Each corner of the lot was marked by a beer can driven into the ground. It was about one hundred feet deep by seventy-five feet wide. With a large lot like that we could have a good-sized house and still plenty of room for a garden. Its frontage looked out at the sea, and about two-thirds of the way back was a picturesque, gnarled tree—shade for a future patio.

"How much are you asking for your lot?" I said (It didn't really matter; I knew he'd made a sale).

"Three thousand dollars."

"We'll think it over and let you know in a day or two," Margie said, but her eyes gave her away. She'd thought it over already.

"Very well," Martín said, "I'll check with you in a couple of days. I have to be getting to work now." He shook hands with me and departed, leaving us standing on the property.

The rest of that day, and the next and the next, all of our time was spent on "our" lot.

"We'll have a big view window across the living room right here, like the Larsons," Margie would say. I'd draw the living room with a stick in the sand. "Then the master bedroom should be here," she'd say, and I'd draw it in. Back at the hotel she'd puzzle over paper and pencil drawing new plans. I was estimating costs. The house had been mentally built at least three different times by the time Verdugo contacted us again.

"We've decided to buy your lot," I told him before he asked, "We'd like to buy it on the 'Thirty Year Trust'. Now, how do we go about it?"

"Well we have to drive to La Paz to the Notary Public," he said.

"Can we go today?" Margie asked.

"Why not?"

The three of us piled into our rented VW and started the drive to La Paz.

The Notary Public [Notario Público] in Mexico is not an elderly lady with a stamp who verifies signatures. He is, first of all, a lawyer with many years of practice. Secondly, he is appointed to his position—a position of great prestige—on the basis of his integrity, knowledge of the law, and reputation. A city the size of La Paz will have only one—or possibly two—Notary Publics to serve the entire area. They are the Title insurance companies of Mexico. The notary has a huge book listing every piece of property in the county over which he has jurisdiction. The book gives the entire history of ownership of that land dating clear back to the ancient Spanish land grants. When one purchases land in Mexico he goes to the notary accompanied by the seller, and the notary checks the book to determine if the property is free of liens and tax bills, and if the seller, indeed, owns it individually. The deal is then consummated in the presence of the notary who enters the name of the new owner in the book and charges him a fat fee. All of these things Martín Verdugo explained to us as we made the sixty mile trek to La Paz.

The office of the *Notario Publico* in La Paz was not nearly as elegant as I had imagined it would be. The waiting room was almost bare. There was an ancient, time-worn desk occupied by an ancient, time-worn secretary, and some bench-like seats around the perimeter of the room. There was no carpeting on the floor, and only one picture on the wall. I've seen Mexican police stations that were more luxurious. The austerity of the place was intimidating. It seemed to imply that this Notary was a no-nonsense individual who rejected frills and dispatched his clients with curt efficiency. Martin asked the secretary if we could see him.

"The *señor* is very busy right now," she replied. "Sit down and wait." She waved us to a seat and returned to her typing.

We sat on a bench where we could see the notary through the open door to his private office. He was portly, middle-aged, and distinguished looking as befit his station in life. But his face was dour—a man devoid of a sense of humor. He was engaged in an interminable phone conversation and twirled his reading glasses nervously as he spoke. When the phone call finally concluded, he dialed another number and began another one. We waited without talking, not liking the sound of our voices echoing off the waiting-room walls.

After about thirty minutes he concluded his second call and buzzed the secretary. She then nodded briefly to us, indicating we could now enter his office. As the three of us approached his desk, I felt as if I were facing a U.S. Supreme Court Justice!

The notary listened impatiently as if he'd heard the story many times before (he undoubtedly had!)

"Your trust," he said, "must be handled through the Bank of Mexico. But I will check the land for you." He stood up, indicating that our

178

interview was at an end. "Come back at four this afternoon."

"*Gracias, señor. Hasta las cuatro,* [We'll see you at four,]" I said, but inside I was irritated. Why couldn't he have checked his damn book while we were in his office? It was only eleven o'clock in the morning and we now had to kill five hours waiting for His Highness to have a *siesta* or something and here we were practically panting to close the deal. I muttered something to this effect as we left the office.

"You will learn," Martín said, "that is the way business is done in Mexico. We never do now what we can postpone for a few hours."

We took Martín to lunch at the La Perla hotel and whiled away the afternoon sipping cool drinks and watching the boats in the bay. It was the longest five hours I can remember, but at last it was four o'clock and we returned to the notary's office. Another half hour wait in his anteroom and the secretary ushered us into the *sanctum sanctorum.*

He was studying a large book open on his desk as we entered and didn't acknowledge our presence at first. We stood hesitantly just inside the door. After a few moments he looked up, waved us silently into chairs, and resumed reading. Then we sat, waiting and listening to the large clock on the wall above him tick-tock the minutes away. Another five minutes or so and he sighed, closed the book, removed his glasses, and looked up.

"The land you wish to buy, Sr. Hunter, is in the Verdugo family through a Spanish land grant. There have been no other owners—"

"*Bien!*" I said, but he shushed me with an impatient wave of his hand.

"In such cases it is necessary to advertise in the newspapers before such land may be sold."

"*Porqué,*" [Why]? Martín said.

"Because such a family as yours has hundreds of relatives all over Mexico, and any one of them may have a claim to your land. They must renounce their claim before you are free to sell it."

I had a sinking feeling. "How many newspapers?"

"In most major cities—one newspaper in each state at least."

"What should the ad say?"

"It must describe the land accurately, give the complete family name, and ask if there are any relatives who claim all or partial ownership of the land."

"*Oy vay gevalt!*" I said.

"*Qué?*"

"*Nada*" [Nothing] I said, "Just an expression."

All three of us left the notary's office crestfallen.

On the drive back to Los Barriles, Martín attempted to convince us to just take a ten year lease on the land. In that way the advertising for relatives would not be necessary. We could still have the house we'd dreamed of.

I resisted. "No, Martín," I said, "I don't want a ten year lease when, with a little trouble, I can own the land for thirty years."

"You are going to advertise, then?"

I sighed. "Yes, I guess we'll have to. It will take some time."

"How about paying me some money to show you really intend to buy my property?"

"You mean earnest money?"

"Yes."

I gave Margie a sidelong glance, and her eyes said, "No!"

"I think not, Martín. But we have a Mexican lawyer in the States, and we'll put him to work on it as soon as we return. If all goes well, we certainly *will* buy your land."

He looked unconvinced. "As you wish."

When we parted at the hotel he said goodbye gravely. I could see in his eyes that he felt he had lost the sale.

The lovely "Baja Feeling" we'd enjoyed all summer evaporated. In its place was a feeling of urgency to return home. We had a television show to sell and the property at Los Barriles to buy. We shoved our departure date up a few days, and soon were flying back to Los Angeles, filled with anticipation.

I hadn't told Martín a complete untruth. We didn't actually "have a Mexican lawyer" in the States, but we knew of one. He had done some work for a friend of mine with financial interests in Mexico. He is a Mexican national living in Los Angeles on a visa, and practicing Mexican law from an office on Wilshire Boulevard. He has the unbelievable name of José Schnaider. Our first order of business when we returned was to visit him. We told him of our meeting with Martin Verdugo and our desire to purchase the Verdugo property, the problem with the advertising, and other details, and engaged his services to close the deal for us.

A checkup by my doctor revealed that I had completely recovered from my heart attack and was able to go back to work, so we plunged into the business of putting our new television show together.

After several months we received a complete report from Jose Schnaider on what we had come to call "our Los Barriles property." He said that the "Thirty Year Trust" law was so new that the Bank of Mexico did not yet know how to implement it. Further, there had been thousands of applications submitted, and the bank was foundering in a sea of trusts it didn't know how to process. It would be a year or more before they would finally get any trusts completed. To make matters worse, it seemed the Verdugo land had a hopeless mess of claimants. The family was so large and widespread, and so many claimed ownership, that it was doubtful Martín would ever be able to sell it to anyone. José concluded his sad report with the advice that we forget the whole thing.

Of course, we were very disappointed, but we took his advice and once again "things worked out for the best." Recently we heard a rumor that the ownership of the hotel had changed hands. Someone had claimed title to all that land (including Verdugo's) under a Spanish land grant and taken over. We remembered the old lady at the abarrotes store and wondered if she were now a hotel owner.

But the corner had been turned. We had actually attempted to buy land and build a house, and now we knew we could—and would—do it. We didn't know where or how soon, but we would have a home in Mexico.

7/ The Pigs
on the Bottom Floor

Our halcyon camper trip down Mexico's West Coast highway to Guadalajara in 1966 was still a pleasant memory, and we often talked of repeating it. In the years that had passed since that trip, we had become a little bit more sophisticated in our knowledge of camping and campers, and we realized that our first "camper" was really very primitive. How nice it would be, we thought, to take that same trip in a camper that had all the amenities—flush toilet, stove with oven, lovely decor, etc. The question was, where to find such a camper? We certainly weren't about to buy one with the "Toy" at our disposal.

Fate provided the answer in the person of a most pleasant Irishman named Bill Sullivan. Bill had invented a remarkable gadget called the Easy-off. It was a device for removing your camper from the bed of your truck. Instead of having to jack up the camper on wobbly hydraulic jacks and drive the truck out from under it, you simply turned a handle on the side of the truck and the camper slid magically off the back and eased onto four built-in legs. To mount the camper back on the truck you merely reversed the process. The Easy-off was so beautifully geared the crank could be turned without applying much strength. Even a child could do it!

We met Bill at one of the sports, vacation, and travel shows where he confided that he was most interested in promoting the Easy-off and would not be at all adverse to a little TV exposure. So a plan was born—Bill would furnish us with a beautiful, modern camper mounted on a truck with an Easy-off. We would then drive it on our big trip to Guadalajara, filming the entire adventure. When we returned from the trip, I would show the film on my program as a travelogue. The audience would enjoy it and it would show the Easy-off in action. Bill, who would purchase the film stock and pay for the processing, would also get to keep the completed film after it had been shown on TV. He planned to show it at various travel shows.

Bill held up his end of the bargain perfectly. When it was time for us to take delivery of the rig, we were absolutely delighted. The camper was brand new and the very ultimate in luxury. We oohed and ahhed over the luxuries—the hot and cold running water, the stove and oven with timer, and especially the flush toilet. This would be a lovely way to travel!

Bill had mounted the camper on his own Dodge truck. It was not a new truck (the odometer read seventy thousand miles) but Bill assured us that he'd had it thoroughly checked and it was in apple-pie condition. The tires seemed a little worn, but there was apparently enough tread left for our trip.

To give Bill a little more exposure than he had bargained for, I decided to incorporate the camper and the Easy-off into my final television show before vacation. At the conclusion of that program I explained to my audience that I was leaving on vacation for a camper trip to Guadalajara, Mexico. I then walked over to one end of the sound stage where the camper, truck, Taco, and Margie awaited. As the cameras televised the action, Margie easily turned the crank and mounted the camper on the truck. Then we all three climbed aboard, waved goodbye, and drove off into the sunset with my theme playing and the closing credits superimposed over our tail lights.

It was a late afternoon start and we knew we could never get to the border crossing at Nogales that evening; but we decided we'd drive until we got sleepy, then park beside the road and start afresh the next morning. Gnawing fried chicken and sipping coffee as we drove, our headlights stabbing out into the darkness, we had passed through El Centro at the southern extremity of the Imperial Valley when we had a mishap. We struck a chuckhole in the asphalt highway and the ancient Dodge headlights bowed their heads dejectedly—their twin beams focusing on the road about four feet in front of the car.

I was just planning to go into my handyman act and fix them when I realized that, for the first time on any of our trips, I had forgotten to bring my tool box. We'd have to find a place to pull off the road for the night, and then continue on in the daylight.

I switched the headlights off since they hindered more than helped, and we strained our eyes in the blackness, searching for some place to pull off the deserted road.

Margie thought she saw a rutted path leading off to the right, so we bumped off the asphalt, drove a few feet into the darkness, and stopped the car. Exhausted, we climbed into the back of the camper and immediately fell asleep—for about two hours. We were awakened by the deafening roar of a railroad train and the ear-splitting screech of its whistle. It seemed to be right on top of us! We both sat upright in bed.

"My God, we're parked on railroad tracks!" Margie cried.

My heart went thump! And then the train was upon us. The camper vibrated, shook, and swayed as the train passed us going fast and close— much too close—to our camper. Poor little Taco was too terrified to bark. She just cowered at the foot of the bed.

My heart was still pounding after it had passed.

"Maybe we'd better move the camper," said a terrified Margie.

I thought a minute. "I'm too tired. Besides, the train missed us and all trains are the same size, so if there are any more, they'll miss us too! Let's go back to sleep."

At least four more huge freight trains roared past us in the night, jarring us awake, shaking our camper like a leaf in the wind, and leaving us with our fearful hearts pounding. When we finally arose at five the next morning we were still exhausted and felt as though we hadn't closed our eyes all night. While Margie started the coffee, I stepped outside to give Taco a stroll, and see how close to those tracks we really were. To the unaided eye it appeared there was no way a passing train could have avoided ripping off the side of our camper. Those hurtling freight cars had been just inches away from us. I forgot to tell Margie these things because when I came back inside she was vomiting in the sink.

At such times I feel so helpless. I want to be a doctor with a quick-acting remedy; I want to be sick for her; I want to show her I understand how she feels; to make it go away. But I can do nothing.

"Oh baby, poor baby," I said, stroking her back.

"Leave . . . me . . . alone!" she gasped between spasms.

Finally the retching subsided and she fell, spent, into the bunk, swallowing hard and staring at the ceiling.

What a hell of a way this was to begin a trip! I sighed and poured myself a cup of coffee.

"Don't drink it!" she said suddenly.

"Why?"

"That's what made me sick."

"The coffee?" I touched it to my lips and tasted. It had a nasty, medicinal taste. I spat it out. "My God, that's awful! No wonder you got

185

sick."

As Margie rested, I puzzled over the coffee. There certainly couldn't have been anything wrong with the newly-opened can, so it must have been the water. I drew a glass of water from the tap and tasted it. The same nasty taste. The answer dawned on me. I remembered reading somewhere that when a camper is new you should fill and drain the water tank several times before actually using it. This gets rid of the chemical coating on the inside. This was a brand new camper and the water tank had never been treated! I explained all of this to Margie and we decided that before we crossed the border we'd have to drain and fill it several times—we'd treat it with baking soda too, to be sure.

Soon Margie was her old self again. We skipped coffee, had cold cereal and milk for breakfast, and departed our unfortunate campground (the water tank draining as we drove).

Within a hour we ran out of gas.

It happened in an archetypal manner. We knew we were low on gasoline, but when we passed a gas station it wasn't the kind for which we carry a credit card.

"I don't want to waste our cash on gasoline north of the border," I said, "There'll be another gas station in a few miles where we can use one of our credit cards."

So we kept going, but no more stations appeared. The tank was getting lower and lower. Surely there'd be a station around the next corner. Nothing. The needle had been on empty for some time and that awful feeling of impending disaster began to creep up within us; then the engine coughed and we coasted to the side of the road. Now there was only silence—except for the happy chirp of crickets who know nothing of failing headlights, roaring trains, polluted water, and empty gas tanks.

Which direction to hitchhike? We knew there was one credit-cardless station many miles back, and we didn't know how far we'd have to continue in this direction to find one. We discussed it briefly, and decided that the odds favored a gas station soon—straight ahead. I left Margie and Taco sweltering in the Imperial Valley heat, took up my position on the road, and extended my thumb. Fortunately, I was picked up by a friendly local citizen who informed me that there was a gas station just five miles down the road. For once, something had worked out right!

The gas station not only accepted one of our credit cards, but the owner very kindly offered to drive me back to the camper in his car so I wouldn't have to hitchhike with a can of gasoline. Soon we were back at the station filling the gas tank completely, and refilling the drained water tank.

We decided not to have the headlights fixed. It's dangerous to drive Mexican highways in the dark anyway. On the way to the border crossing at Nogales, we emptied and refilled the water tank several times until the water tasted sweet, and I purchased a screwdriver and pliers to compensate in part for my missing tool box. We also purchased the all-important insurance at the border. (Mexican public liability insurance is required by law in Mexico. Without it you go to jail if you have an accident—regardless of fault.)

Things were going better now. We arrived at the border in pretty good spirits. The Mexican border guard waved us through with a smile and we headed for the MEX-INSUR office on the other side. As I pulled the camper up in front of the office and parked, there was a loud wrenching sound followed by a sickening crunch!

"What now!" Margie said.

I didn't answer. I just slid out of the cab for a look. Unaccustomed as I was to maneuvering a camper with its superstructure over the cab, I had misjudged the height of our rig. The top right corner of the camper was badly smashed and the insurance agent's sign was dangling by one ear.

Margie got out of the car on her side and gazed at the damage. "His sign was lower than you thought," she said unnecessarily.

"Well it could have been worse. We'll pay the man for his sign, and we'll have Bill's camper fixed when we get home."

The insurance agent was very understanding. "Don't worry about it." he said in perfect English, "I needed a new sign anyway."

We bought slightly more insurance than we needed.

That formality completed, we passed through the city and began the long, hot trek across the Sonora desert. Several miles out on the lonely desert, we began to notice that the car's clutch was slipping, but not badly enough that we couldn't continue.

Normally, the simple act of entering Mexico and pointing the nose of the camper toward a new adventure would have brought on the "Baja Feeling." But such feelings of love, languor, and carefree abandon are greatly inhibited by worry over failing mechanical devices and by responsibility. We had both. The annoyance of the slipping clutch seemed to warn of impending trouble, and we were attempting to film a travelogue.

Making a professional motion picture consists of much more than just squeezing off shots of interesting sights. For instance, transitional scenes must be filmed to show how you arrived at that "interesting sight." Other "takes" must create the impression of a lapse of time. The shots must be made from several angles so you can choose the one that looks best when you're editing the film. Thus, we were forever stopping the truck and dragging the heavy camera and tripod out in the desert heat to film the camper passing by. Being "camera person" out there in rattlesnake heaven became the task of my long-suffering, ever-patient wife. Meanwhile, I coaxed the complaining truck with its slipping gears into the drive-by. It was time-consuming, and it *wasn't* fun. The "Baja Feeling" was so buried, it was almost forgotten.

After several hours of filming our way across the desert, I was feeling par-boiled in the hot cab of our truck. My "camera person" wasn't too thrilled either. Dripping perspiration from every pore in her body, she trudged back to the truck and announced, "I've had it! I'm hot and tired and thirsty and I'm *not* going to work that camera once more today!"

"We've probably got enough transitional footage anyway," I replied, "and I'm really beginning to worry about this damned clutch."

Looking like she's just had a sauna with her clothes on, Margie slid wetly in beside me and we continued driving. The highway began a steep climb upward to the top of a desert bluff and curved around its brow. Just as we started around the curve, the rear tire blew out with a loud boom, and the car went out of control. The wheel spun in my hands as if it were alive and the camper began to sunfish back and forth on the narrow curve, threatening to plunge fifty feet below to the rocks, cacti, and snakes. Strangely, there wasn't a sound in the cab except my breathing as I fought the careening camper. It had happened so suddenly, and startled us so that the adrenalin poured into our blood and brought about a superficial calm. When I finally wrestled the car to a stop on the edge of the cliff, I began to tremble and Margie began to sob. After a couple of minutes we got control of ourselves.

"Well, here's where the Easy-Off pays for itself," I said. "It would be terrible trying to change a tire when you had to jack up both the truck and the camper. But we'll just remove the camper with the Easy-Off and change the tire."

Margie sighed. "Filming it, I suppose."

"I'll film it, Darling. You turn the crank to remove the camper. It'll make a nice scene for Bill."

"I'm beginning to think we don't owe him a damn thing!" she said bitterly, but she complied.

First I filmed the tire, which had been wiped out. It consisted of a few shreds of rubber clinging to the bare rim—great chunks of the tire strewn along the highway behind us. Then I took footage of Margie and me looking at the remains in consternation (you do this by setting the camera on the tripod and letting it run free while you walk into the picture. The looks of "consternation" came naturally!) Next, I filmed Margie turning the crank as the camper moved easily off the truck bed and dropped its four legs onto the hot asphalt.

"Now, get a shot of me loosening the spare tire," I said.

Wordlessly she got behind the camera.

The spare tire was mounted up underneath the bed of the truck. With the camera whirring, I slid on my back underneath the tilting truck and fumbled with the bolts that held the tire in place. At first they resisted my efforts. Then they let go suddenly and the heavy tire came crashing down on top of me, smashing my finger. I screamed in pain and leaped out from under the car, blood spurting all over my shirt.

"Son of a bitch!" I shouted. "Oh son—of—a—bitch!"

Margie grimly filmed every bit of the action and zoomed in tight on my face for the lipreaders.

I was really getting negative vibrations from her. In fact, I could read her mind. She was thinking, "Why did I ever come on this trip? I'd be happier at home without the filming, and a truck that doesn't work right." Further, I was worried about Taco. Taco had gone on a sniffing expedition and strayed quite far away. If she were bitten by a rattler that would be all we needed.

After Margie had bandaged my finger, I said, "Honey we don't have to do any more filming now. Why don't you call Taco, and the two of you get inside the camper where it's cooler? You can mix yourself a drink and enjoy the desert scenery while I change the tire."

She whistled to Taco, who joined her at once, and climbed into the camper without a word. I went to the cab of the truck to get out the tire changing tools.

They weren't behind the seat on the passenger side.

They weren't behind the seat on the driver's side.

They weren't under the seat.

The hood! Some trucks carry tools under the hood. Frantically I raced around and raised the hood of the truck. No tools. I couldn't believe it! I looked in all the same places again.

The second time around, I saw the brackets that were intended to hold the jack and lug wrench. They were empty. It was an inescapable fact. Bill had loaned us his truck unequipped with tire-changing tools! We were stuck. Stuck in the middle of the Sonora desert, with one hundred and ten degree heat bouncing off the black asphalt highway, and we hadn't seen another car for hours. Two vultures circled overhead and came to rest on the bluff overlooking us.

Margie was sitting glumly sipping a tequila over ice when I entered the camper.

"Tire changed already?" she said looking up. Then, seeing my expression, asked "What's the matter?"

I grabbed the tequila bottle viciously and poured myself a straight one before I answered—"There are no tire-changing tools in the truck." I tried to sound calm, but I'm sure there was an edge in my voice.

"I see!" Her voice was like steel. "What do we do now?"

"What can we do? We wait for help, that's all."

"Ben, that could be hours and hours . . . maybe even tomorrow."

"I know. But at least it's a little cooler inside the camper, and we have supplies for several weeks."

She didn't answer. She just looked morose.

And so we waited—mostly in silence—for help. After nearly an hour Margie thought she heard something.

"It sounds like a car approaching from way off," she said.

I listened, but couldn't hear a thing. I climbed out of the camper to listen better.

I heard a sound like the shaking of seeds in a gourd—a rattlesnake's warning—nearby, but that was all. Shading my eyes from the blinding sunlight, I stared intently across the desert, but could only see the sun devils dancing on the landscape. The two vultures were still waiting patiently on the bluff above us. Then suddenly I thought I saw a tiny, black dot moving on the highway in the distance!

"Margie, hand me the binoculars," I said. She passed them out the door.

I put the binoculars on that little dot. Sure enough! It was a Mexican truck of some sort. Now, if they'd only stop for us!

Soon I could hear it plainly and make out its shape. It was a big truck which appeared to be carrying livestock of some kind. As it began grinding its way up the hill toward the curve where our stricken truck and camper perched, I began waving frantically. Slowly it approached, pulled past us, and stopped on the road just ahead with a blast from its air brakes. It was carrying livestock alright. Pigs. Dozens of them. The huge bed of the truck was divided into three floors and the swine were grunting and shoving each other on each of the three floors. Two Mexicans slid out of the cab and approached.

"*Que pasa?*" one of them said.

"*Mi llanta,*" [my tire] I answered, gesturing toward the tire. "*Y no tengo un gato.*" [I don't have a jack.]

"*Tenemos,*" one of them said, went back to their truck and returned a moment later with a heavy truck jack.

"*Oh gracias!*" I said, and reached out to grasp it, but the man continued walking past me to my truck and started jacking it up. Apparently he was going to change the tire for me.

During our brief exchange, Margie had come out of the camper and stood with me, watching. The other man joined his friend.

In no time at all they changed the tire, and our truck was ready for the road. I thanked the men and offered a five-dollar bill.

"*No señor,*" one of the men said, "*El gusto es de nosotros.*" [The pleasure is ours.]

"But you both worked hard," I protested in Spanish, "and a man should be paid for his work."

"Our pay is for driving the truck. On the desert the *ayuda* [help] is free." They turned to go to their truck.

"*Momentito!*" I cried. "Since you will not allow me to pay you, please permit me the pleasure of buying you a beer at the next city."

This they could accept. With a smile and a "*gracias*" they took the five dollar bill, climbed in the cab of their truck, and pulled away.

"You know what?" Margie said watching them depart.

"What?"

"You and I are just like the pigs on the bottom floor of that truck."

"Why?"

"They get crapped on by all the others."

We cranked the camper back aboard our truck and, with gears grinding and slipping, were once again on our way.

The highway completes its desert crossing at the beautiful port city of Guaymas. Normally, it is about a six-hour drive from the border, but with the filming and the breakdown, it had taken us about eight or nine hours. It was nearly dusk on a Saturday night when we pulled into Guaymas, so there was no way to purchase a tire or have the clutch fixed until Monday. Because of our various misfortunes, we were already behind schedule, so we decided to keep going and pray that our balding tires would stay intact and the clutch would continue to function until we reached Mazatlán.

Atop one of the highest hills in the city of Guaymas stands an ancient Spanish fortress in excellent condition. By climbing two stories of precipitous stone steps you can walk its rampart, and gaze out on a panoramic view of the city and its natural harbor dotted with fishing boats at anchor. We were driving past it on our way out of town when we saw a delightful sight—little children using old boards as sleds, sliding down the steep stone steps to the street. A child would climb to the top of the fortress with his board, throw it down, and fall atop it on his stomach. Then with a loud clickety-clack, child and board would begin the descent. Since it was so steep they would be going pretty fast by the time they hit bottom; the board would nose into the hard dirt and the child would go sprawling! Then it was up to the top and over again. There must have been fifteen or twenty children playing this game.

"We've got to have a picture of that on our film!" Margie said delightedly.

I was glad to see my camera assistant back on the job again, so I stopped the car and set up our motion picture company. We told the children the movies were for *Norteamericano* television and they were delighted to perform. Despite the fast fading light, we got great closeups of gleeful, grubby little faces descending the improvised sled-run.

As we worked making setups, takes, retakes, closeups and cover shots, I mused about the difference between Mexican children and American children. Mexico, a poor country compared to the United States, cannot afford luxurious playthings for any but a very few of its youngsters. Children like these invent their own games using a piece of board or some discarded junk item and seem to have just as much fun as our kids—possibly more. I remembered Pedro Camacho's children, how my peanut disappearing act had thrilled them, and how they'd laughed at Margie's game of spitting the watermelon seeds in a hole scooped out of the sand. I thought about my childhood; I remembered the coasters we made using a two by four board and a roller skate and the exciting games we had with milk bottle tops. Those were depression days, and toys were hard to come by. Then I thought of today's toy stores full of wondrous dolls with elaborate wardrobes and mechanical toys that whirr and buzz and move with lights flashing ("Batteries not included"), and I thought that perhaps with the affluence we have in our country we have lost some true values somewhere.

"What were you thinking about?" Margie asked as we drove away. "You never said a word the whole time we were filming."

"I have a friend who says that the phrase 'Batteries not included' may come to be a symbol of our entire society. He's probably right."

Once again we were driving a Mexican highway in the dark—

192

something we'd sworn we'd never do again. And this time we had no headlights! I stared grimly into the deepening dusk, trying to find another place to pull off for the night.

The highway south of Guaymas, like all Mexican highways, does not have a so-called "soft shoulder." It is two lanes wide, and where the asphalt ends it pitches straight down ten feet or more to a deep ditch. Attempting to swerve off these highways can upset a car or leave it standing dangerously on its nose. Every few miles a dirt road branches off the highway providing the only exit. It was such a dirt road we sought as we crept slowly along in the darkness. Now and then, a giant Mexican truck and semi- would hurtle past us going the other direction. Its headlights would be blinding, and the wind generated by its passage would buffet our camper, threatening to throw it in the ditch. I'd freeze on the wheel as I saw it coming, and hope for the best. It was nerve-racking.

After what seemed an interminable length of time, Sharp-eyes thought she spied a dirt road leading off to our right in the blackness. "Now, I'm not *positive*," she said, "so go very slowly and if you feel us heading down into the ditch, stop!" A brilliant piece of logic.

I came to a full stop on the highway, turned in the direction she was pointing, and slowly inched the front wheels off the asphalt. They didn't start downward. So far so good. Now just a little farther, and then a little farther. We both breathed a sigh of relief. It was a dirt road all right. I drove it another fifty feet, stopped the car, and we climbed into the camper. It was pitch black outside. We again eased our nerves with a couple of tequilas. Margie made us our first camper dinner of the trip, we played cards for awhile, then retired.

We were awakened at five the next morning by Taco's snarling. It was her very low, resonant one—a kind of vibration that you can feel in your belly. We knew the sound well. It meant, "There's something amiss outside, and I don't know what it is."

We pressed our noses against the camper window above our bunk and peered into the darkness.

"Do you see anything?" I whispered.

"No. Do you?"

"No."

Then a shadow moved across our line of vision. "*There!* Do you see him?" Margie whispered.

"Yes."

Taco's snarl got louder and Margie reached over, clamping her jaws shut and reducing the snarl to a buzz. He was a *campesino* [peon] wearing white shirt and pants, sandals, and large sombrero, and he was staring at our camper. As the morning light turned the scene to gray we could see him more plainly. He had a large, black mustache. There was water flowing in an irrigation ditch nearby and he made his way over to it, kneeled down, and began splashing the cold water on his face.

"I know," I whispered, "he's been in Guaymas having a big night on the town and now he's on his way home. The water helps the hangover."

"Well, if that's the case," Margie said in a normal tone, "let's get up, have some breakfast, and get going."

We scrambled out of bed to start our day. I drank some juice and donned my clothes while Margie started the coffee. By the time this was done, it was quite light outside so I stepped out to see if our "friend" was still there.

He was still with us alright. In fact it's more accurate to say we were still with *him*! In the pitch blackness the night before we had parked our camper smack dab in the center of his vegetable garden. As I stepped out of the camper, followed by Taco, he was hoeing his garden and humming happily—unconcernedly—to himself. His tiny house was set back from the garden about twenty five feet, and his señora was starting her morning wash.

"*Buenos días,*" I said, attempting to frame an apology in my mind.

"*Buenos días.*" He didn't look up. Just kept on hoeing.

Taco, who doesn't usually take to strangers, ran over to him wagging her tail furiously. He stopped and petted her.

"*Un bueno perro,*" [a good dog] he said.

"*Gracias.* I regret it that we parked in your garden last night."

"*No le hace,*" (It doesn't matter) "The plants will grow. The dog is *francés?*"

"*No. No es francés, es una cruza.*" (Not a French poodle, a mongrel)

Adding insult to injury, Taco broke away from him, squatted over one of his radishes, and fertilized it. I pretended not to see it. "We'll be leaving soon," I said.

"*No le hace,*" he said again.

I called Taco from her bathroom activities, and we got back in the camper. Margie had overheard the whole coversation.

"I just fixed us cold cereal," she said, "so we can move out of his yard as quickly as possible."

We gulped the cereal, washing it down with coffee, locked up the

194

camper, climbed into the cab and started the engine.

"*Adios!*" I called out the window, "and *gracias* for the parking place!"

"*Por nada,*" he replied, and continued working.

With the gears slipping worse than ever, we started down the highway again, the sun blazing through my side of the cab.

The fan belt broke after we'd driven about an hour.

We'd been talking through the next scene we would film and hadn't heard the characteristic snap followed by the flop-flop-flop. The first we knew something was wrong was when the car started to heat up. Fortunately, there was a place where I could pull off the road, so I stopped the car and raised the hood. My heart sank as I gazed at the naked fan belt pulley. We couldn't move another inch without a fan belt—it would burn out the engine. I thought of the Toy resting in the quiet darkness of the garage at home. It always carried extra fuses, wires, oil filter, jumper cables, my well-stocked tool box, and—especially—a spare fan belt, and I cursed this ailing Dodge and my own shortsightedness in not checking it out before we left.

"Fan belt?" Margie asked, leaning out the window.

"Yup. No truck full of pigs can help us now."

"What'll we do?"

"We can hitch-hike to the nearest city and buy one. Or maybe a 'Green Angel' will come along."

"The Green Angels" is a name bestowed on the highway patrol branch of the Mexican Department of Tourism by grateful American tourists. "Green" because their pickup trucks are all that color, and "Angels" because the Tourism Department keeps them patrolling the Mexican highways to assist stranded American motorists. They carry spare parts, gasoline and water, all available at cost to Americans. Their drivers are skilled mechanics who speak some English.

"A Green Angel might not come along for hours," Margie said.

"That's true. But supposing we hitch-hiked somewhere and they didn't have a Dodge fan belt there? I think we'd be smarter just to wait here."

"I suppose so," she said, and sank glumly down in her seat. "What a lovely vacation *this* is."

We sat, watched Mexico wake up, and waited. The familiar sights and smells of the Mexican countryside coming alive revived our spirits somewhat, and for a time we nearly forgot our predicament. The acrid scent of a hundred Mexican fires, the vintage school bus brimming with laughing children, and the farmers tending their fields even brought faint stirrings of "The Baja Feeling." Soon, we were actually chuckling at the incredible string of mishaps that had befallen us in two days. Just then a "Green Angel" came up and stopped.

Two pleasant young Mexicans rifled through their supply of spare parts, discovered they didn't have a fan belt that would fit our car, and told us they'd return with one in about an hour. As we watched them turn around and go speeding off toward Guaymas, I turned to Margie.

"You know what I feel, baby?"

"Tell me what."

"I'm sick to death of ruining our vacation trying to make a travelogue. I say to hell with it!"

"I agree. We'll put the camera away and not touch it for the rest of the trip!"

"Right! And if we can ever get this bucket of bolts going again, we'll just find a beach and camp there."

We climbed into the back of the camper, sipped something cool, and savored the sounds of rural Mexico until the "Green Angels" returned.

Expertly, they installed the fan belt, charged us seven dollars (but refused any other money) and saw us safely off.

The clutch expired just a few miles north of Mazatlán.

It didn't go completely. We just lost high gear. I was still able to drive in low and second gear by speed shifting (you put it into neutral, race the engine, and grind it into second gear as the gears spin). We limped into beautiful Mazatlán in this manner late on a Sunday afternoon.

We decided to force our dilapidated truck as far as Sabalo Beach where we had camped before, make camp, and stay there for the remainder of our vacation. Sometime before we left we could take the truck into the city, buy a tire, and have the clutch fixed.

The beach was pretty much as we remembered it, although not quite as deserted as it had been. A few luxurious homes had been built near our favorite spot so there'd be no nude bathing, and it was plain that the city of Mazatlán was fast encroaching on our paradise. In another year or so there would doubtless be a hotel there and the pristine beauty of the beach would be gone forever. But for now—for the moment—it was ours.

We parked our camper in approximately the same spot as before, and there began several days of the life we love so much. "The Baja Feeling" returned. We played in the warm ocean, took long walks along the beautiful white beach and marvelled at a black sky sequined with myriad twinkling stars at night. The funny crabs that had eaten our coffee grounds and so amused us on the first trip had mysteriously disappeared, but in their place was a stray dog, female and timid, adopted by us and accepted by Taco. We named her "Mama," for she obviously had pups somewhere, and after many overtures and much patience were able to coax her into our camper for a meal. After that she became part of our family. Margie discovered that the seemingly white sand actually had tiny particles—the size of a pinhead—of pink grains in it. She took delight in separating the minute pink grains with her long fingernails and collecting them in a small medicine bottle. We still have that collection today.

The afternoon of the third day, the toilet ceased to function.

Our first clue to the malfunction was the sound it made. When flushing properly, the pushing of the button produced a sound like "Yum-yum-yum." Hearing that, we knew it was obediently swallowing its load and depositing it in the holding tank. This particular afternoon I pushed the button and heard only "Grrrrrrr." I raised the lid for a look and got the bad news.

"That does it!" I yelled, leaping out of the camper.

"What?" Margie was lying in the sun on a beach towel.

"Everything else was bad enough, but now the pot is busted!"

"Maybe we can fix it."

"Not on your life!" I raved, "I won't touch the filthy thing. We're going to take this mess of a rig to a hotel, check in for the rest of our vacation, and then fly home."

"Come on, Darling, calm down. It's so lovely here. Let me try to fix the toilet."

"You want to put your hands inside that thing?"

"Well I don't want to. But it's better than leaving our beach."

I relented. If she was willing to do that, the least I could do was cooperate a little and stop bitching. Using our beach bucket as a container, I dumped the holding tank and carted the unsavory contents down to the ocean. Then, with pliers and screwdriver, I removed the toilet from its moorings and brought it out on the beach where it could be worked on.

"Okay, Margie, the next move is yours."

She studied it a moment.

"Are you sure you want to go through with this?" I asked.

"Absolutely."

Then, like poking a full-blown rose into a sewer pipe, her slender pink fingernails, delicate hand, and slim tan arm disappeared into the bowels of the filthy, constipated toilet.

For awhile she just groped its dark interior.

"Feel anything?" I asked.

"I feel something—I think it's the pump—and it feels like it's clogged with toilet paper." Her hand, stained blue from the toilet chemicals, emerged clutching a handful of very used toilet paper.

Involuntarily, I made a wry face as I pushed the bucket toward her. "Put it in this."

She dropped it in and went back to her work. During the next half hour more clumps and bits of paper hit the bucket.

"I'm going to have to remove this pump," she said finally. "Get me the pliers and screwdriver."

I meekly obeyed and she went back to work. Another hour or so and the recalcitrant pot lay dissembled, its vital parts neatly spread out on the sand as if we were having a garage sale. Blue to the elbows now, she took the parts one by one to the waterfront and cleaned them in the ocean. The malfunction had occured in late afternoon, and by this time it was getting too dark to see. I brought a flashlight out of the camper and, feeling a little guilty (but not guilty enough to touch the damn thing), I lighted her work for her.

"Go get 'em, Tiger!" I said.

Sometime later, the toilet stood reassembled on the beach, clean and gleaming in the moonlight.

"Alright, it's time for the test now," she said.

"Okay, and if it doesn't work we're heading straight for a hotel."

"I agree."

I carried the thing back into the camper, filled it with clean sea water, and hooked it up to the truck's electric system. Then, as we both held our breath, I pushed the button.

"Yum-yum-yum!" said the pot. She had fixed it!

Carrying every cleaning device and solvent we possessed, Margie struggled down to the ocean to try to scrub herself clean. I opened a can of beans and a package of wieners, and prepared our dinner. I didn't want those hands of hers on my food!

To prevent a recurrence of toilet trauma we established a plastic bag to contain used toilet paper. The bag was burned each day, and no more paper was ever put in the toilet. Other than that slight alteration of our routine, the lovely days went on as before.

On Sunday we had visitors. Our coveted solitude was broken by the appearance of an ancient, garishly-painted Ford van. It pulled out on the sand just a short distance from us, and two American hippies got out. We watched resentfully as they stretched, relaxed, and sprawled on our beach, and we wondered how long they would stay.

Later that day we saw them walking along the water's edge picking up something, and our curiosity got the better of us. What were they finding on the beach that we had missed? We speculated fruitlessly and finally decided to walk down for a look. They were gathering tiny little clams. Each one was about the size of a dime or smaller and colored a different pastel hue. We had seen them sprinkled on the wet sand like bits of confetti but had ignored them.

"What are you going to do with those?" Margie asked.

"Eat them," one of the boys replied.

"How?"

"We just collect quite a lot of them, put them in a pot, and boil them. It makes a real nice broth."

Long hair and funky clothes notwithstanding, they seemed to be very pleasant young fellows in their late teens. They explained that they were making a long dreamed-of trip to Central America on a limited budget. They were attempting to save their money for gasoline and other necessities, and this was one way of doing it. That evening we saw them sipping their broth and we resolved to try the tiny clams ourselves some day. It was a pretty good survival trick.

In the morning they were gone, but their visit had given us an idea. We decided to build a fence to keep people off "our" beach. Someone had already erected a barbed wire fence that closed off part of it, but had left an opening that we—and now the young adventurers—had used. We went on exploratory missions in all directions from our camp, picking up sticks or branches that would do for posts. Then we strained ourselves digging post holes in the Mexican sun, and planted posts all across that opening. When we were done, we had created a private beach. It worked beautifully, and no one trespassed on "our" property for the remainder of our stay.

No one, that is, but Francisco and Serge. They arrived the following evening just as we were making a snapshot of a heart-stopping sunset. They walked up the beach toward us—two very small boys carrying all their worldly belongings in knapsacks, like tiny tramps.

"*Buenos tardes,*" they said politely.

"*Buenos tardes.* What are your names?" Margie asked.

The smallest boy did the talking for both of them. His name, he said, was Francisco, and his older brother's name was Serge. Serge, he added, was very shy.

"Y *cuantos años tienen?*" [How old are you?]

He said they were ten and eleven, but they looked much younger to me.

Margie's love of all children, plus the fun of having to speak Spanish, made her continue questioning them. Francisco informed her that they were "having a vacation." Their home was in the state of Sonora and they had saved money all year long for this trip. They had used the last *centavo* they had to buy one-way bus tickets to Mazatlán and were now without money for food or return-trip tickets. They disdained any offer of help.

By this time it was dark, and as we watched the boys prepare for the night, we had to agree they were most self-sufficient. In a very short time they had dug holes in the sand and erected a shelter so strong you could have walked on it! Then they dug a fire pit and started a fire. Feeling they'd had enough of our prying questions, we retired to the camper.

But we couldn't forget Francisco and Serge. After one of Margie's wonderful camper dinners, we decided to spy on them and see what they were doing. We locked Taco in the camper so she wouldn't give us away and, feeling a little foolish, tiptoed across the sand to their shelter. There they were beside the fire, their knees drawn up to their chests for warmth, wiggling their bare toes at the embers. As they talked softly they toasted small pieces of a stale roll by holding them next to the fire with their fingers. They hadn't spotted us, so we crept silently back to the camper.

We tried to play cards for awhile, but Margie's mind was still on the kids.

"I can't stand it another minute!" she finally said. "I'm going to take them a blanket and something to eat."

"Don't give them too much, honey," I said, "they want to do their own thing. They told us they don't want any help."

At my persuasion, she cut the offering down to a bag of penny candies ("They'll need the sugar for energy.") a couple of bottles of black cherry soda pop, and a blanket. They thanked her profusely.

A last peek out the window of the camper before we dozed off revealed the tiny fire on the beach burning low, and a cool, damp breeze blowing in off the ocean. The two little boys were huddled in the blanket, sound asleep.

Early the next morning there was a polite tap at the door. It was Francisco returning our blanket with thanks. He had shaken the sand out of it and folded it neatly before bringing it back. They were going to move on to another beach, he explained. Even the shy Serge managed to mumble "*Gracias, y adiós.*" We felt a little sad watching our small friends walk away down the beach and out of sight.

We had reserved this morning for some badly-needed house-keeping and were about three hours into our chores when we heard whooping and shouting out on the beach. It was Francisco and Serge racing madly toward out camp!

"What's wrong?" I asked as they dashed up breathlessly.

"We are going to be rich! We had much luck today!" Francisco said. "*Mire!*"

He reached in his pocket and removed a complete set of false teeth! They were obviously inexpensive and rather crudely made by U.S. standards.

"Where did you get them?" I asked.

"We found them in the sand. Do you wish to buy them?"

I told him that—fortunately—Margie and I had no need for dentures, or we certainly would buy them.

The questions came tumbling out: What are such teeth worth? Where can they be sold? Would a dentist buy them? Is this real silver?

We fielded their questions as best we could and tried not to sound too pessimistic. We finally concluded that we were sure if they could find the original owner he would doubtless be very grateful and give them a reward. Jubilantly they set forth to ask all the citizens of Mazatlán who had lost these remarkable teeth.

"Good luck!" we cried after them, and Francisco and Serge were gone again—this time for good.

More lovely days slipped by. The troubles that had beset us were forgotten. I even relented and took movies of the area in the event we ever wanted to complete the travelogue. Finally, the day arrived when I decided I'd better get that truck into Mazatlán for repairs. We needed more ice too, so while I was in town I'd buy a few kilos to refresh our deluxe ice box. Margie didn't want to leave her nest on the beach, so we cranked the camper onto the sand and I departed alone. As the complaining Dodge slipped and staggered down the road I looked back and saw Margie waving and smiling from the doorway, Taco at her feet. The camper looked small and forlorn without its truck.

There was a Dodge dealer in Mazatlán, and I had no difficulty locating him. I arrived there about eleven o'clock in the morning. They informed me that repairing the clutch and headlights would take several hours and since they took a siesta from noon until three it would be about 5:30 before

I could pick up the truck. I didn't want to sit around there all day so I asked them to call me a taxi. I decided I'd purchase the ice we needed, and then have the taxi take me back to our camp. He could return to our beach and pick me up later in the afternoon. All those miles in the taxi would cost a lot of pesos, but it would be worth it.

The taxi driver proved to be a pleasant, garrulous type who flashed a broad, gold-toothed smile when he saw his fare was an American and said, "Pliz spik Inglés weeth me. I try learn."

"Okay," I said. "Our first stop is the ice house."

"What eee ise-ouse?"

"*Casa de hielo.*"

"Eet ess not possible to buy . . . how you say . . . *ise?*"

"Why?"

Dee pipe ees broken. Ees no water . . . or ise . . . een de ceety."

"Can't I get ice anywhere?" I said dismayed.

His eyes twinkled. "I have idea—I theenk." So saying, he shifted into gear and we sped away—not toward the ice house in the center of town, but toward the docks. As we drove, I saw trucks dispensing water to the housewives of Mazatlán on each street. The women, carrying buckets, were queued in long lines down the sidewalk. Each one in turn would receive her portion of water, placing the brimming bucket on her head, and walk off without spilling a drop. Walking with easy, measured gait, her back held straight, each of these women had a look of stateliness, grace, and beauty as she performed this simple act. The driver's story about the broken water pipe was apparently true.

Maneuvering through the crowded streets the cabby kept up a constant stream of chatter in his broken English. He told me his name was Antonio Rodriguez, and his wife's name was Rosa. They had four children and another on the way. Also, when he could speak English well enough, he wanted to take his family and go live in the United States where everyone made a lot of money.

I told him we made more money alright but that we also paid heavy taxes to our government, and everything costs more, so his standard of living as a taxi driver might be much the same as in Mazatlán.

"Den I learn to do someteeng else," he said, undaunted.

We pulled up and stopped in front of a fish wholesale house of some sort. You wait een dee car," he said, "I come back queek." He disappeared into the building, and I heard rapid Spanish being spoken, but I couldn't make out what they were saying. In a few minutes he returned to the cab with a large block of ice and placed it beneath my feet.

"That's great, Antonio!" I said, "How much?" I reached in my pocket.

"Ees free. Eet ees . . . how you say . . . *regalo?*"

"Gift," I supplied.

"Sí. A geeft to Benito, my Inglés teacher. Now. You like feesh?"

"Fish? I sure do."

"Okay. We get feesh." He wheeled the cab around with tires squeeking and drove out on the dock where large shrimp boats were unloading their catch. Again he told me to wait in the cab, and he strode up the gangplank to the deck of one of the shrimpers. I could see him engaged in friendly conversation with a fisherman wearing a yachtsman's cap—probably the skipper. Soon the skipper took a small scoop net, reached down into the hold containing the shrimp, and came up with a beautiful four or five pound bass. He handed it to Antonio who thanked him, bid him *adiós*, and hurried back down the gangplank to the cab. The fish was placed on top of the chunk of ice.

"Dey go after *cameron*, get feesh by meestake," he said. "Now you got time? We have sightsee een Mazatlán."

I eyed the taxi meter. Even with free fish and ice this trip was getting expensive, and we still had the long drive out to our camp at Sabalo Beach. "Better not today, Antonio, I've got to be getting back to my camp."

He had caught me checking the meter. "Dee treep ees free, Benito." He snapped off the meter setting it back to zero. "I like spik Inglés. Now we have sightsee, no?"

I sighed. "Okay, Antonio."

We drove along the huge wharf watching the shrimp boats unload, then through the large beautiful city of Mazatlán. Antonio pointed out each of the parks, plazas, and churches. Finally, we made our way out to the sport fishing dock where Americans rent boats and guides for marlin fishing, then north along the *Malecón*, with Antonio praising each of the luxury hotels that lined our route. At long last I got him on the road to Sabalo, but when we finally reached the camper it was past three in the afternoon.

"Neither of us have eaten, Antonio," I said, "so come in, meet my wife, and have some lunch with us."

After protesting politely for a moment, he agreed. He insisted on carrying the block of ice, so I carried the fish as we walked through the sand to the camper. Taco set up a terrible fuss as we walked in. After getting Taco quieted down, I made the introductions.

When the ice and fish were properly installed in the ice box, Margie made sandwiches for all of us, and we settled down for a chat.

Antonio told Margie most of the same things he had already told me about himself, and I told her about the sightseeing trip. We both told Antonio about some of our adventures in Mexico, and we inquired if he knew of any land along the beach available for purchase (we were still looking for homesites)—he knew nothing about the owners of the beach land. Our new friend listened intently as we described certain Mexican cities; he'd never been out of Mazatlán.

The time slipped away and soon it was time to return to the city and pick up the truck. This time we locked up the camper and took Margie and Taco with us in the taxi. She kept up the conversation with the talkative Antonio, allowing me to get lost in thought.

"It's happened again," I mused. "Where in the States would you find a taxi driver willing to give up a whole day's fares just to be hospitable to a couple of foreigners?" Then I thought about the truck drivers with the load of pigs who'd changed the tire for us, and all the other Mexicans we'd met who had helped us or extended their hospitality to us over the years. In the States you so often hear, "They hate and fear Americans," or "They're just after your money." It just isn't so. Not at the people-level anyway. These have got to be the friendliest, most hospitable, generous people I have ever met, I thought when the taxi pulled up in front of the Dodge dealer and stopped.

"I wait here. You see eef peek-up ees ready," Antonio said.

I went inside and checked. It was ready, so it was time for goodbyes. Margie, Antonio, and Taco were standing beside the taxi when I returned.

I spoke in Spanish this time. "Antonio you are indeed a good friend, and if you ever come to the United States you must call me. I would like the pleasure of helping you." I gave him my business card.

"*Gracias*, Benito, but eet was nothing."

"I know there is no fare, but I would like to buy a present for your wife." I handed him ten dollars. "Will you permit me that pleasure?"

"*Gracias,*" he said again, a little embarrassed. We exchanged *abrazos*, then he climbed back in the taxi and started the engine. "Goodbye Benito and Marshe, and good luck!"

We purchased a truck jack from the Dodge dealer for any future emergency and headed back to camp. We'd buy the tire another day.

After returning to the camper on the beach, we decided not to put it back up on the truck just yet. It was fun to walk into it at ground level. I just parked the truck parallel to the camper so we could hook up to the truck's electricity. Then Margie made dinner and we retired happily.

Things certainly seemed to be improving.

But not for long. The next morning dawned dark and cold, and stayed that way all day. The following day was the same. On the third day, still bundled in heavy sweaters, we decided to leave. We'd follow the sunshine and find another place to camp.

Margie took her place at the camera and I moved to the truck and grasped the handle of the crank of the Easy-Off.

"Ready?" I asked.

"Just a minute. Okay . . . rolling!"

Showing by my manner and expression how little effort it took to turn the crank, I began to wind it round and round, and the camper began to move up onto the bed of the truck. It was a remarkable device.

Suddenly, there was a loud thunk! The handle went loose in my hand. With a wrenching, groaning sound the camper slid back on the sand where it had been.

Margie came running over. "What happened?"

"I don't know." I grasped the crank again and began turning it furiously. The whole thing came off in my hand—in pieces!

"What do we do now?" asked Margie.

"Leave the camper here on the beach I guess." I continued to stare at the broken handle of the *Easy-off*.

Margie got up, entered the camper, and came back out with the Spanish-English dictionary. She started paging through it.

"What are you looking up?"

"The Spanish word for 'weld'. Here it is . . . *soldadura.*"

I sighed. "I guess that's the best answer alright. Well, let's get going and find a welder before it gets any later."

Throwing the broken pieces of the Easy-Off into the back of the truck, we climbed in and started the half hour drive into the city. An hour of driving up and down the streets of Mazatlán, and making inquiries finally convinced us that if the people of that city wanted any welding done they had to go someplace else. We knew there was little civilization of any kind north, so we got back on the highway and headed south.

We drove quite a distance and nearly passed the crudely lettered sign that said *"Soldaduria."* I jammed on the brakes and backed up to the tiny shack. Inside, you could see the welding torches and acetylene tanks, but the place was empty. Two small children were playing nearby.

"I'll ask the children where the welder is," Margie said, getting out of the car. She had walked about ten steps when she stopped, screamed, and started running for the truck, her face blanched with terror. She jumped in beside me, slammed the door, and covered her face.

"What is it, Darling? What's the matter?" She was shaking violently.

Margie's father, now deceased, was a simple, hard-working man. He was an excellent mechanic, but his education was minimal—particularly in the field of child raising—and he had three youngsters to raise by himself. When Margie was very small and misbehaved, he would shut her in a dark closet and say, "The spiders will get you!" Because of this she has always had an hysterical fear of spiders.

"I . . . I . . . nearly stepped on a . . . " she shuddered, " . . . tarantula!"

"Oh. I'm sorry, honey." I stroked her head. "I'll go talk to the little kids."

I saw the tarantula on the way to the children. He was a biggie—perhaps three and a half or four inches across. But he was just moseying along the path minding his own business, so I left him alone. Contrary to popular opinion, tarantulas do not jump at you. If sufficiently provoked, they can bite, but their bite is relatively mild.

I asked the children where the welder was, and they pointed to a man lounging in the shade of a tree across the street.

"Papa! Papa!" one of them cried, and the man got up, stretched, and sauntered across the road to where I was standing.

I showed him the sheared off pieces of the camper crank and he saw immediately what needed to be done. He welded the broken parts together and ground the surface smooth in just a very few minutes. His charge was seven pesos (fifty-six cents). Triumphant, and feeling remarkably self-sufficient, we returned to our camper with the repaired crank and installed it.

That's when we discovered another problem.

The place where the steel bar had broken was a kind of universal joint which allowed one end of the bar to move. Our welder had welded it rigid. I strained against the crank with all my might, but it refused to turn.

"Oh no," I groaned. "The damn thing isn't going to work."

Margie began to giggle.

"What's so funny?" Even as I asked, I felt laughter welling up inside me.

"I don't know!" she screeched, and laughed even harder.

It was catching. I began to howl along with her. Laughter—not often heard on this unfortunate trip—wracked our bodies, and soon we were cackling and shrieking, holding our stomachs, and rolling in the sand like idiots.

Finally, exhausted, we just laid in the sand panting, our sides aching, and tears running down our checks. Margie was the first to speak:

"Our troubles are starting to get to us, Darling." We were both hysterical by then.

"I don't care. A little laughter might be just what we needed. I'm going to try that damn crank again."

I got up and again tried to turn the handle. I discovered that by exerting my maximum strength I could make it turn slightly.

"Come over here and give me a hand," I said. "If we both turn hard enough we might make it. If it breaks again we'll just go back to the *soldaduria*."

Together we grunted and strained, moving the crank inch by inch around its axis. Ever so slowly, the camper began to move up onto the bed of the truck. Finally, completely spent and arms aching, we achieved the impossible. The camper again reposed securely on the truck bed.

"And there it stays forever as far as I'm concerned," I panted.

Margie, too tired to speak, just nodded.

"Come on, honey, I know you're tired but if we're going to leave today we'd better get started. We've still got to replace that spare tire. It's absolutely bald!"

"I know," she sighed. "None of them look so hot."

Taco, anticipating departure (as she always does) was waiting for us in the car. We climbed in beside her, took one last look at Sabalo Beach, and pulled off toward the city.

Antonio had told us that the place to buy a tire was a chain store, famous in Mexico, called General Popo, and he'd told us how to find it. As we drove, Margie looked up the word "recap" in the ubiquitous Spanish-English dictionary. The word is *recubierto*. So I was able to walk into General Popo and order *"un recubierto para mi camion"* with great aplomb.

They had one tire and tube our size in the entire store and agreed to install it immediately, so it appeared that we were going to have some good luck for a change.

But only briefly. After a few minutes the attendant returned to inform me that when the tire blew out on the highway we had lost the lock-ring that holds it on the wheel. They had no such part, he said, but would phone other stores in Mazatlán and find one for us.

We settled down for the wait. The girl receptionist at General Popo was young, cute, and—like Antonio—trying to learn English. She plied us with Pepsi and showed us the volleyball and soccer trophies the

General Popo employees had won in intramural competition, practicing her English on us all the while. The time ticked away.

At length, the attendant returned and told us there was no lock-ring of the type we needed to be found in Mazatlan.

"What shall we do?" I asked in Spanish. "Can we continue to drive without it?"

"You would like another Pepsi?" asked the girl.

And another hour passed.

Finally, the attendant returned and triumphantly announced that they had succeeded in making the needed part and the *recubierto* was now installed on our car. We were ready to go. Total cost of the tire, tube, lock-ring manufacture, and all labor was $42.92. I paid the bill and Margie, impressed by the little receptionist's unflagging efforts to keep us amused during our long wait, presented her with a purse-size vial of Arpege. She was thrilled with the gift. Then—feeling like old friends after spending the afternoon with them—we shook hands with everyone at General Popo, bid them all goodbye, and hit the highway north.

Our destination was the San Carlos Hotel—a beautiful spot about five miles north of Guaymas—remembered from our first camper trip. It was not only a beautiful hotel on a spotless, ever-sunny beach, but it marked a milestone for me. It had been at San Carlos where we'd had a flat tire on our first trip, and I had my first intelligent conversation in Spanish with the man at the Goodyear tire store. It would be good to return to this lovely spot again, have a fresh water shower, rid ourselves of this decrepit truck for a few days, and just bask in the sunshine.

We got a very late start so we just drove a couple of hours, parked beside the road for the night, and continued the next day. We completed the eleven hour drive by nightfall. The many problems which had beset us on the trip, coupled with the long drive made the prospect of San Carlos and the delights of a luxury hotel even more appealing. For the last few hours of the trip, it was all we talked about, and when we at last saw the familiar outlines of the hotel and the exquisite beach, it was like coming home—or perhaps reaching heaven! Dusty, dirty, and tired, we checked in and headed straight for the shower, reveling in the inexhaustible supply of fresh hot water. Then, leaving Taco snoozing peacefully on the bed, we enjoyed a magnificent dinner while watching the sunset and being serenaded by strolling violinists, followed by a walk on the beach in the moonlight.

You'd think after all we'd been through we'd have slept late in the

208

morning, but we awakened at six as usual. When staying in a hotel we always like to be served our morning juice and coffee in our room. Then after a quiet coming-alive period we feel better able to face the outside world. The sign on our bedside table informed us that room service began at 7:30.

"I know," I said, "I'll just go out to the camper and fix our juice and coffee there. Then I'll bring it into the room and we can enjoy it here."

"Okay," Margie said sleepily.

I pulled on a pair of Bermuda shorts, and started for our camper in the hotel parking lot. From a distance it appeared our rig was sitting at a very sharp angle. Had I been so tired I'd parked one wheel on top of a big rock or something, I wondered? Nearby the camper a gardener was manicuring an already perfect hedge bordering a flower bed bursting with color; the morning dew still on the petals.

"*Buenos días,*" I smiled at the gardener.

"*Buenos días,*" he nodded.

Then I rounded the hedge and saw the reason for the strange angle of the camper.

"I've got another goddamned flat tire!" I shouted.

"*Qué díce?*" The gardener looked alarmed.

"*Nada.*"

He returned to clipping non-existent twigs.

It was the front left tire this time. It hadn't been a blowout. Exhausted from its many years of service, the ancient, balding tire had simply gasped its last breath during the night and succumbed of natural causes. "We should give it a decent burial," I thought. Then I entered the camper and prepared our morning nectar.

I broke the news to Margie on the way to breakfast an hour later. "The pigs are back on the bottom floor," I said.

"What now?"

"Another flat tire. Front left this time."

She seemed unperturbed. "At least we're in civilization this time. We can have the hotel change it for us."

They not only changed it for us, they took the carcass of "the deceased" to some miracle worker who breathed enough life back into it so that we could use it as a spare. Civilization was wonderful indeed, but I added our second flat to the growing list of misfortunes that seemed to be attending the whole trip.

There followed several lazy days of lounging on the beach and living the luxurious hotel life. I purchased Margie a sexy new bikini in the hotel shop. It was bright pink and very brief. She looked like a lush, tanned pixie on the beach as she giggled or exclaimed over new-found shells. Life seemed lovely indeed, and San Carlos was certainly a heaven on Earth. This, we decided, would be the ideal place to build our vacation/retirement home. Locals informed us that the weather and water were always warm, yet it rarely becomes humid. Guaymas is close by for necessary shopping, and there was even a small, dirt landing strip nearby so we could fly south to enjoy our home on weekends. I resolved to resume the flying lessons I'd been taking a couple of years before, and we began making inquiries about houses or lots for sale.

The manager of the hotel was an American who seemed to be interested in selling us a lot. The lots he showed us were right on the bay just south of the hotel. They were nearly the smallest lots I've ever seen and were ringed with white stones which made them appear even smaller. Those on the waterfront were priced at $8,000, and those inland at $6,000. We remembered Martin Verdugo's gorgeous, wide lots at Bahia de Palmas, priced at $3,000, and said we'd think it over.

Most of our last evening at San Carlos was spent "thinking it over." We talked about it at length. There was no doubt these tiny lots were over-priced by Mexican standards. Yet, at the rate Americans were moving to Mexico, he'd probably get his price. In fact, we reasoned, the value of the lots could even double in a few years. On the other hand if we owned a lot we wouldn't be able to supervise the building on it until I learned to fly. That could be quite a time. Perhaps what we really should buy is not just a lot, but a lot with a house on it. We went to bed that night without making a decision.

At 6:45 the next morning we were aboard the camper again and headed homeward. But just before we left, we wrote a letter to the agent, offering our six unit apartment house in Hollywood as an even trade for a house in San Carlos. We left the letter at the desk when we checked out, but we never heard from him.

With our early start we made it all the way to Tuscon, Arizona, that first day—and without untoward incident. The smooth tires (except for the one we'd purchased), the rebuilt clutch, the Mexican fan belt, and all other parts and appurtenances seemed to function perfectly. We parked in a public rest stop outside Tuscon, barbecued hamburgers, and went to sleep, blissfully unaware of another tragedy.

Morning coffee has always been a ritual with us. I feel those first few cups of steaming brew return my soul to my body after sleeping. Without it, both Margie and I are zombies. It only took a moment to discover after we awakened that we had run out of butane. There would be no morning coffee—not even warm water for washing. It was 5:30 in the morning, and there was no place to buy any. Further, that other important adjunct to morning serenity, the flush toilet, was again not working.

We were too groggy to be dismayed. We used the toilet anyway and just left it to its fate. Then sleepily—stupidly—climbed into the cab of the truck and started driving. The highway, baked in the hot sun the day before, was now covered with dew and there was a musky early morning smell in the air. This made me even sleepier, and I had to fight dozing off at the wheel as we rode along in stupified silence. After half an hour of this we saw the winking lights of a small, all-night cafe. I parked beside it and entered, empty coffee pot in hand.

There were no customers at this hour, and the woman behind the counter was fat, stringy haired, and slovenly. She eyed me suspiciously as I came in.

"Could you fill this pot with coffee?" I asked, holding out the pot.

She didn't take it. "It'll cost ya fifty cents."

"Okay."

She still didn't take the pot. "Have ya got fifty cents?" (My Lord, did I look that bad?)

"Yes I have," I said and slapped two quarters down on the counter.

She whisked them off the counter and deposited them in her apron pocket, then took the pot out of my outstretched hand and filled it. She handed it back to me without a word.

"Thank you," I said.

No reply. I couldn't help thinking about Antonio the cab driver, the receptionist at General Popo, the welder, and all the other Mexicans we'd met and how charming and helpful they'd been. What a contrast!

The coffee had apparently been brewed many hours before and had that characteristic stale taste, but it was coffee! We sat there beside the café and drank every last drop. Then, feeling as if we'd just rejoined the human race, we began our drive again.

We played our "singing game" as we drove. I would sing the bridge or verse of some popular song, and then Margie would have to identify it and sing the chorus. If she succeeded, it was her turn to try to stump me. We have played this game many times on long trips and it makes the time pass quickly. In fact I was concentrating so hard on the game that I made a wrong turn somewhere and we ended up lost in the Imperial Valley.

Temperatures in the hundreds are very common in this area, but this proved to be their hottest day of the year. With no air conditioning in the truck we had to keep the windows open for air, and the rush of hot wind through the cab made it like a blast furnace. Then, when we stopped at a crossing or a gas station, the skin-frying heat and motionless air left us gasping for breath. Sun devils danced on the highway ahead of us and occasionally we could see a mirage shimmering over a field in the unspeakable heat. We purchased Cokes and ice cubes at a tiny market, and guzzled them as we tried to find our way home.

Our wretched trip finally concluded at eight o'clock that evening when we pulled up to our cool, air-conditioned home in the San Fernando Valley. For the first time in my life, I was actually glad to be home from a trip to Mexico.

We spent two days cleaning the camper and resting, and then set out to return the whole miserable rig to its rightful owner. I drove the camper, and Margie tailed me in our car so she could bring me back. Things looked pretty quiet at the Easy-Off sales lot, but I parked the rig, mentally told it goodbye and good riddance, and went into the office to return the keys. Bill was nowhere in sight and his son was seated glumly at the battered desk.

"Where's your Dad?" I asked him.

The young fellow almost wept as he told me Bill had been taken seriously ill, was in the hospital, and the doctors feared his illness might be fatal. I left the keys with him, told him to send Bill our best wishes, and left.

"Poor guy," Margie said when I told her about Bill.

"I didn't have the heart to tell his son about all our troubles."

"Of course not." She thought a minute. "You know I think we have enough footage to put together that movie for Bill, don't you?"

"Oh sure."

"Well, let's do it. That was our part of the bargain you know."

We went to work on it the next day.

When the film came back from processing and I had a chance to view it, I discovered Margie had surreptitiously squeezed off a couple of shots of the patient, waiting vultures when we'd had the blowout on the desert. I decided to splice them into the scene showing our travail at that time. It looked pretty funny—our drawn, worried faces, the shredded tire, and the birds awaiting our demise. The shots of the children sledding down the steps of the fort, some of the scenery along the way, and—most important—quite a few scenes showing the Easy-Off in action all came out very well. It took several weeks to complete the film, but when it was done, it was a fairly good little movie. I phoned Easy-Off to see if Bill was any better and able to view the picture. His condition was still very serious, but I was told that Mrs. Sullivan would come by our house to look at it.

One or two evenings later she arrived. The poor woman looked tired and careworn from the constant vigil at her husband's bed. As the movie unfolded on the screen, it was necessary to tell her a few of our problems because they were in the picture. She listened to the narration and watched the picture without expression. When it was over and I turned on the lights, she stood up to go.

"I don't think we want the film," she said. "I'll be going now."

The door closed behind her and on one more chapter of our Mexican odyssey—in many ways the oddest of them all.

8/ The Dolphin

After our disastrous affair with the Easy-off camper, we four-wheeled contentedly in the Toy for a time. There were still new beaches to be discovered in Baja, and new adventures around each turn in the road. Once, we spent twelve hours attempting to travel a distance of about twenty miles over a small mountain range that hulked between us and the sea. When we finally made it, we discovered the cliffs above the ocean were inhabited by Mexican fishermen. They were harvesting *sargasso*, a type of pink seaweed considered a delicacy by the Japanese. We spent several days with them. Another time we camped in a tiny, picturesque cove in the company of some Mexican lobster fishermen. They sold us huge lobsters for as little as fifty cents apiece, and occasionally took us out in their boats with them. On weekends, we camped in our "secret place" near the border—undetected and undisturbed by anyone. And always, wherever we were, we discussed the possibility of building a home there. Could we get water? Would a generator do for electricity? Could building materials be trucked in? Who owned the land? Would they sell us a lot? And for how much?

Gradually, the unpleasant memories of the Easy-off camper trip became dulled and we only remembered the good parts—the flush toilet was a marvelous convenience (when it worked!); it was surely nice not to have to toil putting up a tent when we arrived at our campsite; and an already made-up bed, a butane stove, and an oven were further delights. The only trouble with a camper, we said, is you can't take it into all those lovely, deserted, inaccessible spots. With a camper and truck you are pretty well confined to driving somewhat established roads. Soft sand?

215

Never!

Then, one night around the campfire, we discussed it again and thought maybe it *could* be possible. We could purchase a four-wheel drive truck and get extra large tires for it. That vehicle would nearly equal our Toy in handling soft sand, steep cliffs, and impossible roads. Then, if we could just find a camper for it that was light enough— and strong enough—we could enjoy our private Edens in luxury. We resolved to look into it.

We didn't look into it at all. I tend to be impetuous in such matters and one day I drove a new truck home!

"Look what I just bought!" I said to Margie.

"A truck! My gosh, it's a monster!"

"It's going to take our camper into the Baja boondocks."

"What camper?"

"Well . . . we'll have to find one," I said.

I had heard about a dealer in the San Fernando Valley who specialized in customizing his pickup trucks for campers, so I'd dropped in for a look around. He just happened to have a four-wheel-drive three-quarter ton pickup with 1200 x 16 tires, an eight thousand pound winch, two extra gas tanks, and various other goodies on it. I purchased it on the spot. The Ford four-wheel drive truck is built with the chassis mounted very high on the frame and looks like a girl lifting her skirts to walk through a mud puddle. With those giant balloon tires, the truck stood even higher.

We had to sell the Toy, so we took out a classified ad. If you ever hear of me advertising anything of mine for sale, be sure to buy it because you will always get the best of the bargain. My price for the Toy was equitable. I hadn't pumped it up for bargaining purposes. But when a pleasant gentleman arrived in response to the ad and offered to purchase the car on the spot, I gratefully included our tent, coleman stove, portable ice box, extra gasoline tanks, tools, parts, and various other appurtenances. (We've since had to purchase some of them again) I don't know why I do things like that—but it made Margie furious!

"My cooking pots? You *gave* him my cooking pots too?" she said incredulously.

"I guess I have a psychological problem," I said lamely.

Now, stripped of our camping gear, we had to find a camper. This time, however, Margie's methodical buying habit prevailed. We took in all the camper-trailer shows. We walked in and out of campers until our feet ached. We picked up all the literature and lugged it home for later reading. We priced this one and that one and consulted some of our friends who were camper owners. (This did very little good because every camper owner swears that his is the best you can buy.)

Our requirements were very special. Many times on our junkets to Baja we had seen the remains of someone's once-proud camper bleaching in the sun. The debilitating vibration of washboard roads, the twisting, tipping, jarring and wrenching of Baja driving had simply torn the camper apart and it had been left to rest . . . in pieces. So our camper would have to be especially well-built and strong, yet lightweight enough to drive through soft blow-sand and deep mud. It was a big order!

After much cautious checking, our search narrowed down to a Dolphin. This camper seemed appropriate, but how could we be sure? It would be tragic to lay out all that cash and then discover that we were forever confined to trailer parks and pavement.

Dolphin campers are not sold by dealers; you have to buy them direct from the manufacturer. So we drove our big blue and white truck over to the factory in Sun Valley, California, for a talk—and a proposition—with the president of the company.

He turned out to be a very pleasant gentleman named Wayne Mertes who smilingly waved us into his small, unpretentious private office.

"We're thinking of buying a Dolphin," I said, "but first we'd like to ask you a few questions."

Our conversation was interrupted by phone calls from time to time and as I overheard him dealing with various situations, I began to realize that this man possessed a solid core of integrity beneath his pleasant exterior, and he had very little patience with those who did not live up to his high standards. It emboldened me to pop the big question:

"What we'd like to do is this, Mr. Mertes. We'd like to rent one of your campers for a weekend and take it out for some tests. I'll run it over the roughest terrain I can find, and if it doesn't break down we'll buy it. What do you say?" (How was that for an attractive proposition!)

"I don't rent the campers," he said mildly, "but you can borrow mine. We'll load it on the truck for you."

"You do understand that I'm going to try to give it a beating?'"

"Yes I do."

As we waited for our truck to be loaded, we tuned in on conversations around us. There were several Dolphin owners waiting for their campers (apparently in for minor repairs) and they were discussing Mertes as we entered the room—there was not an unfavorable comment to be heard.

"It sounds like we've stumbled on the annual meeting of the Wayne Mertes Fan Club!" I whispered to Margie.

217

"It's reassuring," she whispered back.

We also picked up on camper-owner jargon as we listened to these people. The camper by itself is referred to as "the box." When you put "the box" on your truck it comes a "rig." I made a mental note that if we bought the "box" it would be a pleasure to bring it back to the manufacturer for any needed work. Then we heard the familar honk of our monster, and there it stood at the door with an 11-foot 3-inch camper on its backside. It looked like an Hilton Hotel on wheels!

Inside, it was a dream. Soft, warm wood paneling; four-burner range and oven; six cubic foot refrigerator-freezer (we could even make ice cubes on the beach!); room heater; stereo tape deck; huge over-sized bed; enough storage space for U.S. Quartermaster Corps, and that loveliest of all the inventions of modern man, a gleaming flush toilet.

Now, if it could only pass the test!

I knew of a spot just a half-day drive from home where the roads were rutted, strewn with stones, and often muddy. This same area offered some very steep grades too, so I felt it would approximate at least some of the terrain of Baja. We packed enough provisions for the weekend, but since that didn't amount to much weight we asked Margie's sister, Mary Lou, and her husband, Bob, to join us for the weekend and ride in the back of the "box."

Our rig handled the tough road so well it was almost a disappointment. The monster with the hotel on its back surmounted the ruts, stones, grades, and washboard surfaces with anticlimactic ease. As we pitched and bounced on those terrible roads it broke up a card game in progress in the back, but that was the only damage. The shaken passengers in the rear reported that not a single cupboard door swung open; everything was neatly in place. A closer inspection revealed that not a screw or bolt had loosened, and plumbing and electrical connections were all tight. So far so good. But we hadn't tested it yet in deep mud or soft sand, so I resolved I'd head for the sands of the Mojave Desert.

Early the next day we jarred and careened our way down the chuck-holed hillside and made our way to the desert. The spot of soft sand I had chosen was frequented by dune buggy enthusiasts who stared in disbelief as our huge rig steamed across the open desert, the sagebrush whipping at our fenders. They were even more incredulous as they watched me executing S-turns in the softest sand I could find. I was actually trying to get stuck so I could winch out. After about twenty minutes of this, I heard some cries of alarm from the back of the Dolphin.

"Oh-oh, that's it!" I thought, "I've really shaken something loose now."

I had. Bob and Mary Lou were carsick.

On Monday, we returned Wayne Mertes' camper to him as tight, neat, and snug as it had been when we borrowed it. And we ordered one for ourselves—blue and white to match the monster.

Honesty demands a small confession at this point. Deep in our hearts both Margie and I knew that the sands of Baja were much softer than those of the Mojave Desert. We also knew that we frequently traveled on much rougher roads than those where we'd conducted our "test." But we were both so in love with the camper that we weren't about to settle for anything less. As to how well it would really handle the badlands, we'd just head out there and hope for the best! We planned the first Dolphin trip for three weeks after we took delivery.

About this time there was a story among the *campesinos* of Baja. According to the oft-told tale, President Echeverria had flown to the tip of the Baja peninsula with his aides. Then, like a pasha on a Sahara trek, he formed a caravan of limousines and motored north to Tijuana. A bulldozer preceded him all the way smoothing the road ahead of the presidential tires. At the conclusion of the junket, so the story goes, the president declared that before the end of his administration the entire main road of Baja would be paved. I cannot vouch for the truth of the story, but as we contemplated this next trip, road crews were working furiously day and night at each end of Baja to meet somewhere in the middle and establish a new record for speedy road paving. Our beloved Baja would soon be tamed, and we'd have to seek side roads for adventure.

Since the determined workers had already pushed the pavement far south of Ensenada at the northern end, we decided to drive down the coast on the Old Mexico side, passing through the Sonora Desert and stopping at Guaymas. From there we would catch the ferryboat that plies the Gulf and cross over to Baja arriving at the port of Santa Rosalia. Then we would drive south from Santa Rosalia to Bahia Concepción. Using this route, we would be traveling roads as yet unpaved.

Except for revelling in the new found joys of a smooth running, air conditioned truck and the luxurious appointments of the camper, the trip across the desert to Guaymas was uneventful. This was the third time we had crossed that desert and we felt we knew every rock and cactus personally. We paused briefly at the mountainous curve where we had suffered the dangerous blowout on the previous trip and chuckled over the many misfortunes that attended it. We arrived in the Guaymas area in

219

the late afternoon and went immediately to San Carlos Bay.

Those $6,000 lots we had looked at were still unoccupied. They were standing as before, encircled with white rocks and looking even smaller than we remembered them. The beautiful Posada San Carlos hotel looked the same too, and was just as inviting, but we wanted to use our new camper. We found a spot a half mile down the beach from the lots, pulled effortlessly out on the soft sand beach, and made camp. The ferry for Baja was due to leave at noon the next day.

The Mexican Tourist Office in Los Angeles had told us advance reservations on the ferry were not possible and not necessary. However, the next morning at breakfast Margie had one of her famous hunches—"I think we ought to get over there and get our ferry tickets right away," she said.

"But honey, it's only nine o'clock! The ticket office might not even be open yet!"

"I know. But I just have a feeling we ought to be there."

We arrived at the dock a half hour later and purchased the last tickets available for that sailing! If we had been ten minutes later we'd have had to wait three days for the next ferry. The girl at the ticket counter who sold us our passage ($5.60 for us and $39.20 for the camper) explained that the boat wasn't always this crowded, but it was the end of the month and supplies were being shipped to Baja. True enough, there was a three hundred yard queue of trucks waiting to board. They were loaded with every type of produce imaginable—breadstuffs, canned goods, hardware, and other supplies. Baja is not very self sufficient and must depend on mainland Mexico for much of what it consumes. We parked the truck at the end of the long line and began the two hour wait to sailing time.

The ferry's appearance was quite a surprise to me. I don't know what I expected to see, but certainly not an ocean liner! I estimated its length at over three hundred feet. It was triple decked and was pointed at bow and stern—not unlike one of the Matson fleet sailing for Hawaii. Until nearly noon we wondered how they were going to hoist all those cars, trucks (and us!) aboard. Then, suddenly, the bow opened up! It looked like a giant whale opening its mouth, and the vehicles began to move into its jaw, like so many fish!

I began to inch our camper forward at the end of the line. It took me some time to reach my moment of boarding and when that moment came I could see why. The cars and trucks parked in the bottom of the ship were not arranged in neat rows like a parking lot. The head loader, with a skill I have never seen elsewhere, had shuffled and moved them about like a man playing Chinese checkers so that trucks and semis, station wagons, VWs, and other vehicles of every conceivable size and shape were wedged beside each other utilizing every inch of space. As I moved the Dolphin up the gangplank and looked into the dark interior, I could not see one spot left that would accommodate our camper. The ferry appeared to be jammed to the scuppers. But the loader cooly directed me to move back and forth turning the wheels this way and that and soon our rig was wedged in with all the others. The bow of the ship clanged shut inches away from us and we were plunged into total darkness.

The three of us began to pick our way through the darkness toward the stairs leading to the upper deck. Huge chains crisscrossed the deck causing us to trip; giant vehicles hulked above us like menacing shadows. It would sure be a rotten place to have to stay while the ship was at sea. Finally, we stumbled our way to the stairs and mounted them to the upper deck, bathed in blessed sunshine. As we stepped on deck the purser greeted us in English:

"I'm sorry, señora, but you must take the dog back down to your car."

"Whaaat!" Margie said, "the Mexican Tourist Bureau said she could ride on deck with us."

"I'm sorry, señora. They were wrong. The dog must go below."

"Look," I put in, "it's only a six hour crossing and the dog went to the bathroom just a short time ago. She won't make a mess or anything."

He was implacable. "It is a rule of the ship. I'm sorry."

Margie and I looked at each other. "Well, what do you think? I said. "The poor little thing will be terrified, shut up down there in the dark."

"There's nothing we can do about it now." She handed me the leash. "You take her back down and I'll wait for you here."

In the camper I put out the "Taco dish," full of fresh water and some dog cookies nearby for her to find. Then I spread newspapers on the floor in case she had an "accident" in fright. All the time I spoke soothingly to her explaining the necessity for locking her up in the dark down there. She didn't respond a bit. She just stood there with her big, soft brown eyes looking reproachfully at me. When I shut off the light and closed the door on her I had all the gaity and *joie de vivre* of a hangman!

There was a deafening blast from the ship's horn and we were off, the white wake unfurling behind us as the port city of Guaymas faded off astern. The Gulf of California, famous for its often rough water, was as smooth and shiny as a looking glass, and the Midriff islands were clear and stark on the horizon. After watching the Guaymas lighthouse become a tiny dot in the distance, we decided to take a walk and explore the ship.

There were some tidy staterooms—small but with all the amenities—for those who wished to cross the Gulf in luxury. We had elected to cruise steerage class (they call it *Turista*). We figured it was only six hours, and it would be fun riding with the Mexican working folk. The *Classe Turista* consisted of one huge room amidships filled with rows and rows of reclining chairs like you find on airliners, and supplied with a snack stand at one end. As we anticipated, there was a festive, carnival-like atmosphere there. Children were running and shouting; in one corner a boy strummed a guitar and sang to himself; mothers were nursing babies, people chatted, and Mexican music blared from a loud speaker adding to the cacophony. We talked with some of the Mexican passengers and discovered that most of them had their homes in Baja and were returning from business or a holiday on the mainland.

At the forward end of the ship was the *cantina*, delightful with its large view windows affording an excellent view of the sea. We stopped in for a drink and stayed for lunch. Mariachis serenaded us as we sipped tequila and nibbled some of the most delicious broiled lobster I have ever tasted. The tequila, combined with our full stomachs, the fresh salt air, and the soft throb of the ship's engines, made both of us very sleepy.

We decided to go back to the *Turista* section and take a nap, but first I wanted to see how poor little Taco was faring in the belly of the ship.

I found my way through the dark to our camper, climbed the steps and switched on the light as I entered. The dish of water had not been touched, the cookies were uneaten, and the newspaper unsoiled. It appeared she hadn't moved from the spot where I'd left her; those great, smoldering eyes were still looking accusingly at me. I petted and loved her a bit, and explained everything again, to no avail. She wasn't about to forgive me so soon.

"It's only a few more hours, Taco," I said, switching off the light again and closing the door behind me.

Margie was lying back in one of the reclining chairs with her eyes closed when I returned. I slipped into the chair beside her and —in spite of the noise in the room—fell immediately asleep.

Santa Rosalia is a small mining town that came into being back in the 1870s when copper-bearing ore was discovered there. In 1884, the holdings of the independent miners were purchased by a French corporation associated with the Rothschild interests. The company became very prosperous and controlled more than two thousand square miles of the surrounding countryside. Yaqui Indians were brought over from the mainland to work the mines. There was no fresh water so the company laid a pipeline from the oasis of Santa Agueda, ten miles inland. To facilitate shipping of the unrefined ore, they built an artificial port on Santa Rosalia's waterfront.

During the 1920s, the quality of the easily-mined copper ore began to peter out, and the French company decided to sell its interests. They couldn't find a buyer, however, so they just let the mining, and therefore the town, run down slowly to die of natural causes. In 1953, operations ceased entirely and Santa Rosalia became almost a ghost town. Activity returned to the area in 1955 when a Mexican company came in and began mining the manganise deposits in the vicinity. They are still doing so today. Their operation is on a much smaller scale than the previous copper mining company, but at least they breathed a little life back into this dismal Gulf coast town. Santa Rosalia now exists solely for manganese mining and for its artificial port built by the French so long ago.

Margie and I were both awakened by an upsurge of excited talking above the general noise going on around us. Mothers were gathering their children and people were assembling their luggage to disembark. The ship had apparently reached Santa Rosalia and we had both slept nearly all the way across. We yawned, stretched, and strolled out on deck for a seaward view of the port.

We were about half a mile at sea and had an excellent porpoise-eye view of the town. There wasn't much to see. The heart of Santa Rosalia is in the bottom of an arroyo surrounded by barren, desert-like hills. The mesas to the north and south of the arroyo are topped with some larger houses—probably the homes of mining and government officials. The working folks live in little box-like structures along the beach. Most Mexicans choose to paint their homes every color of the rainbow, but these houses were all brown clapboard—colorless. The beachfront itself is dirty, rocky, and thoroughly unappealing and a large, yellowish cloud hovers over the whole city.

"That's Santa Rosalia alright," I said, "Look at the smoke from the smelters hanging above the town."

"It looks yucky."

"It's not 'Marlboro Country', that's for sure!"

"I don't want to camp on that beach either."

"Neither do I. After we get our camper we'll head south and look for a spot."

223

The French built a long rock jetty that extends straight out from shore a couple of hundreds yards, then makes a ninety degree turn south and parallels the shore for a few hundred yards more, creating a bay for Santa Rosalia. With incredible skill, our ship's master brought that great ship into the tiny bay as if he were parking his car in the garage! I didn't realize that a ship of that size could throttle down and move so slowly. It seemed to take nearly half an hour just to move that few hundred yards along the side of the jetty. Finally, he nestled it right up to the dock without the slightest bump.

After the ship had been tied up, the gangplank was lowered, and we were told we had to disembark and return later to get our vehicle, so we joined the other passengers descending to the dock. They were a colorful lot. Suitcases were rarely in evidence, but belongings were carried in baskets, boxes, crates, and occasionally wrapped in a blanket. Men were carrying their children on their shoulders. Boys were carrying their guitars. Here and there a passenger proudly carried a piece of hardware—a shovel perhaps—he had purchased on the mainland.

Finally, the last passenger struggled down the gangplank with his possessions, and the ferry clanked open its huge mouth, revealing the static traffic jam of vari-sized vehicles inside. How would they get them all untangled? Since we had been the last to drive onto the ferry, we would be the last off (they load from one end and unload from the other). As we waited, the tangle of trucks and cars aboard began to come unraveled. One by one, the produce trucks, semis, station wagons and VWs made their way out of the ship.

"Poor little Taco! She must be terrified hearing all those noisy car engines," Margie said.

"I think she's been terrified for the last six hours! I'll try to work my way in to where she is."

I made my way up the ramp and into the vehicle area. The smell of carbon monoxide was unbearable with all the trucks and cars revving up their motors; the sound was ear-splitting. To my surprise, none of the drivers in this massive traffic tangle seemed to be tense, hurried, or angry as drivers usually are in such situations. They waited patiently and smiled, waved, or shouted jokes at each other over the roar of the engines. Or if they were moving out, they courteously braked to let me pass and waved me through. At length I made it to our truck and opened the door. Everything was just the way I had last seen it during the crossing, and the inside of the camper had that musky smell that occurs when any animal is frightened. Taco was still sitting in the same place, but this time she looked at me questioningly and her tail began to twitch slightly.

"It's all over, Taco. We're here. Come on!" I held out my arms.

A bouncing, barking, joyous puppy leaped into my arms happily, bestowing wet doggie kisses all over my face.

If only humans had a puppy's strength to forgive!

It had been 6 p.m. when we landed, and it was now about 7:30, as Taco and I joined Margie on the dock. Taco delivered Margie her A-1 Deluxe greeting, and once again we were ready to travel. I wanted to find a place to camp before dark.

"Before we leave Santa Rosalia, I'd like to see that famous church," Margie said.

"Famous" isn't exactly the right word. "Known to a few people" might better describe Santa Rosalia's one and only tourist attraction. The church is of special interest because it is made entirely of galvanized iron panels shipped to Baja from Europe many years ago. With only a couple of main streets in the town, the church wasn't difficult to find. It was locked up tight when we arrived, but we could peer through one of the windows to see an exquisite stained glass window behind the alter and glimpse the barest hint of a courtyard bursting with blooming flowers. It was an oasis of beauty in the otherwise drab town. We knocked on the walls to prove to ourselves they were really made of iron, and left.

To my disappointment, the road south of Santa Rosalia had already been paved so we were able to zip along without difficulty. After just a short drive we saw a cluster of date palms on the edge of a beach, pulled into the grove, and camped for the night.

The little town of Mulege is an anomaly. Positioned in the center of some of Baja's most forbidding desert terrain, it is lush with flowers and greenery like a bouquet in a cactus garden, or a flower in an old hag's hair. It is situated in a palm-choked arroyo about two miles inland from the Gulf, and divided by a wide river that flows lazily to the sea. Brightly colored flowers are everywhere—crawling over the roofs of houses, blossoming in the streets, and bending over the river. The stores are neat and clean, and the people smile a lot—happy in their tiny Eden. Half a mile up the arroyo is the mission founded by the Jesuits back in 1705; below it is a stone dam and a small lake which furnishes irrigation water for Mulege's rich fields and blooming gardens. Although the streets are unpaved, they are spotless. All around the shaded plaza are large cans for litter which are respected and used by the people. There are several

225

American-oriented hotels in Mulege, and landing strips for flying American fishermen who come down not only for the excellent ocean fishing, but to catch the snook that abound in the river.

The federal prison at Mulege is unique. It is a large, whitewashed building on a hill overlooking the entire arroyo. There is no capital punishment in Mexico, only life sentences, and these prisoners are all lifers—murderers and other felons. Yet, every morning at eight o'clock the gates swing open and the inmates are permitted to descend the hill into town, hold jobs, and be with their wives and families. Then, at five o'clock in the afternoon, the whistle blows, and the prisoners obediently trudge back up the hill to their jail cells. There is no crime in Mulege, and there has been only one attempted escape in over twenty years. In that one case, the escapee was captured and simply turned over to his fellow prisoners. His slow, painful death at their hands has seemed to discourage any further escapes.

Our destination was still Bahia Concepción to the south, and we would probably make it before nightfall, so we decided to take a brief cruise around Mulege and purchase some supplies. The main street led us past the small, flower-bedecked plaza, and under a canopy of hibiscus whose red blooms arched from a roof top clear over the road. From there, the dirt road joined the river and followed it all the way to the sea. It was just two tracks wide with the river bank on one side, and deep, tropical foliage on the other. An occasional waving, smiling pedestrian would leap happily into the flowering bushes to permit us to pass. The livestock wasn't quite as cooperative, and once we had to wait ten minutes for a rooster to complete his pecking in the center of the road. On the river, happy people in small boats fished, paddled around, or just snoozed and drifted. Mulege was a Lotus land, indeed.

The road terminated at a large, older hotel on the beach. We didn't go inside. We just used their parking lot to turn around in and retraced our route back to the center of town.

"I'll take Taco for a walk while you do the shopping," Margie said. So I left the two of them in the beautiful little plaza and headed for the *Supermercado* across the street. Margie wanted me to buy some rolls, and I had in mind a bottle of rum and some limes for daiquiris that night.

The market was clean, attractive, and well stocked. I picked out some rolls, and dozen limes, and a liter of excellent rum and took them to the check stand.

The teenage girl at the cash register looked at my purchases and frowned. *"No ron,"* she said. *"No se permite en Domingo."* [It is against the law on Sunday].

"*Solamente aquí ó otras ciudades tambien?*" [Only here, or other cities also?].

"*Solamente aquí.*" [Only here].

"*Porqué?*"

She shrugged. "*No se.*" [I don't know.]

Handling the bottle of rum as if it were the demon it is reputed to be, she placed it on a lower shelf. I paid for the other items and left, wondering who had decreed that booze could not be purchased on Sunday in this little town.

When I crossed the street back to the plaza, I found Margie deep in conversation with a handsome, elderly gentlemen dressed in white work clothes. He was heavy set with luxuriant white hair and mustache setting off his dark brown face which was lined, reflecting the wisdom of his years. The eyes beneath the bushy white eyebrows were soft and kindly. He looked like someone's grandfather. He was petting Taco as I arrived.

Margie introduced us in Spanish. "Señor Gonzales, this is my husband, Benito."

He stood up and shook hands. "It is a pleasure to meet the husband of this charming *señora.*"

"*El gusto es mio,*" I replied

"Señor Gonzales and I were just discussing living in Mexico," Margie continued in Spanish, "and how it is possible for one to live off the land without money."

"*Verdad,*" the old gentleman said. "There are fish to be caught for one's family, and fruit and vegetables growing wild." He paused and sighed. "But that life is not for me."

"*Porqué, Señor Gonzales?*" I asked.

"Because I live there." He pointed to the whitewashed prison on the hill above.

I couldn't believe that this dear old gentleman was a felon. "A warden, perhaps?" I asked.

He shook his head. "*Un prisonero.*"

I shuddered as Margie asked what I considered a taboo question: "What was your crime?"

It didn't seem to bother him. "*Homicidio, Señora,*" he said simply, "so there I live, and there I will die."

Now that he admitted to being a murderer, I felt not fear, but embarrassment that we had asked and he had told us. I wished that he had lied. Margie apparently felt just as I did and delivered me a look that said, "Let's get going."

I stood up and shook his hand. "*Hasta la vista*," I said.

"*Adios, Señor*," then turning to Margie, he said, "*Vaya con Dios Señora*."

"*Gracias, Señor Gonzales*," she said.

He patted Taco. "*Adios Taco*."

As we drove off down the highway, I could see him in the rear view mirror. He was still seated on the plaza bench, staring sadly after us.

A few more minutes of driving, and it was apparent that the road was going to be paved all the way to the tip of the peninsula. In planning our trip we had misjudged the speed of Mr. Echeverria's racing road builders.

"Damn it, honey, we've been driving nearly four days and we still haven't gotten our rig off the road."

"I know."

"Echeverria and his damned highway."

"A curse on all his limousines! May they have flat tires on country roads."

"And vapor lock in the city!"

Margie thought a minute. "There's one thing we could do."

"What?"

"Just turn off the pavement and go down to the beach. We might even find whatever's left of the old road."

On our left was a steep bank leading down to a soft sand beach. I put the truck in four-wheel-drive, made a sharp left turn, and in a moment we were on the beach. There on our right, hugging the embankment, was the ghost of the old road that had wound its tortuous way around the cliffs and down on the beaches of Bahia Concepción. It had suffered from lack of use and occasional flash floods had gutted it so if anything it was far worse than it had been originally. Gleefully, I turned onto it and we resumed our trek in four-wheel-drive. Now we'd see how the Dolphin survived!

With the deep ruts, chuckholes, sharp stones to stab the tires, and the occasional washboard surface, it was slow going. Even at five and ten miles per hour the camper rocked, swayed, staggered, and lurched, but we heard no telltale crashes in the rear. Now and again the road descended again to beach level and was inundated by the high tide, but we kept going with the seawater sloshing above our hubcaps. On one occasion the sand was so slushy I had to let more air out of the tires to get any traction, but we continued our drive, feeling alone in Baja at last. "The Baja Feeling" was full upon us.

Bahia Concepción is a deep dent in the Baja coastline about twenty-five miles long, ranging up to six miles in width. It consists of a series of small coves with white, sandy beaches looking out at small uninhabited islands that dot the bay. It makes an excellent sheltered harbor for boats escaping the Gulf storms. In fact, a number of the Spanish pearling captains reported finding shelter there back in the sixteenth century. One of them, a man named Lucenilla, visited the bay in 1668, and reported that the shores were peopled with white-skinned Indians who lived on fruits and shellfish. It was these Indians who were Christianized by the Jesuits in 1705 at the mission of Mulege. Passing this way two hundred and fifty years later, we saw no signs of life.

Finally, we rounded the point of one cove, pulled into the next, and— as has happened so often on our trips—Margie cried, "This is it!" I stopped the camper in the center of the beach and all three of us got out to look around.

This cove was larger than some of the others we'd passed. At the northern end was a large grove of mangrove trees, their roots actually stretching out into the water. The bay was as peaceful as a lake and mirrored the few fluffy clouds overhead. Standing on the shore we could look down into the clear, clean water and observe small fish darting about. Straight out from us was one of the islands. It was barren like the rest with sheer sides that looked as if they'd been sliced with a sharp knife plunging down into the bay. It was like a huge stone in a Japanese Shinto pond. And like such a stone, it had no practical use. The Creator simply placed it there to enhance the view from shore.

"What a homesite this is!" Margie said. "Can you imagine a house sitting where our camper is with a view window looking out at that island and the bay?"

"I sure can. Victor Rubio told us he was attempting to buy a large portion of the beaches along here," I noted.

"That's right, he did! Let's talk to him about it when we get back."

Victor Rubio is one of Mexico's most successful and respected stock brokers. He has offices in Tijuana, Guadalajara, and Mexico City, but spends most of his time dealing with American investors at his Tijuana office. He is even approved by the Securities Exchange Commission in the States! We decided a trip to his office would be the first order of business after our trip.

I checked the camper carefully to see if any plumbing, electrical connections, or anything else had shaken loose while we were driving the old road, but it was tight as a drum. Then I dropped the four hydraulic jacks down onto wooden pads on the sand and made the "box" steady as a rock. Next I unfurled our dining fly (a large, grommetted canvas with tent poles and stakes) and put it up astern to provide shade for sitting on the beach. I hooked up the drain hose from the kitchen sink and set it so our waste water would drain harmlessly away from camp. While I did these things, Margie was unpacking and getting her kitchen ready to function. I had just finished setting up our beach chairs under the dining fly when Margie appeared at the door. She had changed into her bikini and looked good enough to devour.

"Would you like to pour?" she said mischievously, and held up a bottle of chilled Chablis.

"Actually, I had rape on my mind."

"Pour now. Rape later."

We sat in the shade sipping the cold wine and watching diving birds plummet into the bay until the sun went down and turned our beautiful beach golden. When we made love on the beach that night the sky was a black canopy studded with a billion-billion stars.

The next day we discovered we were not alone.

Right after breakfast, Margie had been eager for her first "beastie hunt" of the trip. So with shovel, pail, and plastic bag for special shells, the three of us set off south down our beach. As she always does, Taco went ape. She started running this way and that, sniffing seaweed, and barking at our feet with the pure joy of being alive. We didn't find anything interesting to pick up, but were amused by Taco's antics as she dashed about in a doggie display of the exultation we were feeling. At length we reached the extreme southern end of our cove, and were about to turn back when we heard Taco's warning bark and saw him. He had built a little lean-to back in an indentation in the rocks—an "almost-cave," as Margie called it. It was so well concealed from the beach that except for Taco we'd have missed it. He lived alone. His long, double-ended rowboat was pulled up on the sand in front of his dwelling, the heavy oars lying across the thwarts. He was cutting fish on a rock; various sized fish fillets were drying in the sun on rocks and bushes. He looked up.

"Buenos días." He spoke as if two Americans strolling into his hideout at ten in the morning was a common occurence.

"Buenos días," we both replied.

The fisherman was not a young man. Perhaps years of hard, lonely work had aged him prematurely—the heavy stubble of beard aged him too—but he had to be at least in his late forties. He was lanterned-jawed and skinny, bare to the waist, but with each movement of the fish knife the sinews rippled up and down his arms and shoulders. Here was a man who rowed a heavy boat for many hours every day of his life.

"Qué classe de pescado es?" [What kind of fish is that?] I asked.

"Tiburon."

Shark! Why was he fishing for shark? "Es comida?" [It's food?]

"Sí. Machaca."

Speak of food and you capture Margie's interest. "Qué es machaca?" she asked.

He put down his knife and began to explain. Machaca is made from dried meat, he told us; in this case, shark. The dried meat is first placed in water to soften it, then prepared in any one of several ways. The most common method of preparing machaca is to cook it in a white gravy and serve it on toast much as we prepare chipped beef. In Mexico, it is a breakfast favorite. (We tried machaca a year later and found it tasteless but passable.]

As we continued chatting with him he told us his name was Augustino, and he had a wife and four children living in Hermosillo—many miles distant on the Mexican mainland. He worked here on the beach catching and sun-drying the shark until he had a large supply. He would then take the machaca to market and sell it. After that, he would visit his family for a couple of weeks, leave them some money to live on, and return to Baja to fish again. It sounded like a pretty grim existence. We invited him to visit our camp some evening for a glass or two of tequila, then left.

At five o'clock the next morning, we saw Augustino setting out. He dragged the heavy boat down to the water, shoved off, and jumped in. He rowed standing up and facing forward, dipping the long oars into the glassy surface of the water without a sound, and moved steadily out to sea until he was just a tiny black dot on the horizon.

We discovered a huge clam bed that day. It was just a short distance from our camper and in an hour we had gathered enough for a huge feast. We had so many in fact that I decided to use some of them for bait and try a little fishing from shore. The results were astonishing! I would wade out waist-deep in the warm water and cast my line. The bait would no sooner strike the water than a hungry fish would grab it and I'd reel him in. In no time I began to feel like a plunderer because I'd caught more fish than we would ever be able to eat. Even after scaling and cleaning them, they filled both the refrigerator and the freezer!

"No more fishing for you!" Margie declared. "You're too good at it!"

"I'm not that good. It's just that the fishing here is fantastic. But it's fun too. I'll start throwing them back."

"No, don't do that either. I've got an idea." She ducked into the camper and emerged a minute later with what appeared to be a rolled up piece of paper.

"What's that?" I asked.

"Unroll it and see. They were giving them away at the Supermarket before we left Los Angeles, and I thought it might be fun to fly a kite down here."

I brought my camp chair out to the edge of the water and spent hours flying the kite out over the bay from the end of my fishing rod. As it ducked and tugged it felt much like an active fish on the line and I reeled it in and out. Alas, give-away kites are not very sturdy, and after a couple of days in the brisk Gulf breezes it ripped and plunged sadly into the sea. I lost my surrogate fighting fish, but it was fun while it lasted.

Late that afternoon a mystery boat entered our bay. It was a small yacht—I estimated about twenty-five feet long. It was the type that has just two lower bunks forward next to the rope locker, a table that lets down from the ceiling, a kerosene stove, and a head that works with a hand pump. It cruised slowly past our island and dropped anchor about fifty yards away from Augustino's beach at the south end of the cove. We had been following it with the binoculars all the way in, but unfortunately looked in another direction just at the moment it dropped the hook, so we never saw anyone aboard. We waited patiently for someone to come out on deck, put a skiff over the side—it would probably be an inflatable boat—or do something. But no one appeared. We held the binoculars on its portholes hoping to see signs of someone moving about, but could see no movement at all. Later when it got dark we checked again to see lights go on aboard, but it remained dark.

"Now what do you make of that?" I said.

"Maybe whoever it was just swam ashore and we missed him—or them."

"Impossible. We'd have seen them walking up the beach. Whoever brought that boat into the bay is still aboard."

"Well then, what could they be doing?" Margie asked.

A picture flashed through my mind. When I was about nine years old, I worked as a cabin boy on just such a boat. The owner was an elderly man who used to take his pretty young secretary on a cruise to Catalina Island each weekend. At nights he and the secretary occupied the two bunks, and I slept in a sleeping bag in the small skiff he towed astern. As soon as it got dark, I'd quietly draw the skiff up to the side of the yacht and spy on the old gent and his femme through the porthole. They'd be laughing and drinking, and he'd be pulling her clothes off and petting her. I never saw the culmination of this exercise because they always turned off the lights, but my fertile nine-year-old imagination filled in the gaps as I stood with my nose glued to the porthole.

"I bet there's a man and a woman on the boat, and I bet I know what they're doing," I said with an evil wink.

"You're a dirty old man," she laughed.

The next morning the yacht was still anchored in the same place and there was still no sign of life on board. We tired of speculating about its occupants, and went on another "beastie hunt."

This time we headed north along the beach toward the mangrove trees at the other end of the cove. We were wading in about two feet of water when we saw an interesting sight. The night before, after our clam feast, I had dumped the clam shells into the water. Some of them had bits of clam meat left in them, and others had not been touched. Now, in the clear water where I'd thrown them, dozens of tiny little fish were enjoying the clam dinner we had been unable to finish.

"I wonder if I could get them to eat out of my hand," Margie said.

"Why don't you try it?"

Taco and I sat down on the beach to watch (and keep an eye on the yacht at the other end of the cove) and Margie let herself down in the water, allowing herself to drift slowly toward the clam feast in progress. Then her outstretched hand touched a clam.

"They all ran away!" she said disappointedly.

"I figured they would."

"Well, be quiet. I'm going to stay here just like this. If they want the clams badly enough, they'll come back."

We all three began the wait. I wasn't wearing a watch, but it seemed like at least fifteen minutes—perhaps longer—that Margie lay motionless in the water. Then, suddenly, she looked at me excitedly and nodded. I scrambled to my feet for a look. Sure enough, the tiny fish had returned, and two of them were nibbling an open clam in Margie's hand! I wish I'd had the camera with me so I could have recorded the thrilled expresion on her face. She never tired of hand-feeding those fish. All week long we'd dig clams and Margie would take them out to feed her little new-found friends.

But onboard the mysterious yacht there was still no light aboard, and no sign of life.

"My God! When are they going to come up for air!" I said.

"I'm beginning to worry about whoever is on that boat. They might be sick or something."

"Let's wait one more day. Then, if we don't see anyone, we can try hailing them from shore. If that gets no answer, I'll swim out there."

This was the day we made two remarkable discoveries. The first one was oysters growing on trees! I had heard that this occurs in certain places, but never quite believed it. We had walked past Margie's fish-feeding station and clear down to the mangroves when we discovered them. They were growing on the mangrove roots which stretched into the bay and were covered with water at high tide. I immediately started knocking them off with the shovel, but Margie in her eagerness tore them off the roots with her hands. Soon we had a bucket full and retired to the dining fly to enjoy *really* fresh oysters on the halfshell for lunch. Margie's hands were a bloody mess from deep cuts made by the sharp oyster shells.

"Darling, you better put something on those hands." I said.

"Oh, they'll be alright. I'll just bathe them in the ocean."

I know that seawater had great curative powers, but her lacerated hands were red and swollen—infection a good possibility. I resolved I'd let her have her way for the moment, but I was going to watch those sore, bloody hands very closely.

The oysters were delicious. Each one was about the size of a quarter and they were packed together in large bunches like grapes. Using a paring knife, we'd pry the lids off, squirt the little rascals with lemon juice and a dash of Tobasco, then pop them into our mouths with our fingers. We washed them down with chilled sparkling wine from our refrigerator. After that, we napped in the warm sun for an hour or two, and awakened to make our second discovery.

It's more truthful to say Margie made the discovery. The tide had receded during our nap and she got up for a stroll to the waterfront to see if anything interesting had been washed up. Lazily, I got to my feet and joined her. At first we saw nothing. Then, on the hard surface of the wet sand, there appeared a hairline crack. It was a little over a foot long and seemed to be widening.

"Now what do you suppose made the sand crack open like that?" Margie asked.

"Search me. It's drying out, maybe."

"I'll bet there's some kind of a beastie under there."

"I'll go get the shovel so we can dig him up."

234

"Oh, don't bother. I'll use my hands." So saying, she slipped one hand into the wet sand at the beginning of the crack, dug in as deep as she could, and began to scoop along the line of the rupture.

"There is something here!" she said excitedly. "Yuck! It's slimy!"

And then she brought forth one of the strangest sea creatures I have ever seen! It was obviously a crustacean of some sort, but it had outgrown its shell. White, porklike flesh extended several inches out from the shell in all directions. With the orange shell in the center, it had the look of a giant fried egg. It was three or four inches across and absolutely dripping with mucousy slime. As Margie moved the creature from hand to hand inspecting it, her hands became coated with the gooey substance.

"Want to touch it?" she said teasingly.

"No thanks." (She knows I'm squeamish about handling things like that.)

"Why don't you get a bucket of water, and I'll put him in it?"

"Okay." I trotted to the camper, fetched the bucket, and filled it with seawater. She dumped the animal into the bucket and we watched him for awhile to see what he would do, but he did nothing. He just laid on the bottom, apparently contemplating his fate. We forgot him for awhile and spent the remainder of the day loafing and relaxing in the warm sunshine.

The next morning the creature was still lying placidly in the bucket where Margie had placed him, and I decided to try to find out what he was. Because of our penchant for finding weird critters on the beaches, we had long ago purchased a reference book to identify them. The book is *The Erotic Ocean*, by Jack Rudloe, and we always carry it with us. After breakfast, I took it down from the camper bookshelf and began paging through its Latin chapter heads. It took some doing, but I finally located our slimy friend in the chapter titled Phylum Mollusca.

"I think I've found it," I said. "It's called an Ear Shell."

"Ear Shell?"

"Well its other name is *Sinum perspectivum*."

"What does he say about it?"

"You want me to read it aloud?"

"Of course!"

I began to read:

Even when you dig this creature out of its broad, semicircular furrow and examine it on the palm of your hand, you may never realize that it has a beautiful shell tucked away in its mantle. The shell is a delightful, fragile thing of beauty. But who would know that from the sluglike flesh that surrounds it so completely, comprising three fourths of its body size? Only the very tip of the shell may protrude through the mantle, if you let it crawl about your hand for a moment—never mind all that oozing mucus.

"I shall digress on the subject of its mucus for a moment. A professional biological collector who often works with formadehyde of alcohol always has wrinkled, dried and discolored hands because these reagents work on his fingers the way they do on the tissues of the animals. Regardless of the use of rubber gloves, sooner or later your fingers get pickled. *Sinum* (Ear Shell) should be used by the hand lotion people, because nothing softens skin like a good, slimy, mucusy ear shell. I firmly believe it speeds up the healing process and . . . "

Excitedly, Margie interrupted, "Ben! Look at my hands!" She held them out palms up.

It was like a miracle! Her hands which had been laced with deep cuts from the oyster shells the night before were almost completely healed! Only tiny black lines remained where the severe lacerations had been.

"All the soreness and redness are gone—it's almost as if I'd never hurt my hands at all!"

"It's amazing alright. You could have gotten a bad infection."

"But I didn't. Just look!" She extended her hands again.

"I've never seen anything heal so quickly."

"I had that slime from the Ear Shell all over my hands, remember?"

"That must have been what brought about the healing."

We both agreed that if someone could find a way to bottle that slime, or duplicate it chemically, he could make a fortune.

As we were talking, there came a tap at our door. I opened it and saw an odd couple. One was a gentleman I estimated to be in his sixties. He was short and skinny with gray thinning hair. He was barefooted, wearing dungarees and a T-shirt which exposed his scrawny, freckled arms. Towering over him, but clinging to him lovingly was a young girl in her twenties. She was also barefooted, and was wearing bermuda shorts and a bra top. She had a sensational figure and her half-exposed, bulbous breasts drew my eyes like a magnet. Her blonde hair had lost its accustomed coif, and she looked a bit tired and bedraggled.

"Good morning!" the gent smiled. "We're the folks from the boat." He jerked his thumb over his shoulder in the general direction of the mystery boat. (Apparently I had guessed right!)

"I wonder if you know how far it is to Mulege?"

"We were thinking we'd walk there," the girl added, tweaking his ear affectionately.

"I'm not sure," I said, "but I know it's too far to walk."

He laughed a high, squeaky cackle, "Well, in that case, we'll do something else. Come on, Gloria." He turned to go.

"May I ask you a question?" I said.

"Of course. What is it?"

"How did you get ashore from your boat? I don't see any skiff on the beach, and you obviously didn't swim."

He laughed again. "Easy. We saw that fisherman going out in his boat and tipped him to ferry us in. He's going to take us back out later."

So saying, they took their leave, strolling arm in arm down the beach—the sexy young girl and her unlikely Romeo. We never saw them again.

During the entire time we had been on the beach we had eaten nothing but fish. In addition to the clams and oysters, there had been all the fish I caught. Margie barbecued it, fried it, broiled it, served it raw (cerviche), and in cocktails until we both felt we were going to sprout fins and gills ourselves! One evening, in desperation for a new way to prepare fish, she invented a recipe so delicious that I feel constrained to pass it along:

She placed a large fish fillet in aluminum foil. Then she sprinkled it with lime juice (those small, delicious Mexican limes), garlic salt, pepper, and an ample amount of white wine. After that she crumbled a whole oregano over the top and garnished it with raw onion and lemon slices. Then she poured tomato sauce over the whole concoction, folded the aluminum foil over the top, and baked it in our camper oven for thirty minutes. When it was done, it was placed on a plate with the garnishes, and the sauce left in the foil was poured over steamed rice. It was the last piece of fish in the freezer and a fitting finale to a solid week of eating from the sea.

The next evening, Augustino visited us and brought us a gift—one of the largest fish fillets I've ever seen!

"Que maravilloso!" Margie cried with feigned enthusiasm, "Muchisimas gracias!"

Silently, I vowed that neither that fish nor any other creature of the sea would cross my lips for at least a month!

A cool, damp breeze was blowing in from the bay that night, and dark clouds were blotting out some of the stars, so Margie and I had decided to take advantage of the chill to enjoy our first campfire of the trip. It was crackling beautifully.

"Sientese," [Sit down] I said to Augustino, gesturing to a spot beside the fire. "Quiere un tragito de tequila?"

237

"*Gracias.*" He allowed that a little smash of the juice would be most pleasant so I fetched the bottle and some glasses and we all three sat down for a visit, Taco snoozing with her nose toward the fire. Augustino's first question was predictable:

"How much costs such a camper?"

Every Mexican we have met on the beaches of Baja always wants to know what your possessions cost. He'll ask the cost of your car, your camper, your watch, or anything else you have with you. The question is never asked rudely. It is always a simple, direct query expressed with genuine interest. I have never been able to perceive the motive. Is he pricing something he knows he can never afford, or is he salting that item away in his memory bank as "something I will buy when I have much money." Perhaps he is merely attempting to gauge the affluence of the owner. Since I know that the *campesinos* we have talked with will never in their lives be able to purchase such items, and since I don't want to be thought of as "*un rico norteamericano*" (a rich American), I always tend to downgrade the value.

"About five or six thousand, Augustino."

"*Dólares?*"

"*Sí.*"

He nodded wisely, as if he had appraised it at just that figure, and lapsed into silence.

"What of your life, Augustino? Tell us of your family," Margie said.

He tossed off his tequila, and I poured him another one as he began. His wife's name, he said, was Rosa Blanca, and she had been a very beautiful woman when they married many years before. He had then worked as a fisherman at Bahia Kino—a bay near Hermosillo in the state of Sonora. Their first child had died at birth, but the second—a strong, handsome boy and apparently Augustino's favorite—had survived, was now twenty-five years old, and working in a mine in Durango. His name was Carlos and he made very good money. He often sent lovely gifts to his mother. He had married in Durango and had one child.

"Ah, then you are a grandfather, Augustino."

"*Verdad!*" [It is true.]

"What of the other children?"

He sighed. "My second son is poor Davido. He had the crippling disease."

"Polio," I said to Margie. (It is still very common in Mexico).

"*Sí*, polio. He now has twenty-three years but is unable to work. His legs and arms are as if wood. *Entienda?*"

238

We nodded to show we understood, and he went on. The other two children were teenage girls. He said they were cute and silly and laughed a lot, but did not contribute much to the family income. That was why he had elected to fish alone over here at Bahía Concepción. Both the fishing and the market were better, and he had four mouths to feed, plus his own. His wife worked as a servant in wealthy Hermosillo homes, but could not earn much because she could not live in. Her duties with the crippled son kept her at home much of the time. "So it is with Augustino, the fisherman of *machaca*," he concluded, and lapsed into silence again, staring at the fire.

Margie and I fell silent also, staring at the embers. It had been a sad story and we would have liked to have done something to help him, but what could we do? A gift of money—if he would accept it—would have helped temporarily at least. But we couldn't write a check, and the cash we had on hand was needed to buy our gasoline and other supplies. Perhaps, I thought, being able to talk to sympathetic listeners was therapeutic for him.

After awhile he sighed and got to his feet. "I return to my *campo* now. But *gracias* for the tequila and for your ears. It is good to have friends to talk with. A man becomes lonely."

"The pleasure was ours," I said and shook hands with him.

"*Adios Benito y Marshe.*"

"*Adios,*" we said, and he started trudging south on the beach toward his camp.

After he was out of earshot, Margie said "Did you notice? He had tears in his eyes when he left."

I had noticed.

One delightful thing we had discovered about our Dolphin was the superb insulation. Most of those beach days the mercury had hovered around a hundred degrees or more, but the interior of the camper was cool and pleasant—a lovely retreat from the hot sun. On our one chilly evening we found that the Dolphin retained the heat from cooking dinner and was warm and cozy. But as for its performance in off-the-road driving, I was still a bit unsure. It had only been off the road for a relatively short time during our drive from Mulege to where we were camped. I longed to get it off the road again.

"Well, let's break camp and move on to someplace else then," Margie said.

"Where? That damned Echevérria is paving Baja so fast there's no place to go any more."

"I read about a beach in a Mexican magazine."

"Oh? Where is it?"

"It's on the other side—the mainland."

"That means crossing the Gulf in the ferry again. Poor Taco . . . "

"I know. But we have to cross back on that ferry some time. That is, unless you want to drive all the way north on the peninsula."

"No, I don't want that long drive across the Baja desert—even if it's paved." I looked at our unsuspecting pooch curled up on the seat beside me. "The poor little thing will just have to face it I guess. Let's leave tomorrow."

We spent several hours the next morning performing some of the necessary adjuncts to camper life. We dug a hole and dumped the holding tank, recharged the toilet, switched butane tanks, did the dishes, and battened everything down for the drive. We then back-tracked all the way to Santa Rosalia and the ferry, arriving about 1:30 pm. The ferry wasn't due to leave until 6 pm, but this time we didn't want to be the last aboard.

For some reason I have never understood, they require you to go through customs before boarding the ferry, so we made our way to the aduana (customshouse) for our inspection. The customs officer was having his siesta and not expected for several hours, so to kill time we took a walk through the dingy little town, stopped for a drink and a rotten lunch slowly served at the Central hotel, and finally returned to our camper. It was a very hot day but the camper was cool inside so we stayed there playing cards until the customs officer returned to his office. By this time it was 4:30 p.m., and we were both beginning to wish we had never left the beach at Bahía Concepción.

The customs officer inspected our camper, stamped our papers, and we purchased our tickets. Then we got the glad tidings that the ferry was late in arriving from the mainland and wouldn't leave until 7:30 p.m. More waiting.

Departure time came and went, and still the moored ferryboat didn't open its jaws to welcome us aboard. We were getting very hungry. We had originally planned to dine in a genteel manner in the ship's attractive cantina, but we settled for two tamales purchased from a little man with a pushcart.

"They're probably made from burro meat," Margie said, "but I'm so hungry I don't care!"

We never found out what he used for the meat filling, but those tamales

240

were the best we've ever tasted!

Finally at 9 p.m., we got the signal to board. As our camper moved closer and closer to the ferry ramp, Taco's tail got lower and lower. By the time we drove aboard, her usually happy plume was bowed completely between her legs. She knew what was coming. We were about in the middle of the line of boarding vehicles so our camper was jammed in somewhere amidships. Again we attempted to explain to our "child" that this ride below decks was not a type of punishment for some unexplained misdeed (as she probably thought), but a necessary unpleasantness she had to endure by virtue of belonging to the wrong species of creature. Again it did no good, and again we departed wilted by the aggrieved expression on her face.

Old hands by now at ferry travel across the Gulf, we made our way unerringly to the Turista section, flopped in a couple of chairs, and immediately went to sleep. The ship sailed sometime after 9:30.

We reached the port of Guaymas at 4 a.m., and came scrambling out on deck only to discover that we had to lay off shore until the captain of the port awakened, had his breakfast, and escorted us in! Thus, it was 6 a.m. when the ferry finally docked. We went below, received a wild, joyous welcome from Taco who apparently hadn't slept a wink all night, and sleepily drove our camper out to the end of the wharf. Then we climbed in the back, ate breakfast, and did other morning things while we waited for the town to awaken.

The Seri Indians were once called the most primitive people on the North American continent. In fact it is reported that they had a history of cannibalism. At one time they were confined to Tiburon—an island off Mexico's west coast whose waters are alive with sharks. But as time went by, the Seris eschewed their unpleasant dining habits, learned the joys of outboard motorboats and other trappings of civilization, and began to leave their shark-infested waters for happier places. As they appeared on Mexico's coast in ever increasing numbers, the government decided to turn Tiburon island into a Naval base and give the Seris another piece of land to call their own. The land they gave them is a long stretch of coastline extending north from Bahía Kino. Because of its desert-like terrain and lack of water, the Seris didn't take to it, and it remains desolate. It was to this Seri land we were headed.

Soon the sun was fully up and Guaymas began to stir. We drove into town and replenished our larder at one of the supermarkets. Then we hit the highway, drove hard, and arrived at our jumping off place—Bahía

Kino—in the late afternoon.

Bahía Kino is a beautiful little beach resort for the wealthy citizens of the inland city of Hermosillo. It is very clean, with paved streets, artistic street lights, and a number of beautiful homes on the bay. Tiburon Island looms on the horizon, purple and majestic, and there's a sugar loaf rock jutting into the sky at the northern end of the bay. It is most picturesque, with flowers blooming everywhere.

We parked the camper and walked the Bahía Kino waterfront gazing at the beautiful homes and looking for *Se Vende* signs. None of the houses seemed to be for sale, but a number of lots were; a realtor's sign marked each lot. We wrote down the names and phone numbers of the various realtors, keying them to the lots we liked. We would check with the realtors later. Right now our main objective was to get off the road with our Dolphin.

To have pulled our camper out on one of those lots for the night would have been like camping next door to someone's home in Newport Beach or Long Island, so that was out of the question. Then we spotted a neat, attractive trailer park and our lovely camper finally lost her virginity. For the first time she was parked on a cement pad.

Being the off-the-road snobs that we are, Margie and I had always declared we would never take our camper into a trailer park—"I'd rather stay at a motel than do that!" I often said, but we both had to admit that at least for one night it was a pleasant change. The water there was potable, so we were able to refill our water tank. It was nice to hook up to the facilities, and nicest of all to take a fresh water shower after bathing in the ocean for over a week.

The next morning when we were getting ready to leave, we met our first Seri Indians. There were four of them—three men and a woman—attempting to sell us a wood sculpture. It was a figure of a sea bird in flight, very graceful and beautifully done.

"You want buy?" one of them said in English.

"How much?" I asked.

"Twenty dollar."

I had seen many similar sculptures all over Mexico for two and three dollars—six dollars at the most. "I'll give you two dollars," I said, offering two bills. My intent was to let him work me up to four or five.

The Indian just glared at me for a moment as if he loathed me with every fiber of his being, then spun on his heel and stalked off, followed by the others. All four of them had been surly and incredibly dirty. They looked as if they'd been sleeping on the ground with their clothes on all their lives. I felt relieved when they left.

According to a magazine article Margie had read, the road through the Indian reservation began somewhere near the sugar loaf rock at the north end of the bay. From there it snaked its treacherous way north through miles and miles of cactus and rocks—true badlands. According to reputation the road was chuckholed, washboard, and dangerous. It would be a good test for the camper—and the truck too.

We made a couple of false starts, ending up on roads that curved right back into town. But eventually we found the right one and were on our way. At first the road was a disappointment. It was quite wide and so well graded that we were able to zip along almost as if we were on pavement. It led us first to a tiny Indian settlement that boasted a new schoolhouse. We attempted to speak with a couple of the residents, but they just stared at us and turned away. They were filthy with dirt caked on their hair, bodies, and clothes. We waved gaily and smiled as we pulled away but still got no response.

"I believe they're misanthropic," I said.

"Miss and what?"

"Misanthropic. It means they hate everyone."

"I heard someplace that they do. Someone said the Seris don't even bother to learn Spanish."

"Well, we sure bombed out in two languages here!"

Suddenly, I found myself braking down to five miles an hour. The wide, graded road had ceased and it was now beginning to live up to its infamous reputation. Washboard road isn't spectacular to look at—from a slight distance it even appears smooth—but in my opinion it places the most severe strain on a camper. There is mile after mile of teeth-chattering vibration that never ceases until you stop. It loosens bolts, shakes plumbing loose, makes wiring snap, and even causes nails to back out of their settings. We vibrated past another Seri settlement of three houses, not bothering to stop. Again the Indians were filthy and sullen.

"Misanthropes," Margie said.

"You learn quickly."

We endured two more hours on the narrow washboard road that pitched up and down, winding through gullies and surmounting small hills. The only relief was when we came to soft sand and had to drop it into four-wheel-drive to get through. The road moved gradually inland so that we could only catch an occasional glimpse of the sea, sparkling and blue in the distance. Here, in the heat of the desert, it beckoned like a mirage.

"How about stopping for a minute and giving us a rest?" Margie said.

I braked to a stop and shut off the engine. It was dead quiet, but you could feel the presence of unseen desert life in the underbrush around us.

"I feel like I'm vibrating, even though we're stopped."

"So do I. And my hands are numb from holding the wheel."

We got out of the truck, stretched our legs for a few moments, then left the oven-like temperatures for the coolness of the Dolphin's interior. There we relaxed, sipping a Bloody Mary, and listening to the silence of the desert.

"When are we going to get to the ocean, Darling?" Margie said at length.

"I don't know. The road seems to stay inland all the time. I keep expecting it to curve toward the water, but it doesn't."

"I'd sure love to swim."

"Me too." I thought a moment. "Tell you what. What do you say we just turn off the road here and make our way across the open desert until we come to the ocean?"

"Do you think the truck can handle it?"

"I think it probably can. We'll just have to pick our way around the rocks and cactus."

"Well, it couldn't be any worse than that road!"

I walked gingerly through the brush, making lots of noise to scare off the snakes, and took a snapshot of our truck sitting in the desert with the ocean in the distance. Then we climbed back into the cab, turned off the road, and started working our way toward the sea.

We have found that in Mexico's very clear, smog-free air, things appear to be much closer than they are. What seems to be five miles distant is more likely ten miles or more. So it was with the ocean! Unfortunately, I neglected to look at the odometer when we turned off the road so I don't know how many miles we actually covered, but we drove for hours. We lost sight of the ocean for long periods of time due to the deep arroyos, tall desert brush, and the necessity of detouring around large rocks and cacti. The only way I could be sure we were still heading for the Gulf was to constantly consult the compass. The Dolphin swayed and lurched as we plunged down steep embankments and scrambled up the other side in fourwheel drive. It really *was* worse than the road. I was just about to call it quits and stop right where we were for the night when we emerged from a deep arroyo to see the beautiful, sparkling blue Gulf of California fifty yards in front of us. A mound of ice plant two or three feet high formed a natural sea wall, with the white sand of the beach beyond, and Mother Nature was just preparing a breathtaking sunset to welcome us.

"We'll drive over that ice plant and park right there beside it," I said.

Over the ice plant we went, all four wheels spinning, landed on the soft sand of the beach, pulled ahead fifty feet to a level spot and stopped. Without even bothering to make camp, we stripped off our clothes and ran naked to the water for a cooling swim.

The waves were much larger than they are on the Baja side, but the water is just as warm and inviting. I relaxed like a rag doll and allowed the waves to buffet me about for awhile—massaging and healing strained muscles and nerves. Finally, feeling waterlogged, I crawled up on the wet sand beside Margie. She was lying there wet and naked, staring at the sunset and looking like a beautiful, beached mermaid. We just laid there holding hands, watching the last rays of the sun making a path across the water, and reveling in our aloneness.

This part of Mexico's coastline is not a series of small coves as most of the Baja coast is. We were on what seemed to be one long, white sand beach stretching for miles. To the south we could make out an outcropping of land that hinted at the possibility of a cove on the other side, but the vista to the north was just deserted beach as far as the eye could see.

We did the few little chores necessary to set up camp by moonlight, and then I made a gross tactical error. I went into the Dolphin and mixed us a shakerful of daiquiris.

Margie and I very rarely drink too much, but on this occasion we both proceeded to get horribly drunk! We had eaten very little all day and were tired from the grueling drive, which probably made us more susceptible to the ministrations of alcohol. We were feeling no pain after the first round.

"I'd like another one of those good little drinks," Margie said, slurring her words slightly.

"Anything y'say m'dear," I said, and careened into the kitchen bruising my hip in the process.

As I shook the next batch of daiquiris, I though to myself, "Hey man, you're getting smashed!" Then I dismissed the thought and poured.

As drunken conversations often do, ours turned from light banter to deep discussions of enormous importance — so important neither of us would remember them in the morning.

By the time we got to the third shaker, Margie was expounding at length on something, when I began to notice that I was losing most of what she was saying, and her face was weaving in and out of focus.

Moreover, I felt that I needed a breath of fresh air.

"S'cuse me," I said, got up from my seat, and walked right through the screen door, sprawling on the sand and leaving a gaping hole in the screen.

I'll never know how we got to bed that night, but we both had terrible hangovers in the morning, and our beach was covered with snakes. Not hangover illusions; not eels; real honest-to-God snakes striped like tigers!

They all seemed to be dead, but there were hundreds of them all up and down the beach, and the waves were washing more of them ashore every minute. The sun glinting off their tiger stripes made them appear to be furry at first glance. They were water snakes, two to three feet long and incredibly ugly with long, nasty looking fangs. I had read an article about them once. The article had said that their natural habitat was the South Pacific, but there was evidence they were starting to migrate north. It also said that they were one of the most dangerous creatures in the world because their venom was fatal and there was no known antidote for it. I decided not to tell Margie how dangerous they were until we returned home because she'd never go swimming again, but I told her the rest.

"Why do you suppose all these dead ones are washing up here?"

"I don't know. Perhaps a Mexican shrimp boat pulled them up in their nets and just dumped them over the side."

"But we were swimming in that water last night. We could have had them wrapped all around us!"

"The shrimpers probably hadn't dumped them overboard last night," I said, satisfied with my theory.

"Well, I'm going to get them off our beach!" So saying, Margie the compulsive house cleaner, got a stick and began flipping them one by one back into the ocean to be carried away by the outgoing tide. She spent the remainder of the morning doing it.

I took a snapshot of one of the snakes, and then set about the task of checking the camper to see how it had withstood the terrible beating from the day before. I was very thorough and took a lot of time. I put a wrench on each plumbing connection to see if it had loosened; after checking all electrical connections, I went over the camper inch by inch, checking nails and screws to see if any of them had backed out of their settings from the constant, day-long vibration. Two screws on a window sill had loosened a bit, but otherwise the Dolphin's only damage was the large, embarrassing hole in the screen door. Our camper passed everything but the "Drunk Test!"

We stayed out of the ocean and didn't touch booze the rest of that day, barbecued hamburgers by moonlight that evening, and tumbled into bed early.

The next day dawned bright and beautiful. And the next and the next and the next. The snakes were gone. The water was clear, clean, and warm, and the music of the waves was a lullaby. The languor of "The Baja Feeling" engulfed us again. We set up two "rooms" in the sand beside our camper. One was for sitting and staring in the morning, the other for sitting and staring in the afternoon (governed by the position of the sun at those times). Most of the day was spent sitting in one of those "rooms," passing the binoculars back and forth. We even became too lazy for "beastie hunts."

Just to the north of us and far out to sea, was a tiny island—or more accurately a large rock. It was dyed flat white from bird guano, and looked like a scoop of vanilla ice cream floating on the glistening water. We checked it several times a day as if we expected it might one day drift away. We watched the pelicans diving for fish—graceful despite their awkward shape—and occasionally spotted a shrimp boat gliding silently along the horizon. We knew that buying land on an Indian reservation would be impossible, but we talked about the kind of a house we would build here *if* we could, and drew floor plans in the sand.

Some of our friends marvel that the two of us can spend weeks alone together in what they call "God-forsaken spots." They ask: "Don't you get bored with each other? Don't you have fights? What do you talk about?" Perhaps the nicest thing about being alone together is that we don't have to talk at all. If another couple were with us, we would feel obliged to keep the conversation going, but we often sit and stare at the sea for long periods of time without talking at all—content in each other's company. Margie and I never have real fights, but we have some pretty spirited debates now and then. They're fun once in awhile and add to the zest of living. As for our various camp sites being "God-forsaken," we feel the opposite is true. If God is anywhere, it is surely there. Would the Creator of such beauty choose a smog-choked city filled with the creations of man?

So the lazy days passed with the two of us sitting quietly, chatting softly, swimming in the glorious ocean, and making love under God's sky. As usual, little events became memorable. There was the time an injured duck was caught in the breakers in front of our camp. For a time we watched him valiantly trying to swim back to deep water, but each time he tried, a huge comber would catch him and slam him back. After awhile I could stand it no longer.

"I'm going to see if I can swim out there and help that little guy," I said.

"How are you going to do that?"

"Well, he's obviously injured, so maybe I can get close to him. If so, I'll grab him and toss him over the breakers into the deep water."

Margie grabbed the camera and followed me.

I could see the little duck eyeing me warily as I swam closer and closer. Then, suddenly, a huge wave engulfed us both and I lost sight of him. I looked anxiously around and found him again. He was now fifty yards down the beach from me and still in dangerous water. With Margie clicking the camera from shore, I tried another approach. Just as he was almost within my grasp he gave a weak flutter and got away from me. Then another wave swamped us and when I emerged spouting water, the duck was again way down the beach, frightened by my presence, and terrified of its predictament. We were getting pretty far from camp now, but I tried again with the same results. Two more tries and I was exhausted. The little duck was still struggling in the waves out of reach. I gave up and left him to his fate. Margie's snapshots merely show me floundering in the breakers and a tiny black spot just beyound me.

The langurous days had drifted by and at length it was time to start for home. We packed, and made the camper ready for its bone-cracking drive back to civilization. But, alas, we were still filled with "The Baja Feeling" which caused me to violate one of the cardinal rules of off-the-road driving: *Whenever you have driven your rig onto soft stuff be sure to exit at the same place you entered.*

The purpose of this rule is fairly obvious. If you got there by a certain route, you know it is passable and you can back-track. If you attempt to pioneer a route you may get stuck.

"Hey, Darling," I said while the engine was warming up, "instead of getting off the beach where we came in, let's drive along it for a way and find a different way off."

"Oh, that'd be fun!" Margie said.

The engine warm, I put it into four-wheel-drive and compound low and started pulling forward on the soft sand. For twenty-five or thirty feet there was no difficulty, and then the characteristics of the sand abruptly changed. It became the kind of "ball bearing sand" we had encountered years before in the Toy—sand consisting of billions of ground shells that offer absolutely no traction. All four wheels spun and dug in.

"Oh my God! And we're miles from any help," Margie said.

"Don't worry," I said brightly, "I'll just let some more air out of the tires and we'll be going again in a jiffy."

I let the air out until all four tires were nearly flat, climbed in the cab, and started forward again. Like going down in quicksand, the truck and camper sunk in up to the truck bed! We both sat silently for a moment.

Back in the 1950s, I produced and hosted an all-night radio show on KFI in Los Angeles. It developed a large national audience, and is conceded to be the first phone-talk show in the country. However, all of the interviews were not by telephone. I often scheduled in-studio guests, and one of the most popular of these was an intrepid couple named Dana and Ginger Lamb. The Lambs would plunk themselves deep in the interior of a Central American rain forest, or in the middle of a trackless desert somewhere, without food, and would scrunch water out of cactus, build a shelter out of brambles, and live to tell my enraptured audience how it was done. Their *raison d'étre* was to prove that man can live quite nicely in a hostile environment if he has a few skills and uses his wits. As I contemplated our plight, and our dwindling supplies, I fervently wished I could remember some of the survival tricks they had taught.

"Well, Lord and Master, *now* what do you suggest?!" There was an edge to Margie's voice.

"We have two alternatives, Margie. We can leave our rig here and try to walk all those miles back through the snakes, or we can dig out—which I'm sure you'd rather do." I noted my voice was sounding testy too, and I didn't have the confidence that we *could* dig out. That stuff was very, very soft!

We got out the shovel and started digging. To excavate a three-quarter ton truck that's buried that deep takes a lot of digging. I dug until my back ached, and then Margie dug for a while. Whoever wasn't working the shovel gathered brush and brambles from the adjacent desert to place under the wheels. I had to smile in spite of our problems when Margie, who has claustrophobia, slid under the belly of the truck on her stomach and shovelfuls of sand came flying out as if an oversized, busy gopher were burrowing there. The closeness of the cramped quarters must have frightened her, but her desire to get us out of this mess overcame her fear!

We took a break, ate lunch, had a tequila for courage, and resumed digging.

Soon, mountains of loose sand had been dug away, and a neat ramp had been made to drive our rig out of the hole it was in. Then we lined the tire track areas with the desert shrubbery we had accumulated. I prayed it would work.

I was about to start the engine again when I had a sudden thought:
"Oh my God!" I howled. "Oh no!" I put my head in my hands.

"What?" Margie said, alarmed.

"The anchor!"

"*What* anchor?"

"The one we used to have in the Toy. It's here! I forgot all about it!"

"You didn't give it away with all that other stuff?"

"No. I thought we might need it to winch out some day and it's packed.
It's in the rope locker."

I thought Margie took it quite well under the circumstances.

"You stupid son of a bitch!" she said.

I removed the anchor and assembled it, then carried it out to the wet
sand in as near a straight line from the winch as I could—I didn't want the
winch to be pulling us sideways. I buried the anchor deep in the sand with
just the tip of the shank showing, uncoiled sufficient cable from the
winch, and made it fast to the anchor. I started the truck's engine again,
moved it cautiously into gear, and pressed the switch that actuated the
winch. It began to grind and the cable became taut. I held my breath.
The anchor started dragging through the sand leaving twin furrows
behind it. I swore. It wasn't going to work. After all those years of
carrying that stupid anchor with us, it was going to be useless—and we'd
never get off this beach! Then, suddenly, the flukes dug in and the truck
began to move slightly. Very gently I pressed the throttle allowing the
truck's wheels to turn and assist the winch. Slowly—inexorably—it
mounted the ramp and began to move out of the hole. Then, it was being
drawn toward the anchor faster and faster and then we were on hard, wet
sand. We were free!

"Oh thank God!" Margie said, and kissed me. Apparently I was now
forgiven.

I put the blessed anchor back in its locker, closed things up, and we
were on our way at last. I made a one hundred eighty degree turn, and
exited the beach via the route we had used to enter.

The drive through the desert back to Bahía Kino was even more
interminable than the ride out had been. Famished, we stopped once for a
quick supper, then continued jarring the daylights out of ourselves on the
washboard. We arrived at Bahía Kino long after dark, and checked into
the trailer park again.

The next morning, I checked the camper for road damage, and again
found it sound. We left and made record time getting back to Los
Angeles.

The more we thought of our beautiful beach at Bahia Concepción with its warm, placid water, great fishing, and island view, the more we thought we'd like to build a house there, so we placed a phone call to our friend Victor Rubio in Tijuana to see if he'd been successful in purchasing the property—perhaps we could buy a lot from him.

"I'm sorry," he said, "I wasn't able to buy the land. A Mexican politician outbid me. He says he's going to develop it as a tourist area."

As this is written, a large trailer park stands right on the spot where we camped. I hope "Augustino, the fisherman of Machaca," got part of the action.

9/ Ricardo

In the many years that have passed since our first trip in Margie's Tempest, there have been great changes in Baja. The paved highway is now a cement fact; *paraderos* [stopping places] have been erected strategically along the route where travelers can purchase gas and supplies or even sleep overnight; luxury hotels with all the amenities are blossoming; and Americans are traveling the peninsula in every conveyance from campers to Cadillacs. It has become a bit of a challenge to us to find new, isolated beaches, but somehow we always succeed. One such beach is located near San Quintin and named Colonia de Sudoeste.

San Quintin is a natural, almost closed-in harbor about 130 miles south of Ensenada on Baja's Pacific coast. Viewed from the air it resembles a crab's claw with the open end facing south. The seaward side of this claw is a long, sand spit rolling with giant sand dunes and pounded by the cold waves of the Pacific Ocean. This sand spit is Colonia de Sudoeste (Southeast Colony) but there is no colony there. It is devoid of any civilization, and inaccessable except by four-wheel-drive.

We found it by accident in 1974. We were speeding along the new highway in our truck when we spied a dirt track wriggling off to our right in the general direction of the ocean (the highway is quite far inland at this point). On sudden impulse, we turned off and began following the wandering tire tracks for hours across plowed fields dotted with tiny adobe *casas*, up and down hills and through valleys, and fording one fairly large, stagnant pond. Shortly after splashing through the pond we descended into a valley with a snow-white lake. If it hadn't been so hot we'd have thought the lake was frozen. Closer inspection revealed that the whiteness was caused by a very heavy concentration of salt in the water. It was being allowed to leach out in the sun.

From there, the track reared up and delivered some very steep grades which finally terminated on a cliff overlooking a rocky beach. The so-called "road" then continued south along the edge of the cliff. Deep, soft sand almost caused us to bog down several times and the road slanted to such a degree it seemed we were tipping at a 45-degree angle at times (I didn't have the nerve to stop and get out to see how much the angle actually was!) It ended at another cliff, looking down on a spotless, white sand beach. So with Margie and Taco walking and leading the way, down we went, across the sand, and parked our Dolphin next to a large sand dune. According to the map this was Colonia de Sudoeste.

Our beach was over a mile long and guarded at each end by tall rock cliffs. At the toe of each cliff was a reef jutting out into the sea. The reefs were filled with tide pools, and the waves crashed over them, sending spume soaring into the air. The cliff to the south was barren, but the one on the north was topped by a tiny shack, probably inhabited at one time by a fisherman. When we arrived, the shack was deserted so we had the beach all to ourselves. We made camp and slipped at once into "The Baja Feeling."

"The Baja Feeling" often included mammoth make-work projects, and we became involved in one of them the first day. Margie decided that if we had a patio at the back of the camper we wouldn't track so much sand inside, so we set about building it. We gathered great mounds of dried seaweed which Margie spread out on the sand as a bed for the stones. Then, as I worked myself a bit closer to a hernia, lugging smooth stones about the size of half a grapefruit to our camp in pails and boxes, Margie sorted them as to size, and carefully fitted them in place. It took three or four days to complete the patio, but when it was done it was about ten feet square, and boasted our initials outlined in white rocks in the center. It was a work of art, and actually did seem to cut down on the quantities of sand to be swept out of the Dolphin each morning.

Another of our early projects was to go clamming. This area is famous for giant Pismo clams and we had resolved to get a few. Each of us tied a gunny sack around the waist with a piece of clothesline rope. The sack is tied in such a way that one portion is left gaping open so the clam can be dropped into the sack without removing the sack from your body. Then, armed with pitchforks, we waded out into the icy water. Margie plunged her pitchfork into the sand and it clanked.

"I've got one!" she cried, and pulled out a beauty nearly six inches in diameter!

At that same instant I had felt my pitchfork strike something. I reached down in the water and extracted one equally big.

"I've got another!"

"So have I!"

We were finding the giant Pismo clams almost as fast as we could pull them out of the water. We forgot how cold the ocean was, and we forgot that the tide was coming in. As our frantic harvest went on, the water became deeper and deeper and the waves higher. Soon we were thrashing about in water up to our chests and being knocked over by the breakers. Shivering and half drowned, we struggled out of the water and up to camp with enough clams to last for days. We placed them to soak in water overnight so they would spit out the sand, and I cleaned them in the morning.

That led to our next big project: "The Bird Watch." The seagulls had been circling me hungrily as I removed the entrails from the clams and it gave me an idea.

"I'd like to get a *really* close-up snapshot of one of those birds and I think I know how."

"How? With clam guts?"

"Right. I'll put a pile of them in an empty clam shell and place it out there on the beach. Then we can put our beach chairs right beside it and wait for a gull to get hungry enough to come that close to us. Then I'll get my picture."

By the time I had placed the shell full of clam innards on the beach, got the camera, and placed the beach chairs, Margie showed up with sandwiches—Taco trotting happily behind her. We bedded Taco down in the shade of one of the chairs with admonitions to be very quiet, and settled down to wait, about six feet away from our clam bait.

None of this action had been lost on the gulls. From the moment I had placed the shell on the sand, they had set up a terrible squawking and screeching. It was almost as if they were screaming to each other: "Hey man! Look what that dude just set out on our beach!" Time and again one of them would swoop over our heads for a fly-by look at the clam meat and then the screeching would become louder than ever. We took turns holding the camera focused on the spot where a bird would land . . . but none landed.

After about half an hour we noticed something new was afoot. A particularly large gull had laid claim to our clam meat and was chasing the others away. Gradually, the din faded as the other gulls went flapping off to other fishing grounds and Mr. Big-gull had the territory all to himself—and us. He swooped by low over the clam shell a couple of times, reassuring himself that his loot was intact, then he took up a position on a sand dune a few yards away and never took his beady eyes off us. He was going to try to wait us out.

The time dragged on. Once in awhile Margie returned to the camper, but other than that we just sat and waited, camera at ready, conscious of the gull's unwavering stare. It was getting boring, but I was stubborn. I was going to get that picture!

About mid-afternoon he tried to fool us. He suddenly took to the air and flapped off to the south out of sight as if he'd suddenly lost all interest in our bait. But we continued to wait and—a few minutes later—he came winging in from the north on schedule, did his usual low fly-by to have another look at his meal, saw that it had been moved and did the funniest in-flight double-take I have ever seen! We both broke out laughing.

"Up until now I thought Stan Laurel was the master of the slow double-take, but this bird's got him beat!" I laughed.

"I'm going to call him Stanley," Margie said.

Stanley resumed his vigil on the dune, and we resumed ours. More time passed.

In the late afternoon Stanley came up with a new ploy. He leaped into the air and circled once leading us to believe he was going to fly off again. Instead, to our astonishment, he dropped down on the beach just a short distance from us and the bait. He then proceeded to stroll casually back and forth looking out to sea! It was as if he were humming "Tum tum tee tum" and saying, "Lovely day, isn't it? Who cares about clams on a day like this?" Occasionally he'd look our way to see if we were catching his act ("See how casual I am?"). Then he'd go back to his strolling.

The sun was now beginning to set and we'd been sitting out there with that damn bird since noon! I was stiff from sitting, and was now hungry.

"You mean you're going to let Stanley win?" asked Margie with a twinkle.

"Yeah, dammit! I guess so."

We folded the beach chairs and started back towards the camper. Before we had gone fifty feet the gull snapped the meat out of the clam shell and flew off, chomping his well-earned dinner as he flew.

"You win, Stanley!" I shouted at the sky. "You win!"

That same evening, we saw smoke curling into the sky from the fisherman's shack on the cliff and concluded we were no longer alone.

Very early the next morning we saw a tiny figure followed by a smaller one descend from the shack at the top of the cliff to our beach.

"That's the fisherman I guess," I said, "but what's that thing scooting along behind him? It sure isn't a dog."

"I can't tell from this distance." Margie picked up the binoculars and studied the man and his companion for a moment. "Oh God!" She slammed the binoculars down and covered her face.

"What's the matter?" I picked them up and focused on the two dots down the beach. It was a fisherman alright, and he was moving at a rapid pace, but scuttling along the beach behind him like a crab was a little boy. Apparently the child's legs were useless so he hunched along on his posterior pushing with hands trying to keep up with the man. It was a pathetic sight.

"My Lord! You'd think they'd get the kid a pair of crutches!"

"They probably can't afford it—or maybe his legs are too far gone to use crutches. Poor people."

"Well he's learned to move pretty fast that way," I said consolingly, but inwardly I didn't want to see the boy again. It was too depressing.

Margie picked up the binoculars again and watched until they were both out of sight behind the rocks at the far end of the beach.

"His little hands must be like leather," she said. "He scoots across those sharp rocks just as fast as his father can walk!"

"Don't tell me about it."

We finished breakfast and went about our activities. Margie was putting the finishing touches on her patio and I was deeply involved in the construction of a sun dial around our fire pit. The pit was quite deep and protected from the breeze by a ring of large rocks. Using some strong glue we always carry with us, I was sticking shells on the rocks at the various hourly positions. My theory was that when I placed a stick upright in the center of the firepit, its shadow would fall on the shell indicating the time of day. I became more deeply engrossed than usual in my project to blot out the picture of the little child hunching his way along the beach. If Margie thought about it at all she didn't mention it, and the morning passed.

That afternoon I tried a little surf fishing and had exceptional luck. I caught several perch and a good sized corbina just perfect for barbecuing. I cleaned and filleted the fish and Margie slathered them with butter, lemon juice, garlic, and other seasonings, put them in foil, and barbecued them. They were utterly delicious. Then we watched a gorgeous sunset. Later, sitting under the stars while our wood fire crackled I brought up the subject again:

"I didn't see the little crippled boy all day, did you?"

"Nope."

"Do you suppose he and his father are still out on that reef?"

"I don't know. They could have walked past us while we were working on our projects."

"Yeah, I guess so."

There was a long pause while I waited for Margie to say something— perhaps another opinion as to where they might be, how the boy became crippled, or *something*—but she was silent. "How come you don't have any other opinions?" I said finally.

"You said you didn't want to talk about it."

"I guess I really don't." I was solemn.

The next day dawned stormy. During the night huge black clouds had rolled in from the sea; the beach was gray, overcast, and cold. We stayed inside our camper most of the morning reading or playing cards and waiting for the weather to clear, but it got worse. Around one o'clock there was a flash of lightning that turned the beach silvery and shimmered across the entire horizon.

A rolling roar of thunder shook the camper, and the resounding clap echoed in the pit of our stomachs. The storm began. For the next hour we ceased doing anything and just stared, spellbound, at nature's awesome display. The blinding white sheet lightning filled the sky and illuminated the whole countryside brighter than the brightest day. The thunder that followed it seemed to threaten to split the earth wide open. It terrified poor Taco. She just stood shivering, with her tail clamped between her legs.

Perhaps harking back to her heritage as a creature of the wild, Taco finds security in a cave—any makeshift cave will do. So I lifted her up into the bunk and built a cave for her out of blankets. There she remained, with just her nose protruding, for the duration of the storm.

The thunder and lighting continued and soon the wind came—cold and biting—bearing torrents of rain. The wind whipped the rain against the side of our camper with such force it sounded as if some huge monster were hurling great scoops of gravel at us. Though shaking with the increasing violence of the storm, our Dolphin was snug and warm inside, but we felt more alone than ever before—two lone souls at the mercy of the raging elements.

Just before the dark skies turned black with night, the celestial fireworks ceased, the wind died, and rain let up to a steady drip.

"It looks hopeful in the East," Margie said. "Maybe we'll have a nice day tomorrow."

We didn't. The fury of the storm seemed to be spent by morning, but the dark clouds and the dripping rain remained. Bundled up in our warmest clothes, we inspected our camp and found everything sodden but intact. Then we took a brief stroll on the storm-ravaged beach, returned, and again waited for the sun.

"One more day of this rotten weather and I'll feel like breaking camp and heading somewhere else," I said.

"It really *is* looking hopeful in the east," Margie answered.

The next day it began to rain a little harder. We arose early, had breakfast, then sat in the camper doing crossword puzzles until nearly noon.

"What a lousy way to spend a vacation!" I growled. "All we're doing is sitting here waiting for good weather that may never come. What do you say we break camp?"

Margie thought a minute. "I feel like you do, Darling, but wouldn't it be awful to leave here and have the next day be beautiful? Let's stay just one more day."

"Honey, it's been raining for three days now!"

"I know. But look—see over there? There's a tiny bit of sunshine peeking through the clouds—"

I interrupted. "I know what you're going to say. It looks hopeful in the east."

"Well, it does," she said defensively.

The next morning we awakened to a beach bathed in glorious, hot sunshine. The ocean was sparkling blue and we hastened to the water for our first bath in three days. We completed our bath and sprinted back to the camper just in time because the crippled boy and three little girls came down to the beach for a swim. As we hastily donned our clothes, Taco trotted down to the waterfront to join the children, her tail wagging furiously, and soon they were all petting her and talking to her.

"Our Good Will Ambassador is doing her thing again," I said.

"I'm going down and talk to the children too," Margie said, giving her hair a final pat.

"I'll stay here. I want to clean and oil my reel."

Armed with some hard candies we always carry with us, Margie headed down to the waterfront to join Taco and the kids.

My fishing reel didn't really need attention, but I was reluctant to face the crippled child. Even so, I couldn't resist stealing a glance now and then to see how Margie was doing. As usual, she had completely captivated the children. She was seated on the wet sand and four children were gathered around her in a circle talking animatedly. The little boy's useless legs sprawled and curled like wet noodles attached to his torso, and to my horror I saw that his left hand was just a stub. The fingers, frozen together in paralysis, had started to atrophy. It was this club-like arm that he used to push himself along the beach.

After a time, like the Pied Piper of Hamlin, Margie came skipping up the beach to the camper, followed by Taco and the four giggling children—three of them running, the fourth scuttling. The three little girls stood respectfully—the crippled boy sat very erect—as she made the introductions:

"Es mi esposo, Benito."

"Mucho gusto," I said.

"Mucho gusto," they murmered seriously (in the land of macho, a child shows respect for the head of the family!) Then she pointed to each of the little girls as she introduced them. "Belinda . . . Vailer . . . Urbano . . . " Margie patted the little boy on the head, "Y esto es Ricardo!" she said with a flourish, and the little guy beamed.

"Cuantos años tiene, Ricardo?" I asked him.

"Nueve, Señor," he said politely.

Nine years old and gosh what a cute child! His bare torso was brown, lean and muscular from years of assuming the work of his legs. His little brown face set off two of the largest black eyes I have ever seen, and was topped with a swatch of unruly black hair; his smile lit up the beach.

"Las muchachas son sus hermanas?" [The girls are your sisters?].

"No Señor. Mis primas." [No, sir. My cousins.]

I asked a few more questions and discovered that Ricardo did not live in the house atop the cliff. The fisherman was his uncle, and Ricardo was there for a short visit. His home was in an ejido [free public land like a homestead] near San Quintin. The house had seemed deserted to us because the uncle had been visiting Ricardo's family. Now Ricardo would visit his cousins for the rest of the week and then return home. As we chatted I forgot his deformities and was completely enchanted by his dazzling smile and alert little mind. "I could adopt such a child," I thought to myself. Margie brought an end to our conversation:

"Ficase!" [Observe!] she said, and produced one of our old magazines out of the camper.

The "official" interview with the head of the household now concluded, the children gathered around her once more, chattering and pointing at the pictures in the magazine. In these outlying regions of Mexico there are few periodicals of any kind and even fewer pictures, so Margie was offering them a real novelty. *"Qué es?"* [What is it?] they said time and again, and Margie would explain that it was a washing machine, a fancy bathroom, or what-have-you. All of these items were completely unknown to her little guests. At length it was time for them to go. Margie kissed each of them on the nose, causing much giggling; they shook hands with me gravely, and departed with vows to return the next day.

After they had gone, I said, "Well I found out quite a bit about Ricardo, but I wish I'd asked him about his illness."

"I did," Margie said. "It was polio, of course, and he had it when he was very young. He says he doesn't remember being able to use his legs."

"What a shame. Except for that, he's just about the cutest little guy I've ever seen."

The following morning is memorable because of our discovery of the strangest sea creature we have ever found. Except for the three days of the storm, we had taken daily "beastie hunt" walks, and they had been singularly unrewarding. But the seas and beaches are ever-changing and you never know what treasure the next day's tide may bring you, so this morning we set forth again. The storm had washed a lot of seaweed up on the shore and Margie spied him lying nearly buried in an extra large clump. "Ben! Come here! Look what I've found!"

I approached. "What?"

"There!" she pointed. "In the seaweed." She pulled a branch of it back, revealing the animal. "Isn't he weird?"

The main part his body consisted of a round, dark ball about the size of a marble with a sphincter-like hole in the center. Extending out in each direction from this central body were two wings—fragile, purplish, and translucent. Hundreds of tiny feelers emerged from the interior of each wing wriggling and clasping each other.

"You know what he looks like?" I said.

"What?"

"A flying asshole."

She laughed. "Why don't you get the bucket and we'll put him in it. He looks like he's still alive."

I went back to camp, picked up the bucket, filled it with seawater, and returned. Margie carefully scooped it up in a shell, and deposited him in the water. At once, he proceeded to perform fascinating aquabatics! Waving his beautiful wings back and forth he swooped and turned, did loop-the-loops, and gracefully turned around his own center. Sometimes the two wings would touch together like hands in prayer and the feeler from one wing would clasp the feeler from the other ("Is that you, George?")

We both laughed. "He's fabulous!" Margie said. "I'd like to take him home with us."

"I'll bet we can. A thing like that probably survives on plankton, so if we keep his water fresh, he'll have plenty to eat."

We took him up to our camp and deposited him in the shade of the Dolphin, then proceeded to look him up in our book. He simply wasn't there. The author neither pictured nor described anything remotely resembling him.

"I've got an idea," I said. "They say that when you discover an unknown creature of some sort you receive the honor of naming it. Wouldn't it be great if this was a new discovery and we got to name it?"

"You wouldn't!" Margie said, anticipating me.

"Oh yes I would! Right in the middle of all those difficult Latin names scientists like to use would be *Flying Asshole Hunterus!*"

"You know he might really be a new discovery," Margie said seriously, "and I don't think they'd allow *your* name for him."

"Alright then, for the sophistry of the scientific community, I'll put it in Latin. How about calling him *Anus alar hunterus?*"

She clapped her hands gleefully. "I love it!"

He's been known as *anus alar* ever since. We did, in fact, get him home alive, showed him—and pictures of him—to several scientists, none of whom have been able to positively identify him. To this day he does his aquabatics in a salt water aquarium owned by our scientist friend Arnold Newman in North Hollywood.

One afternoon, shortly after we had discovered *anus alar*, Ricardo and his cousins went for a swim again. Wearing only his jeans, Ricardo plunged his arms into the water swimming strongly, his legs trailing behind him like the tail of a kite. He would swim out, catch a wave, and body surf into shore as well or better than children with the full use of their bodies. Then, smiling, wet, and glistening in the warm sun, he and the little girls came up to our camp for another visit.

Now that we were good friends, their visit was much less formal. All of us laughed and played together. They found Taco's name very funny since Mexicans always give their pets human names. Margie found some more magazines which provided lots of conversation, and she magically produced a can of popcorn which made a tremendous hit. The kids taught us the Spanish word for popcorn—*rosetas* [little roses], a much prettier word than ours. By the time they left, Margie and I were even more captivated by little Ricardo.

The days that followed were typical, lazy Baja days in the sun. We sun-tanned, swam, went for walks on the beach, explored the tide pools, and fished.

One day I caught a fairly large perch, and inadvertently became her midwife. I placed the fish on the sand, prepatory to cleaning it when mature babies started to pop out! By pushing on her abdomen I caused more births, and was soon the surprised adoptive father of nearly a dozen fully-formed perch. I lost all appetite for perch at that moment and tossed the whole family back into the sea. I understand that baby perch are often able to mate the moment they leave the womb, so perhaps I was instrumental in increasing the perch population measurably!

Another day we saw two very tough looking young Mexicans coming down the beach from some place south of us. Despite all of our experiences where such people had proved harmless, I felt uneasy when I saw them heading straight for our camp. Taco is a discriminating watch dog—snarling at some and welcoming others—but she snarled and set up a terrible fuss. I glanced about for a shovel or pitchfork that might serve as a temporary weapon, but it wasn't needed. Taco held them at bay a few feet away and I made no attempt to collar her.

"*Quiere comprar langostas ó abulón?*" said one of them. A deep scar on his cheek twitched as he flashed a yellow smile.

"*Somos buzos,*" said the other, holding up a sack.

I had sent Margie into the Dolphin when I saw them coming. Now I stalled for time by yelling to her: "They say they're divers and they want to sell us lobster or abalone, Honey. What do you think?"

"I know. I heard," she said, coming to the window. "Ask them how much."

"*Cuanto?*" I said to the men.

We dickered over the price for a few minutes and I finally decided they were alright despite their appearance. I then grabbed Taco by the collar, made her shut up, and completed the purchase. I bought two large lobsters for $1.50 each and a half dozen abalones for twenty-five cents apiece. That was all they had in their sack, so they just dumped it at my feet, and the lobsters started crawling across the hot sand. I paid the divers and they headed gleefully off in the direction of San Quintin.

"You are walking to San Quintin?" I asked in Spanish.

"*Sí.*"

"Es muy lejos." [it's very far.]

"Sí," they said again.

"What will you do in San Quintin?"

"We will now buy something to eat," they replied in Spanish. Then they were gone.

The lobsters they sold us were out of season, and great globs of golden roe clung to their shells. I have heard that this roe is a great delicacy but—for once—it was an item Margie didn't know how to prepare. We merely removed the roe, twisted off the tails, and barbecued them with lots of butter. They were heavenly. We cleaned, sliced, and pounded the abalone meat and put it in the freezer to take home.

Most of our time, however, was spent laying in the sun, watching the sea change colors, and staring at the sea birds. The visits from Ricardo and his cousins were a daily ritual, and we grew to love all four children. At length, it was the eve of our departure, and the lovely days had passed like a few hours. We had told the children goodbye earlier and sent them off with gifts of hard candies. To our astonishment, the little girls' mother—whom we had never met—sent a gift to us! It was a glass jar filled with especially pretty stones she had painstakingly gathered on the beach. They were packed in the jar with water to increase their luster. Now we sat beside our last campfire watching the stars fill the black sky, and hating to leave our beach in the morning.

"I'm going to miss the kids too," I sighed.

"Me too. They're darling children."

There was a long pause. Something had been turning over in my mind for several days, but I wanted to be sure I really meant it before I said it to Margie. Yes, I decided at length, it's not just a passing emotion—I really do mean it.

"Margie?"

"Yes?"

"I've got an idea. I've been thinking about it for several days."

"I'll bet it's the same idea I've got."

"What is it?"

"Is it about Ricardo?" She looked at me searchingly.

"Yup."

"You've been thinking you'd like to take him back to the States for an operation on his legs."

That was it. Margie is uncanny sometimes. "That's right. We'd have to get his folks' permission, of course. We could keep him at our house in the guest bedroom—"

264

She finished it. "And we'd get the very finest surgeon we could find to see if he couldn't make Ricardo walk again!"

"Right!"

Excitedly we talked over our plans. As soon as we broke camp in the morning we'd talk to Ricardo's uncle and find out where the boy lived. Then we'd visit his parents and tell them of our plans. If the parents approved (How could they say no?) we'd return to the States, line up the doctor and hospital, and make all the other necessary arrangements, then come back here and pick him up. The operation and hospitalization would be expensive, but it would be worth it to see that little guy able to walk. Then, when he was recuperating in our home, what fun it would be to show him our world—a world he'd only glimpsed in the magazines we'd brought with us. Suddenly, our departure time couldn't arrive fast enough!

We four-wheeled our way through the soft sand, and up the steep cliff to where the fisherman's shack stood. He was sitting on the steps gazing at us curiously when we arrived.

"You are the uncle of Ricardo?" I asked in Spanish.

"Sí."

I then explained briefly what we had in mind. To my surprise, the uncle didn't act either pleased or displeased.

"Está bien," [That's fine] he said blandly. "The muchacho will guide you." He got to his feet and entered the shack.

A moment later Ricardo came scuttling out the door. Even though our truck stands very high off the ground, Ricardo swung himself up onto the front seat without help. He was amazing! Then we were off, with Ricardo giving directions from his place in the middle of the seat.

Ricardo's directions took us back to the highway via a much easier route than we had traveled to get there. The dirt road was well packed and hard, without too many bad grades, and we were able to move along at a pretty fast clip. (How had we missed this road coming in?) He instructed us to turn north when we reached the highway, and Margie and I both began memorizing the route so we could find our way back to his house.

It was a very large ejido. There were perhaps a hundred or more houses arranged in blocks criss-crossed by dirt roads deep in powdery, pink dust. The houses were a hodge-podge of adobes, clapboards, and tar paper shacks with dirt floors. None of them had doors or glass windows. Scores of dust-covered children played in the street and we had to drive slowly to keep from hitting them. Cars in the ejido were a rarity and

265

campers even rarer, so they all stared as we drove by.

"*Es mi casa,*" he said, pointing at one of the houses. We pulled up and stopped.

Ricardo's house was adobe, somewhat larger than most, and boasted a six foot high rickety board fence around the backyard. There was no electricity in the *ejido* and his mother was inside in the dark, rolling out tortillas when we arrived.

"*Buenos días,*" I said from the doorway. "We come to speak with the parents of Ricardo."

She wiped her hands on her apron and stepped outside into the sunshine, folding her arms across her ample bosom. She was a plump woman, about forty years old I guessed, and she looked tired.

"*Sí?*"

I explained what we wanted to do for Ricardo.

She listened carefully without a trace of expression on her face. "You must speak to the father," she said in Spanish, then disappeared into the house.

A moment later Ricardo's father emerged. He was tall and slim with graying hair. He wore a large sombrero, and walked very erect. His almost condescending manner caused me to judge him to be a very proud man, indeed.

"*Buenos días, señor,*" I said, and proceeded to go into a detailed account of what we had in mind. This was quite difficult for me to do because I didn't know many of the Spanish words I needed and had to improvise. For "orthopedic surgeon," I said "doctor of bones"; for "recuperation period", I had to say "days of rest"; and so on, but he seemed to understand and listened impassively.

When at last I'd finished, he said "*Bien.* And who are you?"

Good grief! I'd been so excited about our project, that I hadn't even introduced us! To him, we were just a couple of *gringo* strangers coming in off the beach with this wild proposal about his son. No wonder he'd been impassive! I apologized, introduced myself and Margie, and produced my wallet with my driver's license, credit cards, and other forms of identification. He seemed unimpressed until I mentioned that I worked on television. Ah yes, he knew of television. He had seen it once in Ensenada. Now that I had his interest, I started the pitch again with my coined Spanish phrases. I never did a commercial spiel on television with more fervor than this, and at length he began to nod in agreement. Finally I got him to state that I had his permission to give Ricardo the operation, and have the child live with us for six months or more in the States, but he

266

still didn't seem enthusiastic. I then asked him if he had a mailing address. "Sí. I receive the newspaper," he said proudly.

"Then give it to me, and I will write to you when we are coming back for Ricardo."

He had neither paper nor pencil, but Margie produced some from the camper, and he painstakingly wrote his name and *apartado postal*. His name was Manuel Silva. His childlike handwriting was large and cramped, but legible.

I thanked him and we departed, with my head aching from attempting to swim through unfamiliar conversational waters.

For once, the time flew as we drove home from Mexico, because we talked of our plans for Ricardo all the way back. Of course, the item at the top of the agenda was to locate the best orthopedic surgeon we could find. I also wanted to get estimates on what the operation would cost us. That completed, the next chore would be to contact the U.S. Department of Immigration, and find out what red tape we had to go through to bring Ricardo into this country. Meanwhile, Margie was making plans to redecorate the guest bedroom to make it more pleasing to a little boy. We talked of how we'd introduce him to indoor flush toilets, shower baths, hamburgers, Disneyland, television, and many other things he had perhaps never heard of. What a delight it was going to be! The day after we arrived home, we plunged into the project.

I didn't want to "run my fingers through the Yellow Pages" to find a doctor. I wanted a surgeon who was highly recommended by someone I knew, so I started with phone calls to friends. It didn't work. Most of them had never had the occasion to employ the services of an orthopedic surgeon, and those who did had only had relatively minor surgery, and were reluctant to make strong recommendations.

"Why don't you ask on TV?" Margie said.

My many years working on radio and television have firmly convinced me that the audience out there is filled with many compassionate people who will go out of their way to help nearly any worthy cause. I guess that's why telethons were born! So Margie's suggestion seemed exactly right. Surely some viewer of my program would know of some direction we could take to locate the doctor we needed. I tried it the next day, and struck gold with the first phone call I received.

It came from a man named Wayne Baumgartner who was associated with the Burbank Community Hospital. "We have a whole program here at the hospital for helping those Mexican kids. We have all the machinery to get them over the border and we operate on many of them every year," he said.

"You mean the hospital itself brings them across the border?"

"That's right. Just as far as we have beds to accomodate them! And we have some of the best doctors in the country here."

"Orthopedic?"

"Of course—and other fields too."

"That's marvelous! Now what will it cost me?"

"Nothing. It's free. You just have to agree to keep the child in your home during the time he's an out-patient; but everything else is free."

I couldn't believe it! It was just too good to be true. Here we were going to be able to have Ricardo fixed up and it wasn't even going to cost us anything. What wonderful people they must be at Burbank Community Hospital! I pressed Wayne Baumgartner for further details.

He told me that they have a clinic on the American side of the international border at Mexicali. The child would have to be brought to the clinic first for evaluation. Then if it was determined that his case was serious enough, and surgery could help him, he'd be admitted to the hospital for the operation as soon as a bed was available. The hospital made all the necessary arrangements with the Immigration Service. I could hardly wait to tell Margie about it when I got home from the studio that day.

This called for changes in our plans. All we had to do now was drive back to San Quintin to pick up the boy, run him over to the Mexicali clinic, and then stay with him in a motel or something until he could be admitted to the hospital. We were so enthusiastic about the wonderful work being done by this hospital (I have since referred a number of other children there) that we told all of our friends about it.

One of these friends is the well-known actor Frank Cady. Frank is perhaps best known to the public for his running part as the storekeeper in the television series *Petticoat Junction*, but is a fine character actor who has played many different roles in motion pictures and television. Frank had another idea:

"You ought to talk with my dentist," he said.

"Your dentist! Why?"

"Well, he belongs to a group of flying doctors. They fly their own planes down to Mexico all the time to help Mexican kids—even perform operations right on the spot! It might save you that long drive to Mexicali."

Dr. Alden Denman is a successful and busy dentist, but the minute he heard the nature of my phone call, he took time out from his work to have a long talk with me. The name of the group of flying doctors and dentists, he said, is LIGA. It is a large group dedicated to improving the health of our neighbors to the south. All of these highly skilled professionals fly to Mexico at their own expense to administer to the sick. They even pay for the medicines they prescribe! The lame have been helped to walk, the blind to see, and many who were thought to be incurably ill, have recovered their health. On each monthly flight to Mexico they treat about one thousand patients! They have been commended by the Mexican government (small wonder!) as well as by various American government officials.

"Of course we have orthopedic surgeons in LIGA," he said in answer to my question, "Some of the best in the world. How soon would you like us to fly down to see the boy?"

"Would they operate on Ricardo down there or bring him into the States?" I asked.

"Well the doctor would want to evaluate him there. Then I imagine we'd bring him back here for the operation."

"Can you get the child through Immigration?"

"No problem. We've brought hundreds of them back."

It was getting easier than ever! Now we didn't even have to drive Ricardo to Mexicali to the clinic. He could be flown back immediately by LIGA. "I just need time to write to his father and tell him we're coming, Dr. Denman, so let's allow three weeks."

"Whatever you say," he replied.

I had written in Spanish only once—to Pedro Camacho, my fisherman friend at San Felipe—and it had been most difficult. I wasn't going to go through that again! I wrote to Manuel Silva in English, stating that I was bringing some doctors to see Ricardo, and that we might be taking him back to the states for an operation. I also gave him the date and approximate time of our arrival. Then I found a translator to put my letter into correct Spanish. The translator was a charming nun who taught Spanish at Immaculate Heart College in Los Angeles; she refused to accept any money for her translation when she read the letter. I mailed it to Ricardo's father at once, allowing nearly three weeks for delivery.

I knew of several dirt landing strips in San Quintin, but how could we get the flying doctors from the landing strip to Ricardo's home? Here, another friend came to the rescue. Mark Armistead has been a supplier of television crews and equipment for many years in Hollywood, and a long time acquaintance of mine. Coincidentally, he owned a fishing resort in San Quintin named *Cielito Lindo*. It offers bungalow accomodations, a trailer park, restaurant, and an air strip. I phoned his office in Hollywood and asked if he could send word to one of his employees down there to drive us to Ricardo's *ejido* after we landed at his airstrip.

"I'll do better than that!" he said. "I'll go down there and drive you to the *ejido* myself!"

So it was that very early one Sunday morning in September we all met at Van Nuys airport in the San Fernando Valley for our flight to Ricardo. There was the dentist—Alden Denman—and his beautiful wife Patricia. Margie and I would ride in their plane. The second plane would have three passengers: Drs. Robert Johnson, the orthopedic surgeon; Robert Brown, an internist; and his son, Kevin Brown, the pilot. Both doctors were tops in their fields and associated with the Seventh Day Adventist medical college and hospital in Loma Linda, California. Both of the doctors confessed that they were intensely interested in polio cases because there were so few opportunities to treat it in the States any more. (LIGA has been transporting the Salk vaccine to Mexico by the plane-load in recent years.)

"Don't drink any coffee, and be sure to use the toilet facilities before we take off," Dr. Denman said, "There are no potty stops on this flight!"

We did as we were told and then scrambled into his airplane. Both planes took off for Baja just as the sun began to rise. The Denmans were delightful hosts and pointed out spots of interest as the landscape unfolded beneath the plane, but after awhile the conversation died down and I had a chance to think, as I stared out at the clouds.

Many is the time in our Mexican travels that I have occasion to be ashamed of the behavior of fellow Americans. They have been loud-mouthed, critical of Mexico, and seemed to think their possession of the almighty dollar gave them license to treat every Mexican they met as a lowly person. Also, the mere fact that they were in Mexico seemed to embolden them to do things they would never think of doing at home. But this was different! First there had been the Burbank Community Hospital quietly and efficiently spending its funds and doctors' skills in treating the poor people of Mexico. Then I had discovered LIGA, and the unselfish contributions they had been making to Mexico for years. Now here we were, literally thousands of dollars worth of medical skill and aircraft, winging our way to Baja because of one little nine-year-old crippled boy. "It makes me pretty damn proud to be an American," I thought.

We circled and landed at *Cielito Lindo* in San Quintin just before noon—hungry, thirsty, and with bursting bladders! After quick trips to the bathroom, we all headed for the restaurant to enjoy coffee and a delayed breakfast. Margie and I were getting more and more excited as our dream of helping Ricardo came closer to fruition. We were so anxious to get going, we could scarcely eat.

After breakfast, all seven of us piled into Mark Armistead's big white Cadillac, and started for Ricardo's house. Margie gave the driving directions, and I thanked Heaven for her remarkable memory—I had already forgotten how to find his house. As we drove, I wondered what it would be like when we arrived. They would probably have received my letter and would be expecting us. Perhaps they'd be waiting in front of the house with tall Manuel holding his little son. How would they act now that they saw we really meant business? Would the doctors really be able to help Ricardo? Would Ricardo remember Margie and me?

It wasn't as I pictured it at all. Despite the stares of the neighbors as Mark's impressive looking automobile cruised the streets of the *ejido*, no one came out to greet us when we reached Ricardo's house. Neither Señor Silva nor Ricardo was anywhere to be seen. Two small children I assumed were Ricardo's sisters were playing quietly in the backyard.

"*Su padre está aquí?*" [Is your father here?] I asked.

The children looked a little frightened of this army of *gringos* that had got out of the huge white car and entered their yard. They just shook their heads no.

"*Su madre?*" I insisted.

They nodded yes—still without speaking.

"*Por favor, me gustaria hablar con ella.*" [Please, I would like to speak with her.]

The children ducked into the house and in a moment Ricardo's mother emerged, looking much as she had the last time I saw her. She didn't smile.

"*Buenos días, Señora, me recuerda?*" [Good morning, do you remember me?]

She nodded. "*Buenos días.*" She still didn't smile.

"Did you receive my letter?"

"*No. No carta.*"

Ah, that explained everything! Even three weeks hadn't been enough time for mail delivery, so they hadn't been expecting us. "*Tengo los doctores para Ricardo.*" [I have the doctors for Ricardo.]

She still didn't move.

At this point, Dr. Brown broke in, and in fluent Spanish he introduced himself and Dr. Johnson, then asked her to please get the boy. I was surprised and delighted with his Spanish; I had thought Margie and I would have to be interpreters.

Señora Silva ordered the two little girls to get Ricardo and they ran off. Then while we were waiting for him, Dr. Brown quizzed her about Ricardo's illness. How old was he when he became ill? Did she call a doctor? Did the doctor diagnose it as polio? When did they first notice the paralysis? And so on. She answered his questions as best she could, but I thought she still appeared to be troubled about something.

"What do you suppose is wrong with her?" I whispered to Margie.

"I don't know. Perhaps she's just bewildered by all of us barging in so suddenly. They're very simple people."

"Maybe."

Then Ricardo arrived. The two little girls pushed him into the backyard in an odd little go-cart with rickety wheels. It appeared to be a makeshift wheelchair someone had built for him. His legs were curled in front of him and he was sitting upright, looking as bright and sparkly as we remembered him.

"Me recuerda?" [Remember me?] Margie said to him.

He just nodded and stared curiously at all the Americans.

"May we use the bed in the house?" Dr. Brown asked in Spanish.

Ricardo's mother nodded.

Then the two doctors carried Ricardo inside the *casa* for an examination. I noticed with relief that Dr. Brown was speaking softly and patiently to the child and smiling at him as they carried him in.

The examination lasted for quite some time. During this time Margie talked with the *Señora* assuring her that these were excellent doctors, and if anything could be done for Ricardo they would certainly do it. She also talked of our home in Los Angeles and how we would care for Ricardo and how happy he would be. It was all uphill. Señora Silva scarcely responded and volunteered nothing. She just nodded occasionally and said *"Sí."* While this was going on, I stared inside the house trying to see what the doctors were doing. The sunlight streamed through one of the windows, providing dim light in the little house, and I could see Dr. Johnson moving the child's legs back and forth while Dr. Brown talked to him. At length the doctors completed their examination and carried Ricardo back out to the sunshine and his go-cart.

"It was polio alright," said Dr. Johnson, explaining that both legs were badly atrophied. "With surgery and therapy," he said, "we can get braces on him and he might be able to walk with those some day. He'll never walk without braces."

"Well, walking with braces is better than not walking at all!"

"Yes it is. And in the meantime he'll be able to swing along on crutches which is better than he's doing now."

"Why don't you tell his mother?" I said, turning to Dr. Brown, "Your Spanish is better than mine."

He explained it all to Señora Silva at great length. He told her what the surgery would be like, and that they would have Ricardo swimming and going through other therapy to attempt to develop the use of his legs. He concluded by telling her that all we needed now was for them to sign the paper giving their permission.

She didn't react. She acted almost as if she hadn't understood a word he said.

"You talk to her, Ben," the doctor said, "I don't know whether she understood me or not."

I addressed her quite sternly in Spanish. "Señora, what is wrong? You have not smiled since we arrived, and you appear to be troubled. Do you not wish us to try to help Ricardo? If there is something wrong you must tell us."

There was a long pause. *"Hay un otro doctor para Ricardo."*

"Another doctor for Ricardo! Who is this doctor?"

"A *norteamericano.* He came from the beach. Tomorrow he comes for Ricardo."

"What is the name of this doctor?" Dr. Brown asked.

"No sé."

"You don't know his name, but you will allow him to take Ricardo?" She looked flustered. "My husband knows the name."

"Where is your husband?" I asked.

"He works. It is Sunday."

"Where does he work?"

She described a small settlement a mile or so north along the highway. She said Manuel would be there with his cart selling tacos. We all climbed back into Mark's white Cadillac and were off in a whirl of dust for the settlement.

It was just as Señora Silva had said. There were five or six small places of business alongside the highway and Manuel Silva was there with his cart. The tantalizing smell of barbecued goat meat rose from the charcoal brazier on his cart and he was selling the goat tacos almost as fast as he could assemble them. I pushed through the crowd of taco buyers surrounding him, and got his attention.

"Manuel! Soy Ben Hunter. Me recuerda?" I called.

"Sí," he nodded, passed another taco to an outstretched hand, and pocketed the money.

"May I speak with you for a moment? It is about Ricardo. It is important!"

He stepped away from the cart and moved to where Dr. Brown and I were standing (the rest of our party was in the car). "Sí?"

I carefully explained that these doctors had flown all the way from Los Angeles to try to help Ricardo walk and I told him what their prognosis had been. Then I said, "Your wife told us that another doctor comes for Ricardo tomorrow."

He looked puzzled for a moment, then said *"Verdad."* [It is true.]

"What is the name of this doctor?"

His face worked as he tried to think. *"No sé."*

"You don't know his name?"

He shook his head.

Dr. Brown stepped in and introduced himself. "Do you know where this doctor has his office?" he asked in his excellent Spanish.

Again Manuel shook his head.

"San Diego?"

"No sé." He went back to the cart and started selling tacos again. Bewildered, we returned to the car.

As Mark drove us back to *Cielito Lindo,* the two doctors agreed that they certainly could not touch Ricardo if some other doctor had already agreed to treat him. Also, of course, they couldn't do it without his parents' permission.

"I think Manuel was lying," Margie said. "I don't think he's got another doctor. I think he just didn't want Ricardo to be operated on."

At the *Cielito Lindo* I apologized to the doctors for leading them on a wild goose chase. The very gracious gentlemen told us they didn't mind a bit, they'd enjoyed the flight and our company, and at least there'd been a chance they could help someone. And you know what? They made me believe it!

We had a pleasant surprise that day, too. We were all sitting there chatting when a tall, distinguished-looking Mexican gentleman came up behind me:

"Good afternoon, *Señor* Hunter—and *Señora,*" he said in perfect English.

I looked up and saw Gomez.

"Gomez!" I stood up and shook his hand. "What are you doing way south here in San Quintin?"

"I work here now. Mr. Armistead hired me as manager."

"Well, congratulations!"

We had met Gomez a couple of times when he was tending his small store at a tiny fishing village called Puerto Santo Tomás—many miles north. In the interim he had become famous. The popular *Los Angeles Times* columnist Jack Smith had been regaling his large readership with stories about a house Gomez had been building for him in Baja, and thousands of people eagerly awaited each new report in the column.

"Did you finish building Jack Smith's house?" I asked.

"Oh yes. And it's beautiful. Mr. Smith is here today too."

"Where?" I asked excitedly.

"Right there. Gomez pointed to a table in the corner of the next room. Sure enough, there was Jack Smith seated with some friends having a drink.

Jack and I are longtime acquaintances. We have been to many of the same press parties, and he has been a guest on my television show. I dashed over to say hello.

"Jack, I'm sure everyone must tell you this, but I have to say it too. I love your column—it's as important to my breakfast as juice and coffee— but I especially chuckle over the stories about Gomez and your house."

"Everyone does say that, but—believe me—it's always nice to hear," he said.

"Gomez tells me he's finished your house. Does that mean the end of all those funny pieces about him?"

"Well, not quite. I've put them into a book."

"You have! What's the title?"

"I call it *God And Mr. Gomez*. It'll be out in a couple of months."

I wished Jack luck with the book and invited him to do a guest appearance on my show and give it a plug. He did, of course, and was a delightful guest, but I don't think the book needed the plug. The minute it came out it soared to the Best-Seller lists and stayed there for months.

There was little conversation on the flight back to Los Angeles. We all just stared out the window at the incredibly beautiful cloud formations, lost in thought. Margie and I were both thinking about Ricardo. Had his parents lied to us? It certainly seemed likely, otherwise they would have at least known the name of the doctor they said was going to treat him. But if they'd lied, why? If they didn't want the operation for Ricardo, why didn't they tell us when we'd first visited them? These questions and many others swarmed through my head during the flight home.

Back at the airport we thanked all the doctors again, and again apologized for having them give up a Sunday to fly all that distance for nothing. Then we got in our car and drove home, feeling pretty flat.

"Darling, what if the doctors had said they could make Ricardo walk *without* braces. Do you think they'd have let him go then?" Margie asked.

I thought a moment. "No I don't. It looked to me like something was bugging Señora Silva from the moment we arrived."

"I remember you said that." She paused. "Yes, that's true. When I was talking with her she acted as if something were wrong."

"What was wrong was us. They just didn't want us there."

"Then why didn't they say so in the first place?"

I tried to picture that first visit. "Well, if you remember they weren't exactly bubbling over with enthusiasm then. We kind of pushed the thing."

"Stronger than that, Darling. You did a selling job. A big one."

"Yeah, I guess I did," I sighed. We lapsed into silence for the remainder of the trip home.

Margie had it all worked out in the morning. "I tossed and turned thinking about it all night long," she said.

"And?"

"Suppose Ricardo had come to live with us for quite a time. We'd have bought him some nice clothes, right?"

"Right. But so what? We—"

"And taken him to Disneyland. And he'd have been driven in a beautiful automobile, lived in a big house with floors, carpets, indoor plumbing, and running water. We'd have taught him to like hamburgers and hot dogs and lots of foods he'd never even tasted."

"Yeah, I know all that. We even talked about it before. But so what? It would've been fun."

"Yes, it would have been fun for us—and for him. But what would happen when he finally went home to the *ejido*?"

I got the picture. Margie was right. After six months or a year of living the American version of "The Good Life," he would have been discontented with his home. How could an outing at his uncle's fishing shack be compared to Disneyland? He'd be distressed by the dirt floors, glassless windows, and outhouse of his own home. He would no longer enjoy his mother's plain cooking. Yet, it was his destiny to live there in the *ejido* at least until he was grown—perhaps the rest of his life. To be unhappy with your lot in life is far worse than not being able to walk. His parents had been wiser than we thought. They loved him enough to

276

protect him from being exposed to things he could never attain.

We have never gone back to see Ricardo because we don't wish to intrude on their lives again. But his picture is in our scrapbook, and the memory of his cute, merry face will always be in our hearts.

10/ We Take the Plunge

By this time, the idea of owning a house in Mexico was no longer a fantasy. We had a very clear idea of what we wanted in a Mexican home, and we were determined to get it. We had decided that we did not want to live near the border in some American community. We wanted our home somewhere in the interior, and we wished to live in a Mexican neighborhood and become part of the community. We also wanted ready access to shopping, entertainment, restaurants, and beaches. After several evenings of lengthy discussion, we decided on Guadalajara—beautiful city of fountains and flowers—as the ideal site, so I took a month off and we headed there. Our plan was to sample Guadalajara life as residents for a few weeks, then culminate our stay with the big purchase.

Many years before the Spanish conquered Mexico, there was a tribe of Mexican Indians living in the area that is now known as Guadalajara. Nearly all Mexican Indians had a very advanced culture, and this tribe had even developed a medium of exchange. It was a small coin they called *tapatíol*. Because this coin was found only in the Guadalajara environs, permanent residents of the city call themselves *Tapatíos* in the same sense we say "New Yorkers" or "Angelenos." In the days that followed, Margie and I became true *Tapatíos*. We rented a house, shopped at the supermarkets and department stores, played the various golf courses, tried the restaurants, visited the theaters, and learned to find our way around this giant metropolis.

When we felt we knew our way around sufficiently well, we began house-hunting. We read the classified ads in the newspapers and chased out to various neighborhoods looking at houses for sale. Once, while visiting the suburb of Tlaquepaque we spied *El Tular*, the store where we had purchased our dining-room funiture on our first camper trip ten years before. We stopped in to see if it looked the same, and there was its owner, María Elena. We recognized her at once, and she politely said she remembered us also. When we told her we were house-hunting, she told us her house was for sale. The price was right, so we drove out for a look at it. It was on the shore of Lake Chapala in a little community called Jocotepec. The setting was beautiful, and it was very tempting to buy the house, but it was really much too large for just the two of us. We told her she'd be seeing us again anyway because we were going to be fellow *Tapatíos*.

However, just as a beautiful woman may seem less beautiful with familiarity, as time passes, the Queen City of Mexico became less appealing to us. For one thing, it is very large, and its thousands of residents seem to fill every store, restaurant, and boulevard to overflowing. Secondly, we discovered that the Mexican colonial style of architecture which we favored seemed to be the choice of the other Americans as well, while the Mexicans themselves lived in houses reminiscent of Baltimore or Grand Rapids. If we were to live in true Mexican ambience as we desired, we'd have to buy a home in a strictly American neighborhood!

The thousands of Americans residing in Guadalajara keep pretty much to themselves. Few of them speak Spanish or have much to do with the Mexican community outside of dealing with the tradespeople. They have their own—strictly American—clubs, social activities, and even their own English-language newspaper. This was not the type of life in Mexico we had pictured for ourselves at all. We had a lovely month there, but we returned to the U.S. without a Mexican house and feeling somewhat like displaced *Tapatíos*.

It takes a large crew to put together any television show. For my daily show, I am fortunate to have a staff who has been with me for several years. Ira Doud, my senior cameraman; Jerry Cheshire, the stage manager; and several others, under the direction of Bill Chesnutt, make sure the show is technically perfect. Phyllis Gottlieb books all my guests, and Melodie Jackson is in charge of scheduling my announcements.

With our Saturday children's program, *The Elementary News*, it's an entirely different story. Although Margie and I still have an experienced crew for the taping, we, as the co-producers, do just about everything else. I write the show, and Margie books guests, edits videotape, makes cue cards, orders graphics, schedules announcements, and both of us do countless other jobs to get the show on the air.

We plunged back into this routine for a few months, the thought of a Mexican home seemingly shelved.

We have always celebrated a traditional Thanksgiving. Margie prepares a feast, and we invite all the relatives over to share it with us. This particular year, however, she surprised me.

"You know what I'd like to do?" she asked. "I'd like to cook our Thanksgiving dinner in the camper—with just the two of us."

Knowing how she loves a culinary challenge, I readily agreed. It just happened that the studio had scheduled some special programming at Thanksgiving time that would pre-empt my show on Thursday and Friday. We decided to zip down to our "Secret Place" near the border after my show on Wednesday, stay through Sunday, and enjoy our turkey feast there.

We reached our "Secret Place" just after dark, but it was so familiar to us we had no difficulty manuevering the camper through the sand dunes to our favorite camping spot. The moment we came to a stop and I shut off the engine we could hear the music of the waves and see the sparkling flourescence as they curled and crashed on the beach. The sky was black, splashed with stars, and a full moon hung like a giant gold coin above the horizon, making a shimmering path across the water. It was good to be "home."

The morning dawned sunny and warm, and we picked up our Baja beach life as if we'd never left—the only exception was the turkey roasting in the oven. Taco resumed her seaweed-sniffing and crab-hunting while we walked the beach picking up shells for Margie's garage-clogging collection, poked around the tide pools, and eventually returned to camp to sit and stare, reveling in that old familiar "Baja Feeling." As we were sipping drinks, waiting for the Thanksgiving dinner to be ready, I mused over the anomaly of sitting on a deserted beach with the tantalizing aroma of the roasting turkey in the air.

At length, the turkey was done and, to say the least, Margie's feast was spectacular! It was served with a special stuffing seasoned with nuts, fruit, mushrooms, and God-knows-what else, along with homemade cranberry sauce, candied yams, fresh peas, onions in cheese sauce, and other goodies. The whole feast was topped off with slabs of homemade pumpkin pie.

"My God! How did you make all this in a camper?" I said. "You hardly spent any time in there!"

"It was easy. I just did a lot of pre-preparation at home. All I had to do here was cook the turkey and assemble the other things."

"You make it sound easy, but I know it wasn't."

"Yes, it was," she said, but I could see she was pleased.

We ate outside, sitting in beach chairs and basking in the warm sun. It was the most unusual Thanksgiving holiday of my life.

I have a dear friend, Grace Loftin, who publishes an English language magazine about Baja. It's called *Las Californias,* and Grace has been good enough to publish several of my articles about Mexico. We have been long-time subscribers to the publication, and Margie was paging through the latest issue while I gazed at the sea after dinner.

"What do you say we drive to Ensenada tomorrow morning?" she said.

"Break up camp so soon? We just got here!"

"I know. But it's a short drive and we can come back to our camp in the afternoon."

I noticed she was staring at one page in *Las Californias.* Since the magazine features Baja bargains, I assumed she'd found some item she wanted to buy. "Aw come on, honey, you'll have plenty of opportunities to go shopping down there. We came here for a rest."

There was a long pause. "Did you enjoy your dinner?"

"The greatest!"

"Well then just do me a teeny-weeny favor and take me to Ensenada tomorrow. I promise we'll come back in the afternoon."

When we broke camp the next morning, I noticed she carried the magazine into the truck cab with her. That would be so she could find the store where the bargain was, but when we reached Ensenada, we cruised past all the usual shopping spots and she never told me to stop the car. Soon we were at the outskirts of town and heading south.

"I give up," I said, "Where're we going?"

"Wait and see."

I waited, but my curiosity was swelling with each turn of the wheels.

"Now turn right!" she said suddenly.

I made a quick turn and we started down an asphalt road filled with chuckholes. The sign said EJ CHAPULTEPEC—the "EJ" stands for *ejido.* The asphalt dead-ended at a large barnlike building that appeared to be a winery. It looked deserted.

"Turn right here," she said.

The right turn took us onto a rutted dirt road that was pockmarked with extra-deep chuckholes. All I could see ahead were empty fields over-grown with weeds and Ensenada way in the distance, sparkling like a jewel in the morning sun. It was as if we were going off the road to some other camping spot. I stopped the truck in the middle of the road.

"We're not going another foot until you tell me where you're taking us!" I demanded.

"Okay, here it is." She handed me the copy of *Las Californias* magazine.

It was open to a large ad on one of the middle pages. There was a picture of five or six white, red-roofed little houses on the edge of a beach. Each house had a small *palapa* in front of it. An inset in the picture showed a rotund, jolly looking gent and his attractive wife seated in a beautiful living room gazing out the window toward the sea. The advertising copy invited us to buy a home at Nueva España. Below that was a map and directions for finding the place.

"So, we're house-hunting again!"

"Well, I figured it couldn't hurt to look."

I sighed. "I guess not, as long as we've come this far." I started up the truck again and began following the dirt road as it gradually made a long arc toward the beach. A few more minutes and we could make out the little white houses we had seen in the ad.

"The houses look pretty cute from the outside," I said. "They're kind of Mexican colonial style."

"Let's look at the beach," Margie replied.

We stopped the car and strolled out on the beach beyond the houses. It was exquisite! Snow white sand billowed from where we stood, down to the edge of the water. It was spotless—pristine. The ocean water was clean, and so clear you could easily see a bit of seaweed suspended underwater in the green curl of the waves. Beyond the surf, the water turned deep blue, and a purple island perched on the horizon, outlined so sharply in the bright sun that I felt as if I could have picked it off with a beebee gun. South of us, the shore curved out to sea, terminating in a high sloping peak reminiscent of Diamond Head in Hawaii. We decided to call it Emerald Head.

One of the empty houses served as the real estate office, and the sign in the window said OFFICE, not *oficina*. "Americans," I muttered under my breath as we entered.

They were Americans indeed—two of them—and were engaged in an absorbing game of dominos when we arrived. They seemed reluctant to break up the game, even for a possible customer, but after a couple of moves, a large man built like a wrestler pushed his chair back, came over, and shook hands.

"Hi! I'm Bud Murphy. Can I help you?" Then he spotted Taco who had followed us in, and began petting her. "What a nice little dog." Taco wagged appreciatively.

"Are these houses for sale?" Margie asked.

"Some are. Some are sold," he replied, continuing to play with Taco. "Would you like to look around?"

"Yes we would."

"Well, first let me show you the plot plan." He got up and went over to a wall where the plans for a condominium project had been pinned up. "Now, we're right here—that's the office," he said, punching one spot on the map with a pudgy finger, "and those are the houses you see there." He explained that they planned to build many houses and sell them as condominiums. There would eventually be a homeowner's association which would take over the whole project and operate it after all the houses were sold. Then he started showing us the different available floor plans.

"Hey! Have you guys got any coffee?" said a voice from the door.

"Sure. Come in, Ty," Bud replied.

A beautiful woman entered. She was tall, slim, and graceful with just a suggestion of Oriental eyes and cheekbones. Her hair was upswept on top of her head, but looked as if it would fall below her shoulders if she let it down.

"We ran out this morning, and I figured you guys would have a pot full."

"We sure have," Bud said. "Help yourself. And I'd like you to meet the Hunters. They're here today looking around." Then he turned to us. "This is Ty Gillis. She's a native Hawaiian, but she gave up Hawaii to live in Nueva España."

"Nice to meet you, Hunters. Welcome to our little group!" Ty said gaily, and we all shook hands. If you're looking at houses, come on over and see mine—it's right across the street."

"That'll be our first stop," Bud said.

Ty filled her coffee cup, and all four of us trooped across the street to her home. It was charming. From a small entryway we stepped into a large living room with a corner fireplace and large, sliding glass doors opening onto a patio which faced that gorgeous beach. The whole house was a symphony of tile and natural wood. Floors throughout were tiled in warm earth colors with area rugs here and there; the adjoining kitchen and dining room were tastefully done with natural wood cabinets and colorful Mexican tile on the counters and walls. The decor reflected Ty's

Hawaiian heritage. A Hawaiian hikiee (a large, wide, armless and backless couch) was against one wall, and a slim, studious looking gentleman was sprawled on it reading a book.

It was her husband, Allen. He looked up from his book, gave us a nod and a smile when she introduced him, then resumed reading.

Ty took us on a tour of her home showing us the two bedrooms—each with a bath—and raving all the time about the view, the lovely neighbors, and the delights of living in Mexico.

As we strolled through the house my sixth sense was sounding the warning buzzer—*This is it, Bub. You're racing straight for the edge of the cliff and you're going to dive off. You're going to buy a house in an American community near the border—the one thing you said you'd never do. But you're going to do it alright. You can't help yourself!*

Bud Murphy showed us several other houses in the project. He simply unlocked the front door, waved us in, and said, "Here's another one." Then he stood silently as we looked around, only speaking if we asked him a question. There was only one of the beachfront homes like the Gilleses' for sale, and I loved it. If I was going to plummet into a rash purchase like this, that was the one I wanted. But I tend to leave such decisions up to Margie—the home is her domain—so I shut up. Margie had become very quiet and reflective. I knew the wheels were going around in her head, the computer was working, and soon I'd know how she felt. her ultimate decision surprised me.

"I believe I like that one best," she said, pointing at an unfinished house across the street from the ocean front. "What do you think, Darling?"

It was the house I liked the least! Not only was it unfinished and not on the beach, it was poorly planned as well. The view window wasn't a view window at all, it was just standard size and looked out on—of all things—the carport! The patio at the back was postage stamp size and accessible through a dull-looking standard size door. Even the window looking out at the patio was small. I thought Margie had taken leave of her senses.

"Thaaaat house?"

"Yes."

"Honey, it's the worse of the lot—"

"I like it."

"It's not on the beach, it's unfinished, and it's poorly planned. It's a *dumb* house!"

"I like it because it's not finished. We can finish it to suit ourselves. Also, there's a greenway between it and the beach so we can have an ocean view—"

"It'll be a view of the car in the carport!"

She ignored me. "It's only a few feet farther back from the beach than Ty's house."

"But why not right on the beach?" I insisted.

"Well I bet in the summertime there are a lot of people on that beach and they'd all be staring in your window. Besides, if they ever have a real high tide, the water might wash right up on your patio. I like *this* house."

She spoke with such finality I knew further argument was useless. "Okay, Babe, that's your choice."

We returned to the office, signed the papers, and wrote the check. We were to pay $500 now, then a third when construction started, a third when it was half done, and the balance when we moved in.

"Now you'll have to meet our architect," Bud said. "He's your next door neighbor." So saying, he summoned him from the next room.

I looked curiously at the man who had designed the atrocity my wife insisted on buying. Pedro Alonzo appeared to be in his late twenties or early thirties, had black curly hair, a quick smile with flashing white teeth, and dancing eyes that bespoke a delightful sense of humor. When Bud introduced us, I noted that Pedro spoke flawless English, though seasoned with just a trace of Latin accent. Most of all, I sensed in him that indefinable Mexican *macho* that immediately attracts other men and makes women's hearts skip a beat. He was dressed expensively. "Man, does this cat score with the ladies!" I thought.

We chatted for a few minutes, getting better acquainted, then strolled down the block to the shell of a building we had just purchased.

"Alright, now, how do you want to finish the house?" Pedro said.

I got into the act at once. If Margie was going to insist on this house, I was going to do my best to improve it.

"I want all tile floors, and Mexican tiles in the kitchen like the Gilleses' house," I began.

"Of course." He turned to Margie. "We'll go downtown and pick out the tiles you like."

She nodded, seemingly lost in thought.

"Then I want a big fireplace right in the center of this wall . . . here." 1 walked over and made an invisible "X" with my finger on the wall.

"A fireplace there. Okay," he said, and made a note on a pad.

"Then we should have brick, Mexican type arches dividing the room *here* and *here*." I pointed.

"Arches." He made another note. "Anything else?"

I had played my whole scene. "Can't think of anything," I said.

"Mrs. Hunter?"

"I have a question, Pedro," she said. "Why did you put that carport right in front of the window that looks toward the ocean?"

"I didn't design this house, Mrs. Hunter. It was designed by the builder who started the project before we took it over." (I liked him better already).

"I see. Well we won't be using the carport at all, so I'd like you to move this wall of the living room out into the carport area and put a large view window in it. It will make the room much larger and give us a good view of the ocean."

Pedro scribbled more notes.

"Now over here—" She walked to the small window that looked out at the miniscule patio, "take out this window, and put in full, sliding glass doors. That way we can see into the patio from the living room—it opens up the room. Take out the small entrance door and just plaster it up."

"Okay. Sliding glass doors." More notes were written.

"Then we should have beam ceilings, and I want to pick out carpeting for the two bedrooms . . . " On she went. I realized, again, why I always leave these things up to Margie. She had obviously given the entire matter much more thought than I had. When she finally got through rebuilding that house, I could see that it was going to be beautiful, and Pedro had hastily scribbled notes in every pocket.

"What are these changes going to cost, Pedro?" I asked.

He retrieved his notes from various pockets and scanned them briefly. "Five thousand dollars."

I expected Margie to explode and drop the whole thing right then, but again she surprised me. "That's the complete price, Pedro?" He nodded. "That's fine," she said. "When can you start work on it?"

"Oh pretty soon. I have another house to finish first."

Knowing that "pretty soon" can be from one to six months in the Mexican lexicon, I decided to give him a little impetus—"We'll be down next weekend to see how you're doing," I said.

"Okay. See you then."

We told him goodbye, climbed in our camper, and headed back to our camping beach.

The return trip was made mostly in silence—each of us occupied with individual thoughts. My mind was in a state of turmoil. We had acted too impulsively! One minute we were on one of our lovely camping trips, and next we had committed ourselves to buying a house smack dab where we

287

said we never would. My sixth sense had been right! Would we regret it? Would we be happy there? Once the house was completed we'd want to spend our vacations there—that would probably mean we'd have to sell the Dolphin. Would I miss it? The answer to that last question was a resounding "Yes!" but I had no answers for the others. As we drove off the road at our "Secret Place" and our camper began winding sure-footedly through the sand dunes to our favorite camping spot, I loved that rig even more—the way you love something you're about to lose.

Thinking morosely that it might be one of the last, I built a big campfire after dinner that night, mixed a couple of drinks, and again we both stared quietly at the fire. What was Margie thinking? Did she have the same doubts as I? I decided to try to find out.

"What've you been thinking about all evening, Darling?" I asked.

She sighed. "Oh lots of things. I was thinking we could go into Tijuana and buy the light fixtures for our house—they'll be cheaper there. And I was thinking a beige colored tile would look nice on the floor—"

I interrupted. "Don't you have any doubts about buying that house?"

"No. Should I?"

"Well, we bought it so impulsively! We hardly gave it any thought at all."

"Not as impulsively as you think." She looked at me slyly.

"What do you mean?"

She paused as if trying to decide about something. "Oh, alright. I'll tell you. Well, I saw that ad in Las Californias when the magazine first arrived—weeks ago. I decided then that we should come down here and look at those houses—"

"You mean that business about wanting to have Thanksgiving on the beach was just a ruse to get me down here?"

"Well, I thought Thanksgiving on the beach would be fun too. But . . . well . . . yes, it sort of was."

"Oh brother! Have I been had!" I roared angrily.

"Well, I knew if I talked to you about Nueva España at home, you'd go into all that business about not wanting a house near the border and living with other Americans—"

"Yes, I would have!"

"But I thought that maybe if we looked at the houses and they were as nice as the ad, you might change your mind. Besides, at least we're taking that step we've talked about for years. If we decide we don't like living here we can always sell the house at a nice profit in that location."

I could see the truth in that, alright, but I thought, "Who needs

Women's Lib when they get what they want with guile?"

"Are you mad at me?" she asked.

I was beginning to relent, but I wasn't going to show it so soon. "I don't like being deceived. And I have another question for you."

"What's that?"

"When we have the house, what shall we do with the camper? Sell it?" I folded my arms across my chest like a prosecuting attorney.

"Oh, no! I wouldn't want to do that! After we're living there permanently we'll still be wanting to take camper trips. I wouldn't give up the Dolphin for anything!"

She's an amazing woman. In about ninety seconds of conversation she had dispelled all my doubts, and even made me enthusiastic about our purchase.

"Are you still mad?"

She looked beautiful! The flickering light from the dying fire threw sensuous shadows on her long, gorgeous legs, and the stars were reflected in her eyes. "No, honey, you're just all-woman, and that's what I love about you." I kissed her softly, and then the kiss became passionate.

That night the moon seemed brighter, the stars more sparkling, and the whole world more beautiful.

Saturday and Sunday we just played on the beach as always, enjoying the "Baja Feeling," but our conversation was filled with plans for the new house. We resolved that the next thing to do would be to get the floor measurements so we could make a scale drawing at home and plan on how we would place furniture. By Sunday afternoon, we had decided to make a quick trip back to Nueva España to refresh our memories of the house and take those measurements.

We pulled up in front of our house, parked the camper, and I bounded out of the cab and into the house first. Workers were inside (on a Sunday!) and the fireplace and arches I'd ordered were two-thirds completed!

"Margie! Come look!" I shouted gleefully.

She entered, followed by Pedro who had seen us drive up.

"How do you like it?" he said, obviously pleased at having started construction so soon.

"It's beautiful," I said.

"You put the fireplace in the wrong spot!" Margie wailed.

"What? It looks alright to me," I said.

"That's where Mr. Hunter put an 'X' yesterday," Pedro added.

"Yes, but that was before I told you I wanted that side wall moved out into the carport area. The way you've got it now, the fireplace won't be in the middle of the wall at all!"

"Darling, the fireplace is almost finished," I protested.

She was becoming angry at both of us. "I don't care! It's wrong, that's all. I won't have it that way!" She looked at Pedro, and there was fire in her eyes.

Pedro, who had apparently encountered feminine fury before, beat a fast retreat. "I'll change it, Mrs. Hunter." He barked rapid Spanish at the brick setter who immediately began to knock his creation apart. That he had to do his work all over again didn't seem to bother him a whit.

As the bricks clunked to the floor, Margie went into her explanation all over again about how she wanted the room made larger by utilizing the carport area, and how the fireplace should be centered in the new, larger living room. *Now*, did Pedro understand?

"I understood the first time, but that was where Mr. Hunter said he wanted it," he said, shifting the blame to me. "It will be as you wish. How do you like the arches?"

"They're going to be beautiful," I said, hoping I hadn't altered something else she'd requested by demanding them.

"Yes they are," I was relieved to hear her say.

Then another thought occurred to me. "Now that you've started construction, I guess we owe you a third of the purchase price, huh?"

Pedro nodded. "Yes, but next weekend is alright. You don't have to pay it today."

Back in Los Angeles that next week we could still scarcely believe that we were soon to become Mexican homeowners. But, then, it was also hard to believe that they had done so much construction on a five-hundred dollar deposit—and on a Sunday. Any thought that it might have been a dream was dispelled by a middle-of-the-week phone call from Ensenada. It was Pedro.

"I think you need another window," he said.

"Another window? Where?"

"Above the view window in the living room."

"A view window above the view window?"

"Yes."

"Why do we need that, Pedro?"

"Well, you have a very high ceiling, so one window in that wall is not enough. It won't look right," he said firmly.

"Hold the line, Pedro." I cupped my hand over the phone and told

Margie what he had said. "What do you think?"

She shrugged. "I don't know. He's the architect."

"What'll it cost, Pedro?"

"Only eighty dollars."

"Okay. Go ahead and put it in."

The next weekend, instead of going to our "Secret Place," we went straight to Nueva España and parked the camper on the vacant lot behind our house so we could watch the construction taking place. On arrival, we noted that the fireplace had been completed—in the "proper" location this time—and the arches were a graceful *fait accompli*. The side wall of the living room had been knocked down, and the wall to replace it (with holes for two view windows, one atop the other) was completed. Pedro had been right about that second window, it really was an improvement, even though it was too high to see out of.

While Margie strolled to another part of the house, I watched the wall being built. It was astonishing! The walls of the house were apparently made of cement nearly a foot thick, and interlaced with steel rods! As I stared at the fortress-like walls, I could just picture geologists from a distant galaxy landing on our planet in the year 10,000 and finding our house intact.

"So this is how the Earthlings lived, Dr. Ghu!" one would say.

"Yes, and how tall they were! See the height of that second window!"

Our house would give us a kind of immortality.

My musings were interrupted by an alarming cry from Margie: "Ben! Come here! What is that man doing to my house!"

I hastened to her side to discover one of the Mexican workmen seated on the floor calmly chiselling deep holes in one of the walls.

"Why are you doing that?" I asked him in Spanish.

"Para electricidad," he replied blandly.

"The house hasn't been wired for electricity?"

"Of a certainty. One cannot wire a house until one has a house to wire," he said, taking another swipe at the chisel.

"And the plumbing?"

"It is the same."

Later we learned that this is standard practice in Mexico. They erect those incredible cement walls with the lasting quality of a Mayan pyramid, and then proceed to chisel holes and channels in them to accomodate the wiring and plumbing!

I checked another wall and noted with satisfaction that an electric wall plug of the three-hole variety had been installed. The third hole is, of course, for a ground wire and makes for a much safer installation, but I'd never seen them in Mexico before. When we encountered Pedro in the street a few minutes later, I complimented him on that touch of modernity.

"They do look nice, don't they?"

"Well, it isn't so much the looks. It's that it's much safer when your home is ground-wired."

"Oh, there's no ground wire," Pedro said serenely, "We just put in the three-way plugs for looks."

"Just for looks!" I couldn't believe it.

"Of course. Even if the wiring had a short, it couldn't set the cement on fire, could it?"

Grudgingly, I admitted that he was probably right, but Margie was shaking her head. I'm sure she was about to argue with him but just then we were interrupted.

"My God! Ben Hunter! I go to bed with you every afternoon!"

I looked around and saw a cute redhead with a petite figure, dancing eyes, and an impish smile. She was wearing an Hawaiian muumuu and an incongruous pert hat, but on her it looked good.

"How am I?" I asked.

"Marvelous!" Then she spotted Margie. "You must be Mrs. Hunter. I'm Barbie Sylak. I meant, of course, that I watch Ben's show while I'm taking an afternoon rest."

"I thought that's what you meant," Margie smiled. "I'm Margie Hunter. Are you a neighbor of ours down here?"

"Stan and I live in that little house right there," she said, pointing, "and you and Ben are coming there for dinner tonight."

Margie had planned to cook us a dinner in the camper that night, and had been looking forward to it, but there was no dissuading Barbie Sylak, so we finally gave in. Both the dinner and the Sylaks were delightful. Stan was a shrewd gambler, and a clever businessman who made enough money to retire early. We took to them at once, and they have become one of our favorite couples.

Thinking it would be a friendly gesture below the border, we had stocked the camper with a respectable assortment of Scotch, bourbon (both very expensive in Mexico), and mixers before leaving Los Angeles. So the next day we invited all and sundry at Nueva España to step inside the camper for a drink with us. Among our first guests were the two developers, Dewey Bouche and Juan Hurtado. Seated at the dining table, I wrote the check for the first third of the purchase price, then cracked out the ice, glasses, and bottles of what a hillbilly friend of mine calls "Big Mouth." After two or three drinks we all knew each other better.

Dewey Bouche was a rotund, bouncing, boyish blond with a quick laugh and boundless enthusiasm. As he told us his plans for the future of Nueva España, I judged him to be a super salesman—of nearly anything! However, he told us he had been a dairy farmer before the Nueva España venture, and his chubby, rosy cheeks bore it out. I could easily picture him ingesting gallons of foamy, fresh milk in his youth, and I told him so.

"I still do!" he laughed, "Those commercials are true!"

His Mexican partner, Juan Hurtado, was a contrast. Slight of build, with dark complexion, trim black mustache, and flashing white teeth, he was an extremely handsome Latin-lover type. He was impeccably dressed in expensive clothes, and smoked a curving cheroot. He spoke English haltingly with a heavy accent, which only added to his charm, and told us he was the former mayor of a small town in the state of Michoacan. More recently, he had been in business for himself in Mexicali.

In an effort to force people to purchase Mexican-made goods, the government places a very high tax on furniture and household appliances brought in from the states. The duty may go as high as a hundred percent on some items. Nueva España furnished a range with the house, but nothing else, and we had been wondering how to get our household possessions across the border without—in effect—paying for them again. Margie posed the question to our two guests.

"It's easy," Dewey said. "Just load the stuff in your camper and bring it down. They never look inside your camper when you cross the border, do they?

"They haven't yet."

"Well, in case they should, just have a little mordida handy."

"There's one other problem, Dewey," I chimed in. "How the hell am I going to be able to load a big refrigerator into this camper? It wouldn't even go through the door!"

He thought a moment. "Tell you what. I have one in the States, and if you'll buy it from me I'll deliver it here for you."

"What do you want for it?"

"I'll let you have it for two hundred dollars. It's three or four years old, but I put a brand new motor in it. It should last a long time."

I told him we'd look it over on our way back to Los Angeles and let him know whether he'd made a sale. He gave us the address of his apartment near San Diego.

The refrigerator proved to be perfect for our needs, and Margie's experienced eye indicated that it was, indeed, in like-new condition. We telephoned Dewey in the middle of the week and told him we'd take it, and to please deliver it to our casa as soon as the kitchen was ready for it.

At a golf tournament several years before this, I had won—of all the unlikly trophies—a garbage disposer. "What the devil are we going to do with this?" I had asked Margie, "Use it to shred old love letters or something?"

"Let's just put it away. We'll find a use for it some time," she had replied.

As usual, she had been right. The following weekend we carted it— heavy with dust from the garage—to Nueva España to be installed in our sink.

As our camper (again loaded with convivial booze for the local denizens) sloshed to a stop on the back lot, Margie began to chuckle.

"I just don't believe it!" she laughed, "I don't believe it!"

"What?"

"Look! Look at our patio doors!" she pointed.

The sliding glass doors opening onto the postage stamp patio had been installed as Margie had requested, but the standard door that had been there originally was still firmly in place. They hadn't removed it and plastered up the hole.

"That's neat!" I laughed, "We'll have one door to enter the patio, and another one for our exit!"

"Well, that original door has got to go!" she said seriously. "You go find Dewey or Pedro while I look around."

I encountered Pedro on his way down the street to greet us.

"Well, how do you like it?" he said. "It's going to be a beautiful house, isn't it?"

"Well, yes, but there's something I want to talk to you about," I said. "Come with me."

Margie joined us on the patio where I pointed out our solid bank of doors. "Why didn't you take out the old door, Pedro?"

"You need that door to enter the patio."

"Why not use the sliding doors to enter the patio?"

"They're just for light in the living room. It's too much trouble to have to slide them open when you want to go on the patio. The regular door is better."

"Even so, we don't want the regular door, Pedro. I told you that before," Margie said firmly.

He shook his head sadly. "It's too bad. It would be so nice."

"Two doors, side by side, to enter one tiny patio would *not* be nice," I said.

He sighed. "It will be a lot of work to fill up that hole. It will take bricks . . ." His voice trailed off.

"I've got an idea, folks," said a voice behind me.

I turned around and saw the jolly gent I'd seen in the Nueva España ad in *Las Californias.* "Hey, I know you! You're the guy in the magazine ad!"

"Oh, that. Yeah," he said a little self-consciously, "My name is Gene Lange. I live across the street from you."

"Nice to meet you. We're the Hunters. I'm Ben, and this is my wife Margie." We all shook hands.

"As I was saying, I have an idea for you," Gene continued. "Sometimes it gets awfully damn cold here in the winter, and you folks should have a furnace."

Accustomed to the warmer Gulf side of Baja, I had never thought of the need for a furnace. I asked him where we could get one.

"Well, that's where my idea comes in. I have an extra one. I'll sell it to you for what it cost me, and it'll fit right in that spot where you have an extra door."

"And that way Pedro wouldn't have to brick up the hole," I finished. Pedro brightened noticeably.

"Right."

"What do you think, honey?" I asked Margie.

"What does the furnace cost?" she asked.

"I sorta forget," Gene said, "but it was around two hundred dollars—a little over. I've got the receipt at home."

"Let's do it," she said.

"Okay, I'll get it over to Pedro so he can install it for you. Nice to meet you folks." So saying, Gene Lange, savior of patio door-holes, ambled off toward his house.

That same weekend, Margie, Pedro, and I all drove into Ensenada to choose the carpeting for the bedrooms, and the tiles for the rest of the house. My role in this exercise consisted of giving the final—and unnecessary—approval of the colors Margie and Pedro had selected. Deep broadloom in avocado green for the master bedroom, and chocolate brown for the guest bedroom, were the carpet choices. The tiles for the two bathrooms contrasted, but coordinated, with the carpets. The floor tiles in the rest of the house were free-form in shape, and beige. The tiles for the kitchen counters were coffee brown with a typical Mexican pattern worked into them. I hadn't the foggiest notion of how all that would look in the house, but Margie seemed satisfied, so I gave it my approval in the grand tradition of honorary vice presidents everywhere:

"Those will do very nicely. I think you made an excellent selection."

When Margie is involved in anything regarding her home—be it product or service—she becomes a single-minded, resolute perfectionist. I call it her "nesting" syndrome. When she is "nesting," she will spend a dollar's worth of gasoline to return a fifty-cent product that malfunctioned, or she will insist that a workman do his work over and over until it is perfect.

I am just the opposite. If a household product doesn't work right, I just throw it away and resolve never to buy another one. If a workman tries to do his job well and comes up a bit short, I accept it anyway. In fact, I even rationalize his shortcomings for him. This basic difference between Margie and me resulted in some conflict in the weeks that followed.

Other commitments kept us in Los Angeles for a time, but when at last we returned and again parked our camper on the back lot, we were astonished at the changes that had taken place. There were no workers around, and the house appeared nearly ready for occupancy.

Gene Lange's furnace had been installed where that door had been. Bedroom carpets had been laid; tiles were set; the kitchen, viewed through arches, was exquisite with glowing natural wood cabinets and Mexican tiles; the ground-level view window on the ocean side of the house afforded a sweeping vista of the billowing, white sand beach, the blue sea, and the purple island on the horizon. For a few minutes, the two of us just stood there drinking it in, but my reverie was rudely interrupted:

"Oh shit!" Margie said angrily.

She rarely swears, so I knew a major calamity was at hand. "What's wrong?"

"They installed the wrong carpet in our bedroom! That's not the color I ordered!"

"It's green. It looks the same to me," I said hopefully.

"I tell you it's not the same! I know what I ordered!"

"I think it looks nice. Won't this color green do just as well?"

"No. I hate it."

To me, green is green, but I saw there was no use in arguing. "Well, calm down, honey. Just make a note about it, and we'll tell Pedro to change it."

She took a paper and pencil from her purse and noted: "wrong carpet in M. bd/rm."

"We better look this house over carefully," she said grimly.

We strolled into the master bath for a look at the tile work in there. Since it is an inside bathroom, a large fan had been installed in the ceiling.

"I wonder if it works," I said, flipping the switch.

Did it work! It started with a soft whirring sound, and as it gained speed, it roared louder and louder. Soon, speech was impossible, and the sound approximated that of a helicopter taking off.

"I feel like I'm on the flight line at L.A. International Airport!" I yelled.

"What?" she shouted back.

I flipped it off. "That fan is funny! Can you imagine how it will scare the bejeebers out of our guests when they turn it on?"

"It won't scare our guests because they're going to fix it!" Margie said, and made another note: "fan in M/bath."

I stayed in the bathroom checking other points while Margie went to the kitchen—her favorite room—for a closer inspection. I noted that they had neglected to caulk the corners of the shower. That would be another note for Margie's list. Then I heard laughter from the kitchen. Relieved that her sense of humor had returned, I hastened in there to see what the mirth was all about.

"You'll never believe it!" she laughed.

"What?"

"Look at the garbage disposer."

I opened the cupboard under the sink and looked. It appeared to be a perfect installation. It was carefully fitted into the pipeline just as it should be, its hungry mouth against the sink drain. Wires seemed to be hooked up properly. "I don't see anything wrong," I said.

"Turn it on."

I looked. Then I looked again. Then I searched. There was no switch! Perhaps unfamiliar with this American adjunct to The Good Life, the workman had installed the disposer correctly, but left us no way to start it. "That's funny. You better put it on your list, honey, and you can add that the master shower needs caulking."

"Switch for Gar. Disp. Caulk shower M/bth," she scribbled.

As she was writing, the front door opened, and Dewey came in, followed by two of the workers struggling with the refrigerator. They had no dolly, so the big box was being wrestled into the kitchen by sheer Mexican muscle power.

"Here comes your refrigerator, Hunters!" Dewey beamed happily over the duet of grunts and groans.

"Good. Glad to see it," I said.

"How do you like your house? Isn't it beautiful?"

"It sure is. Of course, there are a few little things . . . Margie made a list."

"They aren't *little* things. They're *big* things," Margie said, "and they've *got* to be corrected."

"No problem. Just give me your notes and I'll take care of it," Dewey said reassuringly.

We all fell silent and watched as the perspiring workers inched the large refrigerator closer and closer to its niche between the cupboards on the kitchen wall. Soon it was squared up in the proper spot and ready to shove into place.

"Oh, *damn!*" said Dewey.

The refrigerator was too large to slide in.

"That's amazing, Dewey, you knew the size of your own refrigerator, but you let them build the cupboards so large there isn't enough space for it."

"We'll have to fix it, that's all," Dewey said. "We'll just make this cupboard here about four inches narrower, and then the refrigerator will fit in easily."

"If that cupboard is four inches smaller, it'll be too small to put anything in," Margie said.

"Oh, yeah." The master salesman thought a minute. "I've got it! It'll be just the right size for a spice cupboard! That'll be your spice cupboard."

I was ready to agree with any solution. "That's right, honey, you *will* need a spice cupboard," I chimed in.

"But it will be a tall, skinny one." She paused and sighed. "Well I guess I have no choice."

"Good. It's settled then. I think you'll like it, Mrs. Hunter."

No reply.

Later that evening over drinks in the camper we agreed that the house was at least half completed, and paid Dewey the second installment plus the two hundred dollars for the refrigerator. Before we left for Los Angeles the next day we gave him our note about the needed repairs.

We returned to Nueva España two weeks later with exultation. Surely, by now the house would be completed, we could make our final payment, then move in. Again there were no workers around when we arrived, so we hurried inside for a private inspection. The roomy cupboard to the left of the refrigerator was now the size of a vertical shoe box, and the refrigerator had been installed.

"That little cupboard isn't so bad," I said. "It will make a good spice cupboard, as Dewey said."

"Ben, look!" She sounded exasperated again.

"What now?"

"Look where the switch for the kitchen light is!" she pointed.

The switch for the overhead light in the kitchen was on the wall in the refrigerator niche. With the refrigerator in place, you couldn't reach the switch! "Oh no!" I groaned.

"I'm going to start making notes again," she said grimly, and removed the paper and pencil from her purse.

"Moving that switch will mean hacking more holes in the cement wall," I observed.

"Well, what else would you suggest? The way it is now I'd have to cook in the dark."

I looked over toward the sink and spied a gleaming new switch on the wall. I walked over, flipped it on, and the garbage disposal growled. "Hey, the garbage disposer works fine now. They really did a good job." I was actually becoming defensive for Dewey and company.

"Well, let's look around some more."

The correct carpeting had been laid in the master bedroom, and the master shower had been caulked.

"See, honey? They really are trying hard to please us."

"Turn on the bathroom fan," she snapped.

I touched the switch. We heard a soft whirr, and then, as it revved up, the thundering roar. I turned it off. There was no need for me to say anything—Margie was writing notes again.

As we strolled into the living room, she came to a full stop and stared. "What now?"

"The baseboards. They're the wrong color."

"What's wrong? They look okay to me."

"They're black! We can't have black baseboards!" She made another note.

I had to admit that they did look a little stark, now that she mentioned it. The deep black outline to the white, plastered walls made me think of a death notice.

The Nueva España property slopes gently upward from the beach with the entrance gate at the top of the slope. Thus, it is impossible to arrive at the project without being seen by anyone who happens to be outside, or looking out his window. Once again, our arrival had been spotted from the Nueva España office, and Pedro burst happily into the house just as Margie was writing: "paint the baseboards brown."

"It's all ready for you!" he exclaimed jubliantly. "When are you going to move in?"

"Not quite yet, Pedro, there are just a few more items that have to be changed," I said.

"More than a few," Margie added, "and there may be more!" So saying, she swept out of the room to inspect the guest bedroom and bath.

"She sounds angry," Pedro observed.

"She's not angry, Pedro, but she's very particular. She wants our house to be perfect."

"Of course."

"Ben! Pedro! Come here!" cried an angry voice from the guest bathroom.

We both hurried toward the sound of trouble.

"Look at that toilet!" Margie cried out. "How did that happen?"

Where once there had been a shiny, gleaming, new toilet bowl, there now crouched a relic that appeared to be many years old. It had characteristic brown stains around the inside, and touches of rust on its bolts. It looked as if it might have been sitting in someone's backyard exposed to the elements for several years!

"What happened to our new toilet, Pedro?" I asked.

He laughed good naturedly. "Oh those guys!"

"What guys?"

"My workmen. Sometimes when they need something they pirate it out of another house."

"You mean they needed a new toilet for one of the other houses, so they took ours and left us this one?

"That's right. But don't worry, we'll get you a new one. I know where one is."

"In one of the other houses?"

He just winked.

Margie made me think of a volcano about to erupt. One more flaw discovered in our house and poor Pedro would be engulfed in verbal molten lava! Displays of anger always embarrass me, so I quickly proposed a walk on the beach, and Margie agreed.

The beach was even lovelier than usual. The soft sand felt like velvet beneath our feet, the sunlight sparkled on the white foam of the waves, and a fluffy cloud made a halo around the top of "Emerald Head." We walked along the edge of the water in silence for some time, soaking up the warmth and beauty. Finally, when I sensed that the beach-walk therapy had begun to calm her down, I suggested we sit down for awhile.

"Why? Are you tired?"

"No. But it's so pretty here. Besides, I want to talk to you."

"Alright." She sat down abruptly, and I flopped beside her. "What is it?"

"Darling, you're losing your cool."

"Well, who wouldn't! My gosh, all those dumb mistakes they've made, and the idea of stealing our toilet—"

"I know," I interrupted. "It must be very frustrating to you, honey, and it is to me too. But you've got to remember we're building in Mexico, and things are different down here."

"Pooh! Dewey's an American, and he's the developer."

"That's true, but he is trying to get the job done with Mexican labor, and that's the problem."

"I'm sure he has problems, but that doesn't mean that I want black baseboards, an antique toilet, and switches I can't reach."

"Of course not, and we'll get those things changed. I just mean you shouldn't get so angry with them. Remember *God and Mr. Gomez?* Jack Smith didn't get angry. He was just amused."

"I'll bet he was really angry. He just didn't write about it. Besides, I'm not Jack Smith."

"Well, even if you are angry, Darling, please don't show it. You can get Dewey and Pedro to correct the mistakes without losing your temper. You can catch more flies with sugar."

"A squeeky wheel gets the grease."

"Oh, now we're going to have a battle of banalities. Okay. Throw oil on troubled waters."

"Speak now or forever hold your peace."

"An empty wagon rattles the loudest."

"A rolling stone gathers no moss."

"What's that got to do with it?"

"Nothing. I just couldn't think of another one that fit."

We both laughed, and I kissed her. The volcano had been capped—at least for the moment.

I kissed her again, then we got to our feet and started back toward the casa.

I don't know why I hadn't noticed it before, but when we walked through the front door, it was all I could see.

301

"Look where those damn idiots put the thermostat for the furnace!" I shouted. "It's right on the wall beside it instead of out in the room! Every time it turns the furnace on, the hot air will blow on it and shut the furnace off! I never saw such stupidity!" I raged.

Dewey had the misfortune to be passing by our house at that moment. "Hi Folks!" he waved cheerily.

"Godddammit! Come in here, Dewey!"

For the next few minutes, poor Dewey took the full brunt of my wrath. He fully agreed that placing the thermostat on the wall right next to the furnace was indeed wrong, and assured us that he would order it moved to the center of the room at once.

After he beat a hasty retreat, Margie said slyly, "You catch more flies with sugar."

"This is different!" I growled.

My anger about the misplaced thermostat was short-lived. I rationalized it all again on the way home. Dewey and Pedro were trying hard to please us, and how could they help it if the workers didn't know how to install a furnace? Nevertheless, I resolved that I would join Margie in making a very thorough check of the premises when we returned.

We didn't get back to Nueva España for another two weeks because of a very pleasant diversion. Our children's show, "The Elementary News" had been nominated for an Emmy, and we had to attend the awards ceremony and telecast. Never in our wildest imaginings had we expected to win, and I'm sure our acceptance was less than graceful.

The Emmy presenter opened the sealed envelope, announced our show as the winner, and the television cameras swung around focusing on our table. We looked wildly at each other, jumped from the table, and dashed for the stage in opposite directions! Though I can't remember positively, I believe I tripped over my chair in my hasty exit. Breathlessly, we reached center stage—Margie coming from the right and I from the left. We were handed the Emmy, and the applause quieted down as the audience awaited the acceptance speech.

I stepped to the microphone, acknowledged the applause, and then explained to the audience that " The Elementary News " was really Margie's idea, conceived on a beach in Baja, and therefore she should say a few words. There was another burst of applause as she stepped to the microphone.

"Well, first I want to thank—" she paused, a catch in her throat. She swallowed, and started again. "I want to thank those wonderful—I can't go on!" And she started to cry.

"We want to say thanks to everyone," I said, trying to fill the breach, and led my sobbing wife from the stage.

She was the only boo-hooer on the entire program.

Our next trip back to Baja found Pedro again waiting for us at the house when we drove up.

"Hi Ben and Margie!" he called.

"Hi Pedro," I responded as we got out of the camper, "Did you get everything done on the list I left with Dewey?"

"Almost. We're just finishing up on the thermostat now."

Sure enough, as we entered the house I saw the thermostat's solitary eye staring at us from the center of the living room wall. A deep channel had been gouged out of the cement to accomodate the wiring for it, and a worker was in the process of filling it up and plastering it over. So far, so good.

While I had been inspecting the thermostat, Margie had ducked into the guest bathroom to ascertain the age of the toilet. Now she returned.

"Well?" I said.

"Okay. There's a new toilet in there."

"Good. What's next on the list?"

"The switch for the kitchen light," Pedro supplied. "I had it moved away from the refrigerator to this wall here, where you can reach it."

There it was, gleaming and white, on a convenient wall. But now it was a double-switch.

"I see it's a double-switch now, Pedro. What is the second switch for?"

"Oh nothing. It's just a dummy."

"A dummy switch? Why?"

"For looks."

"Like the three-way electric plugs?"

"That's right. I thought a double-switch in that location would look nicer than a single one. Don't you agree?"

I stole a glance at Margie who gave an almost imperceptible shrug. "Yeah, I guess so, Pedro. Besides, it'll be fun baffling our house guests. They'll always be wondering what that second switch is for."

"Good," he said seriously, "then I guess everything is okay. If you'll excuse me now, I have to check one of the other houses." So saying, he left. I started to laugh. "I think that's neat! We've got a dummy light switch to match the dummy light plugs!"

"Here's something that's not so funny," Margie said.

"What?"

"The fireplace. They didn't put any fire brick in it. After a year of fires we'd burn deep holes in it."

I agreed with her. Mexican bricks are made by hand and as soft as chalk. Margie made a note.

"I see he got the baseboards painted brown as we ordered. Was there anything else on our list?"

"Not that I can think of." She paused. "Oh yes, the fan!"

"I'll check it," I said quickly. If it was going to make its characteristic roar, I wanted to tell her about it rather than have her hear it. It would keep her calmer.

The fan roared.

I quickly shut it off and returned to the living room.

"They didn't weatherstrip the front door," she said as I entered. "Was the fan fixed?"

"Let me put it this way, Darling, Pedro is batting four for five—not a bad average."

She gave me a withering look. "In other words it wasn't fixed."

I nodded, and she made another note.

"Alright, let's look around some more," she said.

We strolled through the other rooms of the house seeing nothing wrong, and ended up in the kitchen where a shiny, store-fresh range had been installed next to the refrigerator.

"Gee, that's a nice looking stove," I said.

"Not bad."

She stared at it for a moment, then reached down and pulled open the oven door. As she did so, the stove rocked violently forward!

"That does it!" she said angrily, "That just does it!"

"Calm down, Margie. I'm sure it can be easily fixed."

"Maybe. But what if I hadn't bothered to try it before we took delivery on the house? We'd be saddled with a rocking stove!"

"Just make a note, Honey."

Although he didn't actually say so, I'm quite sure Dewey had been hoping to get the final check from us that weekend, but we stated firmly (at least Margie did) that the last payment would not be made until everything was completed to our satisfaction. We said we'd return in two weeks to check the house again, and presented him with the notes about the firebrick, weatherstripping, teetering stove, and the fan that tried to lift us—house and all—off the ground.

A weather front moved onto the West Coast the next two weeks, and California was washed by a steady downpour for days. We wondered if it were raining in Baja, and if so, how our house was faring.

The moment we reached Ensenada on our return trip, we could see that Baja had been subjected to heavy rain also. Although the sky was bright blue, and patched with big, fluffy clouds, the streets of the city were still awash, and the dry riverbed that bisects it was a raging torrent. The chuckholed dirt road leading to Nueva España was apparently so hard-packed that the rain hadn't turned it to mire, and our camper splashed through the puddles without incident. Soon we could see our casa, washed clean by the rain, and sparkling white in the bright sunlight. Bud Murphy, Pedro Alonzo, and Dewey Bouche were all standing at our front door waiting for us as we drove up. They were all smiling. "Hi Folks!" they waved.

To me, they looked like three kids who had just brought home good report cards, and I began to relent. "Darling, they've been trying so hard to please us. Let's not be tough on them," I whispered, "Let's just pay them the third installment now. I'm sure they've fixed everything."

She set her jaw. "Are you kidding? And what if we find things wrong after we pay them and move in? Do you think they'll fix them then?"

"I think they probably would."

"Well, I'm not going to chance it. I'm going over that house with a fine tooth comb!" So saying, she got out of the camper and entered the house.

I now began to feel that any further inspections by us were not only unnecessary, but boring. Also, I felt that if Margie was going to do her "fine tooth comb" act, she'd prefer not to have the three of them beaming over her shoulder while she did it.

Having rationalized thus, I said to our smiling friends, "Tell you what, guys, why don't you come inside the camper and let me pour us a couple of drinks while Margie makes a final inspection?"

My suggestion was greeted with enthusiasm, and we all trooped inside the Dolphin for a couple of "belts." Things went well for nearly an hour. We swapped stories, laughed, and sipped cool ones—all four of us forgetting that a very determined woman was going over every detail of that house like a detective searching for clues. Dewey was just reaching the punch line of one of his favorite jokes when the door opened and Margie stalked grimly into the camper clutching a fistful of notes. He broke off the story at once.

"Did you find something?" he said apprehensively.

"Let me put it this way, Dewey," she said irritably, "to begin with, you

305

didn't put a cap on the stove vent and it's been raining on my stove. It's top is actually rusty! Can you imagine that? Rusty! We've told you about that noisy fan in the bathroom a hundred times, and it still sounds like it's going to fly apart when you turn it on. Furthermore—"

"Have a drink, Darling," I interrupted, and poured her one. "I have an idea." The three jolly faces across the table from me had suddenly turned strained and haggard. "Instead of going into all the things Margie found now, we'll go home and put them in a letter to you, Dewey. Then when we return the next time, if everything in the letter has been done, we'll settle up with you once and for all. How's that?"

Relief flooded across Dewey's face. "Fair enough," he said.

February 10

Dear Dewey,

Here's Margie's list. We'll be returning to Nueva España on February 22nd and hope everything will be perfect by then.

1. Put a cap over the vent on the stove so it won't rain on it.

2. Fix the noisy fan in the M/bath (we have mentioned this several times!)

3. The light switch to the left of the fireplace is black. It should be white like the others in the room.

4. The plaster to the right of the fireplace doesn't match the plaster on the left side. It looks like two different houses.

5. Bottom of the bathtub (Where it meets the floor) is completely unfinished. Please put grout in.

6. Front doorknob is loose.

7. House wall next to cupboard in kitchen unfinished. Needs to be plastered.

8. Drawers in master bath too tight. Margie couldn't open them.

9. Somebody chipped the tile to the left of the sink in the master bath since we were here last. Please replace it.

10. Woodwork inside the back closet is unpainted. Please paint it.

That's about it. Looking forward to seeing all of you guys in two weeks—and hopefully moving in!

Sincerely,
BEN HUNTER

I typed it carefully, Xeroxed three copies, and sent them to Dewey so each of the persons we'd been dealing with would know exactly what had to be done.

When February 22nd arrived, and we again pulled our camper onto the lot behind our house, we were greeted effusively by Dewey, Pedro, and Bud—all grinning like kids on Christmas morning. Each of them had his copy of my Xeroxed letter, and each of the ten items had been checked off.

"It's all done! Your house is ready for you!" Pedro cried gleefully, waving his copy of the letter.

"Come inside! We have a surprise for you!" Dewey said.

Excitedly, they led us into our house, and there on the kitchen sink was a huge bouquet of flowers and champagne chilling in a mop bucket!

"It's a house warming present from Nueva España," Bud said.

It was too much for me. I pulled out the checkbook and wrote the final check. We didn't inspect a damn thing.

11/ The End
and the Beginning

Of course, a number of things remained to be done before we could actually move into our *casa*. Foremost on the list was draperies to provide us with some degree of privacy. David and Dee Grone are our next door neighbors in Los Angeles and, fortunately for us, in the wholesale drapery business. We had hoped they would give us at least a slight discount on the drapes, but they didn't. After spending two days in Mexico measuring the windows, and another two days of difficult work putting up the drapes, they refused to accept a penny in payment. "Just call it a housewarming present," Dave said. Friends like that are hard to find.

During those weeks the house had been under construction, Margie and I had carted a lot of small furniture and supplies to Nueva España in the camper and left them in storage for moving day. Now there remained just the larger objects which wouldn't fit through the camper door, so we had to devise a new method of slipping past Mexican Customs officials with them. We removed the camper from the truck and packed the larger furniture on the open truck bed. Then we covered it with a sheet of plastic to keep it clean, and topped the whole load with a heavy, dirty tarp that had been on many camping trips with us. Fishing rods, Coleman stove, and other camping gear were festooned around the load giving us the appearance, we fervently hoped, of a couple of people going on a camping trip. To complete the illusion, we costumed ourselves in camping clothes. Thus disguised for the big furniture smuggling operation, we set out early one morning for the border.

As we approached the border crossing, Margie removed a ten-dollar bill from her purse and I concealed it in the palm of my hand. If they discovered our contraband, the *mordida* would be handy. Then we pulled up and stopped beside the Mexican border guards. It was cold and rainy that morning. Both the guards had their coat collars pulled up around their ears and their gloved hands jammed in their pockets. One of them approached us.

"Good morning!" I said brightly. (We had resolved to speak only English to reinforce our American tourist look.)

The guard just nodded, and took a long hard look at our load.

"Start up!" Margie hissed at me.

I started to inch the truck forward. The guard acted as if he were about to ask us to pull over for inspection. I increased speed.

As we pulled away I heard him say to his companion, *"Pescadores."* (fishermen) We had pulled it off!

For a small tip, the Mexican workers at Nueva España unloaded the truck for us and arranged the furniture as Margie directed. By the time this was accomplished, it was raining steadily, and our house was very cold and damp. Margie was putting down shelfpaper and loading canned goods into her cupboards when there came a knock at the door.

It was Pedro. "Would you guys like some firewood?" he asked.

"Oh boy, would we!" I said.

"I'll bring you a wheelbarrow load," he replied, and left.

"Hey, that was sure nice of him, wasn't it?" I said to Margie after the door had closed.

"I'll say. A fire will be just perfect on a day like this."

"He's really a thoughtful person."

In a few minutes he returned pushing a wheelbarrow full of logs. He took it around to our patio and stacked the wood neatly against the wall out of the rain.

"Hey thanks, Pedro, that's marvelous!" I said.

"That's okay. It's just five dollars."

I thought perhaps I had misunderstood. "Five dollars?"

"Yes," he smiled. "I sell firewood to make a little money on the side. Everything helps, you know."

Feeling slightly deflated, I handed him the money.

"Enjoy your fire," he said, and disappeared again.

The fireplace smoked. Not just a little bit. Shortly after I had lit what was to have been a welcome blaze, the smoke came billowing out of the hearth in great, noxious clouds, filling the entire house, and sending us coughing into the street. After a few minutes' recovery time in the cold

310

fresh air, I dashed back inside, grabbed the burning logs by their unburned ends, and tossed them outside. Then we opened all the doors and windows to clear out the smoke.

While we were standing outside waiting for the pall of smoke to clear out of our house, Pedro came strolling up the street.

"Just look at our house!" Margie said disgustedly.

"How did it get all that smoke in it?" he asked.

"It's the fireplace, Pedro," I said. "It smokes."

"Hmmmmmm." He took a couple of steps backward and scrutinized the chimney. "I think the chimney is too short. We'll make it taller tomorrow," he said easily.

Margie was apprehensive. "I hope it works."

"Don't worry, it will. Actually, I came by to see if we could take you to dinner tonight. We have a favorite restaurant we'd like you to try."

We were tired from the unloading, and the house was still not habitable because of the smoke, so we accepted.

Pedro's wife, Lupe, was one of those rarities—a blond Mexican—and like Pedro spoke perfect English. In all other respects she was completely Latin—as tiny and peppery as a jalapeño, and utterly charming. Pedro's charm increased when he got away from the project, and together they won us completely. They treated us to a magnificent dinner in a fine restaurant, lavished us with drinks and exquisite cuisine, and delivered us to our now smoke-free *casa* in a state of euphoria. Expensive logs and smoking fireplace notwithstanding, Pedro was forgiven.

I was awakened late the next morning to the tantalizing smell of Margie's first breakfast in the *casa*. The "Baja Feeling"—absent these many weeks—began to steal over me again. For a few moments I just laid in bed listening to the breakers beyond our house and savoring it. Perhaps this morning we'd enjoy a leisurely breakfast, and then go back to bed and cuddle for awhile—alone and undisturbed in our beautiful *casa*. Finally I got up, put on a robe, and strolled into the kitchen where Margie stood at the stove.

"Good morning, Darling," I said kissing the back of her neck. "What's for breakfast?"

"Scrambled eggs and bird shit!" she snarled.

The fragile "Baja Feeling" began to fade.

"Well almost. Some birds have built a nest in the vent over the stove and bird droppings are all over everything. It's a mess!"

"Well, it's easily fixed. We'll just ask Pedro to put some wire mesh around the top of the vent so the birds can't get in."

311

"It's something he should have done in the first place! Like the smoking fireplace! Make a note about it while I put breakfast on the table!"

The "Baja Feeling" gone, I made the notes.

I was the first one to christen the new bathroom, and discovered that there was no baffle in the fan-vent over the toilet. Consequently, as I sat there, the chilly morning breezes blew down the vent and played over my posterior. It was like the icy fingers of death toying with my bottom— unnerving! Then the *coup de grace*—when I turned on the fan it sounded as if the Red Baron were flying his Sopwith Camel right through the room. They hadn't fixed the damn fan at all!

"Well, I've got a couple more notes," I growled as I rejoined Margie.

"Don't tell me. They didn't fix the fan."

"That's right. Plus, they didn't install a baffle in the vent, so the outside air blows on your bare fanny. And that air is cold this morning, too!"

She started laughing.

"What're you laughing at?"

"It's a funny picture," she giggled. "You sitting there on the pot trying to keep your bottom warm!"

"It doesn't seem funny to me. If my ass had teeth, they'd be chattering!"

After Margie's laughter subsided, we talked it over seriously and decided that a subtle bathroom fan was simply beyond the reach of Mexican engineering. We would complain about it no more. We have actually become to be amused by our mini-airport, and now refer to a bathroom trip by the euphemism "a ride on the helicopter." As far as the missing baffle on the vent was concerned, that would have to be fixed, and we added it to the growing list.

These landmark decisions had no sooner been reached than we heard a knock at the door and opened it to see Gene Lange standing there with a coffee pot in his hand.

He handed Margie the coffee pot. "It's a housewarming gift. Makes great coffee."

We thanked him and invited him in for a cup. We had met Gene at the time he saved the day by selling us his Sears furnace, and we had chatted with him briefly during the hectic weeks that followed, but we had never had a chance to talk with him at length, to really get to know him, until this morning. We learned that he is a retired civil engineer from Wisconsin. After his retirement, he and his wife jumped into their camper, drove to Baja, impulsively bought a house at Nueva España, and settled down. Since most Baja retirees are from California or Arizona, I suspected their friends back in Wisconsin must consider the Langes an oddity, or very courageous, to retire in "that wild, God-forsaken country."

"Our friends do think we're a little crazy," Gene admitted, "but that's because they haven't seen Baja."

As a man who built roads, bridges, and dams, Gene found Mexican building methods almost more than he could endure. He spent a long time enumerating all the things they were doing wrong at Nueva España, and judging from our experience we were inclined to agree with him.

Many times after that we were to observe Gene pacing up and down the street in front of a house, fuming to himself until his blood pressure was about to peak. Then he would stride over to the workmen and intervene as politely as possible—"Excuse me," he would say, "I know it's none of my business, but if you'd just do it this way . . . " Painstakingly, he would explain the American way of building a wall, setting a stud, or wiring a home. Like school boys stopping their play for a lecture from the principal, the workmen stopped and listened attentively to Gene. When he finally concluded, they would nod, smile, and return to their work—doing it just as before.

Of course, the lecture was in English and the Mexican workmen had probably not understood a word of it. But, even if they had understood, they would never have changed. Gene knew this too, but the sermon on proper building techniques always lowered his blood pressure for awhile.

We met his wife, Silver, sometime later. Like her name, she is pretty, gentle, and serene. While Gene may pace the streets and fume at the builders, she cooks, listens to the song of the sea, and paints sweeping landscapes in oils, quite content in her corner of paradise. Yet, we have discovered, too, that she has great, hidden strengths behind that gentle exterior. She is a perfect balance for her often volatile husband. Like the Sylaks and the Gillises, the Langes have become very close friends.

We were to stay at the casa for two weeks on this occasion. Our purpose was not only to move in and get the kinks out of the house, but to actually taste a bit of our future life at Nueva España. An integral part of this for Margie is to check out the stores. So we sought out Dewey that first morning, told him of the need for a baffle in the bathroom vent, and a fireplace that didn't smoke, then headed into the city for a day of shopping.

We discovered Limons, a modern supermarket in the American tradition, whose clean, neon-lighted aisles were lined with many grocery bargains; a carnicería [butcher shop] where one could purchase a whole beef filet, butchered and aged to perfection, for less than eight

313

dollars; Dorian's Department Store, as large and modern as any in the States, where Margie bought me stunning sport shirts for four dollars each. We also staked out the bakeries, produce stores, tailor, florist, and other tradespeople we'd be doing business with in future years. We lunched off one of the many roadside carts one finds in any Mexican city, and enjoyed a huge, raw clam cocktail with great chunks of delicious clam meat floating in Mexican hot sauce, seasoned with onions, tomatoes, cilantro, and those sweet little Mexican limes.

It was nearly dusk when we finally returned to our *casa*, but even in the failing light we could see that the chimney was considerably taller. It was getting chilly, a cold wind blowing off the ocean. A fire would be nice.

Using a flashlight, I peered up the stove vent and was able to spot the wire mesh around it. The baffle had been installed in the bathroom vent. Pedro had done his work well.

While Margie was putting stuff away in the kitchen, I got one of our expensive logs and built a large crackling fire. In moments it smoked us out of the house again.

I couldn't get angry with Pedro—he had certainly tried to fix it—but we certainly couldn't put up with a smoking fireplace. He and Lupe were having dinner when I knocked at their front door.

"I'm sorry to interrupt your dinner, Pedro, but our fireplace still smokes. I want you to see it."

"It still smokes? I can't believe it!"

"Well, come see." I grabbed his arm and propelled him next door to our smoke-choked *casa*.

Standing in the street, his dinner getting cold, Pedro made his diagnosis: "It's this strong breeze off the ocean that is making it smoke. Tomorrow I'll have my men build a wind break around the top of the chimney."

"Are you sure that'll correct it, Pedro?" I asked.

"Positive."

We were buying our house under the terms of the "Thirty Year Trust" that had been described to us by Jack Larson many years before. The next day Dewey gave us the glad tidings that our thirty year trust deed to the *casa* was ready; he advised us to pick it up and visit the *notario* right away. Remembering the pompous *notario* we had encountered in La Paz some years before, we were pleasantly surprised by Sr. Alfredo Gonzalez Corral. His office on an Ensenada side street is small, but modern and tastefully decorated. Sr. Corral is a tall gentleman with a quiet, assured manner. He speaks in the soft, cultured voice of an aristocrat, and one senses a feeling of great integrity in his presence. Pictures of his handsome family are placed neatly on his uncluttered desk, and expensive oil paintings adorn the walls of his sunny office.

"I . . spik . . very . . leetle . . Ingles," he said, choosing his words with difficulty, "But . . I . . weel . . try . . to . . esplain."

"*Podemos hablar poquito español,*" I said helpfully.

He looked relieved. "*Ah, bien. Entonces hay un problema.*"

A problem with out trust? My heart sank. "*Que es?*"

In a combination of Spanish and English, Sr. Corral explained the problem. It seemed that Dewey Bouche and Juan Hurtado were not the first developers of Nueva España. They had taken over from the original developer who was a Mexican national. This man—for reasons only he knew—had identified our lot as "C'7" and another one as "C7." In other words, the apostrophe in our lot description was all that differentiated it from another. The Bank of Mexico had sent through our papers without that important apostrophe, so we now had legal title to our neighbor's house across the street!

He told us that the lot was free and clear, but also said that we would have to return the papers to Mexico City and have them add the apostrophe.

"How long will that take?" Margie asked.

He shrugged. "*Quién sabe?* Six months perhaps, maybe longer. Things move slowly in Mexico."

With all the tales one hears about the difficulties encountered by foreigners attempting to buy land in Mexico, one feels a bit insecure no matter how legal the land sale seems to be. Thus, those trust papers assumed even greater importance in our eyes. They were the imprimatur of the federal government of Mexico on our purchase. With that official seal, no one could ever take our land away. They were our security. Now the feeling of insecurity was to return for "six months . . . maybe longer" all for the lack of one stupid little apostrophe! We returned to Nueva España, feeling disappointed, insecure, and frustrated.

True to his word, Pedro had installed a brick birdhouse thing atop our chimney to keep the wind from blowing down the flue, but Gene Lange was standing out in the street shaking his head negatively as he stared at it.

"What's the matter, Gene?" I asked.

"I don't think it'll work."

"How do you know?"

"Well, I think the fireplace was built wrong to begin with. No matter

315

what they do to the chimney, it's going to keep on smoking. Mine does."

"Yours does!" I was astounded because Gene had been living there for a couple of years.

"Yup. Everyone's does."

"What do you do about it?"

"Next time it smokes, try opening your patio door a few inches. That'll make it draw better."

We built another fire that night and discovered that Gene was right. It still smoked up the room, but we could make it draw by opening the patio door about four inches.

"I guess we'll just have to live with it this way," I told Margie. "Pedro seems to have exhausted every remedy."

"It's ridiculous! You want a fire on a cold night, but to enjoy it you have to open the door and let the cold air in!"

Ridiculous or not, that's what we did.

The remainder of our two-week stay at Nueva España was spent walking the beautiful beach picking up shells, doing a little surf fishing, shopping in the local stores, and getting to know our delightful neighbors better. They are a gregarious lot and tend to tap at the door any time of the day or night if they look through the window and see we are up. Because of this, there was a little problem beginning to form in the back of my mind. Barbie Sylak solved it simply as we all sat in our bathrobes drinking coffee one morning.

"I'm beginning to get the idea that you and Margie have a pretty active sex life," she said with that cute, impish smile.

"Whatever gave you that idea?"

"Call it ESP. Anyway, I thought you'd like to know one of our Nueva España rules."

"Sex is against the law?"

She laughed. "No. The rule is, when you want privacy just close your drapes. It's an unwritten law, but we all observe it. As long as you keep the drapes closed, no one will knock at your door."

That settled the little problem I'd been worrying about, and we all obey the "drapery law" to this day. On one occasion we opened the drapes and stepped outside to discover Gene Lange had been timing us!

"Three hours!" he marveled, "I just can't believe it! Three hours!"

I never told him that two-thirds of that time had been spent just sipping a glass of wine and enjoying each other's company—talking.

Except for the matter of having to use the fireplace with the door open, the house now functioned perfectly. Further, it was more beautiful than I had ever dared to hope. Margie, however, had been thinking about an improvement. She was thinking that if we purchased the lot behind our house where we'd parked the camper all those weeks, we could add on a playroom. It would be a place where we could keep our books and her handicraft stuff, and I could do my writing. We asked Dewey if he would approve that type of extension in his condominium, and he said "Why not?" We purchased the back lot from Dewey before we left for Los Angeles.

With our house seemingly in good order, we began to lay plans for a housewarming party. It would be a very modest one. Margie would prepare a buffet, and we'd ask two or three couples to drive down for an afternoon open house. If they wished to stay overnight, rather than make the long drive back to Los Angeles, they could do so at a local hotel—at their own expense. But then, as so often happens with party guest lists we kept thinking of other friends we couldn't leave out; soon, the names filled several pages. In the end, we just sent invitations to all of our good friends. After all, we reasoned, how many of them would be willing to make a five hour drive and pay the expense of hotel accommodations just for an afternoon party? Our party would still be small because we would doubtless get many, many turn-downs.

We got one. Everyone else accepted, and we found ourselves faced with the prospect of putting on a party in our small, two bedroom house, for nearly two hundred people! We griped about it good naturedly— Margie began calling our party "The Frankenstein Monster"—but in truth we were highly flattered that so many of our friends honored us by attending.

Of course, the larger party called for a change of plans. Margie couldn't cook for that many, so we'd have to find a caterer somewhere in Ensenada. My bar, though well-stocked, would never be able to moisten two hundred Baja-dry gullets.

We'd have to buy a lot of booze—wholesale, we hoped! And, for a mob like that, there should be entertainment. Mariachis would be the obvious choice, but we'd have to find them and engage their services. So it was that I took another two-week vacation prior to the party to give us time to get ready.

It was raining the evening we returned to our casa, so we decided to try our fireplace. Margie had purchased one of those mesh fire screens that looks and operates like a curtain. They are quick and easy to install, so I put it in place before building the fire. Then into the hearth went the crumpled newspapers, kindling, and the remaining expensive log; the match was struck, the paper ignited, and flames leaped up the chimney. We waited for the smoke to pour into the room—the signal to open the patio door—but none came! We could scarcely believe the miracle that was at hand! Apparently the addition of the fire screen had so changed the characteristics of the fireplace that at last it was actually drawing the smoke up the chimney and discharging it into the rainy Baja night! Were the gods rewarding us for our past travail, or softening us up for what was to follow?

Soothed into tranquility by our now smoothly-functioning home, we slept later than usual the next morning. I was the first out of bed, and when my bare feet landed on the bedroom carpet, water came squishing up between my toes!

"Margie!" I yelped.

Startled out of sleep, she sat up quickly.

"Look!" I paddled my foot up and down making tiny splashes in the broadloom.

"My God!" She leaped out of bed making her own splash. "Does the roof leak?"

"How could it leak? It's solid cement a foot thick."

"Then what caused it?"

"I can't imagine."

For a few moments we both splashed around the carpet looking for the source of the water.

"There it is!" Margie said, pointing to the wall separating the bedroom from the master bath.

I looked. It was so obvious we should have noticed it weeks before. For some time the plaster had been so wet it had been flaking off on the floor. There was only one possible conclusion. A water pipe in the wall had broken and the wall had been soaking up the water. Reaching the saturation point, it had finally begun seeping out onto the bedroom floor.

"I'll get Dewey," I said grimly, reaching for my clothes.

By the time I returned with a worried-looking Dewey in tow, Margie had brewed a pot of coffee, and Barbie Sylak had dropped in for a morning cup with us. The two women were chatting in the living room as Dewey and I walked through.

"Look!" I said, gesturing dramatically at the giant puddle.

Dewey sighed. "Okay, we'll fix it. Don't worry."

"I hope so! And soon!"

"I'll get the plumber right now."

So saying, he left, and I joined the ladies in the living room for solace and a cup.

"Barbie, tell Ben what you just told me," Margie said.

I looked inquiringly at Barbie. "What?"

"I told Margie that the same thing has happened to all of us."

"You——are——kidding!"

"No, it's true. The plumbing in the wall of all the houses broke just like yours did. It absolutely ruined our bedroom carpet."

"Why would they *all* break?"

Barbie shook her head. "I don't know, but they did. I guess the first builder just didn't put the pipes in right."

"My God, what next?"

"I'll tell you what's next," Margie said, "we've got to get that carpet dried out in time for the party."

In a short time a cadre of workmen arrived, removed the tiles from the bathroom wall, and hacked a large hole in it. Then, as we watched in horror, they decided they could reach the offending pipe easier from the other side and began hacking another large hole on the bedroom side of the wall! With gaping holes on either side, our bathroom appeared shell-shocked—like a French farmhouse in a World War II movie. Finally, the workmen found the problem—a joint in the pipe line had just been placed in position without any soldering, welding, or whatever they do. It had simply come apart. They fixed it in no time, poured cement into the yawning holes of the wall, and plastered it over. In a couple of hours the job was completed, but Margie and I were left with the task of drying out the soggy broadloom.

First we soaked up the water with sponges and squeezed them into pails. Then we massaged the carpet with towels. A couple of hours of this routine, and the carpet was no longer sopping; it was just very wet. Fortunately, we had an electric heater, so we raised the carpet off the floor and placed chairs under it for air circulation, then turned on the electric heater and aimed it at the dripping broadloom. This worked fine for awhile—until all the electricity went off. Puzzled by this new problem, we went over to the Lange's house to see if their electricity was off too. It was.

He gave a weary sigh. "It just means that someone around here probably turned on an electric heater."

I explained briefly that we were trying to dry out our bedroom carpet, and why.

"Well you see," Gene explained, "the transformer that furnishes power to Nueva España isn't big enough to do the job. So if you turn on an electric heater when other people are drawing on the power, it blows the transformer. It happens a lot."

"Well what'll we do to get our carpet dry?"

"Just use the heater at a time of day when you're pretty sure no one else is drawing on the electricity. High noon would be a good time—it's nearly dusk, now."

"Oh brother! What next!" (It seemed I was saying that a lot lately).

"Well, next you'll have to wait four or five hours for them to come out and fix the transformer."

We got the carpet dry before the party, but it took a lot of noontime drying periods.

In the meantime, we located a caterer. Chavo (a knickname for Salvador) was not a professional caterer—he was a bartender—but he assured us that his wife was an excellent cook and there would be plenty of good food for everyone. Since most of our guests had never been anywhere in Mexico in their lives, we decided on authentic Mexican cuisine. This is not like the "Number Three Combination" at a Los Angeles Mexican restaurant with the taco, enchilada, and refried beans. The foods we chose were cerviche, escarbeche, carnes asadas, and other unusual favorites we had learned to enjoy over the years. Chavo said he would take care of hiring a mariachi band and purchasing several cases of tequila at wholesale. His bartender would make margaritas for all the guests. As an afterthought, we added a couple of kegs of beer too.

Two hundred people in our small living room would give it the appearance of a live bait tank, so we decided to place tables and chairs out on the back lot, which we now owned, and let some of the party spill over there. It rained hard nearly every day prior to the party, and we just prayed that it would clear up at the last minute. It was coming down in sheets the night before the party, but when the appointed Saturday dawned, the Creator blessed us with a spectacular blue sky scattered with big blobs of whipped cream clouds drifting over the sparklng blue ocean. No more glorious day has ever been seen at Nueva España.

Chavo arrived early that morning with his minions, and our house immediately began to hum with activity. Furniture was shoved against the walls to allow people to pass through the house to the patio and the back lot. Tables and chairs (donated to Chavo by the brewery which sold him the beer) were scattered about the yard; a barbecue for the carnes asadas was set up on the patio and fired into service, and two women started busily making tortillas las manos [handmade tortillas]. A man who introduced himself as Tony was apparently the bartender and set up shop in our kitchen while Chavo and his wife brought delicious dips and other goodies into the house and set up a buffet in our dining room. The guests had been invited for 2 p.m., so at 1:30 the mariachis arrived and began to unpack and tune their instruments on the patio. Then, suddenly, it was 2 p.m. and a deadly quiet settled over the house. The mariachis stood silently at their post; Tony's margaritas were mixed and a regiment of salted glasses stood at attention on the bar; the buffet table was tempting and poised, awaiting assault, and from outside you could hear the soft sizzle of meat on the barbecue. The ship had been battened down. Now we waited for the storm to strike.

2:15 came and no guests had arrived. Then it was 2:20. The mariachis were starting to look restless.

"Do you suppose we have the wrong day?" I said to Margie in a hushed voice.

"It wouldn't surprise me with our luck!" She looked worried for a moment.

Then it was 2:30 and no guests.

At 2:35 there came a tap at the door and we opened it to see Chet Collins, our first invited guest. We almost fell into his arms!

"Where is everyone else?" I asked.

"They're waiting like horses at the starting gate back at the hotel. No one wanted to be first to arrive, so I'm it!"

"Bless you, Chet!" I said.

The mariachis struck up the music, we jammed a margarita in his hand, and began leading him past the array of goodies. For a time, Chet had a party for two hundred people all to himself!

Then they began to arrive. First in a trickle of twos and threes, and then in ever increasing numbers. By 3:15, the house was wall-to-wall people, the patio was jammed with dancers, and the tables behind the house were filled. Some couples had brought their children and/or pets who ran, barked, and played in the forest of legs—it was utter bedlam! Margie and I began making our separate ways through the crowd. It was an interesting human stew we had concocted. There were top-rung Metromedia executives and stage hands; cameramen and directors; secretaries and reporters; movie actors and Mexican workmen; Mexican dignitaries, and our Los Angeles neighbors; our new friends from Nueva España, and Dewey and his crew. Yet they all mixed and got along beautifully—due in part, I suspect, to Tony.

Tony, the bartender, made it his personal responsibiltiy to see that no margarita glass was ever empty. He was constantly leaping through that packed room with a big grin on his face, and a cocktail shaker in his hand. A guest had no sooner taken two or three sips from his drink than the glass was filled to brimming again. One sweet young thing gurgled drunkenly to me, "I don't know why I'm so smashed, I've only had one drink all day!"

Another pretty one (I'm purposely avoiding names) would stop anyone who would listen and declare: "I took off my bra without removing my dress! Wanna see?"

"Who could say nay?" I replied.

With a "Wheeeee!" she flipped her skirt up over her head, and sure enough! I hadn't suspected she was that well built.

One very attractive and dignified lady was spotted wading decorously in the surf—with all her clothes on.

A married couple bid Margie and me a tipsy goodbye, and weaved out to their car. In fifteen minutes they staggered back in.

"Decided to come back to the party, huh?" I said.

"We had a little teeny ol' problem," the girl said.

"Oh? What kind of problem?"

"We jus' ran off the road into the sand and got stuck, didn't we honey?"

Her spouse just nodded and smiled. He seemed beyond speech.

"That's too bad. Who was driving?" I asked.

"Shhhhhh!" She whispered in my ear, "I was, but my husband thinks he was, so don't tell him!"

So far as I know, only one person became ill, and he threw up out in the street. But several guests became lost while stumbling around the beach in the moonlight, and several new—or temporary—romances developed. Everyone was having fun, and there were no difficult drunks or unpleasantries.

Our invitation had specified that the open house was from 2 p.m. until 6 p.m., so at six o'clock the mariachis, Tony, the relentless bartender, Chavo, and all the workers cleaned up and departed. It didn't slow down the party one bit. A volunteer took over at the bar, and the party continued. By 10 p.m. Margie, looking a bit bedraggled, caught me by the sleeve.

"I've had it!" she said in my ear. "I can't stay up another minute."

"Me too. What'll we do?"

"Let's just tell everyone good night and go to bed."

"Okay."

We stood at our bedroom door and shouted above the din: "Good night everyone! Good night! We're going to bed!"

Several people waved and smiled—then the party went on as before. The noise dropped a few decibels when we closed the bedroom door.

I was stripping off my clothes when I heard poor, exhausted Margie weeping in the bathroom. I hastened to her.

"What's wrong, Darling?"

"Somebody shit in my waste basket!" she wailed.

I looked, and sure enough, the waste basket we keep beside the toilet was filled with very dirty toilet paper. Then in a flash I remembered the many bathrooms we have visited in Baja that always have a container beside the toilet for used paper. It's the *rancheros'* precaution against stopped plumbing.

"It was just one of the Mexican workers, honey. He thought that's what the waste basket was for."

"I don't care!" she wept. She was so tired she was inconsolable.

"I'll buy you a new waste basket tomorrow," I promised, carried her to bed, and tucked her in. We never found out how late the party lasted.

After a big party, a house always appears to have been an active participant. The next morning it was quiet and dark in the living room. Elbows striking other elbows had made the floor sticky with spilled margaritas, and dirt tracked into the house had stuck to the mess creating a black patina from wall to wall. Empty tequila bottles stood or laid forlornly on various flat surfaces, and empty or partly-filled glasses were scattered everywhere. The drapes were askew, and a pair of women's silk stockings had been thrown across the back of the couch. Our house looked like a maiden sleeping off a hangover in her party dress.

Margie's good spirits returned after ten hours sleep, but she still couldn't face the filthy kitchen so we went out to breakfast. Immediately on our return we hired two Mexican workers to help us clean up. (They spent a full day scrubbing the floor on their hands and knees). They had no sooner started, when—one by one—some of our guests began to return to thank us for the party and say goodbye. They covered their bloodshot eyes with dark glasses and sat quietly in the sun on our patio recounting some of the amusing incidents of the previous evening.

Everyone seemed to agree that the housewarming had been a huge success. Janis O'Conner, one of our best friends, phrased it best. She said, "Your party will be a benchmark of the year. It was one of those events where we say, 'Now let's see . . . was that before or after the Hunter party?'"

For the week prior to the party, Margie had threatened Chavo with a

323

slow, painful death if we ran out of food. As a result, tons of it was left over, so after our guests returned to Los Angeles we distributed it among the various workers at Nueva España. Then we tallied the consumed food and booze against the party attendance—our guests had consumed two hundred pounds of barbecued meat, two huge barrels of beer, and (are you ready for this?) 1,500 margaritas!

Our casa at Nueva España was officially launched!

Every city in the world has two faces. There is the face that is presented to the tourist, and the face seen by the resident. Since these faces are always very different, judging a city as a tourist is like judging a play from the marquee.

As well as we thought we knew and loved Mexico, living in Nueva España—even as part-time residents—presented a whole new dimension. No small part of this new vista was the people themselves.

If I were casting a movie of Don Quixote, the role of his funny sidekick Sancho Panza would go to a man named Everardo Rocha. Everardo, with his ample stomach hanging over his belt, looks like a plump tamale tied in the middle. His moon-like face is deep brown, shiny, and forever wreathed in a snaggle-toothed smile. He is the maintainance man at Nueva España, charged with picking up the trash, raking the beach, and sweeping sand from the streets, but may usually be seen leaning on either his shovel or broom—a straw sombrero shoved on the back of his jack-o-lantern head. He speaks not one word of English, and his Spanish is spoken with a Mexican hillbilly dialect that makes it difficult even for other Mexicans to understand him. When we first settled at Nueva España we were the only Americans who spoke any Spanish at all, and we could understand about half of what he was saying, so Everardo adopted us as his best gringo friends. Whenever we would arrive at the project from Los Angeles, he would waddle hurriedly from wherever he was working (or leaning) to give us an effusive welcome.

Like so many people, Everardo has great dreams of what he will do some day, but "some day" never comes. He lacks the initiative to take the first practical step to make them come true. He will be a great and successful farmer in the state of Michoacan one day, he tells us, but first he has some things he must do. Of course the first of these things would be to raise enough pesos to buy this dream ranch, and his chances of doing that are virtually nil. If, through some miracle, he did raise enough money for the ranch, he would doubtless spend his time leaning on a hoe instead of a broom, and his produce would never grow.

324

He has great plans for his children too. On one occasion he actually saved enough money to pay a *coyote* [Mexican word for crook] to smuggle his eldest son over the border into the States. According to plan, the boy would go to work for the *gringos*, make much money, and then send for his family. As soon as the whole family reached the land of milk and honey they would be rich in no time and able to buy that ranch in Michoacan. The boy was smuggled over the border successfully and managed to get as far as San Diego before he was nabbed by the immigration authorities and shipped back to Mexico.

One day Everardo's usually happy face looked extremely serious when he came to our door.

"*Qué pasa?*" I asked him.

"I would like to talk with you Benito when I am through work today," he said in his funny Spanish. "*Se puede* to have a *tragito* of tequila together then?"

"*Como no?*" [Why not?]

"*Ah bíen! Hasta los cuatros.*" [Ah good! Until four o'clock then.] He tipped his sombrero and left.   He appeared at the door again promptly at four, but this time he had a little girl with him. She appeared to be about ten years old, soaped and scrubbed within an inch of her life, and dressed in her very best clothes for this visit. She was quite beautiful with startling, clear blue eyes set in her little brown face. Her shiny black hair was tied in pigtails with pieces of orange yarn.

This is my youngest daughter Yolandita," he said.

"Come in," I replied, "the tequila is waiting."

I placed the bottle of tequila, lemon, and salt between us, Margie poured a soft drink for Yolanda, and we all sat at the dining room table. Yolanda sipped her Coke quietly as her father talked. He talked of the fishing, the weather, the coming fiesta, the crops, and the neighbors. I began to think that perhaps I had misread the look on his face that morning. Perhaps this was just a social visit after all. Finally I said, "Did you have something of importance you wished to tell me Everardo?"

He nodded gravely.

"*Qué es?*"

"Yolandita is a very good girl," he began. "She is able to work very hard—and a housekeeper *el mejor!*"

"*Bien.*"

"She will work very hard for you."

So that was it. "We don't need a maid, Everardo."

"Not as a maid. I wish to give you Yolandita. She is pretty, no? She will be your daughter and live with you. Then she will learn to speak English."

"She can learn English in Ensenada. she doesn't have to live with us."

"No. It is better that she live with you. And she will work very hard."

Margie turned to Yolanda. "Wouldn't you be homesick to leave your home—your brothers and sisters?" she asked the child.

Yolanda squared her shoulders and sat up very straight. "I am strong. I will not be homesick. I will live with you and the señor."

"She does well in school too," Everardo added.

She is an adorable child and for an insane moment I thought of taking him up on it. I looked at Margie questioningly. Her return glance said "No way!"

Perceiving that I might be weakening, Everardo launched into a long dissertation on the importance of being able to speak English in Mexico. I lost parts of it, but he seemed to be saying that it was surely the key to financial success in Mexico and that the only way to learn the language properly was to live with Americans, and he wanted this opportunity for his lovely daughter who was so bright and such a hard worker. He concluded his speech by adding that it was expensive for him to feed her, also.

Margie saved the day for us. She suddenly remembered that Marge Sole—one of our American neighbors in Nueva España—was a teacher in the States, and had chosen to give free lessons in English to the children of our area that entire summer. She told Everardo about it, gave him the address of the school, and told him to take Yolanda there. "She will learn much English during the summer," Margie told him, "and she will be learning it from an American."

Marge Sole later told us that Everardo never showed up with Yolanda for those "important" lessons, so one day I asked Everardo why he hadn't sent her to the classes.

"I will some day," he replied, "but now Yolanda is too busy with her piano lessons."

Barbie and Stan Sylak introduced us to Roberto Perez. We had wanted to purchase some wrought iron work, and they said he was the best. He had a little store on the outskirts of town called The House Of Iron. We found that his iron work was more expensive than what you could buy in Ensenada, but also much more desirable. It was very artistic and unusual. We made a couple of purchases, and took a liking to Roberto at once. The feeling seemed to be reciprocated, because on that first meeting he invited us into his house for a drink. There we met his wife

Jean, and in no time we were good friends.

Roberto is a typical, fun-loving, easy-going Mexican with a quick smile, hearty laugh, and an appreciative eye for pretty girls. He's the kind of man you would have expected to remain a bachelor for his entire life. Jean is artistic and magnetic, with flashing blue eyes. She is given to wearing unusual, bangly jewelry, and striking, partially revealing clothes. Some years ago she brought her three children from a previous marriage, moved in with Roberto, and stated, "We're here to stay!" Such was her appeal, that the fun-loving bachelor Roberto married her, became a marvelous father to her children, and built her a palatial home on the shore behind *The House Of Iron*.

Accustomed to old western movies where the Mexican characters (usually played by an Anglo) call each other *compadre*, as our friendship grew I started calling Roberto my *compadre*.

"Do you know what that word means?" he asked one day.

"Yes, it means 'pal' or 'buddy'," I answered.

"No it doesn't. A *compadre* is a co-father. What you call a Godfather of your children—a very special person."

"Roberto," I said, "if Margie and I ever have another child I will make you the *compadre*. Then you will be the Godfather of a miracle!"

He laughed heartily, and from then on told all his Mexican friends he was *compadre* to a *gringo*.

We were planning to add the extra room on our house in about a year, but we decided to surround the back lot with a high wall in the meantime so we could enjoy nude sun bathing. We asked Roberto if he would be the contractor. Even though he wasn't in the contracting business, we felt it would be well to have a good friend oversee the construction for us. Besides, he had told us that he used to be a mason and was used to working with cement blocks, so he'd know whether the job was being done correctly. We offered him five hundred dollars for his work.

We were away from the *casa* for a week, but when we returned we were astonished to see Roberto, stripped to the waist and perspiring buckets, building the wall himself while two admiring assistants stirred the mortar and passed him the blocks. He certainly was an expert at it, and he was moving fast.

"Hey, Roberto!" I said, "We didn't mean for you to build the wall yourself! We meant for you to hire someone to do it."

"I know," he puffed, "but it's good exercise, and I haven't worked with blocks for a long time."

Beer is Roberto's favorite drink, and he is capable of consuming vast quantities, so we bought a couple of cases and kept the cold brew coming his way as he worked. For the better part of a week he showed up at our house every morning at eight, removed his shirt, and worked on the wall. To Jean's distress, he neglected *The House Of Iron* that whole week and left her to contend with the customers. Finally, it was done. Suggesting hidden delights inside its boundries, the great white wall stood tall and sturdy, making our yard safe from prying eyes. Sweat gleaming on his naked torso, Roberto nodded, satisfied.

"How much do we owe you?" I asked him.

"Just the money for the materials and my two helpers. Nothing for me."

"Nothing for you! C'mon, man, you've been working your ass off!"

"It was fun for me Benito. Besides, that's what *compadres* are for," he grinned.

Thirty houses had been completed, or were nearing completion, when suddenly the sounds of building at Nueva España ceased. Dewey Bouche departed, and with him went Bud Murphy, Pedro Alonzo, and all the workmen. Only Dewey's Mexican partner, Juan Hurtado, was left. Rumors were rife about what had happened, but the consensus seemed to be that Dewey had simply run out of money and was unable to finish the condominium. I talked with him once by telephone after that and he insisted that it wasn't true. "I have six hundred thousand dollars all ready to pump back into the project," he said, "I just have to go through some litigation first." I wanted to believe him then, but it's been over four years and he hasn't returned.

It was a shock when it occurred and we got together with the Sylaks, Langes, and Gilliss to talk over the possible ramifications. The first—and most important—point was that our homes and properties were all safe, secured by the Mexican government under the terms of "The Thirty Year Trust." No one could ever take them away from us. Secondly, we began to realize that if Dewey had ever completed his goal of 130 houses, our beach would have been so overcrowded as to be unappealing, and there'd have been no space to park all the cars. Our water supply, which comes from a reservoir, could not have possibly serviced 130 homes, and the electricity is inadequate as it is. It had been unfortunate for Dewey (whom I always liked), but we were all better off by far with the project incomplete. We hoped Juan Hurtado would not attempt to finish it, and we settled down to enjoy its peace and beauty without the constant din of hammers and saws.

The little neighborhood adjoining Nueva España is named Chapultepec.

It is an *ejido* where a man may have the land if he builds a house and lives in it. It consists of a cluster of tiny homes scattered on either side of one main road, a church, and a schoolhouse. The main road itself is dotted with typical Mexican souvenir stands. Each little tumble-down store looks like a clubhouse built by a child—sagging and sprawling, with a tarpaper roof. The stores are flanked by an army of clay pots standing in platoons according to size, painted every color of the rainbow. Baskets, belts, and embroidered shirts hang from the rafters, and the floors are jammed with wrought iron artwork, ceramics, and soapstone novelties. An ancient, dusty counter offers wallets and other leatherwork for sale. The owner's home is usually behind the store and affords an occasional glimpse of a little brown face at a window and the smell of chili cooking.

Chapultepec has become a successful *ejido* and the population numbers several hundred. As it grew from *ejido* to small town, the populace decided that, like any other Mexican town, it needed a park. Thus, during the many months our *casa* was under construction, the men of Chapultepec donated their labor to build the *parqué*. A large lot in the center of town on the main road was cleared, and a *kiosco* was erected. A *kiosco* is an ornate, circular bandstand that every Mexican park has. Then grass and trees (provided free by the Mexican government) were planted, and donated park benches were placed. After many months the park was ready for its grand opening celebration, and everyone from the surrounding countryside was invited.

Joined by close friends from Los Angeles, Dave and Dotty Wiechman, we attended the festivities. A large crowd had gathered on the lawn, children were everywhere, mariachis were playing happy music in the *kiosco*, and the mouth-watering aroma of barbecuing beef filled the air. As we pushed our way through the laughing, milling crowd, we recognized many old friends. Most of our neighbors from Nueva España were there, including Stan Sylak, who had thoughtfully brought along a bottle of tequila which we passed from hand to hand. Nearby was Juan Hurtado and his wife Olga, holding court with their friends. Everardo Rocha, dressed in his best shirt and without the usual sombrero, was busily engaged in socking away a barbecued beef taco. Yolandita was playing with the other children. Guillermo, our Nueva España handyman showed up holding a brand new baby in his arms as his tiny little wife giggled happily. *"No mas,"* he said, "There will be no more children. My youngest son told me so!" And there was Roberto, our door-to-door barber, and Juan, our door-to-door tamale salesman. It was fun seeing our old friends, but even more fun to meet some new neighbors.

Someone introduced us to "Hooks"—that's the only name he goes by. Hooks is a black man, tall, slim, and handsome with a Jamaican Negro accent. He is married to a Mexican woman, and lives near us. He calls his children "my little half-breeds" and they are beautiful, having inherited the best of both ethnic backgrounds. At one point in the festivities his children performed some authentic Spanish dances to the wild applause of the crowd. Hooks is the self-appointed handyman and friend to all.

"If you ever need any tools, Ben, just drop by my place. I've got 'em all, and you can borrow whatever you need," he said.

We met two other happily mixed marriages at the fiesta. One of them was the Yoakums—Mahlen and Margarita. Margarita speaks no English, is tiny, cuddly, shy, and a marvelous cook and seamstress. Mahlen Yoakum, an American, has lived most of his adult life in Mexico. He was an orchestra leader and entertained for many years in the Queen city of Guadalajara. He is now retired and, like his wife, has a gourmet's touch in the kitchen. They live in a tiny green house on the beach just south of us, and pick up a little extra money by operating a part-time, casual cafe in their livingroom/kitchen. Margarita's exquisite embroidery work is on display, and she will custom-make you the most beautiful shirt or dress in all of Mexico.

It has since become our custom to stroll down the beach to their home on a Sunday morning for one of their magnificient breakfasts of *huevos rancheros, frijoles refritos,* and piping hot flour *tortillas.* Some of these Sunday mornings we are able to persuade Margarita to sing for us. Then she will stand beside the refrigerator blushing, and self-consciously fingering her apron as she begins a sad Mexican love song. Soon, lost in the lyrics, her self-consciousness disappears, the room fills with her rich, full voice, and tears come to her eyes. Then we are caught up in the magic of her singing, and when the song is ended, our eyes are wet too.

The other couple we know only by their first names—Ted and Lisa. Ted, the American, seems to have had a background in cattle ranching, and is an excellent horseman. We often see him in his blue jeans, cowboy boots, and ten gallon hat riding his horse at a breakneck gallop down our beach. Lisa is a full bloomed, firy Mexican girl who speaks a little heavily-accented English, but the words come tumbling out over each other in a delightful, gurgling stream of mispronunciations and malaprops. Her eyes flash, and she brims over with Latin charm. Together they own a small motel called the Mona Lisa. It, too, is south on the beach from us, and features a tiny bar overlooking the ocean where one may sip a cold tequila and watch the sunset over the water. We have spent many a happy late afternoon with them there, sipping, watching, and chatting.

We met Paco (a knickname for Francisco) who owns one of the little shanty-house souvenir stands and told us he will earn as much as $2,000 on a good weekend! We met Señora Manzana, who owns another store that specializes in the distinctive black pottery of Oaxaca in the south of Mexico, and offered us the ten percent "residents discount"; the Ortiz family who operate the *abarroteria* [General Store] where we purchase our bottled drinking water; he's also the baker, butcher, and bottled gas deliverer. As we have found so often in Mexico, a casual meeting develops into a good friendship almost immediately. Being friendly with so many of our neighbors made us feel even more a viable part of the community.

For months we just enjoyed it. Days were spent lying on our beach, strolling along the shore picking up shells, and watching Taco chase the sea birds. In the evenings, we visited our Mexican friends in their homes. Then one day we got a new neighbor.

Ty Gillis had purchased two homes at Nueva España with the idea of selling the second one for a profit, so she enlisted the aid of an Hawaiian friend, Lynne Austin, to help her decorate it. Lynne decorated it beautifully, then couldn't bear to leave it, so she bought it from Ty and moved in with her husband.

The Austins are interesting people. Lynne—like Ty Gillis—was born and raised in the islands, but is a world traveler and an avid shell collector. Her house blossoms with intricate, delicate shells from all over the world, and we locals have started calling it "the shell house". Her husband Gwynne wasn't born in Hawaii, but has lived there most of his adult life as manager of Hawaii's various luxury hotels (including the Halekalani and the Hawaiian Village hotels). They have owned their own hotel in Seattle for some years now, but Gwynne is semi-retired and only acts in an advisory capacity in its operation. He is tall and slim, and an avid sportsman. Dearest to his heart is golf, and sailing his beautiful yacht in Puget Sound, so we have much in common since sailing and golf are my passions as well. Since the Austins moved to Mexico so impulsively, with little knowledge of the country or the people, it has been my delight to share some of our Mexican experiences with them.

One day I had just concluded the story about our finding *Anus Alar* on the beach at San Quintin when Gwynne looked quite thoughtful.

"I've got an idea Ben," he said finally.

"What's that?"

"Well I've listened to so many of your stories about Mexico and I think they're really fascinating—"

"Thanks, Gwynne."

"Well, I think you should put them in a book. I bet you could sell a lot of copies."

Epilogue

Our *casa* by the sea has functioned perfectly for a few years now. Of course the electricity still sputters, wavers, and sometimes winks out, but we feel that's part of living in Mexico. Margie purchased some attractive kerosene lamps which are constantly on the alert awaiting the occasional blackout, and their soft light makes interesting shadows on the walls. It's very romantic.

The extra room we planned for the back lot is now complete. It has tile floors the color of the sea, and a large skylight that floods the room with sunshine. It's perfect for my writing and Margie's handicrafts. Roberto Perez's proud wall still guards the remainder of the yard and permits us to cavort nude when the feeling moves us.

We have no telephone, and if a call should be necessary, it's only a couple of miles to the hotel. Several of our neighbors have TV, but we haven't installed a set. To us, the electronic booming from the box destroys the music of the waves. Our dislike of "the tube" may be due to having worked on the other side of it for so many years. We call the view window our TV and can spend hours staring out of it, hypnotized by the ever-changing colors and moods of the ocean.

Recently we loaned our *casa* to some friends while we were away from it. They stayed there a week, and when they returned, they said that they had a long list of all the fun things they were going to do. "We didn't do any of them," we were told. "We just sat on the beach, or in the house, and stared at the ocean!"

"That, Susie dear, is what we call The Baja Feeling," I said.

The Baja Feeling is now with us constantly and we revel in that lovely, langorous, lazy way of life.

Have you heard about grunions? They are tiny little fish somewhat like smelts, that are native to the California and Mexico coastlines. In some mysterious way they know when the moon is full and the tide is just right. On that chosen night they come ashore by the thousands, dancing and wriggling on the beach. If you look closely, you will see that the female grunion has squirmed her tail into the sand and is depositing her tiny eggs there. The male grunions lustfully flop up the beach until they are close to the egg-laying females, twine their silvery bodies around them, and fertilize the eggs. Because this phenomenon occurs in cycles, the scientists are able to predict it accurately, and Californians flock to the beachs on those nights to gather the small fish.

I mention this because we have *just* heard of a place in Mexico where the grunion do their mating dance not by the light of the nearly-full moon, but in broad daylight! They also do it at a time of the month when the moon would be dark, and they do it by the millions! Our Mexican informant told us there will be a carpet of grunions a foot deep as far as the eye can see along the shoreline. He said it is a deserted spot—few Mexicans or Americans know of it. Then he showed us just how to find it.

So we're packing the Dolphin for another camping trip right now. More accurately, I should say Margie's packing it and I'm just sitting here. I got a dirty look from the doorway a moment ago which means she needs help.

So, if you'll excuse me . . .

The casa of Ben and Margie Hunter on the beach near Ensenada.

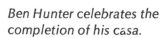

Ben Hunter celebrates the completion of his casa.